The Mediation Process

The Mediation Process

Practical Strategies for Resolving Conflict

Christopher W. Moore

Second Edition

Jossey-Bass Publishers • San Francisco

Substantial discounts on bulk quantities of Jossey-Bass books are available to corporations, professional associations, and other organizations. For details and discount information, contact the special sales department at Jossey-Bass Inc., Publishers (415) 433-1740; Fax (800) 605-2665.

For sales outside the United States, please contact your local Simon & Schuster International office.

Jossey-Bass Web address: http://www.josseybass.com

 Manufactured in the United States of America on Lyons Falls Turin Book. This paper is acid-free and 100 percent totally chlorine-free.

Library of Congress Cataloging-in-Publication Data

Moore, Christopher W., date.
    The mediation process : practical strategies for resolving
conflict / Christopher W. Moore. — 2nd ed.
      p.   cm. — (The Jossey-Bass conflict resolution series)
    Includes bibliographical references and index.
    ISBN 0-7879-0248-9 (cloth : acid-free paper)
    1. Mediation.   2. Conflict management. I. Title. II. Series.
HM136.M684 1996
303.6'9—dc20

96-9959
CIP

SECOND EDITION
HB Printing   10 9 8 7 6 5 4 3

The Jossey-Bass Conflict Resolution Series

The Jossey-Bass Conflict Resolution Series addresses the growing need for guidelines in the field of conflict resolution, as broadly defined to include negotiation, mediation, alternative dispute resolution, and other forms of third-party intervention. Our books bridge theory and practice, ranging from descriptive analysis to prescriptive advice. Our goal is to provide those engaged in understanding and finding new and more effective ways to approach conflict—practitioners, researchers, teachers, and those in other professional and volunteer pursuits—with the resources to further their work and better the world in which we live.

This series is dedicated to
the life and work of
Jeffrey Z. Rubin
1941–1995

Contents

Part Four: Reaching a Settlement

Preface

All societies, communities, organizations, and interpersonal relationships experience conflict at one time or another in the process of day-to-day interaction. Conflict is not necessarily bad, abnormal, or dysfunctional; it is a fact of life. Conflict and disputes exist when people are engaged in competition to meet goals that are perceived to be, or actually are, incompatible. However, conflict may go beyond competitive behavior and acquire the additional purpose of inflicting physical or psychological damage on an opponent, even to the point of destruction. It is then that the negative and harmful dynamics of conflict exact their full costs.

But disputes are not bound to follow a negative course; conflict can lead to growth and be productive for all parties. Whether this happens often depends on the participants' ability to devise efficient procedures for cooperative problem-solving, on their capacity to lay aside distrust and animosity while they work together on their conflict, and on the availability of solutions that will at least partially satisfy all of the parties' interests. Unfortunately, many people in conflict are unable to develop an effective process, deal with the psychological barriers to settlement, or develop integrative solutions on their own. They often need help to do so.

Mediation, one form of third-party assistance in the voluntary resolution of differences, has a long history. However, until relatively recently, there have been few works that detailed what mediators actually do to aid people in conflict.

During the past twenty-five years, I have been actively involved as a mediator of organizational, environmental, family, community, criminal, ethnic, and public policy disputes. I have practiced in the United States and worked as an intermediary, conflict manager, consultant, and trainer in over twenty countries in Africa, Asia, Latin America, Eastern and Western Europe, and the South Pacific.

This broad experience has led me to believe that there are some common mediation principles and procedures that can be applied effectively to a wide range of conflicts. My belief has been confirmed by the expanding experience and literature in the field of mediation. There is now a great need for a "how-to" manual on the general process.

The Mediation Process: Practical Strategies for Resolving Conflict integrates my personal experience and research, detailing what is known about the mediation process as it has been applied in a variety of areas, types of disputes, and cultures. The contents have been greatly expanded since the first edition, to encompass some of the exciting new developments and applications of mediation in the commercial, interpersonal, and public disputes arenas and to incorporate some of what I have learned about the practice of mediation in different cultures. The book outlines how mediation fits into the larger field of dispute resolution and negotiation and then presents a comprehensive, stage-by-stage sequence of activities that can be used by mediators to assist disputants in reaching agreement.

Audience

I have written this book for several groups. First are the practicing mediators who work in a variety of arenas and who have repeatedly expressed their need for a comprehensive description of mediation process and theory. The book should be helpful to practitioners in labor, commercial, family, interpersonal, community, organizational, environmental, and public policy mediation, as well as in many other areas of practice.

Second are professionals—lawyers, managers, therapists, social workers, planners, and teachers—who handle conflicts on a daily basis. Although such professionals may choose to become full-time mediators, they are more likely to use mediation principles and procedures as additional tools to help them within their chosen fields of work. The material presented here will aid any professional who wishes to promote cooperative problem solving between his or her clients.

Third are people who have to negotiate solutions to complex problems. Because mediation is an extension of the negotiation process and, in fact, a collection of techniques to promote more efficient negotiations, an understanding of the mediation process can be tremendously helpful to people directly involved in bargaining. Mediation can teach negotiators how to be cooperative rather than competitive problem solvers and how to achieve win-win rather than win-lose outcomes. An understanding of mediation can also aid negotiators in deciding when to call in a third party and what the intervenor can do for them.

Fourth are trainees and students in both mediation training programs and academic courses on dispute resolution. This book is suitable for use in law, business, social work, counseling, management, education, sociology, and psychology seminars. Undergraduates as well as graduates will find it useful in learning mediation concepts and skills.

Overview of the Contents

Part One provides an overview of the entire process of mediation and dispute resolution. Chapter One describes the broad field of dispute resolution and details how mediation fits in as an important means of handling conflicts. In this chapter, I present a spectrum of conflict management approaches, identify when mediation is appropriate and when it has a high probability of success, and describe the history and range of mediation practice in a number of cultures around the world. Chapter Two examines the mediation process in more depth. I explore variations of mediator roles and procedures, describe a number of types of mediators, introduce the twelve stages of the mediation process, and survey several variables that determine how directive the mediator should be in his or her interventions.

Part Two discusses mediator activities that occur *prior* to joint negotiations between the disputing parties. Chapter Three covers procedures for mediator entry and explores both how an intervenor becomes involved in a dispute and what impact being invited by a sole party, all parties, or an uninvolved secondary party has on the final settlement. Chapter Four describes the process of searching for a dispute resolution approach and arena with the parties. Procedures that can assist disputants in evaluating the various methods of resolving their conflicts are covered, along with the means of deciding which approach to use. Chapter Five presents data collection techniques that mediators can use to gather information about the parties' negotiation procedures and the substantive issues in dispute. Special emphasis is placed on the skills used to intervene in conflict situations. Chapter Six explores procedures for designing a mediation plan. The identification of participants, the physical setup of the session, and strategies for the first session are detailed. Chapter Seven examines procedures for conciliation, the process of emotionally preparing the parties for negotiation over substantive issues. Techniques for responding to strong emotions, perceptual problems, and communication difficulties are discussed.

Part Three explores mediation procedures in joint session with all disputants present. Chapter Eight focuses on beginning a joint session with the disputing parties. Strategies and opening statements for both the intervenor and the parties are described and analyzed. Chapters Nine and Ten examine the steps by which the issues in dispute can be identified, an agenda can be developed, and the substantive, procedural, and psychological interests of the parties can be explored. The useful technique of reframing, or defining, issues and interests is presented. Chapter Eleven presents procedures and strategies for generating settlement options. The technique of proposal-counterproposal is described, as well as more cooperative problem-solving methods.

Part Four covers the conclusion of mediation and the various steps involved in reaching a settlement. Chapters Twelve and Thirteen present procedures for assessing settlement options and reaching final agreements. In these chapters, I explore acceptable bargaining ranges, incremental convergence, leaps to agreement, procedures for building bargaining formulas, and the usefulness of deadlines. Chapter Fourteen discusses how agreements can be finalized. Procedures for drafting settlements, increasing compliance, and monitoring are examined. Chapter Fifteen addresses specific problems that are encountered in some but not all disputes and presents techniques for dealing with them. Both the caucus and mediator power are examined, as are procedures for working with multiparty disputes and for funding mediation. Chapter Sixteen explores some of the developments in the field that have promoted excellent practice. A brief conclusion rounds out the text.

The resources contain a code of professional conduct, a sample agreement, and a list of associations, organizations, and publications of relevance to practitioners.

Acknowledgments

All knowledge is socially produced. Although I bear responsibility for the identification, elaboration, and development of the ideas presented in this book, I have clearly drawn on the experiences and advice of others engaged in the practice of mediation.

The first group of people to whom I am indebted are my fellow mediators. Since 1973, when I first became involved in mediating an intense interracial community dispute, I have worked with four active groups of mediators and conflict resolvers. Each group has contributed significant insights and pushed me to develop my thinking.

First and foremost are my partners at CDR Associates in Boulder, Colorado—Susan Wildau, Mary Margaret Golten, and Bernard Mayer—and our other program staff. They have been my colleagues in developing and practicing many of the ideas contained in this book. Susan Carpenter and W.J.D. Kennedy of ACCORD Associates also provided insights and support in researching and refining mediation theory and practice while I worked as a mediator and director of training for that organization. The members of the Training Action Affinity Group of the Movement for a New Society—Suzanne Terry, Stephen Parker, Peter Woodrow, and Berit Lakey—and my coauthors on the *Resource Manual for a Living Revolution*—Virginia Coover, Charles Esser, and Ellen Deacon—worked with me to develop intervention skills for multiparty disputes and effective training techniques in conflict resolution. Bill Lincoln provided my first excellent exposure to mediation training. Work with academic colleagues was also important. Norman Wilson, Paul Wehr, and Martin Oppenhimer encouraged and supported my research.

The individuals I have mentioned so far are the theoretical and

experiential contributors. Just as important are the people who
prepare the drafts and edit them. My sincere thanks to Nancy Wig-
ington and to Benjamin and Bess Moore, who helped assemble the
final draft.

A final word of thanks to Susan Wildau and Stephanie Judson
for their faith in me as a scholar and reflective practitioner, and
for emotional support during graduate school.

Boulder, Colorado   Christopher W. Moore
March 1996

The Author

Christopher W. Moore is a partner in CDR Associates, an international decision-making and conflict management firm in Boulder, Colorado. He is an internationally known mediator, dispute systems designer, trainer, and author in the field of conflict management.

He received his B.A. Degree (1969) from Juniata College in history, his M.A. degree (1972) from Antioch-Putney Graduate School, and his Ph.D. degree (1983) from Rutgers University in political sociology and development. He was trained as a mediator by the U.S. Federal Mediation and Conciliation Service (1979) and the American Arbitration Association (1976).

Moore has consulted in the field of conflict management in twenty-two countries, including Poland, Russia, Indonesia, Germany, South Africa, Mexico, and Japan. He has also trained U.N. diplomats and foreign service officers in international mediation. In the United States, his work has encompassed negotiated rule-making at the federal and state levels, site-specific disputes in the public policy and environmental arenas, and conflicts over growth management planning, water conservation, wildlife protection, energy development, and air quality. His extensive experience in organizational mediation includes labor-management disputes, cases of alleged discrimination and sexual harassment, and conflicts between headquarters and regional offices. He has also mediated interpersonal and family disputes.

Moore has consulted on the design of dispute resolution systems for, among others, the state of Colorado, the U.S. Army Corps of Engineers and Bureau of Reclamation, the Royal Canadian Mounted Police, the Barangay Justice System in the Philippines, and the Ministry of the Environment and the Environmental Impact Management Agency of Indonesia.

His books include *An Executive Seminar on Alternative Dispute Resolution (ADR)* (1988), *Negotiating Bargaining and Conflict Management* (1982), *Decision Making and Conflict Management* (1981), *Natural Resources Conflict Management* (1982), and *Resource Manual for a Living Revolution* (1976, with others). His articles on conflict management and dispute resolution have appeared in such journals as *Mediation Quarterly, Forum* (National Institute for Dispute Resolution), *Pacifica Review,* and *Cultural Survival.*

The Mediation Process

Part One

Understanding Dispute Resolution and Mediation

Chapter One

Approaches to Managing and Resolving Conflict

Conflict seems to be present in all human relationships and in all societies. From the beginning of recorded history, we have evidence of disputes between spouses, children, parents and children, neighbors, ethnic and racial groups, fellow workers, superiors and subordinates, organizations, communities, citizens and their government, and nations. Because of the pervasive presence of conflict and because of the physical, emotional, and resource costs that often result from disputes, people have always sought ways of resolving their differences. In seeking to manage and resolve differences, they have tried to develop procedures that are efficient, that allow them to satisfy their interests, that minimize suffering, and that control unnecessary expenditures of resources.

In most disputes, the parties involved have a variety of means at their disposal to respond to or resolve their conflict. The procedures available to them differ considerably in the *way* the conflict is addressed and settled and often result in different outcomes, both tangible and intangible.

This chapter begins with an analysis of a specific interpersonal and organizational conflict and explores some of the procedural options available to the parties involved for managing and resolving their differences. Mediation, one of those options, is examined in depth, and a detailed description is given of its historical and present-day applications and variations.

The Singson-Whittamore Dispute

Singson and Whittamore are in conflict. It all started three years ago when Dr. Richard Singson, director of the Fairview Medical Clinic, one of the few medical service providers in a small rural town, was seeking two physicians to fill open positions on his staff. After several months of extensive and difficult recruiting, he hired two doctors, Andrew and Janelle Whittamore, to fill the respective positions of pediatrician and gynecologist. The fact that the doctors were married did not seem to be a problem at the time they were hired.

Fairview liked to keep its doctors and generally paid them well for their work with patients. The clinic was also concerned about maintaining its patient load and income and required every doctor who joined the practice to sign a five-year contract detailing what he or she was to be paid and what conditions would apply should the contract be broken by either party. One of these conditions was a covenant not to compete, or a no-competition clause, stating that should a doctor choose to leave the clinic prior to the expiration of the agreement, he or she would not be allowed to practice medicine in that town or county during the time remaining on the contract; violation of this clause carried a financial penalty. The clause was designed to prevent a staff doctor from building up a practice at the clinic and then leaving with his or her patients to start a private competitive practice before the term of the contract had expired.

When Janelle and Andrew joined the Fairview staff, they signed their respective contracts and initialed all the clauses. Both doctors performed well in their jobs and were respected by their colleagues and patients. Unfortunately, their personal life did not fare so well. The Whittamores' marriage went into a steady decline almost as soon as they began working at Fairview. Their arguments increased, and the tension between them mounted to the point where they decided to get a divorce. Because they both wanted to be near their two young children, they agreed to continue living in the same town.

Each physician at the clinic had a specialty, and all relied on consultations with colleagues, so some interaction between the estranged couple was inevitable. Over time, their mutual hostility grew to such an extent that they decided one of them should leave the clinic—for their own good and that of other clinic staff. Because they believed that Andrew, as a pediatrician, would have an easier time finding patients outside the clinic, they agreed that he was the one who should go.

Andrew explained his situation to Singson and noted that because he would be leaving for the benefit of the clinic, he expected that no penalty would be assessed for breaking the contract two years early and that the no-competition clause would not be invoked.

Singson was surprised and upset that his finely tuned staff was going to lose one of its most respected members. Furthermore, he was shocked by Whittamore's announcement that he planned to stay in town and open a medical practice. Singson visualized the long-range impact of Whittamore's decision: the pediatrician would leave and set up a competing practice, taking many of his patients with him. The clinic would lose revenues from the doctor's fees, incur the cost of recruiting a new doctor, and if the no-competition clause was not enforced, establish a bad precedent for managing its doctors. Singson responded that the no-competition clause would be enforced if Whittamore wanted to practice within the county, and that the clinic would impose a penalty for breaching the contract. He estimated that the penalty could be as much as 100 percent of the revenues that Whittamore might earn in the two years remaining on his contract.

Whittamore was irate at Singson's response, considering it unreasonable and irresponsible. If that was the way the game was to be played, he threatened, he would leave and set up a practice, and Singson could take him to court to try to get his money. Singson responded that he would get an injunction against the practice if necessary and would demand the full amount if pushed into a corner. Whittamore stormed out of Singson's office mumbling that he was going to "get that son of a gun."

This conflict has several different components: the Whittamores' relationship with each other, their relationship to other staff members at the clinic, the potential conflict between Andrew Whittamore's patients and the clinic, and Andrew Whittamore's relationship with Richard Singson. For ease of analysis, we will examine only one of these components: the conflict between

Singson and Whittamore and the various means of resolution available to them.

Conflict Management and Resolution Approaches

People in conflict can generally resolve their disputes by a variety of means. Figure 1.1 illustrates some of these options, which vary in terms of the formality of the process, the privacy of the approach, the people involved, the authority of the third party (if there is one), the type of decision that will result, and the amount of coercion that is exercised by or on the disputing parties.

At the left end of the continuum are informal, private procedures that involve only the disputants. At the other end, one party relies on coercion and often on public action to force the opposing party into submission. In between are a variety of approaches that we will examine in more detail.

Disagreements and problems can arise in almost any relationship. The majority of disagreements are usually handled informally. Initially, people may *avoid* each other because they dislike the discomfort that accompanies conflict, they do not consider the issue to be that important, they lack the power to force a change, they do not believe the situation can be improved, or they are not yet ready to negotiate.

When avoidance is no longer possible or tensions become so strong that the parties cannot let the disagreement continue, they usually resort to *informal problem-solving discussions* to resolve their differences. This is probably where the majority of disagreements end in daily life. Either they are resolved, more or less to the satisfaction of the people involved, or the issues are dropped for lack of interest or inability to push through to a conclusion.

In the Singson-Whittamore case, the Whittamores avoided dealing with their potential conflict with the medical clinic until it was clear that Andrew was going to leave. At that point, Andrew initiated informal discussions, but they failed to reach an acceptable conclusion. Clearly, their problem had escalated into a dispute. Gulliver (1979, p. 75) notes that a disagreement becomes a dispute "only when the two parties are unable and/or unwilling to resolve their disagreement; that is, when one or both are not prepared to accept the status quo (should that any longer be a possibility) or to accede to the demand or denial of demand by the other. A dispute

Figure 1.1. Continuum of Conflict Management and Resolution Approaches.

Private decision making by parties				Private third-party decision making		Legal (public), authoritative third-party decision making		Extralegal coerced decision making	
Conflict avoidance	Informal discussion and problem solving	Negotiation	Mediation	Administrative decision	Arbitration	Judicial decision	Legislative decision	Nonviolent direct action	Violence

→ Increased coercion and likelihood of win-lose outcome →

is precipitated by a crisis in the relationship." People involved in a conflict that has reached this level have a variety of ways to resolve their differences. They can pursue more formal and structured means of voluntarily reaching an agreement, resort to third-party decision makers, or try to leverage or coerce each other to reach a settlement.

Other than informal conversations, the most common way to reach a mutually acceptable agreement is through *negotiation*. Negotiation is a bargaining relationship between parties who have a perceived or actual conflict of interest. The participants voluntarily join in a temporary relationship designed to educate each other about their needs and interests, to exchange specific resources, or to resolve less tangible issues such as the form their relationship will take in the future or the procedure by which problems are to be solved. Negotiation is clearly an option for Whittamore and Singson, although the degree of emotional and substantive polarization will make the process difficult.

If negotiations are hard to initiate or have started and reached an impasse, the parties may need some assistance from a party external to the dispute. *Mediation* is an extension or elaboration of the negotiation process that involves the intervention of an acceptable third party who has limited or no authoritative decision-making power. This person assists the principal parties in voluntarily reaching a mutually acceptable settlement of the issues in dispute. As with negotiation, mediation leaves the decision-making power primarily in the hands of the people in conflict. Mediation is a voluntary process in that the participants must be willing to accept the assistance of the intervenor if he or she is to help them manage or resolve their differences. Mediation is usually initiated when the parties no longer believe that they can handle the conflict on their own and when the only means of resolution appears to involve impartial third-party assistance.

Whittamore and Singson might consider mediation if they cannot negotiate a settlement on their own. We will return to this process later on, once their other procedural options have been evaluated.

Beyond negotiation and mediation, there is a continuum of techniques that decrease the personal control the people involved have over the dispute outcome, increase the involvement of external decision makers, and rely increasingly on win-lose and either/or decision-making techniques. These approaches can be divided into public and private, and legal and extralegal.

If the dispute is within an organization, there is often an *administrative* or *executive dispute resolution approach*. In this process, a third party who has some distance from the dispute but is not necessarily impartial may make a decision for the parties in dispute. The process can be private if the system within which the dispute occurs is a private company, division, or work team; or public if it is conducted in a public agency by a mayor, county commissioner, planner, or other administrator. An administrative dispute resolution process generally attempts to balance the needs of the entire system and the interests of individuals.

In the Singson-Whittamore dispute, both parties might choose to appeal to the board of directors of the Fairview Medical Clinic for a third-party decision. If both parties trust the integrity and judgment of these decision makers, the dispute might end there. However, Whittamore is not sure that he would get a fair hearing from this board.

Arbitration is a generic term for a voluntary process in which people in conflict request the assistance of an impartial and neutral third party to make a decision for them regarding contested issues. The outcome of the decision may be either advisory or binding. Arbitration may be conducted by one person or a panel of third parties. The critical factor is that they are outside of the conflict relationship.

Arbitration is a private process in that the proceedings, and often the outcome, are not open to public scrutiny. People often select arbitration because of its private nature, and also because it is more informal, less expensive, and faster than a judicial proceeding. In arbitration, the parties frequently are able to select their own arbiter or panel, which gives them more control over the decision than if the third party were appointed by an outside authority or agency.

Whittamore and Singson have both heard of arbitration but are reluctant to turn their problem over to a third party before they are sure that they cannot resolve it themselves. Neither wants to risk an unfavorable decision. In addition, Singson fears an external decision that might erode the clinic's prerogative to control the contract process.

A *judicial approach* involves the intervention of an institutionalized and socially recognized authority in a dispute. This approach shifts the resolution process from the private domain to the public. In the judicial approach, the disputants usually hire lawyers to act as their advocates and the case is argued before an impartial and neutral third party—a judge, and perhaps a jury as well. These decision makers take into consideration not only the disputants' concerns, interests, and arguments, but also the broader society's standards and values. The judge or jury is usually required to make a decision based on and in conformity with case law and legal statutes. The outcome is usually win-lose and is premised on a decision regarding who is right and who is wrong. Because the third party is socially sanctioned to make a decision, the results of the process are binding and enforceable. The disputants lose control of the outcome but may gain from forceful advocacy of their point of view and by a decision that reflects socially sanctioned norms.

Whittamore and Singson have both considered using a judicial approach to resolve their dispute. Singson is willing, if necessary, to seek a court injunction that would enforce the no-competition clause in the contract by prohibiting Whittamore from establishing a private practice. Whittamore is willing to go to court to test the constitutionality of the clause. But each sees a risk in this procedure, as the outcome may be highly detrimental to his underlying interests.

The *legislative approach* to dispute resolution is another public means of solving a conflict by recourse to law. It is usually employed for larger disputes affecting broad populations, but it may have significant utility for individuals. In this approach, the decision regarding the outcome is made by another win-lose process: voting. The individual has only as much influence on the final outcome as he or she, and those who share his or her beliefs, can bring to bear on legislators. Furthermore, the win-lose aspect of the outcome is only partly softened by the compromises that go into a bill.

Whittamore has considered using this approach to resolve his dispute. He believes there should be a law against no-competition contracts, and some of his patients agree with him. One patient has even suggested a campaign to pass a bill prohibiting this type of contract. But Whittamore also realizes that a legislative approach to this problem might take a long time—time he does not have at his disposal.

Finally, there is the *extralegal approach*. The approaches examined so far are either private procedures the parties use alone or with the assistance of a third party to negotiate a settlement, or third-party decision making that is either privately or publicly sanctioned. The last category is extralegal in that it does not rely on a socially mandated—or on occasion, socially acceptable—process and uses stronger means of coercion to persuade or force an opponent into compliance or submission. There are two types of extralegal approaches: nonviolent action and violence.

Nonviolent action involves a person or group committing acts or abstaining from acts so that an opponent is forced to behave in a desired manner (Sharp, 1973). These acts, however, do not involve physical coercion or violence and are often designed to minimize psychological harm as well. Nonviolent action works best when the parties must rely on each other for their well-being. When this is the case, one of the parties may force the other to make concessions by refusing to cooperate or by committing undesirable acts.

Nonviolent action often involves civil disobedience—violation of widely accepted social norms or laws—to raise an opponent's consciousness or bring into public view practices that the nonviolent activist considers unjust or unfair. Nonviolent action can be conducted by an individual or by a group and may be either public or private.

Whittamore has contemplated nonviolent action on personal and group levels to resolve his dispute. On the individual level, he has considered fasting or occupying Singson's office until the director agrees to bargain in good faith and give him a fair settlement. He has also considered opening a private practice, challenging the terms of the contract, and forcing the clinic to either take him to court or drop the case. If he goes to court, he could exploit the publicity and place the clinic in a dilemma—dismiss a widely esteemed doctor and earn the wrath of the community and bad publicity or reach a negotiated settlement favorable to Whittamore and avoid the bad press.

One of his patients has suggested organizing a picket or vigil outside the clinic to embarrass Singson into a settlement. If that were to be unsuccessful, the patient has suggested a group sit-in. Whittamore is unsure of the likely effects of these approaches, as well as of the costs.

The last approach to dispute resolution is *violence* or *physical coercion*. This approach assumes that if the costs to the person or property of an opponent and the costs of maintaining his position are high enough, the adversary will be forced to make concessions. For physical coercion to work, the initiating party must possess enough power to actually damage the other party, must be able to convince the other side that it has the power, and must be willing to use it.

Although Whittamore and Singson are very angry with each other, they have not come to blows. Both are physically fit and could conceivably harm each other, but neither feels he could force the issue with a private fight. Whittamore, in the heat of anger, mumbled that he ought to sabotage some of the clinic's valuable equipment, but such an action would go against some of his deeply held values and would also hurt patients. Singson, in a moment of rage and fantasy, also considered violence and wondered what Whittamore's reaction would be if he were to be assaulted by agents Singson could hire for that purpose. He, too, has decided against physical violence as too risky, costly, unpredictable, and unreasonable.

The question remains: which of the approaches represented in Figure 1.1 will Whittamore and Singson choose to resolve their dispute?

Whittamore wants to stay in town so that he can be near his children. He also wants to practice medicine. Establishing a new practice will be expensive, so he wants to minimize his dispute resolution costs. He hopes for a quick decision so that he may leave the clinic soon to avoid more adverse contact with Janelle and to minimize any harm to his personal relationships with other staff members. A positive ongoing relationship with the clinic and its staff is important because the clinic has the only laboratory and X-ray machine in the town. Whittamore also needs to establish a private practice quickly so that he can generate income. Physical violence was a fleeting fantasy. Nonviolent action is still a possibility if the clinic does not yield. Judicial and legislative approaches seem unreasonable at this point because of the cost and the length of time they will take to effect a change.

Singson is also trying to decide what action he will take. He wants to keep management control over the contract process, seeks to solve the problem himself and not rely on outside agents, and wants to minimize such costs as legal fees, patient attrition, and bad publicity. He wants to find an amicable solution but feels that his interaction with Whittamore has reached an impasse.

Whittamore and Singson's conflict is ripe for negotiation. The two parties are

- Interdependent and must rely on the cooperation of one another in order to meet their goals or satisfy their interests
- Able to influence one another and to undertake or prevent actions that can either harm or reward
- Pressured by deadlines and time constraints and share a motivation for early settlement
- Aware that alternatives to a negotiated settlement do not appear as viable or desirable as a bargain that they reach themselves
- Able to identify the critical primary parties and involve them in the problem-solving process
- Able to identify and agree on the issues in dispute
- In a situation in which their interests are not entirely incompatible
- Influenced by external constraints, such as the unpredictability of a judicial decision, potentially angry patients or staff, costs of establishing a new practice, and expenses of recruiting a new physician, that encourage them to reach a negotiated settlement

The above conditions are critical to successful negotiation. However, Singson and Whittamore's relationship also contains elements that will make unassisted negotiations extremely difficult. To overcome these problems, they will need third-party help, and in this case, mediation seems to be the most appropriate dispute resolution procedure to pursue. A mediator may be called into negotiations when

- The emotions of the parties are intense and are preventing a settlement.
- Communication between the parties is poor in either quantity or quality and they cannot change the situation on their own.

- Misperceptions or stereotypes are hindering productive exchanges.
- Repetitive negative behaviors are creating barriers.
- There are serious disagreements over data—what information is important, how it is to be collected, and how it will be evaluated.
- There are multiple issues in dispute and the parties disagree about the order and combination in which they should be addressed.
- There are perceived or actual incompatible interests that the parties are having difficulty reconciling.
- Perceived or actual value differences divide the parties.
- The parties do not have a negotiating procedure, are using the wrong procedure, or are not using a procedure to its best advantage.
- There is not an acceptable structure or forum for negotiations.
- The parties are having difficulties starting negotiations or have reached an impasse in their bargaining.

Because Whittamore and Singson's relationship has some of the characteristics listed here, they will decide to use mediated negotiations as a means of resolving their differences. For the moment, let us leave this case and take a look at the process that they have selected to resolve their conflict. We will return to the Whittamore-Singson dispute in Chapter Two when we explore how the mediation process works.

The Mediation Process

Although mediation is practiced around the world in the resolution of interpersonal, organizational, commercial, legal, community, public, ethnic, and international disputes, and although techniques have been documented in particular applications and case studies, there has been until recently little systematic study or description of specific strategies and tactics used by mediators. The analysis that *has* been done has often been presented on the most general level or is so specific as to limit its broad application.

This book addresses the need for a systematic and practical general approach to mediation. It has three major goals: (1) to illustrate the effects and dynamics of mediation on the practice of negotiation; (2) to develop a theoretical explanation for the current practice of mediation as it has been applied in a variety of issues, arenas, and cultures; (3) to provide practitioners with concrete and effective strategies and techniques to assist parties in dispute resolution. Let us first attempt to define mediation.

A Definition of Mediation

Consider the following scenarios: a mediator from the United Nations enters an international dispute; a labor mediator engages in negotiations prior to a threatened strike; a commercial mediator settles a business dispute; a lawyer acting as a mediator settles a contentious legal suit; a family mediator assists a couple in reaching a divorce settlement. Who are these individuals, and what relationship do they have with the respective parties? What activities are they performing? What are their goals and objectives and those of the mediation process?

As stated earlier, *mediation* is generally defined as the intervention in a negotiation or a conflict of an acceptable third party who has limited or no authoritative decision-making power but who assists the involved parties in voluntarily reaching a mutually acceptable settlement of issues in dispute. In addition to addressing substantive issues, mediation may also establish or strengthen relationships of trust and respect between the parties or terminate relationships in a manner that minimizes costs and psychological harm.

A mediator is a third party, a person not directly involved in the dispute. This is a critical factor in conflict management and resolution, for it is the participation of an outsider that frequently provides parties with new perspectives on the issues dividing them and more effective processes to build problem-solving relationships. More will be said about the variety of possible relationships between the parties and "outsiders" in the next section.

The next aspect of the definition is *acceptability:* the disputants must be willing to allow a third party to enter the dispute and assist them in reaching a resolution. Acceptability does not necessarily mean that disputants eagerly welcome the involvement of the mediator and are willing to do exactly as he or she says. It does mean that the parties approve of the mediator's presence and are willing to listen to and seriously consider his or her suggestions.

Intervention means "to enter into an ongoing system of relationships, to come between or among persons, groups, or objects for the purpose of helping them. There is an important implicit assumption in the definition that should be made explicit: the system exists independently of the intervenor" (Argyris, 1970, p. 15). The assumption behind an outsider's intervention is that a third party will be able to alter the power and social dynamics of the conflict relationship by influencing the beliefs or behaviors of individual parties, by providing knowledge or information, or by using a more effective negotiation process and thereby helping the participants to settle contested issues. Rubin and Brown (1975) have argued that the mere presence of a party who is independent of the disputants may be a highly significant factor in the resolution of a dispute.

For mediation to occur, the parties must begin talking or negotiating. Labor and management must be willing to hold a bargaining session, business associates must agree to conduct discussions, governments and public interest groups must create forums for dialogue, and families must be willing to come together to talk. *Mediation is essentially dialogue or negotiation with the involvement of a third party.* Mediation is an extension of the negotiation process in that it involves extending the bargaining into a new format and using a mediator who contributes new variables and dynamics to the interaction of the disputants. Without negotiation, there can be no mediation.

Conflicts involve struggles between two or more people over values, or competition for status, power, or scarce resources (Coser, 1967). Mediators enter conflicts that have reached various levels of development and intensity—latent, emerging, and manifest. These levels differ according to their degree of organization, the activities of the parties, and the intensity of expression of concerns and emotions. *Latent conflicts* are characterized by underlying tensions that have not fully developed and have not escalated into a highly polarized conflict. Often, one or more parties, usually the stronger one, may not even be aware that a conflict or the potential for one exists (Curle, 1971). Examples of latent conflicts are changes in personal relationships in which one party is not aware of the seriousness of the breach that has occurred; projected staff cutbacks within an organization; developed but unannounced plans for the siting of a predictably controversial facility such as a mine or waste disposal site; or potentially unpopular changes in public policy.

Mediators (or facilitators, another type of third party) working on latent disputes help participants identify the people who will be affected by a change or who may be concerned about a problem arising in the future. They assist in the development of a mutual education process around the issues and interests involved, and work with participants on the design, and sometimes the implementation, of a problem-solving process.

Emerging conflicts are disputes in which the parties are identified, the dispute is acknowledged, and many issues are clear. However, a workable cooperative negotiation or problem-solving process has not developed. Emerging conflicts have a potential for escalation if a resolution procedure is not implemented. Many disputes between coworkers, businesses, and governments illustrate this type of conflict. Both parties recognize that there is a dispute, and there may have been a harsh verbal exchange, but neither knows how to handle the problem. In this case, the mediator helps establish the negotiation process and helps the parties begin to communicate and bargain.

Manifest conflicts are those in which parties are engaged in an active and ongoing dispute, may have started to negotiate, and may have reached an impasse. Mediator involvement in manifest conflicts often involves changing the negotiation procedure or intervening to break a specific deadlock. Labor mediators who intervene in negotiations before a strike deadline are working to resolve manifest conflicts, as are commercial mediators who handle a specific insurance claim over a personal injury. Child custody and divorce mediators also usually intervene in fully manifest disputes.

A mediator generally has limited or no authoritative decision-making power; he or she cannot unilaterally mandate or force parties to resolve their differences and enforce the decision. This characteristic distinguishes the mediator from the judge or arbitrator, who is generally empowered to make a decision for the parties on the basis of a prior agreement by the disputants or societal norms, rules, regulations, laws, or contracts. The goal of a judicial or quasi-judicial process is not reconciliation or agreement between the parties, but a unilateral decision by the third party concerning which of the parties is right.

The judge examines the past and evaluates "agreements that the parties have entered into, violations which one has inflicted on the other," and "the norms concerning acquisition of rights, responsibilities, etc. which are connected with these events. When he has taken his standpoint on this basis, his task is finished" (Eckhoff, 1966–67, p. 161).

The mediator, on the other hand, works to reconcile the competing interests of the two parties. The mediator's task is to assist the parties in examining their interests and needs and in negotiating an exchange of promises and the definition of a relationship that will be mutually satisfactory and will meet the parties' standards of fairness.

The mediator does not have decision-making authority, and this fact makes mediation attractive to many parties in dispute because they can retain the ultimate decision-making power. However, mediators are not without influence. The mediator's authority, such as it is, resides in his or her personal credibility and trustworthiness, expertise in enhancing the negotiation process, experience in handling similar issues, ability to bring the parties together on the basis of their own interests, past performance or reputation as a resource person, and in some cultures, his or her relationship with the parties. Authority, or recognition of the right to influence the outcome of a dispute, is granted by the parties themselves rather than by an external law, contract, or agency.

So far, we have examined some of the characteristics of a mediator. We will now explore some of the functions a mediator performs. The definition above states that a mediator *assists* disputing parties. Assistance can refer to very general or to highly specific activities. We will examine here some of the more general roles and functions of the mediator, and will discuss specifics later, when analyzing intervention activities made during particular phases of negotiation.

The mediator may assume a variety of roles to assist parties in resolving disputes (American Arbitration Association, n.d.):

- The *opener of communication channels,* who initiates communication or facilitates better communication if the parties are already talking

- The *legitimizer,* who helps all parties recognize the right of others to be involved in negotiations
- The *process facilitator,* who provides a procedure and often formally chairs the negotiation session
- The *trainer,* who educates novice, unskilled, or unprepared negotiators in the bargaining process
- The *resource expander,* who provides procedural assistance to the parties and links them to outside experts and resources (for example, lawyers, technical experts, decision makers, or additional goods for exchange) that may enable them to enlarge acceptable settlement options
- The *problem explorer,* who enables people in dispute to examine a problem from a variety of viewpoints, assists in defining basic issues and interests, and looks for mutually satisfactory options
- The *agent of reality,* who helps build a reasonable and implementable settlement and questions and challenges parties who have extreme and unrealistic goals
- The *scapegoat,* who may take some of the responsibility or blame for an unpopular decision that the parties are nevertheless willing to accept. This enables them to maintain their integrity and, when appropriate, gain the support of their constituents.
- The *leader,* who takes the initiative to move the negotiations forward by procedural—or on occasion, substantive—suggestions.

The last component of the definition describes mediation as a voluntary process to reach a mutually acceptable settlement of issues in dispute. *Voluntary* refers to freely chosen participation and freely made agreement. Parties are not forced to negotiate, mediate, or settle by either an internal or external party to a dispute. Stulberg (1981b, pp. 88–89) notes that "there is no legal liability to any party refusing to participate in a mediation process. . . . Since a mediator has no authority unilaterally to impose a decision on the parties, he cannot threaten the recalcitrant party with a judgement."

Voluntary participation does not, however, mean that there may not be pressure to try mediation. Other disputants or external figures, such as friends, colleagues at work, constituents, authoritative leaders, or judges, may put significant pressure on a party to make an attempt at negotiation with the assistance of a mediator. Some courts in family and civil cases in the United States have even gone so far as to rule that parties must make a good faith effort at mediation before the court will be willing to hear the case. Attempting mediation does not, however, mean that the participants are forced to settle.

The Historical Practice of Mediation

Mediation has a long and varied history in almost all cultures of the world. Jewish, Christian, Islamic, Hindu, Buddhist, Confucian, and many indigenous cultures all have extensive and effective traditions of mediation practice. The following examples are indicators of the extensiveness and development of mediation as a means of dispute resolution.

Jewish communities in biblical times utilized mediation—which was practiced by both religious and political leaders—to resolve civil and religious differences. Later, in Spain, North Africa, Italy, Central and Eastern Europe, the Turkish Empire, and the Middle East, rabbis and rabbinical courts played vital roles in mediating or adjudicating disputes between members of their faith. These courts were often crucial to the protection of cultural identity and ensured that Jews had a formalized means of dispute resolution. In many locales, Jews were barred by exclusionary laws of larger societies from other means of dispute settlement.

Jewish traditions of dispute resolution were ultimately carried over to emerging Christian communities, who saw Christ as the supreme mediator. The Bible refers to Jesus as a mediator between God and man: "For there is one God, and one mediator between God and man, the man Christ Jesus; who gave himself as ransom for all, to be testified in due time" (I Timothy 2:5–6). This concept of the intermediary was eventually adopted to define the role of clergy as mediators between the congregation and God and between believers. Until the Renaissance, the Catholic Church in Western Europe and the Orthodox Church in the Eastern Mediterranean world were probably the central mediation and conflict management organizations in Western society. Clergy mediated family disputes, criminal cases, and diplomatic disputes among the nobility. Bianchi (1978), in describing one mediated case in the Middle Ages, details how the church and the clergy provided the sanctuary where the offender stayed during dispute resolution and how they served as intermediaries between two families in a case involving rape. In the resulting settlement, the family of the rapist agreed to provide monetary restitution to the woman's family and promised to help her find a husband.

Islamic cultures also have long traditions of mediation. In many traditional pastoral societies in the Middle East, problems were often resolved through a community meeting of elders in which participants discussed, debated, deliberated, and mediated to resolve critical or conflictual tribal or intertribal issues. In urban areas, local custom ('urf) became codified into shari'a law, which was interpreted and applied by specialized intermediaries or quadis. These officials performed not only judicial but mediating functions. Hourani (1991, p. 114) notes that a quadi "might interpret his role as that of a conciliator, attempting to preserve social harmony by reaching an agreed upon solution to a dispute, rather than applying the strict letter of the law."

In Indonesia, one of the largest geographic areas influenced by Islam and Arab culture, traditional means of decision making and dispute resolution were blended with Islamic practices. The result was the musyawarah process, a consensually based conflict management procedure (Moore and Santosa, 1995). Variations of this process were used, and are still practiced today, throughout the island archipelago to make decisions and resolve disputes on both local and national issues (Von Benda-Beckman, 1984; Slatts and Porter, 1992; Schwarz, 1994).

Hinduism and Buddhism, and the regions that they influenced, have a long history of mediation. The Hindu villages of India have traditionally employed the panchayat justice system, in which a panel of five members both mediates and arbitrates disputes, and exercises administrative functions in addressing welfare issues and grievances within the community.

Mediation has been widely practiced in China, Japan, and a number of other Asian societies, where religion and philosophy place a strong emphasis on social consensus, moral persuasion, and seeking balance and harmony in human relations (Brown, 1982). Buddhist sacred texts describe at least three cases in which the Buddha acted as a mediator (Dhammapada Commentary, n.d.;

Kosambi Jataka, n.d.), and the sangha, or religious community of priests and nuns, has long played a mediation role in Buddhist communities and societies, first in India and China, and later in Sri Lanka, Thailand, Nepal, Tibet, and Japan (McConnell, 1995).

With the rise of secular society in the West, mediation and the range of people acting as mediators expanded. In the business world, guilds and their members practiced mediation, as did burghers in disputes arising in the emerging cities. Though the clergy continued to play a role as intermediaries in local, inter-communal, and interstate relations, the rise of nation-states led to the growth of secular diplomatic intermediaries. Ambassadors and envoys acted to "raise and clarify social issues and problems, to modify conflicting interests, and to transmit information of mutual concern to parties" (Werner, 1974, p. 95).

Mediation also grew in the American and other colonies, and ultimately in the United States and Canada, where religious sects such as the Puritans and Quakers, and Chinese and Jewish ethnic groups, developed alternative procedures for dispute resolution that were of an informal and voluntary nature (Auerbach, 1983). These procedures functioned in parallel with preexisting dispute resolution mechanisms of Native Americans and First Nations peoples, who often used consensus-based council meetings, led by an elder or elders, to resolve disputes (LeResche, 1993).

The Contemporary Practice of Mediation

For the most part, mediators in other ages and cultures were trained informally and they fulfilled their role in the context of other functions or duties. Only since the turn of the twentieth century has mediation become formally institutionalized and developed into a recognized profession. The modern practice of mediation has expanded exponentially worldwide, especially in the last twenty-five years. This growth is due in part to a wider acknowledgment of individual human rights and dignity, the expansion of aspirations for democratic participation at all social and political levels, the belief that an individual has a right to participate in and take control of decisions affecting his or her life, an ethic supporting private ordering, and trends in some locales for broader tolerance of diversity in all its aspects. Change has also been moti-

vated by growing dissatisfaction with authoritative, top-down decision makers and decision-making procedures, imposed settlements
that do not adequately address parties' strongly felt or genuine
interests, and the increasing costs—in money, time, human resources, interpersonal and community solidarity—of more adversarial, win-lose procedures of dispute resolution.

The use of mediation has grown significantly in many countries
and cultures, but it has perhaps grown most rapidly in the United
States and Canada. The first arena in which mediation was formally
institutionalized in the United States was that of labor-management
relations (Simkin, 1971). In 1913, the U.S. Department of Labor
was established, and a panel, the "commissioners of conciliation,"
was appointed to handle conflicts between labor and management.
This panel subsequently became the United States Conciliation Service, and in 1947, was reconstituted as the Federal Mediation and
Conciliation Service. The rationale for initiating mediation procedures in the industrial sector was to promote a "sound and stable
industrial peace" and "the settlement of issues between employer
and employees through collective bargaining" (Labor-Management
Relations Act, 1947). It was expected that mediated settlements
would prevent costly strikes and lockouts and that the safety, welfare, and wealth of Americans would be improved. Federal use of
mediation in labor disputes has provided a model for many states.
Numerous states have passed laws, developed regulations, and
trained a cadre of mediators to handle intrastate labor conflicts.

The private sector has also initiated labor-management and
commercial relations mediation. The American Arbitration Association was founded in 1926 to encourage the use of arbitration
and other techniques of voluntary dispute settlement.

Mediation sponsored by government agencies has not been
confined to labor-management issues. The federal Civil Rights Act
of 1964 created the Community Relations Service (CRS) of the U.S.
Department of Justice. This agency was mandated to help "communities and persons therein in resolving disputes, disagreements,
or difficulties relating to discriminatory practices based on race,
color, or national origin" (Civil Rights Act, 1964). The agency assists
people in resolving disputes through negotiation and mediation
rather than through recourse to street justice or the judicial system
(Klugman, 1992). CRS works throughout the country on such issues

as school desegregation and public-accommodation cases. There has also been a burgeoning of diverse state agencies, local civil rights commissions, and private agencies that use mediation to handle charges of race and ethnic discrimination in areas of employment, housing, accommodations, and consumer affairs (ICMA, 1966). In Canada, the Ontario Race Relations Directorate and other similar agencies in that province have provided dispute resolution services to manage differences between ethnic communities.

There have also been a number of specialized initiatives to apply mediation to the resolution of ethnic and economic disputes within and between various groups. The Navajo peacemakers (Bluehouse and Zion, 1993), Pacific-coast Salish tribes conciliators (Mansfield, 1993), Alaskan tribes intermediaries (Connors, 1993), the Mohawks' Akwesasne Peacemaking Program, and a variety of other tribal groups have developed traditional or modified means of resolving internal tribal differences. On the Hawaiian islands, traditional dispute resolution procedures, the Ho'Oponopono, are being revived to manage differences between a number of ethnic groups (Shook and Kwan, 1988; Barnes, 1994). Programs and projects have been developed in Los Angeles and Chicago to address disputes between Korean and African-American communities, especially those related to conflicts between business owners and customers. In New York, initiatives have been taken to manage African-American and Hasidic Jewish conflicts, and in a number of cities, programs have been developed to respond to tensions between the dominant culture, traditional minority cultures, and Southeast Asian immigrants.

Since the mid-1960s, mediation has grown significantly as a formal and widely practiced approach to community dispute resolution. In the early years of the field's growth, the federal government funded Neighborhood Justice Centers (NJCs) that provided free or low-cost mediation services to the public so that disputes could be resolved efficiently, inexpensively, and informally. In the early 1980s, many of these NJCs were institutionalized and became part of city-, court-, or district attorney–based alternative dispute resolution services. Some community programs also became independent nonprofit organizations and offered a grassroots dispute resolution service in which community members served as solo mediators, co-mediators, or members of mediation or conciliation panels (Lemmon, 1984; Shonholtz, 1984).

In many U.S. and Canadian communities, mediation is being applied in landlord-tenant conflicts (Cook, Rochl, and Shepard, 1980), issues related to homelessness (Nelson and Sharp, 1995), police work with disputants (Folberg and Taylor, 1984), conflicts between citizens and police (Mayor's Office, City of Portland, Oregon, 1994), disputes between elderly residents and nursing home owners, and consumer disputes (Ray and Smolover, 1983).

Canadians have developed community-based programs in a number of provinces. Of special note is the program of the Saskatchewan Mediation Service, based in Regina, which has focused on the provision of services to farm families, including the mediation of debtor-creditor and loan restructuring disputes and interpersonal and operations conflicts on family farms.

In addition to local mediation programs, there are statewide programs in many American states (Suskind, 1986; Drake, 1989). Initially spurred by the advocacy and funding by the National Institute for Dispute Resolution, the number of state-based programs jumped from four in 1984 to twenty in 1995, with some states having more than one program (Khor, 1995). Services provided by state programs include design and implementation of dispute resolution systems, training of state employees in alternative dispute resolution procedures, and mediation of interpersonal, group, and public disputes that involve state government.

Mediation is also practiced in schools and institutions of higher education (Araki, 1990). In this setting, disputes are mediated between students (Volpe and Witherspoon, 1992; Smith and Sidwell, 1990; Burrell and Vogl, 1990; Levy, 1989; Doelker, 1989), between students and faculty, between faculty members, and between faculty and administration (McCarthy, 1980; McCarthy and others, 1984; Crohn, 1985). In the 1980s, the National Association of Mediation in Education (NAME) was founded, to link mediation practitioners and programs in the educational arena.

An interesting aspect of the growth of mediation in education has been the expansion of programs that train youth in mediating peer disputes. These initiatives have made significant impacts on the levels of conflicts in schools (Smith and Sidwell, 1990), and in some cases, a reduction in gang violence (Wahrhaftig, 1995).

Another interesting effort in the area of education is the use of mediation and other collaborative problem-solving skills to handle problems related to decentralized decision making and school-based management (CDR Associates, 1993). In this application, consensus-based decision making assisted by a facilitator/mediator is used as a strategy for the anticipation, prevention, and management of conflict, as well as a process for fostering collaborative day-to-day decisions.

The criminal justice systems in the United States and Canada have utilized mediation to resolve criminal complaints (Felsteiner and Williams, 1978) and disputes in correctional facilities (Reynolds and Tonry, 1981). Mediation in the latter arena takes the form of both crisis intervention in prison riots or hostage negotiations and institutionalized grievance procedures. An interesting growth area in the criminal justice system has been victim-offender mediation programs in which intermediaries help concerned parties to develop restitution plans or to reestablish conflicted interpersonal relationships (Umbreit, 1985, 1994; Fagan and Gehm, 1993; Coates and Gehm, 1989).

One of the fastest-growing arenas in North America in which mediation is being practiced is family disputes (Fisher, L., 1991). Court systems and private practitioners provide mediation to families in child custody and divorce proceedings (Coogler, 1978; McIsaac, 1983; Folberg and Taylor, 1984; Folberg and Milne, 1988; Haynes, 1981, 1994; Irving, 1980; Lemmon, 1985: Saposnek, 1983; Moore, 1988), disputes between parents and children (Shaw, 1982; Wixted, 1982; Vorenberg, 1982), child protection cases (Mayer, 1985; Golten and Mayer, 1987), conflicts involving adoption and the termination of parental rights (Mayer, 1985), spousal disputes in which there is domestic violence (Orenstein, 1982; Wildau, 1984; Ellis and Stuckless, 1992; Barsky, 1995; Corcoran and Melamed, 1990; Girdner, 1990; Erickson and McKnight, 1990), and as an alternative separation process for gay and lesbian couples (McIntyre, 1994; Gunning, 1995). In family disputes, mediated and consensual settlements are often more appropriate and satisfying than litigated or imposed outcomes. Models of practice in this area include mandatory court-connected programs in which disputants must try mediation before a judge will hear the case; voluntary court programs; and forms of private practice such as the sole practitioner, the partnership, and the private nonprofit agency.

Mediation is also extensively utilized within public and private organizations to handle interpersonal and institutional disputes.

The scope of mediation application ranges from one-on-one personnel disputes, problems between partners (for example, in law or medical practices), interdepartmental conflicts, and altercations between companies (Biddle and others, 1982; Blake and Mouton, 1984; Brett and Goldberg, 1983; Brown, 1983; Bazerman and Lewicki, 1983). In the late 1980s and early 1990s, there was a significant growth of mediation services and programs in both the public and private sectors to mediate charges related to racial, ethnic, gender, and sexual-orientation discrimination in the workplace, sexual harassment (Rowe, 1994), and accommodation of people with disabilities (Roberts and Lundy, 1995), as well as to process complaints or grievances in nonunion and unionized settings (Skratek, 1990; Feuille, 1992; Goldberg, 1989; Valtin, 1993). Programs have been developed in a number of federal and state agencies such as the U.S. Bureau of Reclamation and the Army Corps of Engineers ("Corps of Engineers Early Resolution Program," 1993), state governments (deLeon, 1994), and private sector firms (Westin and Feliu, 1988; Rowe, 1995). The federal government, through the Administrative Dispute Resolution Act, presidential memorandums, and regulations for rulemaking, has actively promoted the use of alternative dispute resolution and mediation (Suskind, Babbit, and Segal, 1993).

Closely related to the use of mediation in organizations is the growth of a wider practice of conflict management, institutional decision making, and dispute systems design.

Decision making and dispute systems design is a systematic process for enabling people and developing mechanisms to make decisions and handle serious chronic disputes. The process involves 1) identification of types and causes of reoccurring issues and conflicts; 2) development and institutionalization of a range of decision-making, conflict management, and dispute resolution procedures that will assist parties to make decisions, lower the number of incidents of destructive conflict, and assist them to resolve their differences; 3) matching of issues and disputes with the appropriate decision making, conflict management or resolution procedure; 4) implementation of efficient operations and administrative procedures (of the system); 5) design of effective information programs to educate potential parties about how the range of decision making and dispute resolution processes can assist them to reach settlements and resolve conflicts; and 6) training cadres of people to work in the new system and provide needed services [Wildau and Mayer, 1992].

Many dispute resolution systems, whether newly developed or the result of the expansion of a previously existing system, have involved the implementation of a mediation component. Settings in which systems have been developed include corporations, unionized mines, hospitals, social service agencies, natural resource management agencies, human resource departments, and federal, state, and local governments (Ury, Brett, and Goldberg, 1988; Ziegenfuss, 1988; Slaiku, 1989; Constantino and Merchant, 1995).

Mediation has grown very rapidly since the mid-1980s in the corporate and commercial arenas, where in some types of disputes it has surpassed arbitration as the method of choice. Common types of disputes that have been mediated in this arena include contract disputes, failure to perform, product liability, patent infringement, trademark violations, intellectual property disputes, and a variety of insurance claim issues ("AAA Designs ADR Insurance Procedures," 1984). Leaders in promoting the use of alternative dispute resolution procedures, including mediation, to resolve corporate and commercial disputes have been the Center for Public Resources, the American Arbitration Association, Jams/Endispute, and a number of other national and local private dispute resolution providers, as well as governmental agencies like the U.S. Army Corps of Engineers. The Center for Public Resources is a nonprofit coalition of general counsels of Fortune 500 companies and partners in leading law firms who are seeking alternatives to the increasingly high cost of litigation. Through publications, educational forums, and the Corporate Policy Statement (a pledge signed by corporations to explore and utilize alternative dispute resolution mechanisms as a first resort for settling commercial disputes), they have made a significant contribution to educating North American corporations about the utility of non-adversarial procedures (Henry and Lieberman, 1985).

Court-based mediation programs have been established in a number of jurisdictions in the United States to handle a variety of issues. Starting in the area of family disputes, these programs have expanded to address a wide range of civil cases. In some jurisdictions, courts have prescribed lower limits for financial claims, below which disputants must try mediation before the court will hear the case. Mediators working in these programs are generally either officials of the court or private mediators on contract.

Another court-based mediation initiative that has gained popularity in a number of jurisdictions in the U.S. and abroad is "Settlement Week" (Dewdney, Sordo, and Chinkin, 1994). In this program, the court docket is set aside for a week, and cases are sent to voluntary mediation as an informal and expedited means of settlement. Mediations are conducted by trained professional mediators, lawyers, and judges. The record of success has led to the adoption of this mediation model by a number of jurisdictions across the U.S. and in other countries.

Mediation is also used extensively to resolve a wide variety of large public disputes over environmental and social policy issues (Suskind and Cruikshank, 1987; Laue, 1988; Bingham, 1984; Stamato and Jaffe, 1991). In the environmental arena, mediation has been used to address site-specific conflicts such as those over water project construction, conservation, and operations (Carpenter and Kennedy, 1977; Meeks, 1988; Moore, 1989, 1991; Viessman and Smerdon, 1989), facility siting and locational disputes (O'Hare, Bacow, and Sanderson, 1983; Lake, 1987; Tomain, 1989), and development issues (Sullivan, 1984); wildlife and fisheries management and habitat protection issues (CDR Associates, 1993, 1995); waste management; highway, railroad, and airport siting; hazardous waste cleanup; land management and wetlands protection; and a variety of other local disputes (Bacow and Wheeler, 1984; Talbot, 1983; Cormick, 1976; Lake, 1980; and Mernitz, 1980).

Mediation is also being used extensively by a number of federal and state agencies to develop new regulations through a process of regulatory negotiations, or "reg-negs" (Bingham, 1981; Harter, 1984; Haygood, 1988). In this process, key stakeholders concerned about proposed regulations are convened, and negotiations are conducted by mediators or facilitators to develop consensus recommendations that can be submitted to the sponsoring agency or government entity. The federal agency that has sponsored the largest number of regulatory negotiations has been the U.S. Environmental Protection Agency, although a number of other agencies, such as the Department of Education, the Department of the Interior, the Federal Aviation Administration, the Occupational Safety and Health Administration, the Nuclear Regulatory Commission, and the Department of Agriculture, as well as a significant number of state governments, have implemented similar procedures.

The topics for "reg-negs" have included aggregate resource mining regulations; standard setting for volatile organic compound emissions from finishes used in wood furniture manufacturing; use of disinfectants in drinking water; standards for the disposal of nonhazardous construction debris; rules for fossil collection on federal lands; accessibility of airplanes to people with disabilities; and air emissions standards from small engines.

Closely related to the development of regulations is the mediation of permitting and enforcement actions. Mediation helps concerned parties negotiate acceptable agreements over the conditions for future activity—for example, waste treatment and discharge plans for a new factory or the mitigation or cleanup of past environmental problems. Allocating responsibility among potentially responsible parties at U.S. Superfund hazardous waste sites is a case in point; mediators have assisted concerned parties in apportioning financial responsibilities for cleanup and in negotiating remediation plans.

In the area of making public policy, mediation has been used to facilitate policy dialogues (Ehrman and Lesnick, 1988). Like regulatory negotiations, this process involves convening key stakeholder groups and negotiating consensus recommendations that can then be incorporated into policies or legislation. Some examples of policy dialogues are negotiations to develop growth management plans in California and New Jersey, policies and testing procedures for lowering volatile organic compounds in carpets and carpet-related activities, policies for the protection of oyster beds in the Chesapeake Bay, model national energy policies, and control of storm drainage systems.

In nonenvironmental areas, mediation has been utilized in site-specific cases, regulatory negotiations, and policy dialogues to enable local, state, and federal agencies to coordinate their decisions on such matters as block grants for program funding (Shanahan and others, 1982); development of educational policies; closure or conversion of military bases or weapons production plants; policies on the release of drugs to the public; promotion of biodiversity and sustainability issues; historic preservation of valuable urban properties; municipal social service priorities; funding allocation priorities for the treatment of AIDS (Hughes, 1995); and resolutions of farmer-creditor disputes.

One of the newest areas of growth in mediation is the health care industry (Reeves, 1994; Leone, 1994; Marcus and others, 1995). In the U.S. and Canada over the last decade, this industry has seen a growing number of disputes. Medical malpractice claims cost the industry roughly $15 billion annually in preventive insurance (Quayle, 1991). These suits are damaging to physicians and a threat to family financial security. Studies on the motivations of malpractice plaintiffs have shown that 40 percent felt humiliated by their experiences with the physician, over 50 percent felt betrayed by their doctor, over 80 percent felt embittered by the doctor's response to their complaints/questions, and over 90 percent were "very angry" at their physician. In addition, 24 percent felt the physician was dishonest or misled them regarding the case or incident, 20 percent felt "court was the only way to find out what happened," and 19 percent felt the need to punish the doctor. When asked what could have been done to prevent litigation, 35 percent of plaintiff-patients responded, "apologize or offer further explanations," and 25 percent responded, "correct the error"; by contrast, only 16 percent responded, "pay me compensation" (Dauer, 1994). Because malpractice disputes are often amenable to negotiation to resolve both emotional and financial issues, a number of insurers (Aetna, Allstate, Chubb, State Farm, Cigna, Federated, Fireman's Fund, Hartford, Maryland Casualty, Nationwide, Royal, St. Paul Fire and Marine, Wausau, and others) have begun to offer mediation as an alternative means of dispute settlement (Slaiku, 1989). To date, the process has been highly successful. In Austin, Texas, where a majority of malpractice claims are now mediated, there is an 80 percent settlement rate (Joseph, 1994).

In addition to malpractice cases, there are a number of other health care disputes in which mediation is being applied or explored. They include conflicts between doctors, administrators, and hospitals; HMO, group practice, and partnership difficulties;

disputes between doctors and nurses; insurer denial of coverage; insurer denial of payment; bioethical disputes; credentialing conflicts; and labor-management relations (Joseph, 1994).

Mediation Around the World

The modern practice of mediation is not confined to Western culture, and in fact mediation procedures may be more widely practiced in non-Western societies and countries than in the West (Augsburger, 1992). In general, the world can be divided into direct-dealing and nondirect-dealing cultures. Members of the former value face-to-face interactions, accept conflict as a given, are generally not afraid to directly confront those with whom they disagree, and are comfortable with direct dialogue, debate, and negotiations. Members of the latter generally try to avoid overt conflict, strive to preserve face for themselves and others, and extensively utilize both informal and formal intermediaries. Many non-Western cultures, especially in Asia, Africa, and Latin America, have highly developed informal and formal mediation processes that are integrated into day-to-day interactions for the resolution of conflicts.

Asia

The Asia-Pacific region has been a particularly fertile area for mediation practice. The People's Republic of China has long practiced mediation to resolve interpersonal, community, and civil disputes through People's Conciliation Committees and court conciliation (Ginsberg, 1978; Li, 1978, Li, 1988). The People's Conciliation Committees are institutionalized service providers established by the government; they provide mediation services primarily at the neighborhood, village, town, district, and county levels. The mediators are often retired village leaders with high prestige. The court conciliation occurs in the process of settling judicial cases and is often mediated by the hearing judge. More recently, mediation has been introduced to manage environmental and interjurisdictional disputes between governmental entities, which have been given increasing degrees of autonomy from the central government. Hong Kong, too, has made significant strides in introducing and institutionalizing mediation in the commercial and family areas through the Hong Kong International Arbitration Centre and a number of social service agencies, both religious and secular.

Japan has a long history of using mediation at the informal level, with elaborate systems of go-betweens carrying communications between disputing parties. Mediation is embedded in the business culture, where intermediaries are used as introducers, *shokai-sha,* and as mediators, *chukai-sha,* to smooth business relationships (Graham and Sano, 1984). Japan also has an elaborate system of court-based mediation for both civil and family cases, which is extensively used to address a wide range of issues (Krapp, 1992). Family mediation is mandatory for most divorce proceedings and many parent-child issues. Generally, there is a mediation panel chaired by a judge and two other respected professional mediators, the latter handling most of the sessions. In 1987, there were 13,133 mediators in family courts.

Korea has developed mediation to address family and civil disputes through both independent and court-based mediation programs (Yang, 1988). In recent years, the ruling political party has established the People's Predicament Committee, which performs both ombudsman and mediating functions. The national environmental agency has also developed a mediating committee to address environmental issues.

Thailand, Malaysia, and Indonesia have developed a number of arenas where mediation is used (Muntarbhorn, 1988; Moore and Santosa, 1995; Ihromi, 1988). Thailand has experience in mediation primarily at the village level. Malaysia has developed a formal "conciliation" process, centered on government-appointed mediators, for the resolution of industrial relations and trade conflicts (Aminuddin, 1990). Independent mediators are also used on rare occasions.

Indonesia, which has had a more restrictive government since the imposition of the New Order in 1965, still has maintained the *musyawarah* process for consensus decision making and dispute resolution in many villages and institutions. In addition, labor mediation is offered through a governmental body, the Committee for Labor Conflicts Settlements, which is part of the Ministry for Labor Affairs (Ihromi, 1988). The newest initiative in the area of *musyawarah* and mediation is in environmental dispute resolution. The Ministry for the Environment, the Bureau of Environmental Impact Management, and several nongovernmental public interest groups including Wahana Lingkungan Hidup Indonesia and the Indonesian Center for Environmental Law have supported and participated in a number of mediations over water pollution issues, and the governor of the province of Kalimantan on Borneo is supporting the design and institutionalization of a mediation system for the resolution of environmental disputes. The latter project is conducted in cooperation with the Deutsche Gesellschaft für Technische Zusammenarbeit (GTZ), a German technical assistance agency, and U.S. conflict management practitioners (Moore and Santosa, 1995).

The Philippines and Sri Lanka have developed highly elaborate community-based mediation programs for the resolution of civil and some minor criminal disputes. The Barangay Justice System in the Philippines, which was established by President Marcos in 1978, set up a nationwide system of mediation and arbitration panels in neighborhoods and districts to hear community disputes (Pe and Tadiar, 1988). The mediation panels handle cases in a multistep resolution process that includes efforts by the panel chair to settle the case, a mediation hearing, and if these are not effective, the option of a decision by an arbitration panel. The system now has over forty thousand boards throughout the country.

Sri Lanka's Mediation Boards Commission was authorized by law in 1988. This founding act set up an independent Mediation Boards Commission under the Ministry of Justice and provided for the establishment of mediation panels of respected citizens in districts throughout the island. With the assistance of U.S. experts in dispute systems design and in mediation, the boards have trained over 6,000 mediators and have established over 240 panels. Thousands of civil cases are processed each year (Herat, 1993).

On the Indian subcontinent today, the *panchayat* tradition described earlier is carried on in India, Nepal, Pakistan, and Bangladesh. In India, mediation is provided by legal aid programs in a number of states, and in Gujarat and Uttar Pradesh states, by the *Lok Adalats,* or People's Courts, which offer mediation and conciliation services for matrimonial and civil disputes (Shourie, 1988). In India, many of these systems have been strongly influenced by Gandhian principles of decentralized governance. Nepal, Pakistan, and Bangladesh have also taken steps to enhance, develop, and institutionalize mediation services, primarily at the local levels (Afzal, 1988; Aryal, 1988; Islam, 1988). The Nepalese have developed mediation procedures to handle forest management disputes

(Shrestha, 1995), marital conflicts, and financial transactions. Pakistan and Bangladesh have concentrated on the mediation of family and civil disputes.

Australia, New Zealand, Melanesia

Australia and New Zealand have followed a development path in mediation that in many ways has paralleled that of North America. Initially, mediation in several arenas in Australia was financially supported by government agencies. Community mediation centers have been established in most states and in large urban areas. These centers provide either solo mediation or co-mediation and have primarily addressed smaller civil and neighborhood disputes.

Mediation in Australia has also been developed in the courts—in the family arena (Faulkes, 1988; Renouf, 1991), as a component of a settlement week program, and as part of a Supreme Court pilot project on the resolution of personal injury, mortgaged property, and simple contractual disputes (Dewdney, Sordo, and Chinkin, 1994). Australia also has a very active community mediation sector, with programs in most states (Faulkes, 1990; Stevenson, 1990). Race complaints are also being mediated (Mulcahy, 1992). In addition, mediation is being used to resolve industrial disputes (Interim Rules, 1992) and conflicts between the majority culture and Australia's aboriginal peoples over social service and natural resource issues (Ross, 1995).

New Zealand has developed mediation services to handle a range of commercial, civil, small claims, criminal, family, labor, housing, land, and environmental disputes (Macduff, 1988). In the area of housing, the Housing Corporation of New Zealand has developed extensive services, provided by in-house and external mediators, for resolution of differences between tenants in public housing and between the authority and tenants. The Maori, the indigenous population of New Zealand, have their own traditional means of resolving disputes, *taha Maori,* or the Maori way, which until recently they utilized only within the tribe or kinship group. This process involves a ritualized greeting invoking spirits, ancestors, and common bonds; the creation of an atmosphere for dialogue; a fairly unlimited and open discussion; and a recognition of agreement and reconciliation. More recently, some of these procedures have been used to address Maori altercations with Pakiha (non-Maoris) (Macduff, 1995) and Maori land claims disputes (Wilson, 1992).

In Melanesia, the Tolai villages in New Britain each have a counselor and committee that meet regularly to hear disputes (Epstein, 1971). The role of the counselor and committee is to "maintain conditions for orderly debate and freedom of argument by the disputants and anyone else who wishes to express opinion" (Gulliver, 1979, p. 27). The process is both a "mode of adjudication" and a "settlement by consensus" of the parties (Epstein, 1971, p. 168).

Latin America

Latin American indigenous and Hispanic cultures have utilized mediation historically, and they currently use it to address a range of disputes. Nader (1969) reports on the dispute resolution process in the Mexican village of Ralu'a, where a judge assists the parties in making consensual decisions. Lederach (1984, 1995) describes other mediation models from Hispanic culture that have been transposed to Latin America, such as the *Tribunal de las Aguas* (water court) in Spain. He also details informal mediations to resolve interpersonal disputes in Central America (Lederach, 1988). Riley and Sebenius (1995) and McCreary (1995) describe negotiation, fact-finding, and intermediary assistance in natural resource disputes in Ecuador, Honduras, and Cost Rica. Argentina is in the process of developing family, labor-management, and commercial mediation.

Africa and the Middle East

Mediation is utilized in both traditional and modern African societies, with practices varying from tribe to tribe and region to region. For example, the *moot court* is often a common means for neighbors to resolve disputes (Gulliver, 1971). The Tswana in Southern Africa use headmen and councils, and some tribes in Nigeria use chiefs, to accomplish negotiated resolutions (Comaroff and Roberts, 1981).

In Kenya and Somalia, mediation work has been undertaken by the Mennonite Central Committee and local secular and religious groups to address ethnic and clan disputes (Lederach, 1993). In these interventions, the emphasis has been on building on indigenous processes and the development of culturally appropriate mediation mechanisms to address local disputes.

South Africa has experienced the most extensive development and use of formal mediation processes on the continent. In 1968, the Centre for Intergroup Studies (now the Centre for Conflict Resolution) was founded to create constructive, creative, and cooperative approaches to the resolution of conflict and the reduction of violence. In the mid-1980s, Independent Mediation Services of South Africa (IMSSA) was established to handle an increasing number of labor conflicts in various industries. Its success in that area has led to an expansion into the spheres of racial and political conflict.

In the 1980s and early 1990s, a host of highly effective groups and organizations emerged that were active in community and political conflict resolution. Most notable were the African Centre for the Constructive Resolution of Disputes (ACCORD), Vuleka Trust, Wilgespruit Fellowship, the Negotiation Skills Project (Funda Centre), the Institute for a Democratic Alternative in South Africa (IDASA), and a number of dispute resolution programs at the University of Port Elizabeth and the University of Witwatersrand.

In 1991, the major paries to the conflict in South Africa—the government, the African National Congress, and the Inkata Freedom Party—negotiated the National Peace Accord, a nationwide effort to address the growing violence in the country that was threatening the progress toward democracy. This highly innovative accord established both regional and local peace committees that were to address actual and potential conflicts on the ground through a variety of conflict management approaches, one of which was mediation. Although it encountered enormous structural, political, resource, and logistical obstacles, this national system of dispute resolution made a significant effort in the peaceful transition of South Africa to democracy (Nathan, 1993; Moore, 1993). The boards, staff, and members of the peace committees successfully mediated numerous violent or potentially violent disputes and contributed significantly to the development of positive norms and procedures for peaceful conflict resolution in the country. Since the national elections in 1994, mediation has shifted from a focus on violence to an emphasis on development and reconciliation in South Africa and neighboring countries (Assefa, 1994).

Mediated settlements are also practiced in Arab societies. "A society in which conflicts are frequent must develop mechanisms for settling differences which, if allowed to get out of hand, can destroy the entire social fabric. In the Arab world, mediation on the tribal and village level has for centuries been the traditional method of settling disputes, and the same method has, in modern times, been adapted for settling political and military issues within and between Arab states" (Patai, 1983, p. 228).

Mediation is especially critical in Middle Eastern societies when honor is at stake and any concessions will appear to result in loss of self-respect or face. Therefore, face-to-face negotiations are extremely difficult, and an intermediary is needed to separate the parties and to work out an acceptable arrangement that preserves honor.

In many Middle Eastern and North African societies, intermediary services are performed by a mediator who is a person of respect. In Iraq and among tribal groups in Morocco and Algeria, he may even come from a special descent group with a high status. Generally, mediators in the Arab world must be seen as neutral and impartial, and of high status so that neither of the parties can exert undue pressure on him (Patai, 1983).

Use of intermediaries in the resolution of business disputes is common across the Middle East. Villages in Jordan practice mediation using local community leaders as intermediaries (Antoun, 1972). In Palestinian communities in the West Bank and Gaza, community and political leaders often mediate family, civil, and political disputes (Awad, 1994). These mediators are generally part of the disputants' social network, and help through the mediation process to assert community norms and to reestablish social harmony. In Lebanon, especially during the time of the civil war, a number of political factions provided mediation as a means of managing differences during the time the fighting either prevented access to the courts or inhibited them from functioning (Hamzeh, 1994). Tunisia has an administrator or counselor, a *mouwafak el idri*, who is attached to the office of the premier and handles disputes that citizens have with government officials, and market mediators, or *amine*, who resolve disputes between traders and customers in the public markets.

Clearly, mediation has played a major role in Middle Eastern societies in resolving serious diplomatic disputes and wars. Whether in the Arab-Israeli peace process (Carter, 1982; Rubin 1981), or in the ending of the American hostage crisis in Iran, intermediaries have played a valuable if not critical role.

In Israel, mediation has developed in secular society to resolve commercial, community, and family disputes (Matz, 1991). Several dispute resolution and research centers have been started to study and apply intermediary processes to a wide range of disputes. Among religious Jews, spiritual leaders often play intermediary roles in family, neighborhood, and other community conflicts.

Europe

Western Europe, too, has begun to more widely adopt and develop mediation processes and institutions. Business mediation has a firm foothold in Great Britain, and family and/or community mediation services and centers have been developed in Great Britain, Ireland, the Netherlands, Germany, France, and the Scandinavian countries (Acland, 1990). Norway has developed an elaborate system of Boards of Conciliation, which mediate both civil and family cases (Shaughnessey, 1992).

A number of programs and projects in Ireland have been initiated to address some of the sectarian tensions in the North (Morrow and Wilson, 1993). Germany is currently experimenting with the use of mediation to address a number of environmental, natural resource, and development issues (Weidner and Fietkau, 1995).

Since the end of communist rule in the early 1990s, Eastern Europe and the Confederation of Independent States (CIS) have begun to institutionalize mediation as a means of resolving a range of disputes. Dispute resolution centers, which offer conflict resolution training and mediation services, have been established in Poland, the Czech Republic, Slovakia, Hungary, Bulgaria, Macedonia, the Ukraine, and Russia. Many of these centers have received significant assistance from U.S.-based practitioners who have traveled to the region to provide help in training and dispute systems design (Wildau, Moore, and Mayer, 1993; Votchal, 1993; Shonholtz, 1993). Specific areas of focus for practitioners and centers have been family disputes, conflicts in schools and universities, labor-management disputes, environmental conflict, and ethnic disputes. In this last area, a number of ethnic commissions have been established in Bulgaria and Slovakia, composed of majority and minority group members. These commissions advocate for fair treatment of minorities, conduct educational activities on multicultural relations, act as community problem-solving forums, and provide third-party mediation services (Mayer, Wildau and Valchev, 1995).

Now that some of the history and applications of mediation in a variety of settings, situations, and cultures have been reviewed, we turn to an examination of the mediation process. In the next chapter, we will examine some of the variations in the roles of mediators, their orientations toward influence, the focus or goal of intervention, and the phases and tasks commonly used to achieve resolution of tangible issues and to address problematic relationships.

Chapter Two

┃ How Mediation Works

This chapter examines the various roles of mediators and their relationships to parties. It also explores issues related to the directiveness of intermediaries and their choice of focus between problem solving and relationships. An overview of mediator approaches and activities is also provided.

Variations in Mediator Roles and Procedures

The definition and description of mediation given in Chapter One generally outlines the role of mediators and the processes used to assist parties in reaching voluntary agreements. However, the fact that mediation is practiced in many diverse situations, forums, conflicts, and cultures has led to variations in both roles and procedures.

In general, there are three broad types of mediators, which are defined by the type of relationship they have with involved parties: (1) social network mediators, (2) authoritative mediators, and (3) independent mediators. Table 2.1 illustrates some of the characteristics of each type. To some extent, the type of relationship the intermediary has with disputants also influences the kind and degree of influence that is used to assist the parties. A variety of mediator types can be found in most cultures, although the development of mediation in a specific culture may emphasize or legitimize one form over another.

Social network mediators are individuals who are sought because they are connected to the disputants, and they are generally part of a continuing and common social network. Such a mediator may

Table 2.1. Types of Mediators.

Social Network Mediator	Authoritative Mediators			Independent Mediator
	Benevolent Mediator	Administrative/ Managerial Mediator	Vested Interest Mediator	
• Prior and expected future relationship to parties tied into their social network	• May or may not have a current or ongoing relationship with parties	• Generally has ongoing authoritative relationships with parties before and after dispute is terminated	• Has either a current or expected future relationship with a party or parties	• Neutral/impartial regarding relationships and specific outcomes
• Not necessarily impartial, but perceived by all to be fair	• Seeks best solution for all involved	• Seeks solution developed jointly with the parties, within mandated parameters	• Has a strong interest in the outcome of the dispute	• Serves at the pleasure of parties
• Very concerned with promoting stable long-term relationships between parties and their associates	• Generally impartial regarding the specific substantive outcome of the dispute	• Has authority to advise, suggest, or decide	• Seeks solution that meets mediator's interests and/or those of a favored party	• May be "professional" mediator
	• Has authority to advise, suggest, or decide		• May use strong leverage or coercion to achieve an agreement	• Seeks a jointly acceptable, voluntary, and non-coerced solution developed by the parties

• Frequently involved in implementation	• May have resources to help in monitoring and implementation of agreement	• May have resources to help in monitoring and implementation of agreement	• May have resources to help in monitoring or implementation of agreement	• May or may not be involved in monitoring implementation
• Generally has on-going relationships with parties after dispute is terminated	• Has authority to enforce agreement		• May use strong leverage or coercion to enforce agreement	• Has no authority to enforce agreement
• May use personal influence or peer/community pressure to promote adherence to agreement				

be a personal friend, neighbor, associate, coworker, business colleague, or religious figure (priest, minister, rabbi, Moslem *'ulama*, shaman), or a respected community leader or elder who is known to all parties and perhaps someone with whom those parties have an ongoing relationship. Lederach refers to network mediation using the Spanish term, *confianza* mediation (1995): "Key to why people were chosen were the ideas of 'trustworthiness,' that 'we know them' and they can 'keep our confidences'" (p. 89). He continues, "*Confianza* points to relationship building over time, to a sense of 'sincerity' a person has and a feeling of 'security' the person 'inspires' in us that we will 'not be betrayed'" (p. 89).

The network mediator often has a personal obligation to the parties to assist them as a friend—a desire to help them maintain smooth interpersonal relationships, both in the present and over the long term. He or she may also have a commitment to maintain harmony within the parties' broader social networks.

Network mediator involvement with potential disputing parties often begins long before a specific conflict starts and may extend throughout the life of the resolution process, including the implementation of the agreement. The network mediator's relationship with the parties is ongoing and enmeshed.

One example of a network mediator's activities comes from a dispute I observed in a Philippine community near Manila. A man and a woman had engaged in a heated public argument, the man claiming that money was due to him for his services as caretaker of the woman's garden and chauffeur of her children. He had come to her house twice to collect his pay; on the first occasion, she had been out, and on the second, she had told him she didn't have the money. When he came the third time and was denied payment, he created a noisy scene that roused her neighbors, and as he left, slammed her gate so forcefully that it came off its hinges. She in turn yelled at him and charged him with slandering her good name. They both ended this confrontation knowing that if the conflict was to be resolved, they would need some help.

They tried to think of a third person to whom they could talk, first individually and then together, who could help them resolve their differences and restore the positive aspects of the relationship that they had maintained for several years. Each came up with the name of a respected informal community leader, who was part of each of their social networks. The leader was "related" to both of them: the woman was his *co-madre* or godparent, and the man had grown up with him in the same village and had been his boyhood friend.

The woman approached the leader and obtained his agreement to mediate. He then approached the man and after a long, informal chat, arranged for a joint meeting. This meeting involved discussion of the issues in dispute, the long-term relationship that the parties had had with each other, the need to return harmony to the community, and the concern that each restore the good name of the other in the minds of their neighbors. After an extended discussion, the parties reached an agreement on all issues. Full payment was made for the gardener's services, apologies were exchanged, and each agreed to speak courteously and positively to the other in future conversations, as well as to use courteous language about each other when talking with neighbors about their past problem. (Some of the neighbors attended the open mediation session, saw the results, and were more than willing to spread the word that the relationship had been patched up by the respected leader.)

In this dispute, the authority of the mediator was embedded in the relationships he had with the parties, the trust and respect that the parties had for him as an individual, and his personal knowledge of their histories and the issues at hand. The relationship between the parties and the mediator was in fact the key to resolving the differences.

Although this dispute occurred in the context of Filipino culture, social network mediators are at work in all cultures. They are especially common in interpersonal disputes, whether in neighborhoods or organizations. However, they may also be found in larger public or political disputes; a respected communal or political leader is asked to intervene because of a past or ongoing personal relationship with the parties or because he or she occupies a particular position that engenders trust and respect on the part of the disputants.

The second broad category of mediator is a person who has an *authoritative* relationship to the parties in that he or she is in a superior or more powerful position and has potential or actual capacity to influence the outcome of a dispute. However, authoritative mediators, if they stay in a mediator role, do not make decisions for the parties. For any number of reasons—a procedural commitment to direct decision making by disputants, belief that a solution developed by the parties will result in greater satisfaction and commitment among their constituents, limits on the capacity or authority of the third party to unilaterally impose a decision—these intervenors usually try to influence the parties indirectly and attempt to persuade them to arrive at their own conclusions. This does not mean that they do not, on occasion, exercise significant leverage or pressure, perhaps with a view to limiting the settlement parameters. They may even raise the specter of a unilateral decision, as a back-up to collaborative decision making if the parties cannot agree on their own.

The authoritative mediator's influence may have as its basis personal status or reputation, but it is also generally dependent on formal position in a community or organization, election or appointment by a legitimate authority, rule of law, or access to resources valued by the contending parties. Whether the authority, regardless of form, is actually exercised—and how it is exercised—depends very much on the situation and the intermediary's orientation toward influence.

In general, there are three types of authoritative mediators: benevolent, administrative/managerial, and vested interest. A *benevolent authoritative mediator* has the ability to influence or decide an issue in dispute but generally values agreement making by parties over his or her direct involvement in reaching a decision. A benevolent mediator wants a settlement that is mutually satisfactory, and is not particularly concerned with getting his or her own substantive needs or interests addressed in the resolution. (However, benevolent mediators may have procedural interests of fairness, efficiency, economy, and minimization of overt conflict, and psychological interests of maintaining their personal position, gaining respect from the parties and other observers of the dispute by effectively assisting the parties to resolve their differences, or being seen as a servant of wider community interests for peace and harmony.)

An example of a benevolent authoritative mediator and her activities might be the services rendered by an executive who was involved in settling a workplace dispute. Two department heads were engaged in a hotly argued dispute over how a particular job, which required cooperation between the two departments, was to be handled and performed. They tried to talk directly about the issues but reached an impasse because of strong feelings about the problem and disagreements about how similar issues had been handled in the past. They both agreed to talk together with one of their colleagues, the chief executive officer (CEO) of the company. Although the CEO could ultimately make a decision about the issue being brought before her, she did not at the time have a firm personal or "organizational" opinion about how the problem should be resolved. She was also not constrained by any organizational or legal requirements that would define the parameters of the solution. She did believe that it was better for the parties involved, for their subordinates, and for the organization as a whole if the two disputants reached their own decision on the question at hand. However, she was willing to provide procedural—and if necessary, substantive—advice. After a brief joint discussion with the CEO, who suggested some principles that might provide a framework for an acceptable decision, the coworkers discussed the issues in more detail and developed a mutually acceptable solution to their differences.

A second type of authoritative mediator is the *administrative/managerial mediator.* He or she has some influence and authority over the parties by virtue of occupying a superior position in a community or organization and having either organizational or legal authority to establish the bargaining parameters in which an acceptable decision can be determined (Kolb and Sheppard, 1985). This type of mediator differs from the benevolent type above because he or she has a substantive interest in the outcome, albeit an interest that is institutionally or legally mandated.

Two brief examples of an administrative/managerial mediator, one within an organization and the other with concerned publics, illustrate this type of relationship with the parties. In the first, a male and a female employee in a U.S. governmental agency were arguing over behavior that the woman felt was sexist, demeaning, and harassing on the part of the man. She asked him to stop the behavior, but he failed to do so. Finally, she went to her supervisor, explained her view, and asked that he be told to stop making comments about her appearance, touching her on the shoulder, and constantly asking her to go out. The supervisor, on hearing the woman's description of the situation and learning that the man was a recent immigrant, speculated that the dispute might have arisen because of cultural differences regarding behaviors between the sexes. Nevertheless, in terms of the organization's regulations and the relevant laws, the man's behavior was unacceptable.

After meeting privately with the man, hearing his view of the situation, and explaining the organization's definition of sexual harassment and the types of behaviors that were not considered acceptable, the supervisor decided to have a joint meeting with the parties. She began by acknowledging that the parties had very different views of the situation and the meanings of behaviors. She asked them each to describe how they saw the situation. The woman said that she experienced the man's behavior as demeaning and objectifying, and that she did not like to be touched. The man said that he did not mean to devalue her, that his attention signified liking and admiration, and that touching was part of his life and culture. The supervisor acknowledged these differences but went on to explain what constituted sexual harassment according to the organization's rules and the law. She then requested that the parties discuss how they could interact within these parameters and still remain effective coworkers. Though maintaining the authority to make a command decision, she believed that establishing general parameters for behavior and then letting the parties work out the details was the best way to assist them in developing a solution that they could both accept. The man immediately agreed not to touch the woman. The woman, once she understood the meaning of his compliments and the part they played in his culture, agreed to accept his praise of her attractiveness as long as it was very general. The man asked if it was acceptable to continue to ask the woman out, but both ultimately agreed that dating was currently out of the question in light of their history.

A second example of managerial mediation comes from the Bureau of Environmental Impact Assessment in Indonesia but could have occurred in a number of governmental agencies around the world. The bureau was mandated to control and prevent water pollution from industrial plants and to protect environmental quality. A public interest law group brought a complaint to the agency that a particular company was polluting local waters and that the releases were having adverse impacts on crops and on the health of the people downstream. The agency investigated and determined that the company was indeed releasing effluent that was above the legal limits. The company was notified that it had to control its releases, clean up past pollution, and possibly discuss past impacts with the affected downstream parties.

Company representatives reluctantly agreed to meet with the agency and the affected parties. The meeting was chaired, and ultimately mediated, by one of the deputies in the agency. After being presented with the agency's test results, the company representatives agreed that they might be polluting and that measures needed to be taken to prevent these problems in the future. The government provided some technical assistance to the company and participated in the company's negotiations with the public interest group concerning the technology, procedures, and timing for the installation of pollution control equipment. The company, however, was very reluctant to negotiate on compensation to the downstream interests. The agency could not mandate compensation but agreed with the public interest group that some action had to be taken to address past costs. It strongly suggested to the company that some form of acknowledgment needed to be made that the business had caused the local people serious problems.

Ultimately, in continuing negotiations with the public interest group, the company agreed to make a "contribution" to the community rather than paying "compensation." The company said it was not prepared to publicly admit fault or potentially adverse effects from its past pollution, but would be willing, as a good neighbor, to aid the community in its time of need. The contribution ultimately agreed on was the hauling of fresh water into the community by truck, the exploration of how the village could be hooked up to the water system of the adjacent municipality, and the construction of a new mosque and community center. In this case, as in the sexual harassment dispute above, the managerial mediator had significant authority to make a decision but instead provided the parameters for a general settlement and assisted the parties in negotiating an acceptable agreement within these limits.

The third kind of authoritative mediator is a *vested interest mediator.* This role has some similarity to that of the managerial mediator in that the intermediary has both procedural and substantive interests in the outcome of the dispute. What makes it different is the degree to which the intermediary's interests are advocated. Whereas the managerial mediator establishes the general parameters for a settlement that will meet organizational or legal norms and encourages and assists the parties to work within this framework, the vested interest mediator often has specific interests and goals regarding all aspects of the dispute and pushes these objectives with enthusiasm and conviction (Smith, 1985). Some observers have noted that in this model, the mediator is hardly an intermediary but merely another party who strongly advocates for his or her substantive interests.

The clearest examples of vested interest mediators at work are probably found in the international arena. Henry Kissinger had strong vested interests when he acted as mediator for the Arab-Israeli disengagement negotiations in August 1975 (Rubin, 1981). So did President Carter in his role as intermediary in the Camp David Egyptian-Israeli peace talks (Carter, 1982; Princen, 1992) and the various U.N. mediators involved in the ethno-national conflicts of the former Yugoslavia. The United States has had longstanding political, economic, and strategic interests in the Middle East and has assertively intervened as a broker in attempts to promote stability in the region. The U.S. has played the role of a mediator with muscle. Its representatives have at various times persuaded, cajoled, or aggressively pressured involved parties to seek a permanent peace and have provided both arms and resources for development to help achieve these ends.

The United Nations mediators in the former Yugoslavia, although representing an international organization, sought solutions that met the interests of key U.N. members as well as those of the parties on the ground. Much of their activity involved putting together proposals based on principles established by the U.N. and then trying to persuade the combatants to accept these frameworks (Owen, 1995).

Vested interest mediation differs significantly from a number of other forms of intervention that place a higher degree of emphasis on the parties' reaching their own decision. The latter view is manifested particularly in the independent, impartial mediator, who will be discussed next. Vested interest mediation can be highly effective in certain circumstances and is a common variety of mediation practice, but it might better be called "third-party advocacy."

The *independent mediator* is the final type to be discussed here.

The name derives both from the relationship that the intervenor has to the parties—one of neutrality—and the stance that he or she takes toward the problems in question—one of impartiality. The independent intermediary is commonly found in cultures that have developed traditions of independent and objective professional advice or assistance. Members of these cultures often prefer the advice and help of independent "outsiders," who are perceived to have no personal vested interest in the intervention or its outcome, to assistance from "insiders," with whom they may have more complex and often conflicting relationships or obligations. Members of cultures that favor independent mediators tend to keep the various groups in their lives—family, close friends, neighbors, superiors and subordinates at work, business associates, recreational companions, civic associates, political affiliates, church members—in separate compartments. They may rely on specialists such as therapists, employee assistance counselors, financial advisors, legal counsel, golf pros, ward leaders, and clergy to help them function well and handle potential or actual problems in each area. An advisor or assistant in one arena may have little or no connection with another aspect of an individual's life, and members of these cultures seem to like it that way.

Independent mediators are also most commonly found in cultures in which there is a tradition of an independent judiciary, which provides a model both for widely perceived fair procedures and impartial third parties as decision makers.

This type of intervention has in recent years been called the North American model of mediation (Lederach, 1985), which is really a misnomer. The roots of the process can be found in Western Europe, and specifically Northern Europe, which during the Middle Ages and Renaissance produced the Western models of compartmentalized relationships, professionalism, impartial advice, and independent procedural systems for resolving disputes. Although this type of mediation has been articulated, and perhaps most actively practiced, in North America, the model and its corresponding values are not culture-bound. They have spread around the globe and have influenced the dispute resolution approaches of numerous cultures that have either become acquainted with them as a result of colonial experience or selected them voluntarily because they have been seen to be efficient and fair.

Because impartiality and neutrality are often seen to be the critical defining characteristics of this type of mediation, it is important to explore these concepts in more detail (Young, 1972). *Impartiality* refers to the absence of bias or preference in favor of one or more negotiators, their interests, or the specific solutions that they are advocating. *Neutrality,* on the other hand, refers to the relationship or behavior between intervenor and disputants. Often, independent mediators have not had any previous relationship with disputing parties, or at least have not had a relationship from which they could directly and significantly benefit. They are generally not tied into the parties' ongoing social networks. Neutrality also means that the mediator does not expect to obtain benefits or special payments from one of the parties as compensation for favors in conducting the mediation.

People seek an independent mediator's assistance because they want procedural help in negotiations. They do not want an intervenor who is biased or who will initiate actions that are potentially detrimental to their interests.

Impartiality and neutrality do not mean that a mediator may not have a personal opinion about a desirable outcome to a dispute. No one can be entirely impartial. What impartiality and neutrality do signify is that mediators can separate their personal opinions about the outcome of the dispute from the performance of their duties and focus on ways to help the parties make their own decisions without unduly favoring one of them. The ultimate test of the impartiality and neutrality of the mediator lies in the judgment of the parties: they must perceive that the intervenor is not overtly partial or nonneutral in order to accept his or her assistance.

Kraybill (1979) and Wheeler (1982) address the tensions between impartiality/neutrality and the personal biases of mediators by distinguishing between substantive and procedural interests. Wheeler argues that mediators generally distance themselves from commitments to specific substantive outcomes—the amount of money in a settlement, the exact time of performance, and so forth—but do have commitments to such procedural standards as open communication, equity and fair exchange, durability of a settlement over time, and enforceability. Mediators are advocates for a fair process and not for a particular settlement.

Let us take as an example an independent mediator in a personal injury claim case in North America. The parties, the insurance adjuster, and the plaintiff's lawyer corresponded and talked by telephone, reaching a decision to explore the use of mediation to resolve their differences. They agreed that the adjuster would seek the assistance of a mediation firm that had a reputation for impartiality and experience in resolving this kind of dispute. The firm provided them with the résumés of three possible intervenors. After reviewing this information, the parties eliminated two of the candidates, one because she had previously acted as an arbiter in a case involving one of the parties and had issued an unfavorable opinion, and the other because the number of years he had spent in the practice of mediation was considered inadequate. The mediator who was selected was not known personally to either party but had a significant reputation for being fair, impartial, efficient, experienced, and knowledgeable in handling this type of case.

A premediation interview was held with the chosen mediator, where the parties confirmed their decision to utilize his services and explained the background of the case. They then proceeded to a first joint session. During the subsequent half-day mediation session, the mediator asked both parties to explain their view of the case, helped them to identify key issues and interests, assisted them in generating some possible settlement options in joint session, and then conducted a private meeting with each of them to explore which options were most viable and to break a deadlock on one particularly difficult issue. During both the joint sessions and the caucuses, the mediator asked the parties a number of questions, helped make their interests explicit, and assisted the parties in developing some fair and objective standards and criteria that provided a formula for settlement. He made few, if any, substantive recommendations on how they should settle, and did not indicate his personal opinion or approval of the solution that they ultimately developed.

Variations in Mediator Directiveness and Focus

In addition to the diverse roles and relationships that mediators have with parties, intermediaries also differ with respect to the degree of directiveness or control that they exercise over the dispute resolution process and the relative emphasis they place on the substantive, procedural, and psychological/relationship interests of the parties.

In general, regardless of the type of mediator role being performed, intermediaries vary along a continuum from highly directive to highly nondirective with respect to substantive issues, the problem-solving process, and the management of relationships between the parties. Kolb (1983) described the ideal types at the two ends of this spectrum: the "orchestrators" and the "dealmakers." In brief, orchestrators generally focus on empowering parties to make their own decisions; they provide mainly procedural assistance, and occasionally help in establishing or building relationships. They are less directive than are dealmakers and intervene primarily when it is clear that the parties are not capable of making progress toward a settlement on their own.

In contrast, dealmakers are often highly directive in relation to both process and the substantive issues under discussion. Generally, they are very prescriptive and directive with respect to problem-solving steps, questions of who talks and to whom, types of forum (joint sessions or private meetings), and the types of interventions made. Dealmakers are also typically much more involved in substantive discussions and on occasion may provide substantive information to the parties, voice their opinion on issues under discussion, or actively work to put together a deal that will be mutually acceptable to the parties.

In addition to directiveness, intermediaries vary significantly in terms of the emphasis they place on the purpose or focus of the mediation. Here too, there is a continuum, with some mediators emphasizing problem solving and agreement making on tangible, substantive issues, and others (who sometimes call themselves "problem-solving facilitators") placing more stress on improving the parties' relationships. The latter generally work to establish or build cognitive empathy, trust, and respect. When necessary, they will seek to terminate a relationship with the least possible psychological harm (Bush and Folger, 1994; Rothman, 1992).

In recent years, some practitioners and academics writing about the field have locked themselves into rigid positions on the appropriate degree of intermediary directiveness or the optimal area of emphasis for mediators (problem-solving versus relationship orientation). This narrowness has not been productive. It ignores the range of successful models for practice, the variety of disputes, the specific capabilities of the parties, the expressed needs and goals of the disputants, and the diversity of cultural contexts in which interventions are practiced. A more productive approach would be to explore the specific situation and adapt the process to meet the needs of the parties. This would mean that in some disputes, the intermediary might be highly directive, whereas in others he or she would merely orchestrate the process. Equally, in some conflicts, the mediator would emphasize a more substantive problem-solving focus, whereas in others the emphasis would be placed on establishing or building relationships.

What is characteristic of good practice, and what is needed from effective mediators, is the ability to be a "reflective practitioner" (Schön, 1983). Such a person can match mediation theory and the learnings of others with his or her own past experience in resolving disputes, so that situation-specific approaches and interventions can be developed that assist parties in establishing and building respectful and trusting relationships and resolving issues that divide them.

The Approach to Describing the Mediation Process

As can be seen from the preceding descriptions, mediators can have many types of relationships with disputing parties, and the nature of the connection can significantly influence the process and the types of interventions that are initiated. Because this book is about general processes of mediation and describes a range of mediator intervention approaches that can be used in a variety of situations, it will be helpful for me to describe my own orientation toward these processes and procedures.

Generally, my experience and orientation in mediation are those of the independent mediator who leans toward the orchestrator end of the directiveness spectrum (at least, by North American standards). However, I am familiar with and have worked extensively with intermediaries who have different orientations toward directiveness or the focus of the mediation process. I have also taught intervention approaches and skills to intermediaries who specialized in social network, authoritative, and vested interest assistance. Because of this experience, I recognize the value, complexities, variations, and situational or contextual appropriateness of various orientations.

Writing a book that encompasses all types of mediators and mediation would be very difficult, if not impossible. Therefore, this text is primarily oriented toward describing the approach, strategies, and tactics of independent mediators who lean toward the orchestrator or moderately directive end of the procedural or substantive directiveness spectrum and focus on problem solving as well as on the parties' relationships. This emphasis should not be taken to imply that other types of mediators or their orientations are not valid or effective. However, for the sake of clarity and to facilitate a general understanding of how mediators work, I will describe a specific process that is widely practiced in a number of settings and cultures. In subsequent chapters, I will also describe some of the variations of practice that arise from differences among intervenors, kinds of disputes, and cultural contexts. It is my hope that this method of exploring the mediation process will present both a comprehensible and a cohesive approach to mediation for individuals who want to become effective practitioners.

Mediation Activities: Moves and Interventions

Negotiation is composed of a series of complex activities or "moves" that people initiate to resolve their differences and bring the conflict to termination (Goffman, 1969, p. 90). Each move or action a negotiator performs involves rational decision making in which possible actions are assessed in relation to the following factors:

The moves of the other parties

Their standards of behavior

Their styles

Their perceptiveness and skill

Their needs and preferences

Their determination

The amount of information the negotiator has about the conflict

The negotiator's personal attributes

Available resources

Mediators, like negotiators, may initiate moves. A *move* for a mediator is a specific act of intervention or "influence technique" focused on the people in the dispute. It encourages the selection of positive actions and inhibits the selection of negative actions relative to the issues in conflict (Galtung, 1975). The mediator, a specialized negotiator, generally does not directly effect changes in the disputants by initiating moves, as do the parties themselves; he or she is more of a catalyst. Changes are the combined result of the intervenor's moves and those of the negotiators (Bonner, 1959).

In negotiations, people in conflict are faced with a variety of procedural or psychological problems or "critical situations" (Cohen and Smith, 1972) that they must address or overcome if they are to reach an agreement. All problem-solving groups face these situations, which can be categorized according to size, type, time, and frequency. The largest categories and most frequent problems are hereafter referred to as *stages* or phases because they constitute major steps that parties must take to reach agreement. There are stages or phases for both negotiation and mediation, and for the most part, they parallel each other.

Mediators make two types of interventions in response to critical situations: *general* or *noncontingent* moves or activities, and *contingent* moves or activities (Kochan and Jick, 1978).

Noncontingent moves are general interventions that a mediator initiates in virtually all disputes. These activities are responses to the broadest categories of critical situations and correspond to the stages of mediation. They are linked to the overall pattern of conflict development and resolution. Noncontingent moves enable the mediator to

1. Gain entry to the dispute
2. Assist the parties in selecting the appropriate conflict resolution approach and arena
3. Collect data and analyze the conflict
4. Design a mediation plan
5. Initiate conciliation
6. Assist the parties in beginning productive negotiations
7. Identify important issues and build an agenda
8. Identify parties' underlying interests
9. Aid the parties in developing resolution options

10. Assist in assessing the options
11. Promote final bargaining and agreement making
12. Aid in developing an implementation and monitoring plan

I will examine these activities and stages in more detail later in this chapter.

Smaller routine, noncontingent activities are also initiated by mediators within each stage. Examples of this level of intervention are activities to build credibility for the process, promote rapport between the parties and the mediator, and frame issues in a more manageable form, as well as develop procedures to conduct cost-benefit evaluations on settlement options.

Contingent moves are responses to special or idiosyncratic problems that occur in some negotiations. Interventions to manage intense anger, bluffing, bargaining in bad faith, mistrust, or miscommunication are all in this category of specific interventions. Though some contingent moves, such as the caucus—a private meeting between the parties and the mediator—are quite common, they are still in the contingent category because they do not happen in all negotiations.

Hypothesis Building and Mediation Interventions

For a mediator to be effective, he or she needs to be able to analyze and assess critical situations and design effective interventions to address the causes of the conflict. However, conflicts do not come in neat packages with their causes and component parts labeled so that the intervenor will know how to creatively respond to them. Causes are often obscured and clouded by the dynamics of the parties' interactions.

To work effectively on conflicts, the intervenor needs a conceptual road map or "conflict map" (Wehr, 1979) that details why a conflict is occurring, identifies barriers to settlement, and indicates procedures to manage or resolve the dispute.

Most conflicts have multiple causes. The principal tasks of the mediator and the parties are to identify these and take action to address them. The mediator and participants in a dispute accomplish this by trial-and-error experimentation in which they generate and test hypotheses about the sources of the conflict.

First, the mediator, in dialogue with the parties (either individually or together), observes and identifies elements of the parties' attitudes, perceptions, communication patterns, or ongoing interactions that are producing a negative relationship or hindering a positive one. The mediator tries to determine if lack of information, misinformation, the manner in which data are collected, or the criteria by which it is assessed are at the root of the conflict. He or she identifies both compatible and competing interests, while also exploring any structural causes of conflict, such as differences in authority or resources, or the impacts of time. Finally, the mediator ascertains similarities and differences in the values held by the parties. From all these observations, he or she tries to identify the central causes of the dispute. Often, a framework of explanatory causes and suggested interventions, such as that presented in Figure 2.1, will be used.

For example, in the Whittamore-Singson case presented in Chapter One, the mediator might determine that

1. There are relationship problems between the doctor and the clinic director that need to be addressed.
2. There is a significant amount of data missing on the cost of opening a new practice and on the potential adverse financial impacts on the clinic of losing a doctor.
3. Each of the parties has a variety of interests that need to be explored.
4. A major cause of the problem is structural proximity and day-to-day interaction between the Whittamores.
5. There might be values regarding parents' involvement with children that the clinic staff and Whittamore share.

This information will help the mediator develop a strategy for approaching the problems faced by the disputants and a plan for sequencing his or her activities.

Once the mediator believes that one or more central causes have been identified, he or she builds a hypothesis: "This conflict is caused by *a and probably b,* and if either *a* or *b* is changed or addressed, the parties will be able to move toward agreement." The hypothesis must then be tested.

Testing hypotheses about conflicts involves designing preventions or interventions that challenge or modify the attitudes, behaviors, or structural relationship of the disputants. *Preventions* are

Figure 2.1. Circle of Conflict: Causes and Interventions.

Possible Value-Related Interventions

Avoid defining problem in terms of value
Allow parties to agree and to disagree
Create spheres of influence in which
  one set of values dominates
Search for superordinate goal that all parties share

**Relationship conflicts
are caused by**

Strong emotions
Misperceptions or stereotypes
Poor communication or
  miscommunication
Repetitive negative
  behavior

**Value conflicts
are caused by**

Different criteria for
  evaluating ideas or
  behavior
Exclusive intrinsically
  valuable goals
Different ways of life,
  ideology, or religion

**Data conflicts
are caused by**

Lack of information
Misinformation
Different views on
  what is relevant
Different interpre-
  tations of data
Different assessment
  procedures

**Structural conflicts
are caused by**

Destructive patterns of
  behavior or interaction
Unequal control, ownership,
  or distribution of resources
Unequal power and authority
Geographical, physical, or
  environmental factors that
  hinder cooperation
Time constraints

**Interest conflicts
are caused by**

Perceived or actual competition
  over substantive (content)
  interests
Procedural interests
Psychological interests

Possible Relationship Interventions

Control expression of emotions through
   procedure, ground rules, caucuses, and so forth
Promote expression of emotions by legitimizing
   feelings and providing a process
Clarify perceptions and build positive perceptions
Improve quality and quantity of communication
Block negative repetitive behavior by changing structure
Encourage positive problem-solving attitudes

Possible Data Interventions

Reach agreement on what data are important
Agree on process to collect data
Develop common criteria to assess data
Use third-party experts to gain outside opinion
   or break deadlocks

Possible Interest-Based Interventions

Focus on interests, not positions
Look for objective criteria
Develop integrative solutions that address needs of all parties
Search for ways to expand options or resources
Develop trade-offs to satisfy interests of different strengths

Possible Structural Interventions

Clearly define and change roles
Replace destructive behavior patterns
Reallocate ownership or control of resources
Establish a fair and mutually acceptable decision-making process
Change negotiation process from positional to interest-based bargaining
Modify means of influence used by parties (less coercion, more persuasion)
Change physical and environmental relationship of parties
   (closeness and distance)
Modify external pressures on parties
Change time constraints (more or less time)

activities that a mediator initiates *before* parties interact and that inhibit or prevent them from engaging in unproductive communication or problem solving. *Interventions* are activities undertaken by a mediator in response to unproductive communication or problem solving that arises in a joint session or private meeting after negotiations have begun. Preventions are proactive and interventions reactive initiatives by the intermediary.

Preventions and interventions are often grounded in a theory that identifies a particular cause of the conflict and suggests prescriptive actions. For example, one theory about the cause of conflict has communication as its base. Most communication theories propose that conflict is the result of poor communication in either quantity, quality, or form. The theory postulates that if the right *quantity* of communication can be attained, the *quality* of the information exchanged can be improved, and if this information is put into a mutually acceptable *form*, the causes of the dispute will be addressed and the participants will move toward resolution.

A mediator following the communication theory of conflict might observe disputants communicating very poorly: one barely begins to speak without the other interrupting, or they have difficulty focusing on present issues and constantly digress to arguments over past wrongs that tend to escalate the conflict, turning the dispute into a shouting match. The mediator hypothesizes that one cause of the dispute is the inability of the disputants to talk to each other in a constructive and restrained manner. He or she therefore proceeds to experiment with modifications of their communication patterns (quality, quantity, and form) to see if there is any resulting change in the conflict dynamics. The mediator may suggest that the parties discuss one topic at a time, may obtain permission to monitor the dialogue and prevent interruptions, may establish ground rules about insults, or may even separate the disputants so that they can communicate only through the mediator.

Each intervention is a test of the hypothesis that part of the dispute is caused by communication problems and that if these difficulties can be lessened or eliminated, the parties will have a better chance of reaching an agreement. If the desired effect is not achieved, the intervenor may reject the specific approach as ineffective and try another. If several interventions based on one theory do not work, the intervenor may shift to another theory and begin trial-and-error testing again. The cycle of hypothesis building and testing is the basic process of intervention and conflict resolution (see Figure 2.2).

The Stages of Mediation

Mediator hypothesis building occurs most intensively in the process of conceptualizing the stages or phases of mediation and designing appropriate interventions based on the causes of the conflict and the level of development that a particular dispute has reached.

The stages of mediation are often difficult to identify, and frequently vary across cultures in sequence, emphasis, and approach. Mediator and negotiator activities seem to blend together into an undifferentiated continuum of interaction. Only through careful

**Figure 2.2. Mediator Process of Building
and Testing a Hypothesis.**

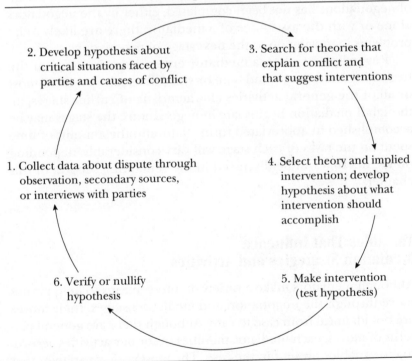

2. Develop hypothesis about critical situations faced by parties and causes of conflict

3. Search for theories that explain conflict and that suggest interventions

1. Collect data about dispute through observation, secondary sources, or interviews with parties

4. Select theory and implied intervention; develop hypothesis about what intervention should accomplish

6. Verify or nullify hypothesis

5. Make intervention (test hypothesis)

observation of negotiations and mediated interventions can distinct stages composed of common and predictable activities be
identified. It then becomes possible to generate hypotheses about
the critical situations and specific problems that a particular set of
disputants may have to address.

The stages of mediator interventions fall roughly into two
broad categories: (1) activities performed by the mediator before
formal problem-solving sessions begin; (2) activities initiated once
the mediator has entered into formal problem solving with the parties, either in joint session or by shuttling between them. Five stages
occur in the prenegotiation work of the mediator, and seven stages
occur after formal sessions have begun (see Figure 2.3).

In each of the twelve stages, the mediator designs hypotheses
and appropriate strategies and executes specific activities. These
initiatives are both sequential and developmental in nature and are
designed to help disputing parties accomplish specific tasks and
overcome barriers that commonly occur at particular points in the
negotiation process. If a critical task appropriate at an earlier stage
of negotiations has not been completed, either by the negotiators
alone or with the assistance of a mediator, there are likely to be
problems in moving on to the next stage of negotiation.

Regardless of when a mediator enters negotiations—at the
beginning, middle, or end—he or she will usually perform most
or all of the general activities characteristic of earlier stages, although if mediation begins late in negotiations, the stages may be
accomplished in abbreviated form. Naturally, the amount of time
spent on the tasks of each stage will vary considerably, depending
on factors that will be discussed in the remaining section of this
chapter.

Variables That Influence
Mediation Strategies and Activities

Although mediators make a variety of interventions to help parties
move through the negotiation and mediation stages, their moves
are not identical from case to case. Although there are general patterns of moves, each mediator modifies his or her activities according to variables present in the case. The most critical variables that
influence both preventions and interventions are

1. The level of conflict development and the timing of a mediator's entry
2. The capability of negotiators to resolve their own dispute
3. The power balance of the disputants and the mediator's role as an equalizer and agent of empowerment
4. The negotiation procedures used by the parties
5. The complexity of the issues negotiated
6. The role and tasks of the mediator as defined jointly by the parties and the intervenor

I will examine each of these variables and how they affect the role of the mediator and his or her application of general and specific strategies.

Conflict Development and Timing of Entry

The level of conflict development, the stage reached in negotiations (or the resolution efforts previously made), and the degree of emotional intensity in the parties significantly influence the tasks that negotiators and mediators have to perform. If a mediator enters a dispute in its early stages, prior to extreme issue polarization or the development of intense emotions, he or she will use a different strategy and set of moves from those that would be used at a later stage, when the parties have been negotiating and have reached a substantive impasse or had a highly emotional interchange. If mediation is viewed as a total process, however, the difference in strategy and activities can be seen primarily as one of emphasis rather than substance; the types of initiatives are the same. For example, conciliation, preparing the parties psychologically to bargain effectively on substantive issues, generally occurs at the beginning of negotiations rather than later. If, however, a mediator enters in the later phases of a negotiation—after impasse, perhaps—he or she will probably have to initiate some conciliatory activities to help overcome psychological barriers to settlement. The mediator will generally have to complete this phase prior to pursuing the substantive bargaining activities that belong to the stage the parties *believe* they have reached.

Capability of Disputants to Resolve Their Own Dispute

Whether the disputants are capable of resolving their own dispute also strongly affects the mediator's intervention strategies. Parties

Figure 2.3. Twelve Stages of Mediator Moves.

Stage 1: Establishing Relationship with the Disputing Parties
- Make initial contacts with the parties
- Build credibility
- Promote rapport
- Educate the parties about the process
- Increase commitment to the procedure

Stage 2: Selecting a Strategy to Guide Mediation
- Assist the parties to assess various approaches to conflict management and resolution
- Assist the parties in selecting an approach
- Coordinate the approaches of the parties

Stage 3: Collecting and Analyzing Background Information
- Collect and analyze relevant data about the people, dynamics, and substance of a conflict
- Verify accuracy of data
- Minimize the impact of inaccurate or unavailable data

Stage 4: Designing a Detailed Plan for Mediation
- Identify strategies and consequent noncontingent moves that will enable the parties to move toward agreement
- Identify contingent moves to respond to situations peculiar to the specific conflict

Stage 5: Building Trust and Cooperation
- Prepare disputants psychologically to participate in negotiations on substantive issues
- Handle strong emotions
- Check perceptions and minimize effects of stereotypes
- Build recognition of the legitimacy of the parties and issues
- Build trust
- Clarify communications

Stage 6: Beginning the Mediation Session
- Open negotiation between the parties
- Establish an open and positive tone
- Establish ground rules and behavioral guidelines
- Assist the parties in venting emotions
- Delimit topic areas and issues for discussion
- Assist the parties in exploring commitments, salience, and influence

Stage 7: Defining Issues and Setting an Agenda
- Identify broad topic areas of concern to the parties
- Obtain agreement on the issues to be discussed
- Determine the sequence for handling the issues

Stage 8: Uncovering Hidden Interests of the Disputing Parties
- Identify the substantive, procedural, and psychological interests of the parties
- Educate the parties about each other's interests

Stage 9: Generating Options for Settlement
- Develop an awareness among the parties of the need for multiple options
- Lower commitment to positions or sole alternatives
- Generate options using either positional or interest-based bargaining

Stage 10: Assessing Options for Settlement
- Review the interests of the parties
- Assess how interests can be met by available options
- Assess the costs and benefits of selecting options

Stage 11: Final Bargaining
- Reach agreement through either incremental convergence of positions, final leaps to package settlements, development of a consensual formula, or establishment of procedural means to reach a substantive agreement

Stage 12: Achieving Formal Settlement
- Identify procedural steps to operationalize the agreement
- Establish an evaluation and monitoring procedure
- Formalize the settlement and create an enforcement and commitment mechanism

who are able to negotiate rationally, who are aware of problem-solving procedures, and who appear to be progressing toward a settlement will require little assistance from a mediator. In this situation, the mediator may lend support to the work of the parties merely by his or her presence or by minimal support of the principal negotiators (Perez, 1959; Kolb, 1983). On the other hand, if parties are in the grip of intense emotions, do not have skills or expertise in negotiations or problem-solving procedures, or have reached an impasse on substantive issues, the mediator will probably be more active and more visible in the negotiations. He or she may assist the parties in productively venting and/or handling strong emotions, framing the specific problems to be addressed, creating an agenda, educating each other about their interests, narrowing the bargaining range, generating and assessing options, and initiating a variety of other procedures or activities that assist the parties in reaching an agreement.

Power Balance Between Disputants

In order to derive mutually satisfactory and acceptable decisions from negotiations, all parties must have some means of influence, either positive or negative, on other disputants at the table. This is a prerequisite for a settlement that recognizes mutual needs (Lovell, 1952). Unless a weaker party has some power or influence, recognition of its needs and interests will occur only if the stronger party is altruistically oriented. If the power or influence potentials of the parties are well developed, fairly equal in strength, and recognized by all disputants, the mediator's job will be to assist the disputants in using their influence effectively to produce mutually satisfactory results. If, however, the influence of each side is not equal and one party has the ability to impose on the other an unsatisfactory solution, an agreement that will not hold over time, or a resolution that will result in renewed conflict later, the mediator will have to decide whether and how to assist the weaker party and moderate the influence of the stronger one.

To assist or empower the weaker party or to influence the activities of the stronger (contingent strategies that do not occur in all mediations) requires very specific interventions that shift the mediator's role and function dangerously close to advocacy. This problem has been debated among mediators (Bernard, Folger,

Weingarten, and Zumeta, 1984). One argument states that a mediator has an obligation to create just settlements and must therefore help empower the underdog to reach equitable and fair agreements (Laue and Cormick, 1978; Suskind, 1981; Haynes, 1981). Another school argues that mediators should do little, if anything, to influence the power relations of disputing parties because it taints the intervenor's impartiality (Bellman, 1982; Stulberg, 1981b).

In examining this question and how it affects the mediator's choice of intervention activities, it is important to distinguish between the situation in which a mediator assists in recognizing, organizing, and marshaling the existing power of a disputant and that in which a mediator becomes an advocate and assists in generating new power and influence. The latter strategy clearly shifts the mediator out of his or her impartial position, whereas the former keeps the mediator within the power boundaries established by the parties. There is no easy answer to this strategic and ethical problem, but it does have an important impact on the types of moves a mediator initiates.

Negotiation Procedures

Negotiation is a form of joint problem solving. The topical problems that negotiators focus on are often called *issues*. An issue exists because the parties do not agree on a particular topic and because they have perceived or actual exclusive needs or interests.

In the Singson-Whittamore case described in Chapter One, the issues about which the two people will negotiate include

1. Can Whittamore continue to practice medicine in a town in which he wishes to live?
2. Will there be a penalty for breaking the contract?
3. If there is a penalty, how much will it be?
4. How will the penalty be calculated, and what factors should be considered?
5. Is there a way that Whittamore can stay at the clinic and still maintain some distance from his estranged wife? (This, after all, is the crux of the problem.)

Note that the description of the issues is in neutral terms that favor neither party, and that the wording describes a problem to be solved rather than a particular solution to be forced by one bargainer on another.

Parties to a conflict select one of two major negotiation procedures to handle issues in dispute: *positional bargaining* and *interest-based bargaining* (Fisher and Ury, 1981). Positional bargaining usually occurs when a negotiator perceives that contested resources are limited and that a distributive solution, one that allocates shares of gains and losses to each party, is the only possible outcome (Walton and McKersie, 1965). Positional bargaining is generally a win-lose or compromise-oriented process. Interest-based bargaining, on the other hand, occurs when negotiators seek integrative solutions that meet as many of the needs of both parties as possible (Walton and McKersie, 1965). Generally, interest-based bargaining is pursued when parties do not see resources as limited, and when solutions can be found in which all parties can have at least some of their needs met.

Positional bargaining derives its name from the practice of selecting a series of positions—particular settlement options that meet the proposing party's interests—and presenting these to an opponent as *the* solution to the issue in question. A party's position may or may not be responsive to the needs or interests of other negotiators. Positions are generally ordered sequentially so that the first position is a large demand and represents a negotiator's maximum expectation of gain should his or her opponent acquiesce. Each subsequent position demands less of an opponent and results in fewer benefits for the initiating party. Characteristically, positional bargaining commits parties early in negotiations to very specific solutions to issues in dispute and often reduces the flexibility to generate other equally acceptable options.

Positional bargainers generally reach agreement because they have identified a solution that meets enough of an opponent's interests to induce settlement. However, positional bargainers often fail to maximize the satisfaction of either party's interests because the settlements are compromises or adoptions of one party's proposal, rather than the product of a joint effort to find mutually beneficial solutions.

In the Singson-Whittamore case, Whittamore's possible positions might include: "I refuse to pay any penalty for breaking the contract because the no-competition clause is not constitutional." Singson might respond with counterpositions: "Pay the penalty fee immediately or move out of town" or "You must pay the penalty, but we can negotiate on the due date." If an agreement is reached, the parties might settle at a point between these two extreme positions.

Disputants often adopt positional bargaining when

- The stakes for winning are high.
- The resources (time, money, psychological benefits, and so on) are perceived to be limited.
- A win for one side appears to require a loss for another.
- Interests of the parties are not or do not appear to be interdependent and are contradictory.
- Future relationships have a lower priority than immediate substantive gains.
- Parties assume that positional bargaining is *the* way to resolve problems, are not familiar with other approaches to negotiation, or other approaches are deemed to be inappropriate or unacceptable (Moore, 1982b).

Interest-based bargaining differs from positional bargaining in its assumptions about the substantive issues to be negotiated, the contents of an acceptable solution, and the process by which an agreement is to be reached.

In interest-based bargaining, the negotiators do not necessarily assume that the substantive resource in question—money, other resources, time, behavior, and so on—is limited. They do not assume that the resource must be divided into shares in which one bargainer is a winner and the other a loser. The attitude of the interest-based bargainer is that of a problem solver. The goal of negotiation is to find a solution that is mutually satisfactory and results in a win-win outcome.

Interest-based bargainers believe that settlements in negotiations are reached because a party has succeeded in having his or her interests satisfied. *Interests* are specific conditions (or gains) that a party must obtain for an acceptable settlement to occur. They are of three broad types: substantive, procedural, and psychological.

Substantive interests refer to the needs that an individual has for particular goods such as money and time. Substantive interests are often the central needs on which negotiations focus.

Procedural interests refer to the preferences that a negotiator has for the way that the parties discuss their differences and the manner in which the bargaining outcome is implemented. Possible procedural interests might be that each person have the opportunity to speak his or her mind, that negotiations occur in an orderly and timely manner, that the parties avoid derogatory verbal attacks, that the process focus on meeting the mutual interests of all the parties rather than forcing a party to agree to a predetermined position advocated by another, that the plan for implementing the agreement be worked out in detail prior to final settlement, or that a written document or contract should result from bargaining.

Psychological interests refer to the emotional and relationship needs of a negotiator, both during and as a result of negotiations. Negotiators want to have high self-esteem, want to be treated with respect by their opponent, and do not want to be degraded in negotiations. If the relationship is to continue in the future, the negotiators may want to have ongoing positive regard from the other party for their openness to future communication.

In the Singson-Whittamore case, Whittamore's interests include

1. Remaining in town so that he can see and parent his children
2. Continuing to practice his profession
3. Avoiding contact with his estranged wife
4. Maintaining amicable relations with the clinic and its staff
5. Minimizing the amount of initial penalty payments to the clinic so that he has enough money to start his own practice

Some of Singson's interests include

1. Avoiding monetary loss and patient attrition when a doctor leaves the staff
2. Maintaining clinic management's prerogative to set the terms of an employment contract
3. Avoiding a precedent in which a doctor leaves the clinic before the expiration of a contract and begins a practice in town
4. Avoiding a lawsuit

Interest-based bargaining begins with an understanding of each of the interests of the two parties, not statements of positions. Often, the parties identify their interests and those of other disputants in private and then hold a joint meeting to share their results. Parties discuss and modify their interests on the basis of these early discussions. Once the interests have been revealed, explored, and accepted, at least in principle, the parties can begin a mutual search for solutions that will meet their needs. Reaching an agreement requires negotiators to develop settlement options that meet at least some of the substantive, procedural, and psychological needs of all parties.

Interest-based bargaining seeks to identify and address the particular interests of all parties rather than achieve a victory of one party at the expense of another, as is the case in positional bargaining. The procedure in interest-based bargaining is one of mutual problem solving, similar to what happens when two people work together on a puzzle. The parties sit side by side and attempt to develop a mutually acceptable picture or settlement.

Mediators can help parties conduct either positional or interest-based bargaining more efficiently and effectively. As the goal of mediation is to help parties reach a settlement that is acceptable to all, mediators generally have a bias toward interest-based and integrative solutions.

Parties often engage in a positional process that is destructive to their relationships, does not generate creative options, and does not result in wise decisions. One of the mediator's major contributions to the dispute resolution process is assisting the negotiators in making a transition from positional to interest-based bargaining. This process will be discussed in more detail in later chapters.

Complexity of the Issues

Disputes come in a variety of levels of complexity. The simple landlord-tenant case in which two parties argue over a security deposit is very different from a child custody and divorce dispute that involves multiple issues and very complex psychodynamics between the disputants. The latter case may in turn be very uncomplicated in comparison with multiparty disputes, such as one involving the U.S. Environmental Protection Agency, product manufacturers, and environmentalists over new federal air pollution regulations or a complex commercial negotiation between major telecommunications companies over the provision of services.

Mediators must design intervention strategies that respond to the complexity of the specific dispute. In one case, detailed data collection procedures involving multiple interviews over a period of months may be required to understand the causes and dynamics of the conflict, whereas in another, a simple intake interview at the first joint session with the parties is sufficient. In some disputes, the mediator must break a particularly difficult impasse, and when successful, may withdraw and encourage the parties to continue and complete negotiations on their own. In others, the mediator may play an active role throughout negotiations and provide the major procedural framework. In exploring the stages of mediation in later chapters, it will be important to consider the complexity of the dispute to determine the amount of initiative and the level of intervention required from a mediator.

Role and Tasks of the Mediator

The final variable that affects the activities of a mediator is the definition of the tasks and role that he or she is expected to perform in the negotiations. This definition is formed both in the mind of the mediator and in the declared preferences of the parties for specific kinds of assistance.

Mediators vary significantly in the way they define their role and involvement in promoting successful negotiations. The differences are generally rooted in mediators' judgments about how much they should focus on process or substance.

One school argues that mediators should focus primarily on the process of negotiations and leave substantive content as the exclusive domain of the parties (Stulberg, 1981b). Procedurally oriented mediators define their role this way for a variety of reasons. First, they believe that the parties are often better informed about the substantive issues in dispute than any third party could ever be. They maintain that the best decision is that arrived at by the parties. Second, they believe that what the parties need is procedural help, not substantive advice or a decision by an outsider. Third, they hold that the parties' commitment to implement and adhere to a settlement will be enhanced if those parties make the substantive decisions themselves, as opposed to having a deal forged by the intervenor. Finally, they believe that a focus on the process and an impartial stance toward substance build trust between the intervenor and the disputants, decrease the risk to the parties of involving another party (the mediator) in the substance of the dispute, and make the disputants more open to procedural assistance.

Many labor-management mediators, especially intervenors from the Federal Mediation and Conciliation Service, subscribe to this view (Kolb, 1983). They see themselves as "orchestrators" of a process that enables the parties to make their own substantive decisions.

Some environmental mediators also follow this procedurally oriented definition of the mediator's role. Bellman (1982), while raising concerns about a substantive agreement with which he disagrees, ultimately sees the terms of the settlement as the prerogative of the parties. He sees himself primarily as a process consultant.

The procedural orientation can be found among some family mediators, too. They argue that in a divorce, for example, the parents generally know what is best for both the children and the family system as a whole (Phear, 1984). The parents do not need a substantive expert to tell them what to do. What they need is procedural help to assist them in problem solving.

The alternative school of thought argues that although the mediator is impartial and neutral, this does not mean that he or she should not work with the parties on substantive matters to develop a fair and just decision (as fairness and justice are understood by the intervenor). Suskind (1981, pp. 46–47), an environmental mediator, argues that intervenors should be involved in substantive decisions when (1) "the impacts of negotiated agreement [will affect] under represented or unrepresented groups"; (2) there is "the possibility that joint net gains have not been maximized"; (3) the parties are not aware of the "long term spill-over effects of the settlements"; and (4) the precedents that they set "may be detrimental to the parties or the broader public." Suskind further notes that "although such intervention may make it difficult to retain the appearance of neutrality and the trust of the active parties, environmental mediators cannot fulfill their responsibilities to the community-at-large if they remain passive" (p. 47). Some labor-management mediators belong to this school. These "dealmakers" intervene substantively when the parties are uninformed, ill-prepared to negotiate, or unaware of mutually acceptable substantive settlements (Kolb, 1983).

Child custody and divorce mediators also have representatives in the second school. Saposnek (1983) argues that the mediator should advocate the unrepresented interests of the children in negotiations between the parents and believes that the mediator should intervene and influence the substantive outcome if those interests are violated or not taken into consideration. Coogler (1978) advocates engagement in substantive negotiations and advocates that the mediator write a letter of nonconcurrence to the court if he or she seriously disagrees with the settlement.

There is a spectrum along which mediators place themselves in defining their degree of involvement in the procedure and substance of negotiations. At one end are those who advocate mostly procedural interventions; at the other are advocates of substantive involvement by the mediator that may include actually forging the decision. Between them are mediators who pursue a role with mixed involvement in process and substance.

I lean strongly toward the process end of the spectrum because I believe that the parties should have the primary responsibility for self-determination. On occasion, however, the mediator has an ethical responsibility to raise critical questions about substantive options under consideration by the parties. These occasions include cases where the agreement appears to be extremely inequitable to one or more of the parties, does not look as if it will hold over time, or seems likely to result in renewed conflict at a later date, or where the terms of settlement are so loose (or confining) that implementation is not feasible. I believe the mediator should also intervene in cases involving violence or potential violence to one or more parties, either primary or secondary.

Depending on the role that is assigned to the mediator (whether self-assigned or defined by agreement with the parties), he or she will have to determine which types of interventions to perform. In this process, the mediator must decide on (1) the level of intervention, (2) the individual or group to be targeted by the intervention, (3) the focus of intervention, and (4) the intensity of intervention.

The *level of intervention* refers to the degree to which the mediator concentrates on helping negotiators move through the general problem-solving stages, as opposed to particular idiosyncratic problems that are pushing the parties toward impasse. In some disputes, the parties may need assistance to break a particular deadlock, whereas in others, they will require the help of the mediator throughout the bargaining process.

The *target of intervention* refers to the person or people to whom the mediator directs his or her moves. Should moves be directed to all parties, to a constellation within the group such as a sub-group or team, or to a particular person? In a postmarital dispute, for example, will it be best for the mediator to focus on changing the ex-wife's move, the ex-husband's, or both, or should the focus be on the entire family system, including children, ex-spouses, step-parents, and grandparents? In a community dispute, should the mediator focus on the spokespersons, specific team members, the team as a whole, or the constituents of the parties?

The *focus of intervention* refers to the particular critical situations at which the mediator directs his or her moves. The mediator may focus his or her energies on changing the *psychological relationship* of parties to each other. This is often referred to as a conciliation. He or she may aim at creating the psychological conditions that are necessary for productive negotiations. Alternatively, the focus might be on changing the *negotiation process* or the procedure that is being used by one or more people to solve the dispute. Another option is to focus on the process for moving from one stage of negotiation to the next; for example, a mediator might help a party make a proposal that will be acceptable to the other side.

The focus could be on changing the *substance* or *content* of the dispute. The mediator may look for ways to explore data, to expand the number of acceptable options on the negotiation table, to narrow the choices when the parties are overwhelmed with possibilities, or to integrate proposals made by the disputants.

I will now turn to a detailed examination of the stages of mediation and the general moves mediators make in their efforts to promote agreement. Chapters Three through Seven describe activities that are often conducted prior to formal problem solving or a joint meeting of the parties. Some of these endeavors are generic conflict management initiatives that may be performed by the mediator and the parties as means of deciding between a number of potential resolution processes; others, such as those in Chapters Six and Seven, are more mediation-specific. Chapters Eight through Eleven describe the mediation process in detail, from the first session to the final agreement.

Part Two

Laying the Groundwork for Effective Mediation

Chapter Three

Managing Initial Contacts with the Disputing Parties

Mediators enter disputes as a result of (1) direct initiation by the parties, (2) referrals by secondary parties, (3) direct initiation by the mediator, or (4) appointment by a recognized authority such as a government official or agency. Each of these means of entry poses specific strategic choices regarding mediator activities and may affect the quality, type, and probability of a settlement.

Direct initiation by a party or parties is probably the most common mechanism by which a mediator enters a dispute. The request for mediation may come from a single party, a subgroup or coalition of parties, or all the disputants. It may occur before or after the start of negotiations. The source of the request and the timing of the proposal for mediation may have a significant effect on the dynamics of negotiations. I will first explore requests for entry of a mediator made by single parties and subgroups of disputants and then examine requests made by all involved parties.

A request for mediation by a single party, whether an individual or a team, can have a variety of effects on the dynamics of negotiation and on subsequent strategies of the negotiators. One party commonly either proposes mediation to an opponent or takes unilateral action to obtain a mediator. For example, a husband may call a mediator and request help in negotiating custody arrangements with his estranged wife, or a government agency may request assistance in negotiating with a public interest group. If the parties have not started to negotiate, the request for mediation may mean that discussions are preferable to avoidance, stalemate, or alternative approaches to dispute resolution such as going to court. A request for mediation may also signal a desire to cooperate for mutual benefit, a willingness to make concessions, or a belief that total victory is not possible.

People in conflict are often reluctant to ask for a third party's assistance; they are afraid that their request for intervention will weaken their negotiating position and damage the possibility of a satisfactory outcome. Reluctance to call a mediator is especially strong once parties are in the midst of negotiations and have reached an impasse. Theodore Kheel, a labor mediator, describes the problem faced by a party who is initiating the entry of a mediator: "If you've reached an impasse, it can be assumed that both sides have put forth what they claim will be their final offers. In that situation a proposal by one side or the other to bring in a mediator is obviously a signal that side is willing to go still further" (and grant more concessions, for instance) (Shapiro, 1970, pp. 41–42). Reluctance to appear weak or to make additional offers often discourages a request for a mediator. If such a request is made, the party from whom it comes has probably been following the traditional negotiator rule, "Always save something for the mediator" (Downing, 1960, p. 62).

Similar problems to those just described hold true for subgroups or coalitions of parties who request mediation. However, risks may be mitigated when more than one party makes such requests. The initiative can be framed in terms of the needs of all disputants rather than those of a single party, thus lowering the expectation of new concessions.

A proposal for mediation, especially in interpersonal or community disputes, raises the possibility of procedural rejection by another party. Several studies have examined the rate of refusal to initiate mediation in community and interpersonal disputes. Cook, Rochl, and Shepard (1980) found that people refused mediation services in 1,898 of 3,911 cases—a refusal rate of 48 percent. Pearson (1982) found a rejection rate of 50 percent among divorcing couples in Denver, Colorado, who were offered free mediation services. Davis, Tichane, and Grayson (1980) found that in felony offenses among acquaintances, 32 percent of those referred to mediation failed to report, and 12 percent refused outright to participate in the process.

Researchers have attributed the rejection of mediation services to (1) unfamiliarity with the process, (2) rigid adherence to a win-lose approach to dispute resolution, (3) intense emotions that block communication, and (4) habitual attachment to judicial means of dispute settlement (Cook, Rochl, and Shepard, 1980). Single-party requests for mediation services generally seem to result in fewer instances of mediation.

Given such rejection rates, what should the mediator do if approached by only one party? After talking with the initiator, he or she must contact the responding party. In some situations, the mediator or agency will mail a letter to the responding party, explaining the process of mediation and its advantages, liabilities, and cost, and stating that the mediator will call within a short time to answer any questions and to discuss whether the party is interested in using the process. This letter serves to prepare the responding party for the mediator's call and provides an opportunity to consider the viability of mediation before any discussions with the mediator take place.

When calling the respondent, the intervenor should not assume that there is a willingness to mediate. Most people are not familiar with the process, and the intervenor may therefore need to educate the respondent before a commitment to mediate can be elicited. Adequate time should be allowed for the explanation and for questions from the respondent. The approach should not be a "hard sell"; the respondent should be able to freely select or reject the option and should not feel pressured to use the mediator's services. The parties' personal commitment is crucial to successful settlement.

One mediator uses a paradoxical approach to demonstrate the merits of mediation. Instead of promoting the process himself, he asks the respondent to explain why he or she should use mediation. The respondent is thereby placed in the position of mediation advocate.

In some situations, especially those involving cultures in which writing or the telephone are not the preferred means of making an initial contact, the mediator may visit the disputants in person as a way of establishing a connection. This first visit may be facilitated by an introduction from a mutual friend or associate.

In cases in which the mediator is approached by both parties, a significant psychological step toward a cooperative resolution to the dispute has been made.

> Implicit in such an invited third-party role are two assumptions: first, the disputants are sufficiently motivated to address their conflict that one or both of them are willing to enlist the services of a third party; and second, the third party is regarded as sufficiently attractive by one or both disputants that this party is invited to intervene rather than some other individual. From the third party's vantage point, an invited role is desirable both because it suggests that the disputants are ready to work and because the third party is placed in a unique position to exercise influence [Rubin, 1981, p. 11].

To date, no data exist that correlate joint initiation of mediation with successful intervention. However, mediators generally find that a cooperative initiation of mediation by all parties minimizes escalatory dynamics between the disputants at the beginning of the intervention and indicates willingness to solve the dispute to the satisfaction of all.

Referral by interested secondary parties is another way that mediation services are obtained. Secondary parties fall into two categories: first, persons or groups who have no direct stake in the settlement of a dispute but are concerned about the general ramifications of continued conflict; and second, parties who, although they are not principal actors, do have tangible investment in the settlement of a dispute.

Examples of the first type are close friends or neighbors who referred parties to a mediator—or vice versa—and a private foundation that was concerned about general community turmoil that could result from escalating conflict (Lansford, 1983). These parties did not have a direct stake in the outcome but do want the dispute settled.

Secondary parties who have a more direct interest in the settlement also initiate activities that facilitate mediator entry. For example, in one particular workplace dispute, two managers were in conflict over how a job was to be performed. A third manager—a peer—was uncomfortable with tension in the office. He talked to a fourth person in the office, a woman with no authority over the disputing managers, and asked her to intervene.

Lincoln (1976) described a school desegregation conflict in which a mediator was invited by the mayor and the school superintendent to mediate between two hostile groups of students—one black and the other white—that were threatening to vandalize school property and physically harm each other. Although the secondary parties were not directly involved in the negotiations, they clearly had high stakes in the outcome.

Occasionally, secondary parties have authority over the people in conflict and will intervene to encourage disputants to mediate. Mediation organizations often establish referral relationships with judges, lawyers, court clerks, police officers, and personnel in planning departments, social service agencies, and educational and public interest organizations to route disputes to mediation.

Some secondary parties may not only refer cases to mediation but also influence the probability of settlement. Bench referrals by judges, prosecutors, public attorneys, and police officers generally have a higher rate of settlement than referrals by community social service agencies, legal aid organizations, or governmental agencies (Cook, Rochl, and Shepard, 1980). The prospect of a litigious alternative is undoubtedly a significant factor in the influence of certain referral sources on the probability of settlement. Parties know that if they do not reach an agreement in mediation, the case will probably go to court, an undesirable alternative in many instances.

Interventions initiated unilaterally by the mediator are not unusual in complex community disputes that are public in nature, involve multiple parties, and do not have a set of defined primary actors who can request mediation. In this form of entry, the mediator usually learns of the dispute from published written material or an interested secondary party. After careful examination of the dispute, the mediator takes the initiative to contact one or more disputants and offer his or her services. Entry of this type is complicated by the fact that the mediator may have difficulty building credibility with disputants, may lack their psychological commitment, may be subject to ethical issues related to the perception of "ambulance chasing," and will need to consider the possible effect of the intervention on the coalescence of power among the parties involved.

Gerald Cormick and Jane McCarthy, mediators of an environmental dispute concerning flood control and land use along the

Snoqualmie River in Washington State, became involved in this way. They entered the conflict on their own initiative and assisted the primary parties in identifying and including additional disputants. "In determining whether mediation would be acceptable to the disputants, Cormick and McCarthy discovered who the key participants were by asking everyone involved: 'Can you name 10 or 12 persons who if they could agree on something, would have stature and influence enough so that you, who are in disagreement, could reasonably support them and any agreement they might reach?' Those named most often became part of the group that would meet with Cormick and McCarthy to work out a compromise" (Dembart and Kwartler, 1980, p. 47).

This uninvited form of entry is often the only one available to mediators who perceive that they may be helpful to disputants but also understand that the latter may not be aware of mediation as a means of dispute resolution.

Appointment is another means of entry. In institutionalized labor disputes, mediation is often legally required before the parties can proceed to other means of dispute resolution, and mediators are appointed by state or federal agencies. There are some interpersonal, community, civil, and court-related disputes in which government agencies may mandate the process, appoint mediators, or do both.

In the marital conciliation court system of California, for example, parties in child custody cases are required to try mediation before court action (Comeau, 1982). There are also numerous instances in which elected officials have appointed a mediator to respond to a community dispute (Dembart and Kwartler, 1980; Lansford, 1983; Clark-McGlennon Associates, 1982).

In the Whittamore-Singson case presented in Chapter One, both parties attempted unassisted negotiations and were not successful. Singson was familiar with mediation and had his lawyer ask a mediator to propose the process to Whittamore. The mediator sent Whittamore a letter of introduction, followed it up with a phone call, and then scheduled private meetings with both Whittamore and Singson to explore whether they wanted to use the process. When they indicated that they did, he instructed them to proceed with data collection on the case.

Tasks of the Mediator in the Entry Stage

Regardless of how a mediator enters a dispute, he or she must accomplish certain specific tasks in the first stage of the mediation process. These include (1) building personal, institutional, and procedural credibility; (2) establishing rapport with the disputants; (3) educating participants about the negotiation process, the role of the mediator, and the function of mediation; and (4) gaining a commitment to begin mediating.

Building Credibility

Mediators must build credibility with those in conflict by developing their expectations that the mediator and the mediation process will help them successfully address the issues in dispute. In general, there are three types of credibility: personal, institutional, and procedural.

Personal credibility refers to the mediator's possession of certain personal characteristics that both mediators and disputants have long seen as crucial to the success of the intervention process (Davis and Gadlin, 1988). Landsberger (1956) found that disputing parties in labor negotiations, when asked to name desirable attributes of mediators, mentioned

Originality of ideas

An appropriate sense of humor

The ability to act unobtrusively in a conflict

The ability to create the feeling of being "at one" with the disputants and concerned with their well-being

A willingness to be a vigorous salesperson when necessary

Control over his or her feelings

Persistent and patient effort

The ability to understand quickly the dynamics and complexities of a dispute

Some specific knowledge of the field in which he or she is mediating

Activities by mediators that allow them to personally exhibit these qualities will generally reinforce beliefs held by disputing parties that the mediator has personal attributes that will assist them in resolving the dispute.

Institutional credibility refers to the reputation of the organization that employs the mediator. Such credibility is based on an organization's history of successful performance in the particular field of dispute resolution for which a mediator is needed, a history of unblemished impartiality among personnel, and often a background of neutral—or at least, not overtly biased—sources of funding. Institutional credibility may be a crucial factor in the acceptance or rejection of mediators or mediation organizations. Mediators wishing to build institutional credibility may

1. Produce brochures describing their expertise and services
2. Present a list of former clients to prospective users (subject, of course, to client approval and the limits of confidentiality)
3. Offer examples and explanations of the types of disputes they have mediated
4. Present credentials of membership in recognized dispute resolution associations
5. Disclose organizational funding sources to demonstrate institutional impartiality

Two case examples illustrate the importance of building institutional credibility. A company executive considered using a mediation service to assist him in settling a community dispute to which he was a party. The mediation firm was asked to make a presentation about its services to some of the involved parties. During the meeting, the executive looked at the firm's brochure and began to put pluses and minuses next to the names of the firm's board members according to his perception of whether they would be positively or negatively disposed toward his interests in the dispute. When he counted the marks, he noticed that they came out even, and he accepted the firm's claim to impartiality.

In another case, an environmental group wanted the names and telephone numbers of other public interest groups that had used a mediation organization to settle conflicts over mining. The organization provided the data to build institutional credibility.

Procedural credibility refers to the belief of the disputants that the process the mediator has proposed has a strong likelihood of success. Some mediators are reluctant to describe the procedures by which they propose to resolve a dispute. By claiming that they respond differently to each conflict or by arguing that mediation is an art form rather than a series of scientific interventions, some mediators shroud their practice in secrecy and leave the disputants ignorant of the mediation process. Mediators following this approach argue that procedural credibility is enhanced by mystifying the process. However, this is not the majority view on the issue.

The practice of obscuring the mediation process has been sharply criticized by those who advocate a candid education of the parties about general mediation procedures that might be used in their dispute. Clear procedural descriptions enable the parties to make informed judgments about the viability of the process, and they demonstrate how the procedure might work in the particular case. In building procedural credibility, the mediator should stress that successful resolution rests primarily on the disputants themselves and that the best possible process will not guarantee that recalcitrant parties will come to terms.

An example of procedural credibility building occurred when mediators from my company, CDR Associates, were asked to intervene by the Public Utilities Commission of Colorado in a dispute over the creation of a new rule on telephone access charges. As the process of negotiated and mediated rulemaking had a very limited history in Colorado, and none of the major parties had ever engaged in such a process, the mediators conducted an educational session for the disputants in which case histories and procedures used for regulatory rulemaking in other settings were presented. Successful case studies built procedural credibility and enabled the parties to visualize how the process might work for them.

Establishing Rapport with the Disputants

Personal, institutional, and procedural credibility is merely the starting point for a mediator's entry into a dispute. The greatest factor in the acceptability of an intervenor is probably the rapport he or she establishes with the disputants. *Rapport* refers to the degree of freedom experienced in communication, the level of comfort of the parties, the degree of precision in what is communicated, and the quality of human contact. Rapport is clearly influenced by the mediator's personal style, manner of speech, dress, and social background; by common interests, friends, or associates; and by the amount of communication between the mediator and the disputants. Mediators often talk about the need to develop some form of bond with the parties. This may be accomplished early in the mediation by identifying common personal experiences such as recreation, travel, children, and associates; by talking about common values; by genuinely affirming one or more of a disputant's attributes or activities; or by demonstrating one's sincerity through behavior.

In an intervention a few years ago, I was encountering significant difficulty in building rapport with a party over the telephone. He answered most questions, even open-ended ones, with yes or no answers or a grunt. Finally, he asked about the weather where I was in Colorado, and I knew that was the opening. On learning that it was snowing, he began to reminisce about time he had spent in the mountains. I followed up with a few open-ended questions about his experiences, and after a few minutes, we discovered that we had both done winter camping. The beginning of rapport had been established.

In another case, Kakwirakeron, a Mohawk leader in a dispute involving Native American land claims at Moss Lake in upstate New York, described the manner of Rowley, a mediator with the American Arbitration Association, as follows:

> When I first met Rowley I remember the white hair which he has, and the type of face he has is to me an honest face. And he always had the ready smile, which is a genuine smile, not just for the show of it. He had a manner, a very easy manner which is easy for us to identify. He really doesn't have a mask on. He is not trying to put on a show or an air of importance. He is just honest and straightforward and our first impression of him held up all the way through [Kwartler, 1980, pp. 15–16].

Educating Participants About the Mediation Process

To build initial procedural credibility, the mediator should explain enough about his or her role and mediation procedures to create a willingness in disputants to try the process. In the later phases of a mediator's efforts to enter a dispute, he or she will spend additional time educating the parties about the particular negotiation and mediation process. This educational effort should be undertaken to (1) minimize surprises that might result from misunderstandings about the negotiation and mediation processes; (2) clarify the sequence of steps so that disputants know what to expect and know what roles they will be playing; and (3) gain both conscious and unconscious feedback from the participants, reflecting their feelings and reservations about the intervention procedure. Although the goal of mediation is not primarily an educational exercise, it is still a process designed to *teach* participants how to solve their problems. Disputants must thus have at least a minimal understanding of the process for the intervenor to be successful. Some of the matters that the parties should understand include

- The role of the mediator (neutrality and impartiality as appropriate for the particular type of mediator role being performed)
- The way information or data about the dispute will be collected
- The procedure that will be used to "work" on each issue
- The limits of confidentiality in the mediation process
- The potential use of joint sessions and of caucuses (private meetings)
- The possible forms that an agreement, if reached, might take

Before committing themselves to mediation, the parties should assess all the procedures available to them to resolve their dispute. Careful explanation and evaluation of the alternative approaches enhance the probability that mediation, if it is selected, will be successful.

Gaining a Commitment to Mediate

The mediator must believe that there is a common commitment by the parties both to the process of negotiation and mediation as a means of resolving their dispute and to the mediator as an assistant in this effort. The commitment to the process and to an intervenor has been referred to in organizational development literature as a "psychological contract" (Schein, 1969, pp. 81–88). A psychological contract is a tacit agreement between mediator and disputant that their relationship exists for the purpose of settling the dispute and that it will be based on certain core values, such as openness and honesty.

At this point, mediators usually have to make a strategic decision about how explicit or formal the commitment process should be and what form it should take. In some situations and cultures, oral agreements to participate may be all that will be necessary. In others, the contracting may be more formal.

Formal contracts often specify fees, expected time expenditure, and specific services to be or not to be performed. Mediators vary considerably in the degree of formality they introduce into mediation contracts. Some want an explicit signed statement that the parties are committed to achieving a jointly satisfactory solution with the mediator's assistance. Others rely exclusively on more informal documents.

In some disputes, an attempt to gain overt commitment to mediation, either oral or written, may lead to a failure to begin negotiations at all. Mediators occasionally delay asking the parties to formally commit to mediation until a series of successful procedural and substantive decisions has been made. In this approach to achieving commitment, mediators first seek agreement that they can talk with one or more parties alone or in informal joint meetings. In these conversations, the disputants may discover common interests that can be built on to develop rapport between the parties and later, perhaps, to form substantive agreements. Such common interests are used to initiate formal discussions.

Between the two extremes of explicit written commitment and informal oral commitment is a strategic third option. Through questioning of and discussion with the disputants, a mediator may discover specific conditions under which conflicting parties will be willing to negotiate. These might include understandings about how the parties will interact in negotiation, the timing and location of sessions, or specific symbolic gestures that are demanded before discussions can begin. The mediator may work with the parties to meet these behavioral preconditions for negotiation. By setting the stage and building a commitment contract, the mediator can encourage involvement without seeking a formal statement to that end. This approach has the advantage that parties do not have to overtly commit to the process to begin dialogue. However, it also has drawbacks: a precedent may be established that requires the mediator to constantly overcome limits or hurdles thrown up by participants who are not committed to the process; and the parties may balk at formalizing their commitment to any agreements.

In some large public disputes, mediator entry may initially be for data collection, and a party's participation in this phase of the process does not mean that a mediation will result or that the interviewee will necessarily be a participant. This form of entry is often called "convening" and will be described in Chapter Five. In this scenario, the intermediary wants to collect data that will be used to determine if mediation is desirable and feasible; invitations to participate and the commitment process that has been described will occur later.

Implementation of Entry

So far, I have explained the four general means of entry and the tasks to be accomplished by the mediator during this stage of intervention. I now turn to specific ways in which mediators initiate contact with disputants. These include letters, phone calls, personal visits, and third-party introductions. Depending on the mediator, institution, type of dispute, and characteristics of the disputants, various combinations of the above may be effective. Some mediators and mediation organizations make first contact with clients by phone, whereas others rely more heavily on personal interviews. Frequently, a combination of letter, brochure, and phone call is used to build credibility, describe the process, and gain commitment to mediate.

In complex disputes in which access to the main actors is tightly controlled or limited by some barrier such as race, channels of authority, or even physical inaccessibility (examples are volatile community conflicts and cases involving highly bureaucratic and hierarchical organizations), a secondary party may be used to introduce the mediator to one or more disputants. These introductions may be invaluable to the intervenor seeking entry into a closed dispute.

Two types of intervention activity are usually considered when determining the point at which a mediator should enter a dispute: data collection and problem-solving mediation activities. Although both types of intervention require entry by the mediator, their impacts on the dispute are quite different.

Data Collection

Entry to gather preliminary data about a conflict can be initiated at almost any time in the development of a dispute, although information may be more difficult to collect during certain phases of conflict development, such as the early escalation stage before the parties have decided to negotiate, or the stage in which negotiations have commenced but the parties do not believe a mediator is necessary.

The major strategic decisions about intervention for data collection focus primarily on whom to talk with, the sequence of interviews, and the content of interviews. More will be said about entry strategies for data collection in Chapter Five.

Problem Solving

The timing of mediator intervention to solve problems, as opposed to collecting data, is one of the most intensely debated topics in the dispute resolution field (Simkin, 1971; Kerr, 1954; Carpenter and Kennedy, 1979; Pearson, 1984). Some mediators argue that early intervention limits hostility and emotional damage. It may also alleviate the tendency for parties to polarize on substantive issues. Early entry may enable the mediator to prevent the development of a hard-line commitment on one side to options that are unacceptable to the other.

Another argument for early intervention concerns procedural advantages. Polarization often results when disputants fail to understand productive means or procedures to resolve their controversy. Early intervention can discourage unproductive negotiation behavior, can route the parties toward behavior or procedures that will result in settlement, and can deter energy-draining responses that may escalate a dispute and create barriers to settlement based on poor process rather than substantive differences.

Arguments for later mediator entry into a dispute center on

parties' needs to mobilize their power, to equalize the means they have to influence each other, and to occasionally demonstrate their coercive power before negotiations. Later entry may also allow for polarization to develop that often clarifies issues; provide time for the parties to vent emotions; and allow the parties themselves to request the assistance of an impartial mediator after they have exhausted their own procedural and substantive options.

Proponents of later intervention argue that parties need time to mobilize their forces and gather their means of influence in order to affect the other parties involved (Cormick, 1982; Crowfoot, 1980). They claim that early entry hinders this process; that the weaker party, who is not as well prepared for the conflict and therefore has less influence, may be overwhelmed; and that an unfair settlement may be either reached or imposed. Mobilization of resources might include visiting a lawyer and obtaining advice on the strength of a legal case, conducting research necessary for informed negotiations, mobilizing a community group to protest a particular policy, filing a case in court, or planning a strike.

Early-entry adherents generally do not disagree with those advocating late entry about the needs of parties to mobilize and, whenever possible, equalize power. Failure to gather the necessary data before negotiations is tantamount to playing a game of poker without looking at the cards. Failure to assess legal power or, when appropriate, extralegal action before negotiations can enable one party to take advantage of another.

Advocates of early entry diverge from their colleagues who advocate late entry on the question of demonstrating coercive power. They argue that mobilization and exercise of coercive options should be separated. Early-entry advocates point to experimental research (Rubin and Brown, 1975) demonstrating that the exercise of coercive power, although it may promote negotiations, does not necessarily promote cooperative behavior. This finding seems to be corroborated by research on outcomes of actual negotiations. Pearson (1984), for example, found that couples in divorce settlement mediation who had used coercive court mechanisms to obtain temporary orders had a lower rate of settlement than those who had not used legal coercion before settlement negotiations.

Late-entry advocates counter with valid case examples in which the exercise of force—by means of legal suits, strikes, or demonstrations—has been necessary to demonstrate a party's power and, in some cases, to force an opponent to negotiate. Last-minute pressure has clearly inclined parties toward agreement and has motivated them to request a mediator's assistance.

Mediators who look for easy answers regarding questions of power and timing of the impartial party's entry will probably find none. The best answer is that these factors depend on the case. If parties can mobilize power so that they are informed and so that the other side knows that they are dealing with a prepared and powerful adversary, the power may never need to be exercised, and the mediator may be able to intervene before a crisis exacerbates relationship problems or inflicts costs that provoke escalation. Early entry in the case may prevent unnecessary damage to either of the disputing parties. On the other hand, if the parties have unequal power, need a confrontation to mobilize resources, or must test each other's strength before good-faith bargaining can begin, mediators are advised to delay entry.

The argument for a period to vent emotions is also not contested by early-entry proponents. They do, however, maintain that unstructured and prolonged venting, which may occur if the mediator delays entry, may result in hostile or unproductive behavior that causes unnecessary psychological barriers. The final argument, which relates to the "ripeness" of a dispute for settlement, is an extremely important strategic issue that bears directly on the timing of intervention. Numerous mediators and negotiators have observed that disputes go through specific cycles, and that resolution of issues often cannot occur until disputants have performed ritual acts (Douglas, 1962). Mediator entry too early in a dispute, it is claimed, damages this developmental cycle.

Late-entry proponents argue that parties are not psychologically or strategically prepared to use an intervenor's services until they have reached an impasse and recognize that they cannot reach a settlement without third-party assistance.

The safest rule postulates that a mediator should not enter a negotiation until there is a bona fide deadlock. The reason is self-evident. A premature intervention by the mediator relieves the parties of the pressure under which they are working. The reciprocal pressure is the basic force that keeps the parties moving through proposals and counterproposals. Entering the situation before a genuine deadlock is reached creates an atmosphere of relaxation in the parties, and consequently, the mediator has no basic element to keep the parties moving. Requesting the services of a mediator before the bona fide deadlock is usually a trick used by one or both parties to extend the negotiations. An intervention at this time will discourage the parties from reaching an agreement. One or both parties will relax their efforts while the mediator gets his fingers burned [Perez, 1959, p. 717].

Proponents of early entry, on the other hand, argue that the development of psychological readiness and motivation for settlement can often be accelerated by an efficient mediation process introduced early in a dispute. Early introduction of mediation can decrease levels of frustration, diminish polarization, and promote positive results. Success, rather than mutual frustration, can then become the driving force in negotiations.

The timing of entry is clearly an important strategic decision for mediators. At the current stage of research, not enough is known to specify in an unqualified manner the conditions under which early entry is superior to later intervention. Mediators should assess whether early entry is likely to be more detrimental to the disputants than delay. If the answer is no, an early intervention is probably the safer route.

Chapter Four

Selecting a Strategy to Guide Mediation

In Chapter One, I presented several approaches to conflict management and resolution. These spanned a continuum, with conflict avoidance at one extreme and physical violence at the other. As one moved from left to right in the diagram (see Figure 1.1), the approaches became progressively more directive and coercive. My concern in this chapter is with the processes people in conflict use to select a particular approach or combination of approaches along this continuum. Of particular concern is how and under what circumstances people select mediated negotiation as the principal way to manage or resolve conflict.

Related to the selection of approach is the selection of an arena. Arenas are locales for conflict management and resolution that vary on several dimensions: publicness and privacy, informality and formality, institutionalization and noninstitutionalization, and voluntariness and coercion. Any given approach can be acted out in a variety of arenas. For example, mediation can occur in a private setting that is informal, voluntary, and uninstitutionalized—as in child custody and divorce settlements conducted by a mediator in private practice. Alternatively, mediation can be conducted in a highly public setting with standardized behaviors and rituals, formal rules for participation, and an institutionalized structure. This is the type of arena used when the U.S. Environmental Protection Agency and other concerned parties engage in a negotiated rulemaking, or "reg-neg," to formulate new, consensually based regulations.

Parties need to select both the approach and the arena they think will best meet their needs and satisfy their interests.

Approach and arena selection is a relational decision, in that it occurs as a result of interaction between the people in conflict. Parties may use the same approach and arena, may partially coordinate their approaches or arenas, or may use entirely different approaches and arenas. To achieve a termination of the conflict, the parties must usually coordinate at least some of their dispute resolution activities.

A mediator can assist parties in selecting and coordinating approaches and arenas. He or she is often more aware of approaches and arenas than are disputing parties and can therefore educate them about alternatives in the early stages of prenegotiation and assist them in selecting an appropriate means of conflict management and dispute resolution that will best meet their needs and capabilities.

The Mediator-Disputant Relationship and Decision Making

The roles available to mediators in helping disputants make decisions about conflict approaches and arenas are similar to those from which lawyers must select. Hamilton (1972, p. 41) outlines three philosophical stances that a lawyer may take in advising and counseling clients:

A. Collect the facts, explain how the law applies, analyze, recommend a best course, or courses, of action, and argue for its adoption.
B. Collect the facts, explain how the law applies, analyze, explain the course of action open to the client, and leave the decision entirely to him.
C. "B" above, except with discussion of the ramifications of the course of action and the situation until the client is able to make his decision.

Mediators must choose among the same three stances, with the exception that they do not interpret the law.

The majority of mediators probably see their role as defined by option C, in which the task is to assist disputants in making their own decision based on information supplied by the mediator about the opportunities available through various approaches and arenas. Most mediators view their relationship with the disputant as collaborative; information is shared to develop the wisest and most considered decisions possible.

The Approach and Arena Decision

Mediators do not automatically assume at the beginning stage of intervention that mediated negotiation is the best approach for conflict management or resolution. It is only through a careful assessment process that the disputants and the mediator may jointly arrive at this conclusion.

There is no one decision-making procedure that is appropriate in all disputes for determining whether mediation is the best approach. Mediators can, however, assist disputants in accomplishing some of the following tasks:

1. Identifying the interests or goals that must be satisfied in a potential settlement
2. Considering the range of possible and acceptable dispute outcomes
3. Identifying the conflict resolution approaches that may assist disputants in reaching individual, subgroup, or collective goals
4. Identifying and assessing criteria for selecting an approach
5. Selecting and making a commitment to an approach and arena
6. Coordinating, if necessary, the approaches used by the disputants

In the following sections, I will explain each point in more detail.

Interests to Be Satisfied

At this point, the mediator often talks with the parties separately and will encourage them to carefully examine their own interests and those of other parties to arrive at answers to the following questions:

1. What interests (substantive, procedural, and psychological) must be met by a conflict management approach and resolution?

2. What interests are mutually incompatible or overlap with the interests of other parties?
3. What interest is there in an ongoing relationship?
4. What forms of actual or potential power do the parties have that would allow them to impose their will on other disputants in order to achieve their interests?
5. How important or salient are the various interests to each actor in the dispute?

The analysis of interests enables the parties and the intervenor to determine whether any common interests exist and to assess the purity of the dispute (Kriesberg, 1973). *Purity* refers to the degree of exclusivity of interests. A pure conflict is one in which all interests are incompatible—for example, no settlement options are available that can satisfy one party's interests without sacrificing those of another. A mixed conflict allows for some satisfaction of all interests. If a conflict is pure, parties have little to negotiate. If it is mixed, negotiation and mediation are appropriate approaches to dispute resolution.

For example, if divorcing spouses both demand legal custody of their child and there are no provisions in their jurisdiction for joint custody, the conflict could be pure: neither party could win legal custody without the other losing. On the other hand, if both parents want to share their relationship with the child and are interested in allocating time equitably, the conflict is mixed and suitable for negotiation.

Possible Dispute Outcomes

After identifying the interests involved in the conflict, mediators usually work with each party separately to assess potential—and in some cases, probable—conflict outcomes. Thomas (1976) identifies five possible outcomes to any given issue in dispute. Clark and Cummings (1981) elaborate on Thomas's themes. Their combined results are represented in Figure 4.1. For the sake of clarity, this figure represents a dispute with only two sides and illustrates a conflict from the viewpoint of Party A.

Figure 4.1. Possible Outcomes of a Dispute as Viewed by Party A.

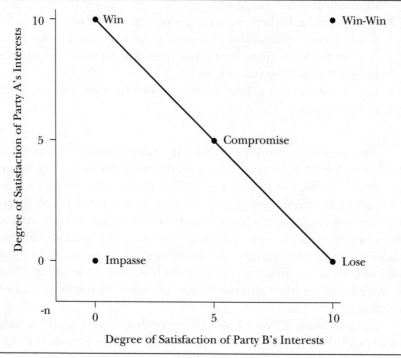

Win-lose outcomes occur in the upper left and lower right corners of the chart. The difference is in which party wins. Win-lose outcomes are most common when

- One party has overwhelming power.

- Future relationships are not of great concern.

- The stakes for winning are high.

- One party is extremely assertive and the other is passive or not as aggressive as the "winner."

- Satisfaction of the interests of the disputants is not dependent on their mutual cooperation.

- One or more parties are uncooperative and are unwilling to engage in cooperative problem-solving negotiations in which interests can be mutually satisfied [Moore, 1982b, p. V–3].

Impasse outcomes are present in the lower left corner. These outcomes result when parties are not able to come to an agreement. They occur when

- Both parties choose to avoid the conflict for whatever reason.
- Neither party has enough power to force the issue.
- There is lack of trust, poor communication, expressive emotion, or an inadequate resolution process.
- The stakes for winning are low or neither party cares about the dispute.
- The interests of the parties are not related.
- One or more of the parties are uncooperative [Moore, 1982b, p. V–3].

Compromise outcomes are illustrated by the central portion of the diagonal line. Such outcomes occur when all parties give up some of their goals to obtain others. They are likely to happen when

- Neither party has the power necessary to win totally.
- The future positive relationship of the disputants is important but they do not trust each other enough to work together for integrative solutions with mutual gain.
- The stakes for winning are moderately high.
- Both parties are assertive.
- The interests of both parties are mutually interdependent.
- The parties have some leeway for cooperation, bargaining, and tradeoffs [Moore, 1982b, p. V–3].

Win-win outcomes occur when all parties feel that their interests have been satisfied. Conditions for win-win outcomes are present when

- Both parties are not engaged in a power struggle.
- A future positive relationship is important.
- The stakes are high for producing a mutually satisfactory solution.

- Both parties are assertive problem solvers.

- The interests of all parties are mutually interdependent.

- Parties are free to cooperate and to engage in joint problem solving [Moore, 1982b, p. V–3].

Mediators discuss with parties various possible outcomes and how they meet the interests of the disputants. Ideally, the outcomes and interests should match.

Range of Approaches

Once a party has assessed its interests and those of other parties and reviewed potential dispute outcomes, it must select a particular approach to reach the desired end. Approaches are general procedures for resolving disputes; they include such options as unassisted negotiations, negotiations with the assistance of an advocate, conciliation to handle emotional or relationship barriers, facilitation, mediation, arbitration, and litigation.

Approach selection depends on a variety of criteria, including the outcome that is desired and the strategy that is to be used. Mediators review general strategy options open to the parties and how these strategies may be applied within the context of a given approach. Strategy assessment is usually conducted by the mediator privately with each party.

There are five general strategy options: competition, avoidance, accommodation, negotiated compromise, and interest-based negotiation. Figure 4.2 describes strategy options as viewed by Party A.

Competition

In some situations, a party's interests are so narrow that they can be met by only a few solutions, none of which are acceptable to other parties. Such a party may choose a competitive approach and strive for a win-lose outcome, especially when it has more power than its opponent. Competitive approaches include litigation, arbitration, and extralegal activities such as tactical nonviolent direct action and violence.

In deciding to use a competitive approach, a party should weigh the costs as well as the benefits of its conflict behavior:

Figure 4.2. Conflict Strategies as Viewed by Party A.

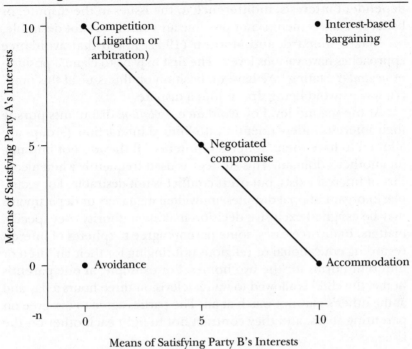

- Will the party get what it wants over the long term as well as short run?
- Will competitive behavior destroy relationships that will be important in the future?
- Does the party have enough power to guarantee a win? What happens if it loses?
- Will competition provoke competition in other areas?
- Will a competitive strategy lead to the most desirable solution? [Moore, 1982b, p. V–4].

Avoidance or Stalemate

Conflict avoidance can be either productive or unproductive in satisfying interests. People avoid conflict for a variety of reasons:

fear, lack of knowledge of management processes, absence of interdependent interests, indifference to the issues in the dispute, or belief that agreement is not possible and conflict is not desirable.

Blake, Shepard, and Mouton (1964) noted that avoidance approaches have various levels. The first may be to claim a position of *neutrality*. Stating "We have no position on this issue at this time" is a way to avoid being drawn into a dispute.

At the second level of avoidance, *isolation,* disputants pursue their interests independently, with limited interaction. Groups are allowed to have their "spheres of interest" if they do not impinge on another's domain. This strategy is used frequently when a conflict of interest exists, but overt conflict is not desirable. For example, in organizational disputes, individual managers or departments may be assigned exclusive decision-making authority over specific matters. In divorce cases, some parents agree to spheres of interest regarding educational or religious upbringing for their children or different norms for the two homes. For example, at one parent's home, the child is allowed to watch television three hours a day and at the other's may not watch at all. The parties agree to disagree on parenting styles, and they contract not to fight each other on the issue.

People or groups that have been repeatedly defeated frequently use *withdrawal* to ensure their continued existence and to avoid any conflict that might lead to another defeat. Withdrawal means total dissociation of disputants. This strategy does not encourage or promote mediated negotiations.

Accommodation

Accommodation occurs when one party agrees to meet the interests of another at the expense of its own needs. An accommodation strategy is pursued when

- Sacrifice of some interests is required to maintain a positive relationship.

- It is desirable to demonstrate or foster cooperation.

- Interests are extremely interdependent [Moore, 1982b, p. V–5].

A positive accommodative approach may be pursued when there is hope that a more collaborative process or benefit trading may occur later on other issues. For example, when a developer voluntarily agrees to spend additional funds to add an amenity demanded by a dissatisfied homeowners' group, he is accommodating himself to their needs. He does not have to spend the money but decides that a positive ongoing relationship is worth the expenditure.

Accommodation may also be pursued for negative reasons:

- Parties lack the power necessary to pursue an alternative strategy.

- Parties are passive or unassertive.

- Parties have a lower investment in the outcome [Moore, 1982b, p. V–5].

Negotiated Compromise

Bargaining to reach a compromise is selected because

- The parties do not perceive the possibility of a win-win situation that will meet their needs and have decided to divide and share what they see as a limited resource.

- Interests are not seen as interdependent or compatible.

- The parties do not trust each other enough to enter into joint problem solving for mutual gain.

- Parties are sufficiently equal in power so that neither can force the issue in its favor [Moore, 1982b, p. V–5].

Many out-of-court settlements are negotiated compromises. A judicial decision is risky for both sides because it is not clear who will win. Parties and their advocates frequently split the difference to ensure that each gets some of what they want, and each party shares some of the loss.

Interest-Based Negotiation

In contrast to competition and compromise, in which the outcome is seen as division of fixed resources, interest-based procedures seek to enlarge the range of alternatives so that the needs of all parties are addressed and met to the greatest extent possible.

Interest-based procedures work best when

- Parties have at least a minimal level of trust in each other.

- Parties have some mutually interdependent interests.

- Equal, but not necessarily similar, means of influence exist, or the party with the superior power is willing to curtail the exercise of power and work toward cooperative solutions.

- Parties have a high investment in a mutually satisfactory outcome because of mutual fear of potential costs that might result from impasse.

- Parties desire a positive future relationship [Moore, 1982b, p. V–5].

Each of the preceding strategies can be pursued in the context of several approaches and arenas.

Parties must match their strategy with their interests and link it with an approach that offers the best prospects of satisfying them. Mediators should help parties to decide if they want to compete, avoid, accommodate, compromise, or seek a cooperative settlement. Once the party has selected a general strategy, it chooses an approach that best implements the strategy. Of all the strategies described, compromise, accommodation, and interest-based negotiation are the most compatible with the negotiative approach.

Selection of a general strategy to guide a negotiation approach does not mean that other strategies will not be used to respond to particular aspects of a dispute. For example, a party may choose to compete on central or core issues but to avoid or accommodate on others. Selection of a general strategy is merely a guide for subsequent negotiations. Strategy will often change once the parties have started discussions and have become more informed about issues, interests, and means of influence of other parties. Parties commonly select a competitive strategy, decide to negotiate, and then shift to a strategy of compromise or interest-based negotiations.

Mediators aid parties in matching interests, approaches, and strategies by helping them identify and assess an approach's potential for reaching a satisfactory outcome. Generally, a mediator should suggest, and help a party assess, more than one approach and strategy so that he or she does not seem to be advocating a particular method of resolution. The mediator may also discuss possible arenas that may be combined with an approach. For example, a party might consider litigation as a means of forcing a party to negotiate. The mediator might explore with the party the use of the threat of litigation to promote settlement negotiations.

Criteria for Selecting an Approach and Arena

After presenting possible approaches and arenas, the mediator can assist the parties in identifying relevant criteria that should be considered in making the selections. Criteria may be different for interpersonal, commercial, organizational, and public disputes. There are, however, many similarities. Some of the criteria or variables for selecting an approach or arena are cost, time, the relationship between the disputants, the internal dynamics of the dispute, and power.

The question to be asked with respect to *cost* is: What will be the costs (direct costs, salary costs, delay costs, lawyer fees, and so on) of pursuing each approach or arena?

As far as *time* is concerned, the questions will include

- How long will it take to settle the dispute using each approach or arena?
- Is a rapid or a delayed settlement desirable?
- Are there any critical deadlines or time constraints to be considered? Does a deadline pose an opportunity or a crisis for one of the parties?
- What is the most advantageous time to settle?
- Do the parties need more time to mobilize resources or build credibility and commitment among a constituency for a particular course of action?

With respect to the *relationship between disputants*, the key questions will be

- Is the conflict a single-encounter dispute, or is it occurring in the context of an ongoing relationship?

- What type of relationship is desired at the end of the dispute?
- How will the use of various approaches and arenas affect the ongoing relationship?
- Do any of the proposed approaches and arenas seem unfair or in conflict with relationship or community norms?
- What effect will selection of an approach or arena have on the public image of the party or parties? Do the various options enhance or detract from public credibility?
- Will the selection of a particular approach or arena affect future conflicts of this type?

The questions to be asked about *internal dynamics,* according to Crowfoot (1980), are

- Is the individual or organization stable and effective enough to pursue various approaches?
- Will the approaches involve the membership of the organization? How and at what costs or benefits?
- Will a particular approach or arena build or unify membership and the organization?
- Does a particular approach build self-acceptance, confirmation, essentiality, and a psychological feeling of success or failure (Argyris, 1970)?
- Do the individuals or organizations have the necessary leadership and skills to pursue a particular course of action?
- Do the individuals or organizations have the time, energy, and financial and emotional resources to pursue a particular course of action?

The relevant questions about *power,* as identified by Simokaitis (n.d.), are

- What power or means of influence do disputants have to make the other side give them what they want?
- How powerful does the party believe the other side perceives it to be?
- What possible allies and other sources of power might the party be able to tap?

- What might happen to limit the party's power?
- What are the limits on the power of the other disputants?

Once decision criteria or variables are identified, the mediator should assist a disputant in assessing how important each criterion is, and how it affects the selection of a particular approach and arena. Mediators may assist parties in making this assessment by providing a structure for a cost-benefit analysis (Moore, 1982b), by developing a decision tree (Behn and Vaupel, 1982) that identifies strategic choices and possible outcomes, or by helping participants assess probabilities of outcomes through an analysis of similar cases or trends (Bellows and Moulton, 1981).

An initial statement by parties that they want to mediate should not necessarily be taken at face value. A careful assessment of their interests and their criteria for selecting an approach and arena may reveal that they are not willing to make the substantive, procedural, or psychological offers that would be required by a negotiated settlement. In these situations, the mediator should advise the parties that other approaches to resolving the conflict may be more appropriate.

Commitment to Approach and Arena

Once all approaches and arenas have been compared according to the criteria, the mediator should assist the parties in making a final selection. Careful assessment of valid information about potential outcomes from each procedure usually helps people build internal commitment to a choice of action. "Internal commitment means the course of action or choice that has been internalized by each member so that he experiences a high degree of ownership and has a feeling of responsibility about the choice and its implications. Internal commitment means that the individual has reached a point where he is acting on the choice because it fulfills his own needs and sense of responsibility, as well as those of the system" (Argyris, 1970, p. 20).

Internal commitment to negotiation with the assistance of a mediator will help the parties in dispute to struggle together to reach an agreement. If the mediator has done his or her job well, assisting the parties in selecting mediated negotiations will have moved them closer to a resolution.

Coordination of Approaches and Arenas

Approach and arena selection by one disputant does not mean that the same approach or arena will be selected by other disputants. The approach and arena assessment process must be conducted with all of the primary parties in a dispute.

Mediators may assist parties who are operating with different approaches or in different arenas in coordinating their conflict resolution efforts so that they can cooperatively reach a solution rather than spend unnecessary time, money, physical energy, or emotional effort on unproductive conflict activity. For example, Party A wants to negotiate a settlement on one issue, but not while litigation is being conducted on another. The mediator may help Party A defer litigation until after the negotiable issues have been discussed.

In collective bargaining situations, where negotiation is the accepted and preferred means of settling conflicts, the parties are less likely to encounter the coordination problems that arise in interpersonal, organizational, or community disputes. In the latter types of conflicts, disputants often lack either a common approach or a common arena. They may in fact have no prior history of interaction and therefore no traditional or accepted way of resolving conflicts. In these types of disputes, the mediator can play a critical function in assisting the parties with the coordination of their conflict resolution efforts.

There are, however, situations early in the negotiation process in which perfectly coordinated procedures are not attainable. These situations arise when parties

- Are not psychologically prepared to commit themselves to a particular approach
- Are not dissatisfied with the approach currently being used
- Want to try noncoordinated activity, hoping for a win-lose outcome in their favor, before cooperating
- Feel that a coordinated approach offers them no advantage

The first part of this chapter will examine methods of data collection. The second part will explore how information is integrated and analyzed. The chapter focuses primarily on data collection and analysis in disputes between more than two people or parties. However, the process is basically the same for conflicts between only two individuals.

The amount of time spent on data collection depends on the complexity of the dispute. An interpersonal conflict clearly requires less time to be expended in data collection—perhaps an hour or two with each party—than does a complex social policy dispute in which months may be needed to gather relevant information.

Data collection can be conducted before negotiation or once negotiation has begun. Because I prefer to perform preliminary data collection before joint sessions, I will assume in this chapter that the mediator is meeting with parties separately before starting formal mediation in joint sessions.

Useful and accurate data collection depends on several factors:

1. A framework for analysis and adequate background information
2. An appropriate method of data collection
3. An appropriate person to collect the data
4. A strategy for data collection and for building rapport and credibility with involved parties
5. Appropriate interviewing approaches that encourage valid responses
6. Appropriate questions and listening process during interviews

Framework for Analysis

All conflicts involve specific people, relatively predictable dynamics of development, competing interests, and tangible and intangible issues. These common components of disputes allow a general framework to be created that is useful in generating questions and explanatory hypotheses about a given dispute.

Mediators may use categories in Figure 2.1 (see p. 60) as a basic framework for analyzing a conflict. Relationship problems, data disagreements, competing interests, structural barriers, and value differences should be considered as potential causes of conflicts.

In addition, factors that promote positive relationships, points of data on which the parties agree, compatible or nonexclusive interests, structural variables that enhance constructive interaction, and common or superordinate values should be identified as factors that may be encouraged or enhanced to promote agreement.

Data Collection Methods

Mediators use several procedures to collect data: direct observation, review of secondary sources, and interviewing. These procedures are used either individually or in combination to provide more accurate or complete information about a given conflict.

Direct Observation and Site Visits

A mediator may watch a couple fighting at the beginning of a mediation session, may attend and observe a public meeting, may visit a proposed development site, or may attend a company briefing to gather firsthand information on how the parties react and interact in a conflict.

Observation goals vary from dispute to dispute. The focus can be on any of three levels: individual behavior, interaction within subgroups, and interaction between groups. From observation, the mediator can determine social class, status, power, and influence relationships; communication patterns; and group routines that will influence the conduct of a conflict.

Consultation of Secondary Sources

Secondary sources are materials that provide information about a dispute without direct observation or interviews. Helpful secondary sources may include financial records, minutes of meetings, maps, organizational or government reports, newspaper or magazine articles, tape-recorded or videotaped presentations, and research conducted on the issues or people involved in a dispute.

Interviewing

The most common way for many mediators to gain information is to interview involved parties. There are two broad types of interviews that may be used in mediation: data collection interviews and persuasive interviews (Stewart and Cash, 1974). The first type is used to collect relevant information, the second to persuade disputants that a particular procedure or outcome is desirable. The focus of this discussion will be on data collection interviews.

Such interviews may be conducted either before or during joint meetings. Some mediators prefer to hold a preliminary data collection interview with each individual or party before a joint meeting. This provides the interviewer with information necessary to understand some of the people, issues, and dynamics of the conflict before interacting in a joint session. Preliminary interviews often provide the mediator with more information about the dispute than is known by any one party. This knowledge enables him or her to plan how the parties will educate each other about issues and interests in joint sessions; it also identifies information that needs to be exchanged to clarify misperceptions, fill in data gaps, and help the parties reach agreement.

Data collection interviews also serve to introduce the participants to the mediator. The personal and organizational rapport and credibility that are built during the interview strongly influence the amount and quality of information gathered and the receptivity of the disputant to the mediator's later interventions. Rapport is often more easily developed in one-on-one interviews than in joint sessions.

Finally, data collection interviews allow an exchange of information about the mediation process. A mediator can use the data collection interview to describe his or her proposed process in more detail and to solicit procedural or substantive suggestions from interviewees. A dialogue on processes for conflict management may be the first step toward collaborative problem solving.

Data collection interviews may also be conducted at the start of joint meetings. Data collection is then performed in the presence of all involved parties. Such interviews allow the parties to educate each other, provide an opportunity for the mediator to watch how the disputants interact, and enable the mediator to verify that information presented in the joint meeting is consistent with that provided in the earlier private interviews.

Data Collector

Many mediators delegate the task of conducting the initial interview to an "intake" worker, whose findings form the basis of a case file. Although this arrangement may save time for mediators, it may also hinder the subsequent development of rapport and credibility between the mediator and the disputants. Usually, the mediator will have to follow up with his or her own brief data collection interview to build rapport with the parties.

In some conflicts, mediators or their agencies may prefer to collect data and mediate in teams. Male-female or lawyer-therapist teams are often utilized in child custody and divorce cases. In complex public policy or environmental disputes, interviewer-mediator teams may be involved. Co-mediators should take care in data collection to work together as much as possible, to frequently exchange any information that they obtain individually, and to minimize the possibility of working at cross purposes.

In some disputes, assignment of mediators to a particular type of conflict or interviewee may be an important move in securing fuller information from a respondent. Gender, age, race, social class, status, and previous relationship with the interviewer may affect the amount of information that can be obtained. For example, a woman disputant may feel more comfortable relating an incident of domestic violence if one of the mediators is a woman. In some interracial disputes, a minority mediator's presence has made a difference in the willingness of parties to be involved.

Usually, the more the respondent identifies with the interviewer or mediator, the better he or she will respond to the intermediary's influence. Mediators can often manage their own dress, speech, and manners, and can use these attributes to enhance the possibility of interviewer-respondent identification.

Data Collection Strategy

A strategy is a conscious approach for solving a problem. In this context, the problem is how to get enough information about a dispute from the parties so that the intermediary can develop an intervention plan that will assist them. The information includes identification of key parties and a strategy for approaching them.

Identification of Parties

In many interpersonal and organizational disputes, parties are easy to identify, and the mediator can easily determine whom to interview. In divorce cases, for example, the husband and wife and perhaps the children will be targeted for interviews. The same is true in two-party commercial or insurance claim cases, but it is not always the case in cross-cultural cases, where extended family members—parents, uncles, aunts of the disputants—and numerous other concerned parties may need to be involved in order to resolve a dispute.

In conflicts in which there are multiple disputants and the parties are not well organized or highly visible, the mediator may have to identify main actors before data collection can begin. In public disputes, mediators use procedures similar to those used by researchers in community power-structure research (Aiken and Mott, 1970). The methods about to be described are used alone or in combination to assist mediators in identifying critical individuals, groups, and organizations that must be involved in a dispute resolution initiative.

The *positional approach* (Jennings, 1964; D'Antonio, Loomis, Form, and Erickson, 1961) identifies the main formal institutions or organizations involved and targets the people who fill their key positions. The chief executive officer of a company, members of a county commission, or the elected president of a public interest group all occupy positions of authority. The assumption of this approach is that those in key formal positions of authority in the institutions or organizations involved in a dispute are those who will make decisions about how the conflict will be handled and resolved. In many cases, this may be true, although positional power holders may not have the authority to decide any given issue. Formal leaders of social, economic, and political institutions may not be as important as an individual without a formal position who can mobilize a group of supporters, make a technical decision, or initiate a lawsuit.

The assumption of the second identification method, the *reputational approach* (Walton, 1966; Hunter, 1953), is that people with a reputation for having power are indeed powerful. Mediators ask a group of reliable informants, "Who are the central people who should be interviewed about this conflict?" These informants are often knowledgeable observers of the dispute—but not active participants—or other primary parties. Names gathered in this process are cross-referenced, and the people who are most frequently mentioned are considered to be central to the dispute.

The weakness of this method, similar to that of the positional approach, is that perceived power does not necessarily mean actual power. Only through interviews can the two aspects of power be correlated.

The third identification method is the *decision-making approach* (Polsby, 1960; Dahl, 1961). In this method, the mediator seeks to ascertain who within an organization or group has been involved in previous decisions on issues similar to the one in question—and at what level they have been involved. The assumption is that certain people are likely to be repeatedly involved in the same type of issue. This method depends on the mediator's ability to review prior decisions and to identify the people who took part in them. It focuses on those participating in a conflict, the processes they have used in the past to influence decisions, and the development of conflict relationships over time.

All these approaches for identifying the key people in a conflict have merits and weaknesses, both in their theoretical assumptions and in their applications. Mediators will usually find that a combination of approaches produces the most reliable data on potential interviewees.

Sequencing of Interviews

After the interviewees have been targeted, mediators should consider the sequence of interviews. In interpersonal disputes and occasionally in other conflicts, the party that initiates mediation is interviewed first. These parties are often more amenable to providing information than those who are responding to another's initiative.

Because the sources of data in conflict situations are individuals under actual or potential emotional stress, great care should be taken to determine a sequence of interviews that will not antagonize anyone.

In multiparty disputes, the mediator will have to develop a more detailed process for sequencing interviews. Often, he or she may have to contact secondary or less involved parties before talking to the principals. This helps to identify disputants, generate a more accurate picture of the conflict, practice questioning techniques, and obtain valuable information on the most suitable interviewing approach before talking with the main actors. Secondary parties are invaluable resources in disputes, because they often have a more objective view and may also be able to introduce the interviewer to other parties to the conflict. For example, in a university dispute, a department's secretary may be highly informative on the dynamics of faculty members and students and the critical interests and issues that concern them.

The mediator should frequently ask a secondary party, "Who is it important for me to talk with?" and "Who should be talked with first?" Inclusion of interviewees in interview sequencing decisions often gives the mediator valuable information about those most central to the dispute. In some instances, an interviewee may offer to call a friend and provide an introduction.

When secondary sources have provided sufficient data for the mediator, he or she should develop a strategy and a sequence for interviewing the central figures. Questions that frequently guide the sequencing include

- Who are the most powerful or influential people in the dispute?
- Who will be offended if he or she is not interviewed or is not interviewed first?
- Who should be interviewed earlier so that his or her cooperation can be used to induce others to participate in interviews?
- Who is the person most likely to talk about the problem?

Before interviewing the central individuals, the mediator may conduct research on what roles they play in the conflict, what positions they have held on similar issues, their likes and dislikes, and their personal traits. This information may expand the potential for data collection in the interview.

Timing of Data Collection Interviews

Data collection can be conducted before or at the time of joint sessions. Questions that mediators can ask themselves to determine if a premediation data collection interview is necessary include

- Are the parties extremely hostile toward each other? Is there a potential for violence?

- Do the parties have widely divergent viewpoints on the issues in conflict?
- Do their styles of communication in joint session inhibit a clear exchange of views on the issues in dispute?
- Are multiple issues involved?
- Are issues extremely complex?
- Is there a likelihood that additional data or factual information may be needed before a joint session?
- Does one of the parties appear to be weaker than another?
- Does one party express fears of being dominated by another?
- Is one party unclear about the mediation process or the role of the mediator?

A yes to any of the preceding questions indicates that a premediation interview for data collection may be appropriate.

If a mediator decides to use a premediation conference, he or she should carefully explain to all parties the purpose of the interview, its duration, the scope of issues to be covered, and limits of confidentiality of data revealed in the sessions. Most mediators hold to the standard that information exchanged in the premediation data collection meeting and in later separate caucuses is confidential and will only be revealed publicly or in joint session with the consent of the disputants. However, others make exceptions to this rule, most notably when criminal conduct, child abuse, or risk of physical harm is involved.

Some mediators opt to conduct all their initial interviews in joint session, with all disputants present. This choice may be based on strategy, convenience, time constraints, complexity, limits on confidentiality, or a desire to avoid suspicions of partiality. The forum for data collection may also be constrained by the wishes of the disputants—one or more of whom may not wish to meet separately because of distrust of the mediator—or by political factors, such as rules on open meetings or sunshine laws. More will be said in Chapter Eight about conducting data collection interviews at the start of a joint session.

Development of Rapport and Credibility

The first five to ten minutes of any data collection interview may be the most critical to building rapport and establishing personal credibility. This has been called the "social" stage of the interview

(Survey Research Center, 1969). (Clearly, the cultural context of the dispute and the relationship of the mediator to the party will greatly influence the length of time and the content of this activity.) In this brief period of informal conversation, the mediator should try to present himself or herself as an open, warm, intelligent, and interested person. A mediator should first take some time to have an informal conversation on noncontroversial topics of mutual interest. This conversation should not include subjects that might create distance or dissonance between the mediator and the disputant.

Once the initial phase of developing rapport has been completed, the mediator begins the process of credibility building referred to in Chapter Three. A mediator builds credibility from the moment he or she makes the first phone contact, but the face-to-face interview provides an additional opportunity to do so. Mediators usually decide in advance how much to explain about themselves, the mediation organization, their relationship to the various parties, and the mediation process before going on to direct questioning. Disputants may need to know more about the process and the mediator with whom they will be working before they can enter into trusting communication.

The mediator must also motivate the participant to respond. This will be easy or difficult depending on the participant's disposition toward the issue in dispute, the procedure, and the mediator. Responsiveness is often facilitated by rapport building and by the discovery of commonalities between mediator and participant. For example, in collecting data for an environmental case on acid drainage from an old coal mine in rural Pennsylvania, I interviewed an elderly coal miner who sat as a member of a county water board. I asked him about his family's history in the area and then allowed lots of time for him to talk. I did this not only to learn more about the man and his background but also to give myself an opportunity to mention that my grandparents, too, had settled in the area; he could then feel that we had something in common. Some of the motivation strategies that mediators can use to elicit information include

- Explaining the importance and worth of the data to the mediation process so that the disputant feels that he or she can make a genuine contribution toward a positive change

- Stressing the need to hear all views, especially those of the interviewee
- Explaining the benefits of participation
- Answering questions that may decrease resistance to participation
- Demonstrating a positive personal interest in the disputant's concerns, problems, or viewpoints

Most mediators use a combination of these motivation strategies.

Interviewing Approach

The interviewing approach often significantly affects the kind, form, and detail of the information that is collected. It also influences who is in control of the process and content of the data collection effort—the party being interviewed or the mediator.

Focused Versus Nonfocused Interviews

In some data collection interviews, the mediator determines specific areas about which he or she wants to obtain information through prior secondary source analysis. In other cases, mediators are more interested in conducting general exploratory interviews that may become more focused after the disputant has shared his or her perception of the conflict.

Advantages to interviews with specific foci include

- The ability to focus on issues that are deemed relevant by the mediator
- The greater ease of filtering extraneous or irrelevant information
- The ability to gain the most helpful information in the shortest amount of time

The major drawbacks are that

- The mediator may bias the information received by encouraging the disputant to give answers he or she thinks the interviewer wants.
- The mediator may miss valuable information the participant would have revealed if the questioning had been more comprehensive.

- The mediator's conception of the conflict, rather than the participant's, may become the dominant framework for defining the dispute.

A mediator should carefully decide what he or she needs to know and then design an interview format that will achieve those goals.

Structured Versus Nonstructured Interviews

Mediators usually use two types of interview formats to collect data from disputants or other parties with relevant information: structured and nonstructured.

Structured interviews are designed to collect the same or similar information from each of the disputants so that their answers are quantifiable and comparable. This requires a list of standardized questions or categories of information.

Nonstructured interviews are used for exploratory data collection when the same information is not required from each disputant, when there may be resistance to structure by the interviewee, or when the mediator has not accumulated enough information to narrow the focus to specific categories or questions. Nonstructured interviews resemble ordinary conversations except that they have more focus and less equal exchange. In this form of interview, both the mediator and the disputant have greater freedom to influence the direction of the information exchange.

In selecting the most appropriate form of interview, mediators consider which will produce the desired information, encourage the respondent to share knowledge, and create the rapport necessary for later information gathering or intervention.

The Interview Format

Mediators should plan a format for both individual and joint data collection interviews. Although formats may differ somewhat for these two interventions, many of the strategic questions are the same. The following considerations should be addressed:

- In joint meetings, who should speak first to either make an opening statement or present his or her story?
- What information exchange format should be used?
- What time constraints should be placed on speakers?

- How will the mediator gain a procedural agreement on the data collection process?
- How acceptable is emotional expression?
- How will disagreements or discrepancies in data be managed?
- In joint sessions, how will the mediator prevent psychological burnout or boredom in the party who is not speaking?
- How will interruptions be managed?

Although there is not enough space to answer all these questions, several of the most critical are addressed here.

Who speaks first? This question applies only to joint data collection meetings. Mediators use several criteria for determining who presents his or her view first:

- Who initiated the dispute or conflict?
- Who initiated the mediation?
- Who wishes to change the status quo?
- Who is not emotionally capable of waiting to explain his or her case?
- Who is the weaker party?

General practice usually allows the initiator or claimant to go first, as this party has brought the dispute to mediation (Stulberg, 1981a). Often, the first party to speak is the one who wishes to change the status quo. For example, in labor negotiations, the union generally goes first with proposals to change the current contract or initiate a new one. An exception to the above practice may be made when one of the parties is so emotionally engaged in the conflict that he or she cannot wait for another party to present their viewpoint first, when one party is weaker and may gain some internal psychological strength from going first, or by mutual agreement of the disputants.

What format should be used for information exchange and data collection? There does not seem to be one format that mediators use consistently. One common procedure is to allow each party a specific period of time in joint session to present its case to the mediator and the other party. The only interruptions allowed are requests from the mediator for clarification or more information. In joint meetings, other parties may often be allowed or encouraged to ask questions and obtain clarifications at the end of each interview.

Another procedure used in group disputes is for a disputant who has the trust of most parties to outline the dispute and its history, and for other parties to voice any disagreements with this account as it is proceeding. These points of disagreement may later become agenda items for discussion.

A third approach is to conduct a joint meeting with multiple parties or a team so that a group view of the problem may be obtained. Although group interviews are often a highly efficient way to get information from a number of people at one time, they can also result in the group view influencing or jaundicing the otherwise independent and diverse views of individuals. In group interviews, the accuracy of the views expressed should always be checked by giving participants the opportunity to contact the mediator privately to voice any privately held views. (I often give group participants my business card and encourage them to call me if they have any new thoughts on the subjects we have discussed.)

How are anger, interruptions, and disagreements over data to be managed in joint session? Because data collection usually occurs either before joint sessions, at the start of negotiations, or after the mediator has entered a dispute as the result of an impasse, the parties are usually experiencing significant feelings during the time allotted for information exchange. In individual interviews, mediators may accept emotional expression more than in joint sessions. More will be said about this in Chapter Seven.

Interview Questions and the Listening Process

Effective interviews require both good questions and good listening on the part of the mediator. The balance between these communications skills, of course, depends on the purpose and structure of the interview. In both structured and nonstructured interviews, there is a great degree of variety in how questions are asked and the degree of mediator directiveness (see Table 5.1). Questions generally are of two types: closed and open-ended (Stewart and Cash, 1974).

Table 5.1. Types of Questions or Responses.

Type of Response	Definition	Example
Elaboration Question	A request for more information related to something respondent has already said.	A. We are interested in co-parenting but don't know what it entails Q. Can you say more about what concerns you?
Active Listening	An exact statement or paraphrase of what the respondent has said. The restatement often focuses on the emotional content of a message and is more of a response than a question.	A. I'm very upset about the condition of the road and what they did to it. A. You are very angry that they damaged your property.
Direct Clarification Question	A direct request for information to clarify vague or ambiguous information.	A. We do not want multiple-family homes in our neighborhood. It spoils our single-family-home lifestyle. Q. Is it the idea of multiple-family homes that bothers you or the number of people or units in each one that is important?
Inferred Clarification Question	Clarification or information that was implicit in previous response.	A. The meeting was held over at the Federal Bulding. Q. At Frank Williams's office?
Summary Question	A question that summarizes previously stated information and requests that the respondent verify the data.	A. We purchased the property as a cooperative venture, wrote an agreement that required an equal input of money, and they subsequently violated it by not making agreed payments. Q. You purchased property, made a financing agreement, and then the partners failed to follow through?

Table 5.1. Types of Questions or Responses, Cont'd.

Type of Response	Definition	Example
Confrontation	A question that points out a discrepancy in data presented by the respondent. (This should be used with care because it can create resistance from the interviewee.)	A. I want to have Smith pay for the cost of replacing my windshield and all the trouble he has caused me. That amounts to $250. Q. You say you want to have him pay $250 in damages, yet you stated earlier that your brother handled the installation and that the glass cost only $100. What exactly were your time and energy expenditures on this problem?
Repetition Question	An exact restatement of a previous question.	Q. How much will impact mitigation cost to restore the land to its previous state? A. Oh, I'm not sure with the price of water, seed... Q How much will impact mitigation cost to restore the land to its previous state?

Closed Questions

Closed questions, which call for a yes or no answer or a specific statement of fact, allow the mediator to narrow the focus so that he or she may obtain concrete information on a particular aspect of the dispute. The most closed format is a leading question such as, "Didn't you see the people move the truck onto the site the afternoon of August 27?" Mediators often avoid closed or leading questions early in interviews because they may create animosity toward the mediator on the part of the interviewee and may therefore reduce the amount and quality of information that is offered (Richardson, Dohrenwend, and Klein, 1965).

Open-Ended Questions

A mediator wants to gather as much information about the conflict as possible and to identify the disputant's perceptions about the problems to be addressed. That information is frequently difficult to obtain because of distrust or guardedness on the part of those in conflict, or because the respondents have not defined the situation in the same terms as the mediator. Mediators use open-ended questions to help overcome these limitations. Such questions allow the interviewee to share as much information as he or she wishes without feeling pressured. In addition, they enable the interviewee to share his or her perception of reality without being subjected to an alien framework of analysis; there are no probing questions with an implied or prescribed answer.

In interviews based on open-ended questions, mediators should not create a highly structured discussion. The goal is for the interviewee to do most of the talking. After asking an open-ended question, the mediator should simply listen. Active listening (see Table 5.1) with content or emotional feedback may also be useful as a clarifying technique (Gordon, 1978).

Sample open-ended questions include

- What is the background to this situation? (*Situation* is preferable to *conflict* because of the negative connotation of the latter.)
- What are the issues (or problems) that concern you?
- What kinds of decisions are to be made?
- Who (individuals, agencies, or groups) would have to be involved to reach a wise and implementable decision? What does each party think about the problem?
- What common interests and concerns do you and other people in this situation have?
- What do you think should be done to avoid or resolve this situation? Under what conditions would you be willing to work with the other people on this problem?

Note that many open-ended questions begin with *what* and *how* rather than *why*. Asking "why" questions may make a person feel that his or her beliefs have to be justified and may put him or her on the defensive (Richardson and Margulis, 1984).

Failure to Answer Questions

Occasionally, an interviewee will fail to answer a mediator's question. The possible reasons are numerous:

- Failure to understand the question
- Overly complex wording of the question
- A multiplicity of questions in one sentence
- Excessive scope or complexity of the problem posed
- Reluctance to reveal private or privileged information
- Effects of intense emotion on thinking capacity
- Lack of trust between disputant and mediator

By carefully recording answers to questions, observing nonverbal behavior, or questioning directly, the mediator should be able to determine why a respondent does not answer.

Recording Answers. A mediator often receives more information in an interview than can possibly be remembered. To prevent losing important data, mediators usually decide before the session what data-recording methods they will use. The two primary recording techniques are written notes and sound/video recordings. Each method has its benefits and costs.

Written notes require rapid notation so that content and emotions can be easily retrieved during analysis. The writing method must be accurate enough that points of information are not lost but unobtrusive enough that the writing does not distract from the interview. The following are some guidelines for mediators relying on written recording:

- Ask the disputants for permission to take notes.
- Clarify with the disputants how notes will be used and whether they will be confidential or open to the public.
- If an interview has a planned sequence of informational categories, have a prelabeled page for each category.
- Take notes in an abbreviated or shorthand form.
- Maintain eye contact with the respondent as much as possible during the interview (if this is culturally appropriate) and do not concentrate on taking notes.

- Take notes consistently throughout the interview. Do not write in a noticeably different manner when an especially important or complex point is explained by the respondent. This prevents biasing the disputant by giving special attention to a particular area of questioning.
- Read the notes back to the interviewee, when appropriate, to verify accuracy.
- If appropriate, use a team consisting of one interviewer and one recorder. The roles can be reversed during the interview.

Sound or video recording of interviews is another way to obtain complete interview records. Tape-recording is by far the most accurate data collection and storage system but is often time-consuming to listen to and costly to transcribe, and it may inhibit interviewees.

If sessions are to be tape-recorded, mediators should obtain permission from disputants, explaining how the tape will be used and who will have access to it. Mediators may gain greater cooperation by offering to turn off the recorder if a disputant is uncomfortable discussing a particular subject.

Conflict Analysis

Conflict analysis is the synthesis and interpretation of data collected by the mediator from interviews, direct observation, or an examination of secondary sources. The mediator's central task during this stage is to integrate and understand the elements of the dispute: people, dynamics, issues, and interests.

Conflict analysis activities are often difficult to identify as a separate component of mediation because many mediators, working alone, do not perform any visible or external activities to indicate that they are analyzing a dispute. From all appearances, they often move from data collection to proposing an acceptable mediation procedure. However, when a group of mediators is working together on dispute analysis, their activities are more visible.

Data Reporting Between Co-mediators

Data reporting refers to the exchange of interview information between interviewers or mediators if more than one person is collecting data. Several techniques are used to facilitate reporting.

The simplest is probably a periodic team meeting in which mediators make brief oral reports on people they have interviewed and information they have obtained. Time should be allowed for questions from other interviewers and for suggestions on improving the interview procedure and format. Such formal meetings, however, may take up too much time if there are many interviewers or interviews and the dispute demands rapid intervention.

Information may also be disseminated by circulation of written transcripts or recordings of interviews or reports of the interviewer's impressions. Mediators often find that writing down their reflections while traveling from an interview is an effective procedure for interpreting data and sharing them with others. This technique promotes synthesis and summarization of salient points, making the information more manageable.

Integration of Data

In complex disputes, interviews often generate a tremendous quantity of information. Structured recording and cross-referencing systems may have to be used. There are a variety of tools that mediators use to integrate their data.

Data About People. One way to organize data about the people in a dispute is to make a *participant list* showing names of potential and past interviewees and the organizations with which they are associated. Such a list helps mediators keep track of those who have been interviewed, when they were interviewed, and who remains to be questioned. It also allows mediators to determine when individuals representing a particular category of disputant—such as a family member, a company representative, a city council member, a lawyer, or a federal regulator—should be interviewed to balance views on an issue and to ensure that all viewpoints have been presented. Among the helpful elements that may be included in participant lists are the name of the interest group to which the person belongs and the degree to which he or she can influence the course or outcome of the dispute (Table 5.2).

Data About Relationships and Dynamics. The second category of information to be integrated is that concerning the relationships of the conflicting parties. In order to understand a dispute, a mediator must have a grasp of historical events and trends that have led to the present conflict. Two tools are often used to describe the

Table 5.2. Interest Group or Individual Participant List.

	Industry Group		Government Group		Public Interest Group	
	Person	Interview Date	Person	Interview Date	Person	Interview Date
Main Groups or Individuals (High Influence)	1 ___	___/___	___	___/___	___	___/___
	2 ___	___/___	___	___/___	___	___/___
	3 ___	___/___	___	___/___	___	___/___
	4 ___	___/___	___	___/___	___	___/___
Secondary Groups or Individuals (Moderate Influence)	1 ___	___/___	___	___/___	___	___/___
	2 ___	___/___	___	___/___	___	___/___
	3 ___	___/___	___	___/___	___	___/___
	4 ___	___/___	___	___/___	___	___/___
Interested Parties with No or Low Influence	1 ___	___/___	___	___/___	___	___/___
	2 ___	___/___	___	___/___	___	___/___
	3 ___	___/___	___	___/___	___	___/___
	4 ___	___/___	___	___/___	___	___/___

development of conflict relationships: timelines and case study scenarios (Coover, Deacon, Esser, and Moore, 1977).

The time line is a chart on which a mediator records significant events that have influenced a conflict's development (see Figure 5.1). Time line entries include specific communications, failures to communicate, interviews, press releases, public meetings, elections, direct actions, and the initiation of litigation. In addition, they may include larger events such as changes in public awareness on an issue, economic trends, a major government policy change, or international events that influence the dynamics of the dispute. Time lines may also project into the future and identify critical data or action that will affect the conflict dynamics.

Some mediators write brief dispute case histories to help them identify and order historical events. Later, these case studies or scenarios may be used to present to the parties a view of how the conflict developed, so that a common understanding of the background of the dispute can be cultivated.

Data About Substantive Issues. The final category of data that must be organized and integrated pertains to the substance of the dispute: issues, interests, positions, and potential settlement options.

One tool that mediators use to order and analyze conflicting interests is an issue, position, interest, and option chart. This chart is used to plot a disputant's stated issues and positions in an organized manner and then identify the underlying interests that lie behind those positions. The chart also identifies potential settlement options. By identifying interests, the mediator can assist the parties in generating a range of solutions that may be mutually acceptable.

Verification of Data

Data collection, especially when conducted in separate meetings, may generate contradictory information. Data may have been incorrectly heard or recorded by the mediator, or the respondent may have intentionally or unintentionally given misinformation. Disputants also have different perceptions or definitions of the problem. The mediator must try to understand and correct information discrepancies if a successful intervention is to be launched.

The first step in investigating discrepant data is to determine

Figure 5.1. One-Month Time Line.

Parties	Time and Events			
	Week 1	Week 2	Week 3	Week 4
1. Company	Files plans with planning department	Visits affected homeowners		Attends public hearings
2. Planning Department	Receives plans			Holds public hearings
3. Public Interest Group	Meets to discuss company plans	Develops counter-position and press release	Meets with homeowners	Attends public hearings
4. County Commissioners		Notified by planning department of citizen opposition to project	Talk with citizens	
5. Local Landowners	Meet to discuss company plans	Meet with company	Meet with public interest group	Attend public hearings

if the incongruity is due to a problem in the questioning or recording process. This may entail reviewing original notes, cross-referencing interviewee responses, referring to secondary sources, or initiating follow-up interviews or questions.

Occasionally, mediators may recontact a disputant to clarify a point. This is usually done in a low-key manner, without placing judgment or blame on the disputant. For example, "I don't understand, there seem to be two explanations of this point. Can you clarify this for me?" would be appropriate to challenge a discrepancy in the information. The respondent always needs a way to maintain dignity in the process of clarifying conflicting data.

Interpretation of Data

So far, most of the conflict analysis procedures discussed have pertained to data organization. I will now discuss the most difficult aspect of conflict analysis: the interpretation of information. In order to proceed, the mediator must create a conceptual map of the conflict and develop a set of hypotheses such as those discussed in Chapter Two. There is no one procedure used by mediators to interpret information about a dispute. Listed below are several thought processes that may be useful, depending on the type of dispute. These procedures are linked to the categories presented in Figure 2.1 (pp. 60–61).

Some mediators begin to dissect and analyze a conflict by dividing the unnecessary or unrealistic causes from those that are genuine or realistic (Coser, 1956). *Unrealistic causes of conflict* include

- Strong emotions that are not based in objective reality
- Misperceptions about motivations of other parties
- Stereotypes
- Miscommunication
- Unproductive repetitive behavior that negatively affects another party
- Attempts to force an agreement on values when such concurrence is not required for settlement
- Confusion over data
- Competitive behavior induced by a misperception that interests are mutually exclusive

Genuine causes of conflict include

- Real disagreements over what data are important or how they are collected or assessed
- Actual competing substantive, procedural, or psychological interests
- Structural constraints on the parties, such as competing roles or unequal power or authority
- Destructive behavior patterns caused by external forces such as environment or time constraints
- Different value systems that are difficult to reconcile but must be addressed to reach settlement

By dividing the causes of conflict into unnecessary and genuine categories, the mediator makes it possible to first address the problems that are tangential—the unrealistic ones, for instance—and then focus on the realistic causes of the dispute.

A second analysis process requires the mediator to carefully analyze the causation categories represented in Figure 2.1 and then target the cause that will be central to successful dispute resolution. For example, consider the following case where poor communication and inadequate communication structures are a primary cause of the conflict. In a complex dispute involving closure of a local school because of declining enrollment, the only means by which parents can express their grievances is a hearing process before the school board. But public hearings frequently promote conflict because of their one-way communication structure and the tendency of participants to voice extreme positions. A new forum or structure is needed that will enable the community and education officials to effectively discuss the impacts of the closure on the neighborhood and the system. Creation of a new structure may induce productive dispute resolution.

This same procedure can be used if a dispute over data is deemed to be the primary cause. For example, in a complex water dispute in Colorado, the parties disagreed over critical basic data—how much water was available, how much was needed, and where resources were located. Negotiations could not proceed until these issues were resolved. One party had much of the information in a computer model but would not disclose it because it was proprietary and would affect the party's economic capacity to obtain additional resources. The mediator worked with the parties to help develop a parallel computer model that would answer the necessary questions about water resources but would not require disclosure of privileged information. The two models were submitted for comparison to an independent and mutually acceptable water resource consulting firm. It verified that each model was based on valid premises and came up with similar conclusions regarding the amount of water available and the location of sources. The disputants were able to use assumptions developed through the computer modeling process to agree on basic data without violating proprietary constraints.

Conflict analysis is complex and will be different for each case. This step, however, is critical to designing an intervention plan.

Presentation of Data and Analysis to Disputing Parties

In most two-party mediations, the mediator will use the data collected in individual interviews and organized in his or her own mind to design a mediation strategy. Often, the information will never be directly shared with the parties.

However, in complex multiparty or public disputes, the mediator may want to organize the data into a "convening report" that is shared with the parties to help

- Organize their thinking
- Increase their understanding of the dispute
- Make them aware of each other's interests
- Describe the issues to be discussed
- Identify possible problem-solving processes for future joint sessions
- Build a commitment to begin the exploration of possible settlement options by mentioning options suggested by parties

Convening reports can be effectively used to identify both points of agreement and issues that need to be discussed.

Convening reports are often expected or required by public agencies that are initiating mediation as means to resolve public disputes. In fact, such agencies may divide the dispute resolution process, and contracts for intervention, into a convening portion and a mediation portion. They may also use the convening report to determine if adequate conditions have been met to proceed with formal mediation. For example, the U.S. Environmental Protection Agency will generally proceed to mediation in regulatory negotiations or policy dialogues only if there are a limited and identifiable number of parties, the issues are clear and definable, there is a limited time period in which to act, and there is some sort of political pressure that encourages parties to reach an agreement.

If the agency's criteria for proceeding are known by the mediator prior to preparing the convening report, the report's content can be structured to address the specific concerns and considerations that the agency will use in its decision making. If these criteria are not known, the mediator may suggest appropriate criteria and list the pros and cons of proceeding. Ultimately, of course, it is up to the parties to decide whether they will move forward to the next stage of the mediation process.

Chapter Six

Designing a Detailed Plan for Mediation

Once a mediator has gained a commitment from the parties to mediate, and information has been collected and analyzed, the task that remains before any direct intervention is the design of a mediation plan. A *mediation plan* is a sequence of procedural steps initiated by the intervenor that will assist negotiators in exploring and reaching an agreement. The plan's detail depends on the type and complexity of the conflict, the extent of the mediator's knowledge of the dispute, available planning time, and the amount of control over the negotiation process the disputants have delegated to the intervenor.

Mediation planning occurs throughout a dispute, but in the beginning of the intervention, the mediator may be especially active. If the mediator has scheduled separate data collection interviews with disputants before joint negotiations begin, he or she may have time to reflect and develop a plan before the parties come together. If, however, the first data collection is performed with all the parties assembled, and they expect progress in the same session, the mediation plan may have to be designed at the first meeting.

Many mediators prefer a more deliberative planning process that allows them time to consider all the options and formulate a comprehensive strategy. Others prefer to design the plan as the issues and dynamics unfold. Clearly, there is not one right way to design a mediation plan. Mediators must select the process with which they are most comfortable or that is best suited to the particular situation.

The mediator may develop mediation plans either in cooperation with the disputants or, if one of two conditions is met, without consulting or involving the parties (Argyris, 1970). First, if the issue or problem under discussion is not very important and "does not involve the clients' feelings of self-acceptance and competence and where the problem is clearly out of range of competence of the clients" (p. 27), the mediator may decide to intervene unilaterally. Second, if the dispute is extremely intense and the disputants feel hopeless or paralyzed in their efforts to change their interactions, the mediator may take control of the process.

Whenever possible, the parties should be involved in the design of the mediation plan, as this strengthens their commitment. If the process is designed by the mediator alone, the parties may feel that it is external to them. An example of joint procedural planning by the mediator and the parties occurred during the negotiation of a new growth management plan for the state of California. The mediators asked each party to designate a representative to sit on a small process design task group whose function was to design, with the mediator, the procedures for discussion of the issues in dispute. Once developed, procedural proposals were submitted to the group as a whole for approval and implementation. Involvement in designing the negotiation procedures and mediation plan increased the parties' ownership of, and commitment to, the process and created stronger advocates for the interventions that were suggested by the mediators.

In designing a mediation plan, mediators should consider certain critical questions:

1. Who should be involved in the mediation effort?
2. What is the best location for mediation?
3. What physical arrangements need to be made?
4. What procedures will be used?
5. What issues, interests, and settlement options are important to the parties?
6. What are the psychological conditions of the parties?
7. How will rules or behavioral guidelines be established?
8. What is the general plan for the first joint negotiations in the mediator's presence? How will specific agenda items be identified and ordered?

9. How will parties be educated about the process, and how will they arrive at agreement to proceed with negotiations?
10. What possible deadlocks could occur, and how will they be overcome?

This chapter will examine these questions and discuss planning activities assuming that they will be accomplished before the first joint session conducted in the mediator's presence. This approach will provide an opportunity to examine the design of mediation plans in some detail. Later chapters will focus on the implementation of the activities designed during this stage.

Participants in Negotiations

In many disputes, the parties who should participate in negotiations are readily apparent. In divorces, husband and wife should be present; in labor-management disputes, union and management representatives should attend. In other disputes, however, the identities of the central parties are not as clear. For example, in a child custody case concerning visitation rights revision, the second wife of the divorced husband may want to participate in negotiations. In commercial cases involving bankruptcy, multiple creditors may want to be involved. In large-scale community land use disputes, multiple parties may be interested in the issues and may want to participate.

Although the mediator usually should not decide who the disputants are or who will participate in negotiations, he or she may help the parties decide who should be present and when. Occasionally, a mediator may assist a party in selecting a spokesperson to represent a group or in identifying a person who will be both effective in communicating a group's interests and acceptable to the other side. When a group or organization is disorganized, the mediator may also assist in designing a decision-making process to select a negotiating team or spokesperson.

A case in which a mediator played a role in helping a group determine who should be at the table to represent their interests was a federal regulatory negotiation. The formal leader of one of the parties, a coalition of groups, was perceived by other parties as being verbally abusive, unreasonable, and untrustworthy. They announced that if this person represented the coalition, they would refuse to participate. The mediator persuaded the coalition to increase the number of spokespersons it would send to the negotiations, as a means of broadening the "voices" at the table, providing wider credibility, and controlling the member perceived as difficult.

In general, participants in the negotiations should include those who

- Have the power or authority to make a decision
- Have the capacity, if they are not involved, to reverse or damage a negotiated settlement
- Know and understand the issues in dispute
- Have negotiating skills
- Have control of their emotions
- Are acceptable to other parties
- Have demonstrated commitment or are willing to commit to bargaining in good faith
- Have the backing and support of their constituents

One mediator was asked by city officials to intervene in a dispute between a landlord and numerous tenants in a large apartment complex. She entered the apartment building's common room where the residents had gathered and found them vocal, angry, and prepared to harass the landlord. She asked them who their spokespersons were. They had not thought to select any. She then asked for a list of issues they wanted to discuss, and they shouted out a few items. She told the group that their meeting and show of force had demonstrated their seriousness to the landlord, but that they now had to organize themselves to be effective in negotiation. She suggested that they select four or five people who could speak for the group and would have authority to negotiate. She mentioned some of the criteria listed above for selecting spokespersons, and after some resistance and milling around, the tenants picked a team. Compromises had to be made on membership to ensure that all views were represented and that no one would work against the group's interests. Once the team was selected, the mediator asked the representatives to identify the issues deemed important and to prepare to negotiate on them.

As part of a bargaining strategy, one party occasionally may refuse to send a representative who has the authority to make a final decision. This action may be an attempt to insult the other party or to deny them recognition or legitimacy—a signal that one's own party does not consider the issue as important as the other party does or a means of insulating a decision maker from the dynamics and direct pressure of negotiation (Schelling, 1960). Negotiation etiquette usually requires people of equal rank or status to be present. When faced by a discrepancy in decision-making authority between negotiators, mediators may (1) push for the substitution of a decision maker with equal authority or (2) make explicit the differences in authority between two or more sides and develop an understanding of the decision-making and ratification structure to be used by the party without a decision maker present. To thus clarify the decision-making process before negotiations begin can minimize unnecessary conflicts and later claims of bargaining in bad faith.

Friends, Witnesses, Constituents, and Secondary Parties

Parties often want to have friends, witnesses, constituents, or secondary parties present at negotiations. (This is especially true in cultures based on collectivism and group decision making, in contrast to those that value individualism and individual decision making.) There is no one rule or practice mediators follow to respond to such requests. Some mediators ask that friends, witnesses, and constituents remain outside negotiations unless they have a particular function or role to perform (Stulberg, 1981a). Others allow observers who are informed of the limits of their participation. This occurs commonly in cultures other than those dominant in North America and Western Europe; in such cultures, friends and observers are often used by the mediator and the parties as option generators, witnesses to ensure the fairness of the agreement, and ensurers of the implementation of an agreement. Occasionally, the mediator will not have a preference or procedural rule regarding the presence of additional parties at negotiations and may leave the final decision to the disputants.

Lawyers, Therapists, and Other Resource Persons

Disputants often want resource persons with specialized skills present at negotiations. These secondary parties may assist the disputants in exchanging accurate information, providing emotional support, or may participate as surrogate negotiators.

Lawyers are a special category of resource persons. They provide numerous types of services to disputants (Bronstein, 1982; Riskin, 1982). They may be legal advisers providing information about possible settlement ranges or judicial decisions should the dispute be brought to court; they may act as strategists, general advisers, or surrogate negotiators for disputants who are disinclined or unable to represent themselves.

Lawyers who advise or coach disputants may or may not be present at negotiation sessions. If they are not, and if the issues being negotiated involve legal questions, the mediator should encourage parties to consult with them before, during, and after negotiations so that there is a clear understanding of disputants' legal rights and of possible settlement parameters. The mediator may request that lawyers who are not directly negotiating on behalf of a client remain silent in joint session and confine their activities to consultations with their clients in caucuses or private meetings. Alternatively, lawyers may be allowed to participate fully as either conegotiators or as direct advocates for parties, the latter retaining only final decision-making authority. The degree of lawyer involvement depends on the case, the will of the parties, and the intervenor's style.

Lawyers who negotiate on their clients' behalf may create special problems for mediators. Although many lawyers have a cooperative style and are experienced in interest-based bargaining, others are familiar only with hard-line positional bargaining (Williams, 1983). Lawyers who have been trained to develop an argument that supports a singular outcome may couch settlement options in right-or-wrong, yes-or-no terms. Negotiation depends on cooperative and integrative decisions rather than either/or options for success. The different demands of litigation and negotiation may on occasion make the lawyer a liability to the process of seeking a mutually acceptable resolution.

Mediators may sometimes decrease adversarial tendencies in mediation by encouraging parties to retain lawyers for legal advice but not for service as surrogate negotiators.

From time to time, disputants in North America request the presence of therapists in negotiations. This is not unusual in family or interpersonal disputes. Although mediation is not a therapeutic process, it may benefit from the presence of resource persons who can provide emotional support or psychodynamic insight. Mediators should be open to the involvement of therapists in negotiations if it is acceptable to all parties and if it can be demonstrated that the therapist can help disputants with emotional and psychological problems (Haynes, 1981). However, some restrictions on therapist participation may be appropriate.

Disputants may also request that accountants, engineers, financial planners, technical experts, or researchers be allowed to participate in negotiations. Such resource persons may provide disputants with a helpful professional perspective on issues (Fisher, 1978), with information that will prevent unnecessary conflict over inaccurate or conflicting data, or with a way to mediate data disputes (Straus, 1979). Mediators often suggest that specialized resource persons such as property assessors, accountants, and scientific experts be introduced into mediation to provide new information to disputants.

Media

Mediation in the U.S. is generally considered to be a private means of dispute resolution. In fact, research evidence indicates that negotiation is often effective because of the private nature of the controlled communication (Folberg and Taylor, 1984; Freedman, Haile, and Bookstaff, 1985). Private negotiations may allow for greater candor and may decrease the posturing so often found in public adversarial relationships.

However, before mediating a dispute of public interest, the mediator and the parties should decide if the meetings are to be open or closed, and how inquiries from the news media about media presence and the provision of information will be handled. On occasion, the media have been excluded from negotiations because of potential negative effects they may have on the behavior of disputants or the public. The presence of reporters can encourage posturing for a constituency rather than serious negotiation. Premature or inaccurate revelation to the public of the substance of negotiations can also create conditions that make joint problem solving impossible.

In other public disputes, in which large interested and involved constituencies want to be present, it may be difficult or impossible to maintain privacy by means of closed meetings. Furthermore, public decision makers may be precluded from participating in closed negotiations by "sunshine laws" that require all discussions to be public. Although mediators and many negotiators assume that closed negotiations are crucial, a large number of negotiations of public disputes have been successfully executed in the public view, including a series of public policy dialogues, regulatory negotiations, and mediations of site-specific disputes sponsored by a variety of federal, state, and local agencies. There has also been significant experience with open negotiations on the interpersonal level. The Community Boards in California (Shonholtz, 1984) and several Canadian mediators (McWhinney and Metcalf, 1984) have conducted open mediation with significant success. Most interpersonal mediations conducted by the Mediation Boards in Sri Lanka and the Barangay Justice System in the Philippines are also conducted in open meetings. However, such meetings for interpersonal disputes are the exception rather than the rule in North America.

Mediators should assist the parties in determining whether negotiations are to be closed or open to the public and to design, when appropriate, methods of public education about the substance of a dispute and the procedure disputants are using to resolve their differences. If meetings are to be closed, the mediators may propose specific procedures to release information (Lansford, 1983). Parties often agree to a common press release that is issued on their behalf by the mediator. Other publicity about mediation progress may include periodic meetings with the press and public presentations by the parties outside the negotiation sessions.

Location of Negotiations

The location chosen for negotiations may significantly affect the interaction of the negotiators. In considering where to meet, a mediator should select, or persuade the parties to select, a neutral location where neither party has strong emotional identification or physical control of the space. The benefits and costs to the parties and the mediator of neutral locations are as follows:

Benefits

- Interruptions can be controlled.
- Neither side can manipulate the use of space.
- Distance from the site of the conflict and from other distractions can be maintained.
- Distance from the usual environment may promote the psychological distance needed for an open-minded exploration of issues.
- Potential for bugging or eavesdropping is limited.
- All parties have the same psychological handicap of being in a new location.

Costs

- Negotiators may be separated from necessary information.
- Parties are separated from their emotional support system.
- Parties may have to bear the cost of renting facilities.

Disputants occasionally refuse to negotiate at a neutral site and want to mediate in their own territory. Or they may want to continue negotiations at a site established before the mediator's entry.

Mediators have two major strategic options when confronted with a demand by one party to negotiate in its territory. They can (1) discuss and make explicit the costs and benefits of such a decision, stressing the possible negative impacts on settlement; or (2) persuade other parties to accept the recalcitrant party's request while identifying costs or benefits to the parties who are not in their own territory.

Benefits

- The guest party can demonstrate its good faith and willingness to be flexible.
- Asking the host party for information may be easier, and it may be more difficult for him or her to refuse.
- The guest party can more easily make demands on the host party's time and space if the host party does not cooperate.

Costs

- Unfamiliar surroundings may disorient the guest party.
- Lack of access to sources of information may weaken the guest party's case.
- The host party can be interrupted and called away at any time.
- The host party can receive strategic phone calls.

The mediator may also refuse to mediate the case, but this response is extremely rare.

Physical Arrangement of the Setting

Physical arrangement of the negotiation setting may also affect the dynamics and outcome of negotiations. The disputes that erupted over seating arrangements and the shape of the table at the Vietnam peace negotiations held in Paris in the early seventies indicate the impact that physical arrangement can have on negotiations.

Physical arrangement refers to seating patterns, the shape of the table, the amount of physical space allocated to and between disputants, physical objects that indicate authority or differences in power, and space for public or private interaction. Social science research presents important findings on seating arrangements and conflict behavior. Filley (1975) observes that adversaries tend to seat themselves opposite each other, and that this physical arrangement seems to produce more polarized and competitive behavior than side-by-side seating. Sommer (1965, 1969) postulates that undifferentiated seating locations for disputants, so that they neither are arranged opposite each other nor possess seats that indicate greater or lesser power, produce more evenly distributed leadership and less one-sided exercise of power.

Barriers such as tables between disputants are another variable. The following case illustrates how, in U.S. culture, tables are often equated with doing serious business. The intervenor conducted several sessions in an informal setting without a table. One day, mediation was scheduled in a conference room with a large wooden table. One disputant remarked, "Well, we now have a negotiating table. We can get down to business." They did, and settled that day.

The table's shape may be used to indicate the status of a party as a discrete entity with its own "side." Furthermore, a physical place at the table may grant recognition and legitimacy to a party and its views. Such was the case in the Vietnam peace talks held in Paris.

In volatile disputes, maintaining a safe distance and using a table as a physical barrier may be crucial in preventing dispute escalation and physical violence. Several years ago, the U.S. Air Force Academy negotiated with a union that provided services to the facility. The negotiations were protracted and became heated. Finally, one negotiator reached across the narrow negotiating table, seized the position paper of his opposite, and tore it into small pieces. The table prevented physical violence but was not large enough to prevent this negative interchange.

In addition, the shape of the table and seating arrangements may be used to blur differences between disputants. Round tables are often used by mediators because there is no physical indication of a boundary between representatives of the disputing parties.

In some disputes, mediators may eliminate tables or barriers between disputants to increase physical proximity or to promote informality (Stulberg, 1981a). In interpersonal disputes, a living-room setting without tables may be more appropriate than a formal conference room. One mediator reported that in a deadlocked interpersonal dispute that had been mediated in the intermediary's office at a table, a shift of venue to her living room, with sofas, a coffee table, and finger food during the discussions, changed the whole tone and dynamics of the session.

Additional important physical arrangements are waiting rooms and facilities for caucuses (Stulberg, 1981a). Mediators need waiting rooms so that they do not have to associate publicly with one of the parties before joint meetings; disputants may perceive such fraternization as partial behavior. In volatile situations, mediators may also use separate waiting rooms for antagonistic or hostile parties.

Caucus rooms are facilities where mediation participants can meet privately during negotiations. Caucus rooms should be near the site of joint negotiations but far enough removed so that they provide visual and auditory privacy.

It is important when working in separate caucus to ensure that the parties are really separated. In one of my earlier cases, I requested a caucus with the parties and asked one party to leave and wait in a conference room down the hall. He left, I closed the door and completed the private meeting with the other party. Later, when I went to the door and opened it to bring the absent party back for his caucus, he fell into the room. He had not gone to the waiting room but had been in the hall trying to listen. This underlined for me the importance of ensuring that the parties and the mediator really are in a private setting.

Caucus rooms are crucial in managing conflicts in which intense emotions are displayed or in which a potential for violence exists (Schreiber, 1971). Mediators often use entirely separate rooms for each party in disputes that involve actual or potential violence. The mediator can carry messages and work out a settlement between disputants, and if necessary, the parties may be kept from all direct contact.

Mediators should consider the type of dispute and the psychological and emotional condition of the disputants and should select a physical arrangement that will be conducive to resolution. When negotiations have been held before the mediator's entry, the mediator may try to make minor modifications to the physical setting to induce psychological shifts in the disputants or may move them to an entirely new setting.

Negotiation Procedures

Before developing a mediation plan for joint negotiations, mediators should evaluate what the conflicting parties know about negotiation procedures and ascertain what approaches—positional or interest-based bargaining—have been used or are likely to be used. If the mediator conducts private meetings to collect data before the joint sessions, this information is usually easy to obtain. If it is not possible to gain information on the preferred negotiation procedure of the parties, the mediator should design a series of contingency plans that will enable him or her to respond to any combination of negotiation procedures.

There are four possible combinations in a two-party dispute:

- Both parties use positional bargaining.
- Both parties use interest-based bargaining.

- One party uses predominantly positional bargaining and the other uses predominantly interest-based bargaining.
- Both parties use a mixed procedure depending on the issue and their interests.

If the dispute involves more than two parties, the number of permutations increases.

Mediators frequently have a procedural bias toward interest-based negotiation procedures because the interests of all parties are more likely to be satisfied with this process. When mediators encounter parties who have previously engaged or are planning to engage in positional bargaining, they should, if possible, develop a mediation plan that will shift the parties toward interest-based bargaining as rapidly as possible. This may involve a briefing or discussions about the interest-based bargaining process or, in multiparty disputes, training sessions on how cooperative negotiations can be initiated. Mediators from CDR Associates and several other conflict management firms have conducted a number of successful joint training seminars in the industrial relations and public policy arenas that have presented interest-based bargaining procedures and skills to parties preparing for negotiations. Participants have reported that these workshops have greatly assisted them in making a more rapid transition from positional to interest-based bargaining.

Issues, Interests, and Settlement Options

Designing a mediation plan requires a mediator to identify issues and interests with which disputants are concerned, the salience or importance of these issues and interests, and potential settlement options. Anticipating these components of a dispute enables the mediator to design an effective procedural plan but *not* a specific mediation settlement. Mediators differ greatly on how specifically they link the interests of the parties to the mediation plan. Some intervenors, "dealmakers," design a plan that will lead toward specific solutions addressing interests that they have identified and consider important to the parties. Other mediators, "orchestrators," design a plan in which the parties identify their interests and develop their own negotiation procedures and outcomes (Kolb, 1983). I usually prefer the latter procedure.

Psychological Conditions of the Parties

An assessment of the psychological readiness of the disputants to negotiate should accompany a mediator's consideration of the parties' substantive concerns and procedural preferences. The mediator should review some of the relationship variables—level of emotion, accuracy of perception, amount of miscommunication, and extent of repetitive negative behaviors—that will influence or have influenced the dynamics of the negotiations. He or she should then design appropriate procedures to reduce potential negative impacts and enhance positive ones. More will be said on these topics in Chapter Seven.

The mediation plan should include a tentative sequence of activities for the first joint negotiations that is responsive to potential psychological or relationship issues. The sequence is tentative because it cannot be implemented before the parties accept the proposed activities. I will now describe a number of activities that can help a mediator set the tone, define an agenda, establish rules or behavioral guidelines, and obtain commitment to negotiate.

It is generally important to establish a positive and harmonious tone at the start of negotiations. Positive working relationships between the parties depend on their attitudes toward themselves and each other. The presence of a neutral third party can often significantly assist in the development of a positive, open, direct, and businesslike approach.

Tone setting usually begins with introductions. Setting the stage for the first joint session should include scheduling time for the mediator and the parties to introduce themselves to one another. In cases in which parties in dispute are groups or organizations, the mediator may also provide time for descriptions of group affiliation and concerns.

After introductions, the mediator will usually schedule time for his or her opening statement—a description of what is to come. Stulberg (1981a, pp. 42–43) lists the advantages of conducting an effective opening statement:

A. It establishes the ground rules and your role in the hearing.
B. It establishes your control over the hearing.
C. It serves to put people at ease.
D. It conveys to the parties a sense that the mediator is confident and skilled, thereby inviting them to trust both the mediator and the process.
E. It serves to reconcile any conflicting expectations regarding what the party believes he could obtain through mediation and the reality of it.

Mediators often begin their opening remarks with a congratulatory statement that affirms the willingness of the disputants to negotiate and to try to cooperatively solve their problems. A reference to their interdependence is often mentioned at this time. Stulberg maintains that "the very first sentence or question in mediation needs to address what the individuals have in common or what they like and respect about each other. Emphasizing mutual dependence on one another heightens the need for overcoming the obstacles that brought them in. It also helps participants to look for the good in each other rather than letting their anger blind them. Conflict is much easier to handle if it rests on a positive foundation" (1981a, p. 22).

After tone-setting activities, the mediator may allow time to review how he or she was asked to assist the parties in the dispute. If the mediator represents a mediation agency, he or she may explain the procedures and goals of the agency and the services it provides. The mediator may also describe his or her background and qualifications, but mediators usually try to convey their qualifications by their manner rather than reviewing their professional work, educational background, or affiliations.

At this time in intervention planning, mediators should demonstrate personal credibility, trust, and a businesslike manner by explaining, for instance, what mediation is and the mediator's role. The manner and process of explanation will convey the mediator's command of negotiation procedures.

Mediators commonly cover the following items in their description of mediation and the mediator's role (Moore, 1981):

- Mediation is a process whereby a third party helps people in conflict to identify issues about which they disagree, uncover needs which must be met by a settlement, generate possible solutions, and reach decisions.

- Mediation is voluntary. The people are there by choice, and the mediator has no power to force a decision on the parties involved.

- The people in the conflict will decide how the conflict will be terminated.

- A mediator is impartial (optional or inappropriate in some situations or cultures). He or she has no investment in a particular substantive settlement. The mediator is a facilitator of the process, not a judge on the issues.

- A mediator is neutral in that he or she has no relationship with any of the parties which will bias his or her impartiality or commitment to all of them (optional or inappropriate in some situations or cultures).

Mediators should also inform parties of their right to use legal procedures and seek legal advice (if appropriate). Offering this information should not, however, be construed as providing legal advice or practicing law. Disputants retain their right to terminate negotiations and pursue a legal route to redress their grievances until they sign an agreement that may become a legal contract. Participation in negotiation or mediation does not deny a party the right to consult legal counsel. Disputants can confer with a lawyer at any time, and many mediators request that all decisions be reviewed and perhaps be drafted by counsel before the parties sign the document (Folberg and Taylor, 1984).

In addition, mediators should explain the limits of confidentiality of the proceedings. Information exchanged between negotiators or between the negotiators and the mediator in joint sessions or in caucuses is usually confidential. On occasion, mediators have parties sign release forms in which the parties state that they will not subpoena a mediator or records of the negotiations for a later court case.

Ground Rules and Behavioral Guidelines

In some negotiations, a carefully designed procedure may be enough to incline disputants toward a productive resolution. In others, the negotiators may need to establish behavioral guidelines that detail how they will act toward each other and how the parties will handle particular problems that arise in the course of negotiations.

Behavioral guidelines that should be considered by mediators and parties include

- Agreement on the speaking order of the disputants
- Rules on how disagreements over data will be managed
- Agreement on the time frame for the negotiation session or sessions
- Agreements on observers and witnesses
- Rules preventing attribution of motives or slanderous statements
- Rules regarding interruptions
- Procedures for breaks or intermissions
- Procedures for initiating caucuses or private meetings

Behavioral guidelines may be proposed either by the mediator or by disputants. If they are initiated by the mediator, the parties must agree to their implementation. The mediator should be careful not to create a dynamic in which he or she is the authority and the parties are obedient subjects. To work effectively, guidelines must be agreed on by consensus.

Behavioral guidelines may be made the subject of the first negotiations to occur in mediation. Parties may be willing, for a variety of reasons, to discuss behavioral guidelines and agenda formation procedures prior to discussing substantive issues. Doing so

- Enables the parties to establish rules for interaction that may make the parties feel safer

- Allows parties to practice making agreements on problems that are neither substantively important nor as emotionally charged as the issues in dispute

- Demonstrates that agreement is possible [Moore, 1982b, p. VI–33]

I will explore the process of negotiating behavioral guidelines in more detail in Chapter Eight.

The amount and detail of guidelines vary tremendously among mediators. Coogler (1978), a leader in divorce mediation, has turned the explanation of procedures and guidelines into an elaborate component of the mediation process: disputants with whom he mediates must accept a list of sixty rules before negotiations can begin. Although Coogler occupies an extreme position, establishing behavioral guidelines is common practice, and most mediators may suggest a few to provide safety and direction for the parties.

Plan for First Joint Negotiations

Once the mediator has planned the first joint session's general format, he or she should define the process for identification of specific agenda items. The mediator usually has enough information from data collection and conflict analysis to be able to formulate a proposed negotiating agenda.

In most cases, mediators should provide the parties with an opportunity to make their own opening statements—presentations at the start of negotiations in which the parties present the problem or conflict history, identify the needs they must have met for a satisfactory settlement, and occasionally, express strong emotions. Opening statements may be the first opportunity for the mediator to watch the disputants interact face to face. Mediators learn much about disputants, issues, interests, positions, options, and conflict styles by observation at this stage. Foreknowledge of the issues and interests that parties will focus on in the opening statement assists the mediator in planning the order in which issues will be managed and what the subsequent problem-solving process will be for each item. The following (adapted from Moore, 1982b, pp. VII–19–19) is one agenda-planning procedure many mediators use:

1. The mediator should gather all potential agenda items from disputants prior to the negotiation session. This may be done orally or in written form.

2. The mediator should clarify in his or her own mind the goals or outcomes desired by the parties for each item. He or she then should determine which items are information-sharing items, which discussion items, and which are items that require a decision.

3. The mediator should make a tentative division into high-priority, medium-priority, and low-priority items, as well as items that can be held over for a later session. In defining priority, the mediator should take into consideration the time value of the item

(does this decision have to be made tomorrow so that work can proceed next week?), the importance of the item (substantive importance and emotional importance), and the parties to whom it is important (all parties, a subgroup, an individual, or a superior). High-priority items should usually be scheduled for discussion, at least in principle, at the first session and should not be deferred.

4. The mediator should make an estimate of how long it will take to achieve the defined goal for each agenda item and establish possible time blocks for the topics.

5. Agenda items should be ranked according to the likely difficulty of achieving the defined goal: hard, medium, and easy.

6. The first item on the agenda should usually be one of high or medium priority—substantively, emotionally, or in terms of time value—to most of the disputants and one the mediator expects will not require a long time to reach agreement on or to achieve the stated goal. This item should be easy for the parties to work on. The mediator should place the item with these qualities first because he or she wants the disputants to have a chance to achieve success in a short time early in negotiations. An early success will make the disputants feel more positive toward the process and toward their ability to work together, and it will indicate the possibility of future success in negotiations.

7. The second item often concerns a more difficult topic and may take longer to reach its goal. Successful completion of the first item will have prepared people for work on more complex issues.

8. Short and long items, and hard and easy ones, may be alternated so that the participants feel that the negotiations are progressing toward a productive end.

9. The agenda should allow some time for identification of issues to be addressed at a later session and for discussion of future logistics.

Education of Parties

After completing a mediation plan, the mediator should decide how he or she will educate the parties about the process and gain their commitment to try it. If the mediator has worked with disputants on the design of the plan, gaining final approval is not a problem, but if disputants are not familiar with negotiation and mediation procedures or are too embroiled in the substantive issues in the dispute to focus on process, the mediator may have to educate the parties about the procedure he or she has designed.

Mediators occasionally take an active educational role before joint sessions to prepare disputants for what is likely to occur. The goal is to obtain the commitment of the parties to the procedure before the joint session. Other mediators make their procedural proposals or suggestions during the first session and assume that they will be accepted or that alternative procedures will be negotiated with disputants. The procedure for agreement on process usually depends on the particular parties involved, the issues in dispute, and the conflict dynamics of the case.

Possible Deadlocks

The final aspect of designing an intervention plan is the mediator's identification of potential problem areas that may cause an impasse. Fisher (1978) identifies several problem areas that often deadlock negotiations: (1) substantive problems, such as too few or too many favorable options; (2) procedural problems, such as an absence of process or the wrong process; and (3) problems with people, such as strong emotions, stereotypical labeling, or miscommunication. Early identification of potential problems and contingency plans to avoid or overcome them are central to mediation planning. Mediators can prepare themselves by imagining problems that might occur in the joint session and then developing several contingency plans for responding to each of them. I will discuss a variety of problems and the moves mediators use to handle them in later chapters.

Chapter Seven

Building Trust and Cooperation

Negotiation has long been recognized as a psychological process. Even by the mid-1970s, Rubin and Brown (1975) had identified over five hundred studies on negotiation that examined individual psychological variables and group dynamics. In this chapter, I will discuss mediator activities that minimize unnecessary conflict and build a positive psychological relationship between disputing parties. This process is called conciliation.

"Conciliation is essentially an applied psychological tactic aimed at correcting perceptions, reducing unreasonable fears, and improving communication to an extent that permits reasonable discussion to take place and, in fact, makes rational bargaining possible" (Curle, 1971, p. 177). *Conciliation* is the psychological component of mediation, in which the third party attempts to create an atmosphere of trust and cooperation that promotes positive relationships and is conducive to negotiations.

Although I will discuss conciliation here as if it were a separate stage of negotiation and mediation, conciliation in practice is an ongoing process that occurs throughout negotiation and mediation. Five types of problems commonly create negative psychological dynamics in negotiations:

1. Strong emotions
2. Misperceptions or stereotypes held by one or more parties of each other or about issues in dispute
3. Legitimacy problems
4. Lack of trust
5. Poor communication

I will discuss each of these problems in turn and explore some common intervenor moves employed to respond to and change them.

Strong Emotions

Several authors have noted the different emotional stages that disputants move through in the process of conflict development, deescalation, and settlement (Douglas, 1962; Kessler, 1978; Ricci, 1980; Daily, 1991). At the start of negotiations, people often feel angry, hurt, frustrated, distrustful, alienated, hopeless, resentful, betrayed, fearful, or resigned to unsatisfactory conditions. For rational discussions on substantive issues to occur, the impact of negative emotions must be managed and minimized by either the disputants themselves or by an intervenor. If not handled early in negotiations, feelings—whether openly manifested or felt and not spoken—may later block a substantive agreement or inhibit the formation of more positive relationships.

For a mediator to assist parties in reaching an agreeable solution, he or she must work at least to minimize or neutralize the effects of negative emotions and, if possible, to create positive feelings between disputants. Before examining conciliation procedures used to influence emotions of disputants, I will diverge briefly to examine two sources of emotions in conflict situations.

Unrealistic and Realistic Conflict and Emotions

Coser (1956) distinguishes between unrealistic and realistic conflict. Unrealistic conflict exists when parties act as if they are in dispute even though no objective conditions for conflict exist. Realistic conflict is the result of genuine conflicts of interest. Coser's concepts of unrealistic and realistic conflict can also be applied to human emotions. Frequently, parties in conflict have unusually strong feelings that may not be merited by the actual situation. A conflict without a realistic base for negative emotions is in direct contrast to a dispute in which emotional responses are the predictable outcome of circumstances.

Many people have had the experience of meeting someone for the first time and immediately forming an intense dislike for that person. There is no previous relationship between the people, yet there is a strong negative reaction. This dynamic has been variously referred to as restimulation (Jackins, 1978) and negative transference (Freud, [1920] 1943).

Restimulation refers to the surfacing of feelings similar to those generated by a relationship or events in the past. Old feelings are triggered by a new encounter, which may or may not be similar to the earlier relationship or event. Although the new situation may not provide an objective base for restimulated feelings, it is the mechanism that resurrects past emotions.

An example may illustrate restimulation more clearly. An environmental group had for several years struggled with a public utility over the terms and conditions for operating a hydropower dam. During the negotiations, personal relationships between the environmentalists and the company's spokespersons became tense and fairly hostile. Ultimately, the utility agreed to take some of the group's interests into consideration and reached a hard-fought negotiated agreement. A year later, a new public relations director at the utility—a man who was very open and committed to good company-community relations and public involvement in decision making—announced that the company planned to revise the operations of a second dam, which was unlike the first in both its construction and its situation. He also stated that the utility wanted to employ some of the operations procedures that had been hotly debated during the previous negotiations. The announcement was met with outrage by the environmentalists, who launched a personal attack on the public relations director. Even though he had values and approaches to problem solving that were very different from those of his predecessor, he was treated just the same way. Old feelings had been restimulated by a situation that looked like the earlier one but was in fact dissimilar. The new situation may have merited a strong response from the environmentalists, but the intensity of their emotions was more than likely provoked by restimulated feelings related to past events.

Transference, and in particular *negative transference*, is the carryover or generalization of learned responses from one particular relationship to another. In the Freudian sense, transference occurs when the power dynamic of a previous relationship is transferred to a new one. The new relationship may or may not be similar to the earlier one. For example, in a couple's dispute, the wife may transfer emotions about a controlling father on to her husband even though the husband may be quite unlike the father in his personality and manner of relating.

Restimulation and transference may result in an escalation of feelings that may or may not be merited by the objective conditions of the disputants. Mediators need to know how to respond to these sources of strong emotions. More will be said on this point later in the chapter.

Realistic feelings, in contrast to restimulated feelings, are the direct result of clear and present conditions that could normally be expected to intensify emotions. For example, if two parties in negotiation begin to yell at each other and make derogatory remarks about each other's integrity, the direct insults will usually result in strong emotions. This is not restimulation but a direct response to the immediate circumstances. (Obviously, a person could also be restimulated if he or she has been directly insulted in the past, but the current events do merit the strong emotions that the disputant feels.)

Ideally, parties will manage both realistic and restimulated feelings. However, when people experience and express strong emotions, a third party may be needed to mitigate or manage their adverse impacts. Although the mediator is not a therapist, he or she must be familiar with psychological techniques to assist parties in managing their emotions.

Responses to Intense Emotions

For the most part, conflicts involve negative rather than positive feelings. In considering conciliation strategies, I will focus attention on mediator interventions that neutralize negative emotions or enhance positive ones between disputants.

Emotions are highly complex physiological and psychological responses to external stimuli. They may manifest themselves in neuromuscular, cardiovascular, respiratory, hormonal, or other bodily changes. The mediator must often respond to both the physiological and the psychological basis of emotions, and he or she should bear in mind that feelings cannot necessarily be "resolved"—that is, dispelled by objective solutions. Mediator responses to emotions consist of three separate steps: recognizing that a party has a strong emotion, diagnosing the emotion, and selecting an appropriate intervention strategy to assist the party in managing the emotion. Mediators should watch for signs of strong emotions that may hinder productive bargaining. Tone of voice, pacing of words, facial expressions, changes in posture, and body movements are all clues to the presence of underlying emotions.

Mediators frequently have little difficulty recognizing that a party is experiencing an emotion, but they may not be able to identify it or determine how intensely the party feels about the subject under discussion. *Active listening* often facilitates identification and diagnosis of emotions. Rogers (1945) first identified this form of interaction as a means of conducting social research, and Gordon (1978) and Creighton (1972) later elaborated on it as a method of responding to the emotions of people in conflict. Active listening is a communication technique in which a listener decodes a verbal message, identifies the precise emotion being expressed, and then restates the emotional content of the message to the speaker using the same or similar words used by the speaker. For example, the mediator might respond, "You were really frustrated and hurt when the city did not respond rapidly to your permit request." The disputant then has an opportunity to verify the accuracy of the mediator's perceptions of his or her feelings: "Yes, I felt frustrated! I had complied with all the requirements, but they still wanted more data." It is important that the listener accept the speaker's emotions without necessarily agreeing with the speaker or holding the same beliefs about the issues in question.

Active listening performs several functions in responding to people's feelings:

- It assures the speaker that he or she has indeed been heard.
- It allows the speaker and listener to verify that the precise meaning of the message has been heard.
- It demonstrates the acceptability of expressing emotions.
- It allows the speaker to explore his or her emotions about a subject and to clarify what he or she really feels and why.
- It may also perform the physiological function of encouraging the release of tension through the expression of emotion.

Mediators can use active listening in caucuses and joint sessions to assess whether the expression of emotions is a negotiation tactic to influence another party to make concessions, whether it is posturing for other disputants or constituents, or whether it is a genuine expression of feelings. The more the mediator and disputant interact, the more difficult it is for disputants to maintain insincere emotional postures.

It should be noted that active listening may be a culture-specific process in that it will not work or be appropriate with certain individuals or groups or within particular cultures. Members of cultures that prefer to avoid overt display or discussion of emotions in front of parties with whom they disagree will resist active listening and may feel that responding to its use will result in loss of face for themselves or their opponent. Mediators should take care when using active listening in indirect-dealing cultures or in those that are not comfortable with the direct expression of emotions.

Once the mediator has accurately diagnosed the content and intensity of a disputant's emotions, he or she should decide how to assist the party in managing the feelings productively. Although conciliatory moves are close to the practice of therapy, the mediator is in fact not attempting to change or rehabilitate a disputant through a clinical or casework approach. The mediator merely assists parties in managing their emotions so that they can negotiate on the specific issues in dispute.

There are three general categories of strategy to respond to intense emotions: (1) approaches that provide creative opportunities for parties to express their emotions; (2) strategies for suppressing emotions; and (3) strategies for removing the objective cause of the emotions by meeting substantive needs or interests. I will discuss the first two strategies in this chapter. Strategies for removing the objective cause of emotions will be discussed in Chapters Nine through Fourteen.

Strategies for Venting Emotions

Strategies for venting strong emotions are usually pursued because the mediator believes that (1) the party needs a physiological release for repressed emotions and is unable to focus on substantive issues until this physiological release has occurred (Jackins, 1978; Bach and Goldberg, 1974); (2) the party needs to express his or her emotions to another party as an educational move to demonstrate how strongly he or she feels about an issue; or (3) direct expression of emotions is culturally expected and acceptable. If a mediator decides that parties need to vent emotions for any of these reasons, he or she usually decides when, where, and how the emotions might best be expressed.

Emotions that threaten to be highly destructive to a delicate negotiation process, strong emotions that are the result of restimulation, and manipulative emotional outbursts are often best expressed in a caucus with the mediator. Emotions are also channeled into a caucus when the recipient of the emotions may not be capable of responding to a direct expression. In a caucus, the emotions can be vented safely, outside the presence of other parties. Physiological release can be attained, an assessment can be made of what is genuine emotion and what are restimulated emotions, and the expression of manipulative comments can be curbed without risking the damage that could result from a direct negative interchange. Mediators often initiate a caucus for the venting of emotions once parties have begun negative venting in joint session. Mediators also initiate caucuses specifically for the purpose of provoking parties to release emotions.

Venting in joint session may, however, be a functional process important for achieving productive negotiations. Douglas (1962) observed that ritualized venting in the early stages of labor-management disputes appeared to be almost a prerequisite for the parties to move toward negotiation of substantive issues. If the mediator decides to encourage the parties to vent their emotions, or if venting occurs spontaneously in joint session, his or her central concerns should be how to prevent the process from escalating and how to prevent negative dynamics in the relationship of the parties.

Several intervention strategies in response to this problem are common. Mediators may encourage parties to establish ground rules regarding acceptable behavior. These rules may exclude such practices as character assassination, attribution, projections regarding motivations, and direct personal attacks. Mediators may also encourage parties to vent about the *interests* in dispute and not about the *people* who advocate them (Fisher and Ury, 1981). A third approach is for the mediator to verbally identify and preempt unproductive venting and to encourage or suggest ways in which disputants can express the same concerns in a less volatile manner. This strategy often means preparing a party in caucus for a verbal interchange in joint session. Humor is a fourth way that mediators can assist parties in venting and yet limit the negative effects of anger (Landsberger, 1956).

Venting in joint session has value only if it provides a productive physiological release for one or more parties without damaging the delicate relationship between disputants, or if it serves to educate a party about the source or intensity of emotion around a particular issue. When venting is conducted to punish another party, it will probably result in a deterioration of the relationship of the parties. When this occurs, the mediator should encourage the party to move to a caucus, both as a defensive measure and as a means of directing the destructive feelings into safe channels.

So far, I have advocated emotional venting as a mechanism for creating attitudinal change. Although this may indeed occur in some cases, there is no concrete evidence that emotional release necessarily has a direct correlation to a perceptual or attitudinal shift. The one incontrovertible effect of venting is, however, a tendency toward increased relaxation after the emotional outburst. This physiological effect alone may justify a mediator's efforts to provide an opportunity for parties to vent.

Strategies for Suppressing Emotions

I have discussed mediator strategies that encourage emotional expression as a means of furthering better communication and removing sources of unnecessary conflict. In some situations, however, encouragement either in joint session or in caucus may be counterproductive and may lead to unnecessary escalation (Berkowitz, 1973; Hokanson, 1970; Steinmetz and Straus, 1974). Straus (1977, p. 233) argues that "in general, aggression against another (either verbally or physically) tends to (a) produce counter aggression, (b) impedes getting to the real problem, and (c) if it does succeed in squelching the other person, reinforces the use of aggression as a mode of interaction." When there is a history of violence, when one or more parties have a low degree of impulse control, when the mediator does not believe that he or she can control an escalation of emotions, or when the expression of strong emotions is culturally unacceptable, it may be preferable to structure negotiations so as to limit emotional expression. Structures that limit emotional exchange include explicit guidelines about how parties will communicate, rules that limit communication between disputants and encourage them to talk only to or through the mediator, and physical separation of the parties so that they have few or no face-to-face meetings. The mediator in this last model performs a type of shuttle diplomacy and conveys messages between the parties.

Misperceptions and Stereotypes

Conflicts are often escalated or deescalated on the basis of parties' perceptions of each other. The mediator's role in the conciliation phase is to decrease perceptual barriers to negotiation. This is usually accomplished in four stages:

1. Identifying perceptions held by a party.
2. Assessing whether the perceptions appear to be accurate or inaccurate.
3. Assessing whether the perceptions are hindering or furthering a productive substantive, procedural, or emotional settlement.
4. Assisting parties in revising their perception of other disputants when they have characterized the disputants with stereotypes or other image distortions, and in minimizing the negative impacts of such misperceptions.

The Mask-Mirage Analogy

Curle (1971, p. 209) observes that "many of man's feelings about others derive from his feelings about himself. Since these feelings are often intricate, contradictory, and not fully grasped at the conscious level, his attitudes towards others are correspondingly obscure and irrational." Curle explains that individuals conceal from themselves and others true representations of themselves and, in place of these, present a mask that expresses how they would like to perceive themselves or how they would like to have others perceive them.

Curle argues that when a person uses a mask, the image he or she holds of other disputants is often that of another mask or a mirage. A mirage is an image based on the psychic needs of the observer rather than on real or objective characteristics of the observed.

How does the mediator recognize this mask-mirage dynamic? First, through interaction with disputants, the mediator will often be able to penetrate the fronts the disputing parties present and to identify the discrepancies between who the disputants really are, how they want to be seen, and how they are being perceived by other combatants. Because the mediator does not have an investment in a particular outcome and cannot dictate a settlement, disputants are often honest with him or her; they have little to lose in exposing their real selves to the mediator (Goffman, 1959). (This does not mean that parties always let down their masks for mediators. And when they do not, mediators may accept the false images being projected. Mediators should take great care not to be drawn into believing that the image is the real person.) Because mediators possess this access, they may have an unusual opportunity to view disputants speaking and acting sincerely. Such observation allows them to identify misperceptions between disputants and assess the accuracy of their views.

Several types of action are available to parties and mediators seeking to modify the way parties are perceived. The disputants or mediator can (1) demonstrate that parties share similar attitudes toward an object, event, idea, or third person; (2) encourage association between parties to provide an opportunity to reveal undisclosed commonalities; and (3) encourage a party to associate with (or disassociate from) objects, ideas, or people that his or her opposite likes (or dislikes).

Demonstrating Similar Attitudes

"Similar attitudes toward an object (event, idea, third person) set up forces toward attraction between persons" (Walton and McKersie, 1965, p. 225). Similar attitudes can be cultivated by identifying personal points in common, encouraging use of similar language, defining a common problem, focusing on the benefits to both parties that will result from mutual success, emphasizing a common view of outsiders, and deemphasizing differences between the parties.

Personal points in common may include geographical or educational background or intellectual, recreational, or religious concerns. For example, several disputants in an energy development project modified their perceptions of each other when they discovered that they had all been involved as participants in, or coaches of, high school wrestling teams. The common experience of an enjoyable sport blurred the adversarial relationship between them. Parties themselves can often identify personal points in common, but if they do not, the mediator may initiate moves that make the parties aware of their commonalities. Mediator moves may be either indirect, such as the casual mention of a common factor, or more direct and structured. Some family mediators, for example, ask divorcing couples to describe how they first met and what they liked about each other to create a sense of positive history for a current negative relationship.

Parties often hold misperceptions of each other because they use different language. They may be using different words to convey the same meanings or may actually be speaking from an entirely different world view. Coordination of the language of the parties may also align their perceptions.

The mediator can encourage parties to use the same language or can translate the communications of the various parties to foster mutual understanding. The mediator may often assist a party in reframing or restating a message in another way to facilitate accurate communication and positive reception. This process will be explored in more detail in Chapter Nine.

Identifying a dispute as a common problem that can be resolved for any party only through mutual cooperation can also induce a positive attitudinal shift. For example, identifying common problems of landlords and tenants as issues of predictability and "stability of living situation and rent" may enable the parties to reach agreement on the terms of a lease. Mediators often must point out common problems to a party who is trapped in an adversarial mirage and sees little in common with an opponent.

Identifying mutual benefits of success is closely related to identifying common problems. Divorcing parents may modify their perception of each other if they believe that their children may benefit from an amicable rather than hostile divorce. Disputing spouses may see happy and well-adjusted children as a mutual benefit.

Often, mediators must directly identify the mutual benefits to be gained by common action because the parties may not recognize them.

The way an event, idea, or third person is described can also promote either discord or attraction between parties. By deemphasizing differences, a party can minimize the amount of negative perception an opponent has of him or her. Mediators often perform the valuable function of minimizing differences by reframing disagreements between parties.

Encouraging Common Association

Parties can be induced to change their perception of each other by developing common positive associations. Mediators should determine if parties have undisclosed commonalities that are likely to be revealed or enhanced by increasing their interaction. If this is the case, parties may be encouraged to work together. The opposite, however, may also be true. If the parties have few similarities, association may increase polarization. Mediators may separate and maintain the distance of parties who have little in common or traits or beliefs that may escalate the conflict.

Encouraging Association/Disassociation with Objects, Ideas, or People

Parties can either associate themselves with, or disassociate themselves from, objects, ideas, or people that another disputant likes or dislikes. Mediators may encourage either association or disassociation, depending on their assessment of various perceptions of the parties. In some instances, association may be more important and positive than disassociation, while in other disputes, the opposite may be true.

Reinforcement of Perceptual Change

Another approach to perceptual change focuses on rewarding or punishing a party's behavior to induce perceptual change. This approach has three central premises: (1) the more frequently one person's activity rewards the behavior of another, the more often the latter will demonstrate the behavior; (2) the more valuable the reward activity is to a person, the more often the person will demonstrate the rewarded behavior; and (3) if one person's activity punishes the behavior of another, the punished behavior will probably be suppressed (Walton and McKersie, 1965).

This approach assumes that by rewarding positive behavior and punishing negative behavior, a person can influence the behavior, if not the perception, of another. Procedures for rewarding an opponent's behavior include extending compliments, expressing appreciation, returning favors, and increasing or stressing positive benefits (Walton and McKersie, 1965). Punishment behaviors include reminding an opponent of his or her role obligations, threatening the opponent's self-concept, and issuing direct threats and sanctions (Walton and McKersie, 1965).

Positive reinforcement or rewards are moves usually preferred by both mediators and negotiators because they do not trigger as many negative reactions (Stevens, 1963). In general, mediators should elicit and stress the benefits of reaching an agreement with the other party before detailing the costs of not doing so. Emphasis on the positive can incline parties toward agreement, whereas emphasis on the costs of not settling may set up resistance because of negative pressure or sanctions.

Occasionally, however, mediators must direct the attention of the parties to negative measures of reinforcement. The utility of a mediator's reference to a party's use of negative means of reinforcement or possible negative consequences of a continued behavior depends on several variables. Generally, the threat of punishment, or the risk of incurring costs for rejecting terms for agreement, will only under certain circumstances induce a party to change his or her mind.

Punishment or threat of punishment seems to work only in specific situations. If, for example, a party has anticipated the costs or punishment that he or she might receive as a result of a particular action, has factored them into the overall calculation of whether the action should be undertaken, and has found the punishment to be manageable, the threat is likely to have little effect.

Fisher (1964, p. 32) observes that "other considerations . . . suggest that inflicting pain on an adversary may be worse than useless. There is a common tendency to treat sunken costs as invested capital. The greater the costs we impose upon our adversary, the greater the amount they will regard themselves as having committed to this course of action." Parties therefore resist settlement

because of the energy and resources they have invested in a conflict. Mediators may assist parties in rationalizing a change in
resource expenditure so that settlement can be reached. Mediators should take great care when emphasizing the negative consequences of a failure to settle. Stressing the negative, even when one
party has the capacity and will to carry out a coercive threat and
the other is incapable of defending himself or herself, may create
resistance on the part of the latter and escalate the dispute. Mediators often use soft negative reinforcement by implying, not
directly stating, that a threat may be posed by another party. For
example, the mediator might say, "I don't know whether he will go
to court, but he could, and that might hurt you." This phrasing
uses negative coercion, creates doubt, and pressures the party to
reevaluate his or her view without directly threatening the party.

Legitimacy Problems

The most difficult perceptual problems, for both negotiators and
mediators, are probably those that deal with legitimacy and trust.
Legitimacy refers to a party's acceptance and recognition that an
opponent, an opponent's issues or interests, and even an opponent's emotions are genuine and reasonable and conform to recognized principles or accepted rules or standards. Without a
perception of legitimacy, negotiations may never begin.

A classic case in point is the perceptual change on the part of
the Government of Israel and the Palestine Liberation Organization (PLO) regarding each others's legitimacy. From the founding
of the Israeli state in 1949, these parties repeatedly refused to recognize each other's legitimate right to exist and to have a state in
the Middle East. This condition led to wars, terrorist bombings,
assassinations, economic sanctions, forced removals, imprison-
ments, property destruction, and various nonviolent actions on the
part of each party to convince the other to recognize its legitimate
interests. In the early 1990s, a shift of perception, which had been
developing over time, suddenly became more visible and explicit.
How did this happen?

The changes appear to have resulted from (1) protracted interaction, both formal and informal, between the parties; (2) the stub-
bornness of each side in pressing for the recognition of its rights;

(3) mobilization of power by each party (accompanied by increasing risks and costs) to force the other to recognize the legitimacy of its interests; and (4) recognition that a continuation of the status quo was unsatisfactory to all sides. This led to a breakthrough in informal mediations in Oslo, Norway, and ultimately to the formalization of a peace accord.

This chapter is most concerned with persuasive rather than coercive means of perceptual change and with encouraging parties to accept the legitimacy of the other party's issues, interests, and emotions. I will explore the use of coercion in Chapter Fifteen. Here I will explore each of the areas of legitimacy—party, issues, interests, and emotions—and the ways in which disputants shift perceptions by means of persuasion.

Legitimacy of Person or Party

A party recognizes another party as legitimate when the former is willing to talk with the latter. Negotiations often fail because one party does not perceive another as the legitimate spokesperson or bargaining agent for the opposing view. This can be the case in family disputes, union disputes, or international relations. The refusal of the U.S. and Israel to recognize the PLO as the legitimate bargaining agent for Palestinians and the corresponding refusal of the PLO to recognize Israel stood in the way of peace talks in the Middle East for years. The refusal of one birth parent to recognize the legitimacy of a stepparent's participation in negotiations may hinder or block postdivorce negotiations between birth parents.

Changing perceptions about the legitimacy of a person or party as a bargaining agent for one side of an issue can be accomplished in several ways. First, if the unacceptability of the negotiator is due to misperception, clarification of communication may remove the barrier.

Second, if the problem with legitimacy results from the procedure by which negotiators were selected to represent a conflict group, the procedure can be explained or the mediator can assist the parties in developing a procedure acceptable to all of them. Acceptable procedures ensuring that a negotiator genuinely represents and can ensure the commitment of a constituency often remove barriers to the recognition of legitimacy. Mediators can and should assist the parties in improving procedures.

Third, perceptions about a particular negotiator can often be changed by direct discussion about images and perceptions. Blake, Mouton, and Sloma (1961) have succeeded with this approach in labor management disputes. Mediators can also assist parties in changing their personnel and thus changing an opponent's perceptions.

Some parties may not be persuaded to change legitimacy perceptions, and coercion may be the only way to obtain recognition. When this perceptual deadlock occurs, mediators occasionally discuss with the party whose legitimacy is questioned the coercive means likely to be most effective with the other party and to cause the least damage to the relationship of the parties.

Legitimacy of Issues and Interests

Legitimacy of issues and interests can be created in a variety of ways. Fisher (1964), drawing from his observations of international negotiations and mediation, suggests that a party can

- Change the wording of the issue
- Redefine the issue in terms that are favorable or acceptable to the other party
- Ask that another person with authority recognize the legitimacy of an interest
- Have another person advocate an interest
- Ask for a focus on another issue that has greater chance of being recognized as legitimate
- Be more specific
- Be more general

Mediators can assist parties in making all the above moves by either indirect or direct suggestions.

Legitimacy of Emotions

Legitimacy of emotions refers to the acceptance of a party's right to hold or possess specific feelings, not to whether another party agrees with them (Gordon, 1978). As long as a dispute persists about whether the substantive issues or behavior of an opponent objectively merits a particular emotion, the possibility of productive negotiations will remain low. The mediator should try to interpret the emotions to the other side and explain why they are appropriate or important to the person expressing them. He or she should also inform the party that is denying legitimacy that it is not necessary to agree with the emotions in order to proceed with negotiations. All that the party must do is accept that they exist and acknowledge that, for whatever reason, an opponent does feel a particular way. Acknowledgment may be all that the person having the feelings needs in order to proceed with a productive dialogue.

Lack of Trust

Conciliation involves not only minimizing the impact of negative emotions and perceptions but enhancing positive feelings and perceptions. The importance of trust in conducting productive negotiations has been identified by numerous researchers and practitioners (Deutsch, 1958, 1960; Rapoport and Chammah, 1965; Zartman and Berman, 1982). *Trust* usually refers to a person's capacity to depend on or place confidence in the truthfulness or accuracy of another's statements or behavior.

In negotiations, trust is very closely related to the mask-mirage images of disputants. "To believe everything the other person says is to place one's fate in his hands and to jeopardize full satisfaction of one's own interests. . . . On the other hand, to believe nothing the other says is to eliminate the possibility of accepting any arrangement with him" (Kelly, 1966, p. 60). At the start of negotiations, when the mask-mirage dynamic is strongest, the parties and the mediator face the challenge of creating perceptions, if not actual behavior, that induce trust between disputants.

Base of Trust

Trust is based on the experiences of the negotiators with past negotiations, the similarity of current issues to those in past negotiations, past experience with a particular opponent, rumors about a current adversary's trustworthiness, and the opponent's current statements or actions. Mediators often must respond to all these variables in the process of building minimal trust between the parties.

The past experience of a negotiator, his or her personality, and his or her needs, beliefs, values, and predispositions toward other parties will strongly affect his or her ability and willingness to trust another party. Mediators usually do not make any efforts to change or modify a negotiator's psychological makeup based on experience with previous negotiating opponents. However, the mediator may attempt through careful questioning to modify and clarify a negotiator's perceptions of the current negotiation and may assist him or her in identifying similarities and differences between the present situation and the past. Because mediation is future-oriented, in that the goal is to establish a new relationship or define future terms of agreement, the mediator often pushes parties to defer judgment about a present situation or party and to limit the intrusion of past judgments or biases into the current case until they are proved to be valid.

A negotiator's past interaction with an opponent can provide a base for either trust or distrust. Mediators negotiating with parties who have a history of negotiations between them may begin the trust-building process by asking questions that assess whether a positive or negative relationship has been built over time. If the parties have a positive trust relationship, have been able to depend on the other party's veracity and count on the other party to follow through on agreed commitments, the mediator's task becomes simpler. In this case, the mediator may merely remind the parties of their positive and productive history or may ask them to recount transactions in which trust in each other has been rewarded.

The latter technique may often be used effectively even when little trust exists between the parties, but the mediator has been able to identify a past positive interaction. For example, in difficult divorce mediation cases, mediators have asked spouses for specific instances when they have been in conflict, have trusted each other, and have found the other spouse to be trustworthy. By this means, the disputants are reminded of occasions when the other has responded to cooperative gestures with reciprocation rather than exploitation. The mediator must thus be able to enhance the positive aspects of the relationship.

Should the mediator discover that parties have a negative relationship and that past trust has not been reciprocated, he or she can assist the parties in determining if the breach of trust arose from a misinterpretation or an unintentional misunderstanding. If it did, accurate communication may remove the perceptual barriers to a new trusting relationship. If, however, the trust of one party was misplaced, and intentional exploitation rather than reciprocity resulted, the mediator must pursue a different strategy and start from a point of no or little trust to build a positive relationship between the parties.

Mediator-Negotiator Moves to Build Trust

Trust in relationships is usually built incrementally over time. Through a succession of promises and congruent actions that reinforce the belief that commitments will be carried out, negotiators gradually build a relationship of trust. Mediators may assist negotiators in building a trusting relationship by encouraging them to make a variety of moves designed to increase credibility. Some of these moves include encouraging negotiators to

- Make consistently congruent statements that are clear and do not contradict previous statements (Creighton, 1972)
- Perform symbolic actions that demonstrate good faith in bargaining (Fisher, 1978)—for example, providing for an adversary's physical comfort, negotiating at a time or place that is convenient for another party, making a minor concession that indicates a willingness to negotiate
- Place themselves in a subservient position in relation to another party so that they incur a minor risk. This demonstrates trust because it places a party's well-being in the hands of an opponent (Pruitt, 1981)
- Ask for help, thus acknowledging the need for assistance from other participants (Fisher, 1978)
- Exhibit a genuine concern to help other participants reach their objectives while retaining the ability to reach their own (Zartman and Berman, 1982)
- Demonstrate that there will be an earlier return of benefits to the agreeing party than had been previously expected (Zartman and Berman, 1982)

- Show that they are willing to undergo punishment or incur costs if they do not follow through on their promises (Zartman and Berman, 1982)
- Avoid making threats to an opponent or making promises that are unbelievable or unrealistic (Zartman and Berman, 1982)
- Make incremental agreements in which success can be measured along the way (Fisher, 1978; Zartman and Berman, 1982)
- Demonstrate an understanding of the other side's concerns, even if they do not agree with those concerns

All these moves should be carried out by the parties. The mediator, however, can be a catalyst for them.

Mediators can also make specific interventions that will build trust between parties and change their perceptions. Some of these moves include creating situations in which the parties must perform a joint task, translating one party's perceptions to another, vocally identifying commonalities, verbally rewarding parties for cooperation and trust, and facilitating a discussion of their perceptions of each other (Fisher, 1978).

Structured Procedures to Address Issues of Trust and Respect

On occasion, intermediaries may want to introduce more elaborate and explicit procedures to address issues of trust, respect, and cognitive (as opposed to emotional) empathy. Although not historically common in problem-solving mediation, and though more akin to therapeutic or group dynamics interventions, these procedures can, when appropriate, be incorporated into a mediation process when it appears that attitudinal issues or extremely difficult historical relationships between parties are likely to block discussion or agreement making, thereby perpetuating the conflict.

In general, these approaches involve parties in explicit dialogue about their relationships and attitudes. The following are two common approaches:

1. Parties are asked to develop a profile, in list form, of how they perceive their attitudes and motivations in a situation, how they

perceive the other party, and how they think the other party perceives them. The results can then be shared in joint session and can act as a catalyst for discussions about the bases of the perceptions, the past history that has given rise to them, and the actions necessary to change them and build more respectful and trusting relationships (Blake and Mouton, 1961).

2. Individuals in a two-party dispute or stakeholder groups in multiparty conflicts are asked to privately develop a vision of an ideal working relationship between the parties, expressing this in terms of attitudes and behaviors. The parties are then asked to work in joint session, sharing their visions with each other and seeking a general consensus on the attitudes and behaviors they would like to see in their future relationship. The parties then separate and develop privately a list of attitudes and behaviors that have historically blocked, or are currently blocking, the achievement of their joint vision. When this task in completed, the parties come together again to share their ideas. They discuss the barriers, reach agreement on those they consider to be the most important, and then move to the third phase of the process, problem solving. The problem-solving phase has the parties identifying and agreeing on concrete actions they can take to improve their working relationship. The final phase of the process is working out ways to implement and monitor the jointly developed solutions and setting a time to reconvene, discuss progress being made, address any new problems that may have emerged, and if necessary, fine-tune earlier agreements (Blake and Mouton, 1984).

Other procedures for dealing with attitudinal, respect, trust, and cognitive empathy problems have been developed by Burton (1969), Kelman (1991), Fisher and Brown (1988), and Rothman (1992). The goal of the problem-solving workshops designed by these practitioners is to create a positive environment conducive to conflict resolution and to transformation of the relationship between the conflicting parties to one of understanding and cognitive empathy—both in the short term and the long term (Kelman, 1991). Other practitioners, including Bush and Folger (1994) describe transformative strategies for small-group and interpersonal disputes.

Poor Communication

Communication is certainly a central component in negotiation. The amount, form, and quality of communication, as well as the identities and qualities of the communicators, are usually strong influences on the outcome of negotiations.

The common assumption that if parties are talking, they will work out their differences is not necessarily true. Deutsch (1969, p. 12) describes the communication of people in conflict: "Typically a competitive process tends to produce the following effects: communication between the conflicting parties is unreliable and impoverished. The available communication channels and opportunities are not utilized or they are used in an attempt to mislead or intimidate the other. Little confidence is placed in information that is obtained directly from the other; espionage and other circuitous means of obtaining information are relied upon. The poor communication enhances the possibility of error and misinformation of the sort which is likely to reinforce the pre-existing orientations and expectations toward the other."

Unproductive communication can lead to a breakdown of interaction between the parties or the inability to start negotiations at all. Mediators often structure communication or assist parties in doing so. Mediator moves to modify communication involve controlling or assisting the parties in determining

1. What is communicated
2. How a message is communicated—in terms of both syntax and means of transmission
3. By whom the message is communicated
4. To whom the message is delivered
5. When a message is delivered
6. Where a message is delivered

I will examine each one of these points in detail.

What Is Said to Another Party

The content of a message that a speaker conveys to a listener can be substantive information, such as data regarding issues, interests, or positions; procedural information concerning the way a negotiator does or does not want an activity to be conducted; or information about the negotiator's emotional state.

Mediators manage what negotiators say in several ways. First, the mediator may meet with the party before joint sessions or during caucuses to assist him or her in determining what information should or should not be shared with other disputants. The mediator's knowledge of the likes and dislikes of other parties often assists him or her in making suggestions about the communications in joint meetings that will best meet the needs of all parties. The coaching role of the mediator is often important.

Second, the mediator can influence what is said by a party in joint session by translating it into language that is both understandable and acceptable to another party. This process, often called reframing, will be discussed in more detail in Chapter Nine. After a message is delivered, the mediator may make efforts at clarification to ensure that the listener fully understands its content and implications. I discussed active listening, one means of message clarification, earlier in this chapter, and I will discuss other clarification techniques in Chapter Nine. It is enough to say here that clarification usually includes restatement. If the message has been restated in one of a variety of forms, the speaker, whether negotiator or mediator, can determine if it has been accurately received. Restatement allows for corrections and modification by the speaker to ensure accurate communication. The mediator's role in clarification may extend to the interpretation of messages.

Third, the mediator can shift what is being said by structuring communication channels so that parties are allowed to make only limited and managed statements (Young, 1972). For example, the mediator may allow parties to talk only on particular subjects, may interrupt parties making statements that another party will not positively receive (for reasons either of substance or of emotional tone), or may even prevent direct communication by keeping the parties in a caucus. If a caucus is used, the mediator may filter information that flows between the parties, allowing through only content that builds toward agreement (Maggiolo, 1972). He or she may also suppress communication on issues that do not seem important to the parties, or that might antagonize them.

How Messages Are Communicated

Mediators may also help determine how a message is communicated. *How* refers not only to the medium—written, oral (in person or by phone), and so on (Cohen, 1980)—but also to the sender's syntax.

By managing how parties communicate, the mediator can vary both substantive and emotional content of a message. For example, written messages eliminate unproductive nonverbal communication and may be more explicit. They also take more time both to prepare and to respond to, thus allowing parties to deliberate longer on what they send and receive.

Direct oral communication between parties may be good for some negotiations and poor for others. In some cases, the mediator may want to deliver a message because the recipient is more likely to accept it from him or her than from the other party. In such cases, the mediator is also able to control and formulate what is to be communicated.

Who Communicates a Message

Mediators often take the initiative to manage who communicates in negotiations. In some disputes, a negotiator may deem a message more or less acceptable depending on who sends it. If, for example, a mediator discovers that one group is disconcerted by a member of another group, he or she may advise the initiating group that their message will be better received if delivered by someone else.

Who Receives a Message

Communication may be accepted or rejected, depending on whom it is directed to. Because the mediator is aware of the structure of negotiating teams or their constituents, he or she may be able to suggest to whom a communication should be addressed. Variables that mediators should consider are

•Who has the power to decide?
•Who is psychologically ready to hear the message?

- Who are the moderates in the group?
- To whom in the bureaucratic hierarchy should the message be addressed?
- What is the protocol for delivering messages?

When a Message Is Delivered

Timing of communication is often important. *When* something is said is frequently more important than *what* is said. In one case, a manufacturer entered contract negotiations with his workforce. After careful analysis, he determined what wage increases the union wanted and decided to comply. In his opening offer, he proposed to meet the union's demands. The union rejected the offer, not because it did not meet their expectations but because it was offered too soon. The union had expected to fight for the increase. The offer's timing led to a strike that damaged both labor and management.

Mediators can often control communication timing by either encouraging or inhibiting discussion by one party until the other party or parties are most receptive. For example, one labor mediator kept parties apart in caucus and delayed joint meetings until their private discussions had progressed to the point that they would be able to agree in joint session (Shapiro, 1970).

Where a Message Is Delivered

Where a message is delivered may also be important. An extreme demand made in joint session when the opposing party's entire group is present may meet with a stronger objection than if the proposal had been made in a private and more informal setting. A psychologically relaxing setting may induce a party to settle in some situations, whereas in others an uncomfortable setting may induce resolution. For example, mediators occasionally conduct all-night negotiating sessions in unfamiliar settings. Former Representative Timothy Wirth used this strategy in his efforts to induce agreement between the Denver Water Board, the U.S. Environmental Protection Agency, and environmental groups on the siting of the Foothills water treatment facility in Denver, Colorado (Burgess, 1980). Time and setting can be used to influence recalcitrant negotiators. Mediators can often manage the negotiation and communication settings to enhance productivity.

Nonverbal Communication

Nonverbal communication—gestures, use of space, and manipulation of objects—may be intentional or unintentional, but it still conveys messages. Henley (1977) argues that nonverbal communication may be the principal way that people communicate dominance, authority, and status. If a mediator is to assist parties in effective nonverbal communication, he or she must be aware of all its various forms and how it can be channeled to the benefit of all parties.

Gestures, Eye Contact, and Demeanor

Nonverbal gestures clearly can communicate a tremendous amount of information about a disputant's attitude and data about the power relationship between disputants. Hinde (1972) reported that people often communicate superior attitudes toward others with unsmiling or disdainful facial expressions, erect posture, and staring. People may communicate anxiety, on the other hand, by tense, rigid posture and hand-wringing.

Gestures are often difficult for parties—and mediators—to control, being frequently initiated by the subconscious. Mediators may attempt to control nonverbal communication either directly or indirectly. Direct control may take the form of asking parties, variously, to (1) face or look at each other when they are speaking (if strategically or culturally appropriate); (2) look at and speak only to the mediator to avoid eye contact with an opponent; (3) stop tapping feet or fingers when they are frustrated; or (4) adjust their body positions so that they are sitting in postures likely to induce cooperation rather than competition. Handshakes at the conclusion of negotiations are in some cultures one way to nonverbally affirm an agreement.

The use of caucuses is one way to eliminate the effects of gestures and other nonverbal signals. When negotiations are conducted through caucuses, all messages are transmitted by the mediator.

Although controlling gestures and eye contact of disputants may be difficult, the mediator may engage in nonverbal communication that conveys particular messages to the parties. The mediator can use eye contact, handshakes, and body language to convey to disputants either engagement and approval or disengagement and disapproval.

In one case, a contractor and a homeowner were engaged in an intense conflict over compensation for a fault in house construction. They became verbally abusive and pointed and shook fingers at each other. The mediator stood up very slowly, took off his glasses, and began to slowly pace around the room. He suggested that the parties look at the issue another way. He stopped and pointed to a chart on the wall that listed information about the house in question. The mediator's movements and gestures, because they were more active and interesting than those of either of the disputants, attracted their attention, drawing their focus away from each other. The mediator's manner—calm, deliberate, rational, serious, and focused—also changed the emotional tone of the disputants and encouraged them to seek a more rational approach to their problem.

In conclusion, mediators can manage the gestures of disputants by direct requests or separation or by means of indirect signals transmitted by the mediator's own gestures or eye contact. There is a caveat, however. Nonverbal communication is often culturally or racially bound; signals take on different meanings among different cultures and races (Kochman, 1981; Van Zandt, 1970). Mediators should take great care to adhere to cultural norms when they attempt to modify their own gestures or eye contact or those of disputants. A violation of such norms can lead to a deterioration or breakdown in communication between disputants or between disputants and the mediator.

Use of Space

Mediators also initiate moves that control the environment in which parties negotiate. *Environment* refers to physical distance between the parties, or between the parties and the mediator, and also to the way individuals are physically positioned in relation to each other.

In a seminal work on nonverbal communication, Hall (1966) observed that Americans have norms regarding acceptable proximity between people for particular types of interactions. He identifies four general categories of relationships: intimate, personal, social, and public. The first three are relevant to negotiations. A distance of zero to six inches indicates extremely intimate interaction. It often includes body contact and may result in playful wrestling, affectionate touching, or gestures that comfort or protect. A distance of 1.5 to 2.5 feet is the acceptable proximity for people who have a close personal relationship, and is characteristic of parents and children or close friends. Henley (1977) notes that this is also the limit of physical domination. Social distance—four through seven feet—is the normal distance for working colleagues. It is a distance for more formal settings in which people do not engage in intimate or personal relationships.

Although these zones are culturally based, mediators must be familiar with them because they establish norms that, if violated, may trigger changes in the dynamics of disputes. Parties tend to become uncomfortable if acceptable distances are violated and will usually initiate behavior to reestablish a spatial norm; they may even become hostile.

A case illustrates the role of physical space and settlement. Two co-mediators were talking with a party in caucus. One of the mediators stressed the negative impacts of not settling the case and crowded the physical space of the party by leaning toward him. There was no room for retreat, because the party was literally up against the wall. The party refused to change his negotiating demands. The other co-mediator suggested a break to allow time for consideration of the proposal. During the recess, this co-mediator suggested that the other mediator allow the party more physical space. The other mediator agreed, and when the caucus was resumed, the party began to move around, leaned forward, and accepted the proposal.

Mediators often take the initiative to maintain spatial norms in order to prevent conflict escalation. They may allow parties enough room in the negotiating setting to avoid crowding; they may ensure that there is enough space between disputants so that they cannot harm each other; and they may even position themselves midway between the parties to provide a physical buffer and to physically demonstrate the mediator's impartiality. Occasionally, however, a mediator may violate spatial norms for negotiations in order to destabilize parties.

Certain aspects of spatial organization (such as seating arrangements, discussed earlier) and the location's degree of formality are both closely related to physical distance between negotiators or between negotiators and the mediator.

Some mediators manage the degree of formality to promote more cooperative negotiation or to emphasize the seriousness of the issues. Some court-related mediation programs may tend to reinforce a quasi-judicial perception of the mediation process by locating negotiations in a courtroom or judicial building, a lawyer's office, or a police station and maintaining a highly formal setting: sparse furnishings, few personal items, institutional furniture, and so on. Such an environment seems to reinforce formality, seriousness, and a businesslike approach to negotiation. It may subliminally suggest the gravity of the proceedings and may psychologically reinforce commitment to the agreement later.

Some mediators, however, prefer informal settings such as their personal offices, a neutral and uninvolved third party's home, a restaurant, or a relaxing public setting such as a resort or retreat center. Mediators assume that informal settings will encourage parties to be more relaxed and comfortable, as the parties will not be forced to manage an alien environment as well as controversial issues.

Mediator moves to either increase or decrease the formality of the negotiating setting are, of course, contingent on the situation.

Use of Objects

Messages in negotiations are often conveyed by physical objects, such as clothing, sunglasses, handkerchiefs, documents or reports, briefcases, and even firearms. Mediators may attempt to enhance conciliation by either (1) promoting or inhibiting the use by negotiators of objects that may influence settlement or (2) using objects themselves to influence disputants toward settlement.

The most important objects that negotiators use to influence other parties are their clothing. Clothing can produce either affinity or alienation between negotiators. Mediators may suggest to parties appropriate attire that may encourage another party to settle. In cross-cultural disputes, personal attire may often be a barrier to a party's acceptance of another's trustworthiness or seriousness.

Clothing can also influence the mediator's acceptability and credibility with a party. Several years ago, a group of professionals asked me to intervene in an interracial high school dispute. I wore jeans and a work shirt to the interview with conflicting students. My attire reduced the differences between myself and the students. The same attire, however, caused a controversy when I went to discuss the intervention with the professionals right after speaking to the students. They did not equate professional mediation services with informal attire.

Mediators also may request that the parties bring to sessions particular objects that may enhance psychological cooperation—financial records or contested objects (televisions, cars, clothing, and so on)—so that parties can refer directly to the objects. Mediators must also occasionally discourage the use of objects that have negative effects on negotiation. For example, certain negotiation projects require that all firearms be left at home or checked on arrival.

Part Three

Conducting Productive Mediations

Chapter Eight

Beginning the Mediation Session

In this stage of intervention, the mediator will assist the negotiators in beginning a productive exchange of information about issues in dispute. If the parties have been meeting before the mediator's entry, he or she may abbreviate some of the component moves of this stage. Nevertheless, most of these moves will appear near the start of the first joint meeting held in the mediator's presence. My discussion of the various moves and strategies mediators use in this stage will assume that the parties have not yet held a joint meeting.

The mediator's major tasks in this phase of intervention parallel those of the negotiators. The mediator wants to

- Begin establishing a positive tone of trust and common concern
- Externally provide, or assist the parties in developing, a procedure that encourages emotional expression but prevents destructive venting
- Externally provide, or assist the parties in developing, a structure for mutual education about their key interests and the issues they would like to discuss
- Provide a structure that enhances the possibility of accurate communication

In Chapter Six, I discussed the general strategy or conceptual plan that mediators pursue when opening negotiations. I will now examine implementation of the strategy in more detail.

Opening Statement by Mediator

Disputants usually enter negotiations in various states of emotional stress. Argyris (1970) notes that people are more likely to accept change—and negotiation means change—voluntarily if the negotiating climate enhances self-acceptance, a confirmation of personal worth, feelings of essentiality, and a psychological sense of success. Maslow (1968) points out that an individual's safety needs must be met before higher needs can be addressed.

The mediator's first activities in this phase of intervention should set a positive tone and meet the basic needs of safety. A mediator accomplishes this nonverbally through the physical arrangement of the parties in the room and verbally with his or her opening statement. The opening statement usually contains approximately eleven elements. These include

1. Introduction of the mediator and, if appropriate, the parties
2. Commendation of the willingness of the parties to cooperate and seek a solution to their problems and to address relationship issues
3. Definition of mediation and the mediator's role
4. Statement of impartiality and neutrality (when appropriate)
5. Description of mediation procedures
6. Explanation of the concept of the caucus
7. Definition of the parameters of confidentiality (when appropriate)
8. Description of logistics, scheduling, length of meetings
9. Suggestions for behavioral guidelines
10. Answers to questions posed by the parties
11. Joint commitment to begin

In Chapter Six, I discussed the general content of the mediator's opening statement. I will now explain how it is presented in practice, using as an example the Whittamore-Singson case presented in Chapter One.

Mediator Introduction

First, the mediator introduces himself or herself and the parties (if applicable) and explains how he or she became the mediator in this negotiation:

Good morning, Dr. Whittamore and Dr. Singson. My name is Rita Montoya, and I have been asked to be your mediator and to assist you in discussing the issues that have brought you to mediation. I work as a mediator for CDR Associates and have a background in helping people work out their own solutions to situations they would like to change.

The mediator, by choosing to refer to himself or herself with a social or professional title such as Ms. or Dr., to give his or her full name, or to use only the first name, sets the tone for the degree of formality in the proceeding.

Affirmation of Willingness to Cooperate

Second, the mediator should commend the willingness of the parties to cooperate and to try mediation to settle their differences.

I would like to congratulate you both for coming here today and trying to reach your own agreement on some issues that may have been hard in the past to discuss. It is an affirmative indication on your part that you want to take responsibility for making your own decisions.

The mediator may want to ask people how they feel (if culturally appropriate), ascertain their emotions through their verbal or nonverbal messages, and acknowledge their emotional condition. The mediator may acknowledge or restate what he or she sees and hears to test perceptual accuracy and demonstrate that he or she understands the emotions of the disputants. The point of recognizing emotions here is not to make a therapeutic intervention but to release stress by talking about emotions. Early acknowledgment that disputants are uncomfortable often helps them dissipate tension so that they can relax and focus on the substance of negotiations.

Definition of Mediation and the Mediator's Role

Third, the mediator should define mediation and the mediator's role in dispute resolution. The mediator may have discussed this with each party in prenegotiation interviews, but it is psychologically important for all parties to hear the same information from the mediator in the presence of other disputants. This ensures that everyone has the same information and minimizes the risk of different interpretations of what the mediator has previously said.

If the parties are extremely tense at the start of negotiations, they may not be able to hear or retain all the mediator's comments. Although this is a drawback to presenting the information at this time, the mediator should still explain to the parties why he or she is there and what he or she proposes to do. This can protect the mediator from later charges of having brought the parties together under false pretenses and outlines precisely what the parties can expect from the intervenor. An explanation of mediation and the mediator's role at this stage may also give the mediator leverage later in negotiations, when he or she can refer to the role definition presented at the start of the session.

Mediators in the community sector and in interpersonal disputes usually try to explain mediation and the mediator's role in the most informal language possible. Explanations vary considerably, but they usually cover (1) a brief description of what the parties will do during the current session; (2) what a mediator is; (3) what the mediator can do for the parties; and (4) the potential outcome of mediation. For example,

During the next meeting or two, you will be engaging in discussions and searching for a joint solution that will meet your needs and satisfy your interests. We will also be discussing how your mutual relationship, and your individual relationships with other clinic staff, can best be handled so that the current situation does not adversely affect other people, the functioning of the clinic, or the provision of quality services to patients, which both of you mentioned in premediation discussions as being important. My role as mediator will be to help you identify problems or issues that you want to talk about, help you clarify needs that must be met, assist you in developing a problem-solving process that will enable you to reach your goals, keep you focused and on the right track, and generally help you define a new relationship that each of you will find more comfortable and acceptable.

Next, the mediator should describe his or her authority relationship with the disputants:

As I told each of you previously, mediation is a voluntary process. You are here because you want to see if you can find solutions to issues that concern you and to discuss your future relationship. My role is to assist you in doing this. I do not have the authority, nor will I attempt, to make decisions for you. I will try to stay out of discussions of specific substance or content. My role is to advise you on procedure, and on how you might best talk about these issues. If you reach an agreement, we (or I) will write it down in the form of a memorandum of understanding. This agreement can become legally binding if it involves issues covered by law, or it may be left as an informal agreement. If you want to make your settlement legally binding, you may want to consult a lawyer at the end of mediation. He or she can draft the agreement and put it into the form of a contract. If you do not reach a settlement, you are free to pursue other means of dispute resolution that you feel are appropriate. You do not lose any rights to go to court if you use mediation and are unable to reach an agreement.

Statement of Impartiality and Neutrality

When acting as an independent mediator, the intermediary should explain that he or she is impartial in his or her views and neutral in his or her relationship to the parties.

Before proceeding, I would like to clarify both my position on the issues at hand and what my relationship has been with both of you. During this mediation, I will be impartial toward the substance of issues. I do not have any preconceived biases toward any one solution or toward one of you over the other. My relationship with each of you has consisted of (preconference meetings, business association, previous advisory role, and so on). I do not believe that this relationship will jeopardize my capacity to act as an impartial assistant to you in resolving this dispute. If at any time you feel that I am acting in a partial or one-sided manner, please bring this behavior to my attention, and I will try to change it. If at any time you feel that I am not able to remain impartial and am unable to assist you, you may cease negotiations, find another mediator, or pursue another means of settlement.

In claiming impartiality toward issues and neutrality toward the parties, the mediator should disclose any relationship with one or more disputants that might bias his or her behavior or raise a question in the minds of the disputants as to whether the mediator can in fact remain impartial while assisting in discussions of the issues at hand. If disputants feel uncomfortable about the mediator's relationship with one or more parties, the mediator's past experience with similar issues, or a known aspect of the mediator's private life (political activity, professional or economic relations, or social affiliations that might jeopardize neutrality), they should have the opportunity to ask questions, obtain clear answers, and select a replacement mediator if necessary.

Disputants may not initially believe a claim of impartiality in a highly polarized conflict. There is a tendency to see the dispute in bipolar terms—"You are either for us or against us"—and anyone not taking a vocal position toward one side or another is suspect. Naturally, the parties will have to see impartial behavior before they believe that a mediator is unbiased in attitude. The goal of the mediator at this point is to gain nominal approval from the parties to proceed with negotiations.

Description of Mediation Procedures

Next, the mediator should describe the procedures to be followed. If he or she has worked these out with the disputants in the prenegotiation interviews, this description is no more than a reiteration of what has been previously agreed. However, if the mediator has taken the initiative to design negotiation and mediation procedures independently of the parties, he or she should present the proposal in a way that the parties are most likely to accept. The strategy, of course, must be adjusted to meet the idiosyncrasies of the particular parties. The following is a common description of negotiation procedures:

At this time, I would like to briefly describe the process that I propose you follow to begin the session. This proposal is based on your suggestions in our premeeting discussions. Both of you have a significant amount of information about the situation that you are responding to. Although I have briefly spoken with each of you about these matters, I do not have the detailed understanding that each of you does. I suggest that we begin the discussion today with a brief description from each of you about the situation and issues that brought you to mediation. This will educate all of us about the issues you want to discuss and the interests that are important to you and give us a common perception of the problem. Each of you will have a chance, roughly fifteen to twenty (or other specified time) minutes, to present your view of the situation. I request that you not interrupt the other while he or she is explaining a viewpoint, and that you hold your questions until the end of the presentation. A pencil and a pad have been provided for each of you. I would suggest that you note observations or questions as they arise so that they do not get lost prior to the question-and-answer time.

During your presentations, I may ask some clarifying questions or probe your description so that I can gain a greater understanding of how you perceive the situation. My probing is not to put you on the spot but rather to broaden our mutual understanding of the problem. At the end of each of your presentations, there will be a time for the other person (or parties) to ask questions of clarification. This is not a time to debate the issues, but an opportunity to clarify issues and perceptions about the problem(s) at hand.

At the end of the presentation and questions, we will turn to the other (or next) person (or party) to repeat the process until a representative of each view has had an opportunity to speak. At that point, we will clearly identify both the issues that you would like to discuss in more depth and the interests that you would like to have satisfied. Once we are clear on the interests and have described our task in terms of meeting as many of your individual and joint interests as possible, we will develop some potential solutions and assess whether one or more of these options will meet your needs. Note that your goals will be to develop mutually acceptable options that will address the issues at hand and your current and future relationship. Mine will be to assist you with a process that will help you accomplish this end.

The mediator should clearly explain the stages of the problem-solving process and should take care not to present himself as an authority figure. It is the disputants' process, not the mediator's. The process description is a procedural suggestion, not an order.

Explanation of Caucus

Next, the mediator should explain the concept of the caucus with each party:

There may be a need, at some time in the course of our meetings, for each of you to take some time for yourself away from the joint meeting (and confer with other members of your group, if it is a group dispute) or to meet with me individually as a mediator. This type of break or meeting is not unusual. It allows you time to refocus and reflect on your short- and long-term goals, handle strong emotions, explore options or proposals, gather your facts to develop new settlement options, or reach a consensus within your group (if applicable). At times, I may call such a meeting, but you may initiate one also. If I call a separate meeting, it is not to make a deal but to explore issues that might be more comfortable for you to discuss in private. What is discussed in these separate meetings will be considered by me to be confidential. I will not reveal what we have talked about with the other party (or parties) unless you instruct me to do so.

Little more is said about caucuses at this time because in some situations, the thought of private meetings may make one or more of the parties uncomfortable. Disputants often fear clandestine deals or coalitions between the other party and the mediator. I will explain the uses of caucuses in more detail in Chapter Fifteen.

Definition of Confidentiality Parameters

At this point, the mediator should describe his or her understanding of the confidential nature of the negotiation session. Confidentiality, though often considered to be both an important aspect and indeed a functional necessity of mediation, is not universally guaranteed or necessary. Some states in the United States provide legal guarantees of confidentiality between disputants and mediator (Freedman, Haile, and Bookstaff, 1985; Comeau, 1982; Folberg and Taylor, 1984). Other states do not allow for confidentiality and, on occasion, may request data or subpoena mediators to testify in postmediation court proceedings when the parties have failed to reach an agreement. Mediators should describe the limits of confidentiality as it is provided for in their state or agency so that disputants know the limits of their privacy. The following is an example of a statement concerning confidentiality:

These sessions will be considered by me to be confidential in that I will not discuss them publicly with any person not involved in this dispute. I will attempt to maintain this confidentiality to the best of my ability. On occasion, I may want to discuss this problem with a colleague so that I may gain greater insight into the conflict. I request that you grant me this privilege as it will enable me to better assist you in reaching an agreement. If I do so, I will not use either of your names in describing the situation.

At this point, some mediators ask parties to sign a confidentiality statement or a waiver and consent form (see Resource B) designed to protect the mediator from a future subpoena demanding either an appearance in court or the presentation of his or her notes as evidence in a lawsuit.

Description of Logistics

The mediator should now describe any relevant logistics: the time schedule for the entire process, the length of sessions, and note taking. The mediator often estimates how much time will be necessary to settle the dispute. Parties need to know this in order to assess the costs and benefits of mediated negotiations. An initial commitment should be gained from the parties for the allotment of a specific period of time to the first session. Later meeting dates and times can be established as needed. Some mediators in complicated cases have obtained a time commitment for several sessions, as such cases require more time for data collection and for the education of the parties about the issues in dispute. It may also take several sessions to achieve any substantive progress or to lower the psychological barriers to settlement.

The mediator should seek permission from the parties to take notes, explaining that the notes are for his or her own reference and that they will remain confidential. The notes are not an official transcript of the meeting but might at a later time be used to construct a written memorandum of understanding or a settlement document.

Suggestions for Behavioral Guidelines

At this time, the mediator should shift his or her focus to behavioral guidelines that will facilitate an orderly discussion. Guidelines that mediators may suggest include procedures to handle interruptions, agreements about the role of witnesses and relationships with the press, conditions for smoking, identification of those with whom disputants may discuss negotiations, delineation of what can or should be disclosed by the parties, and so on:

> *At this point, I would like to suggest several procedural guidelines that other negotiators have found helpful in their discussions. I would like to suggest that each of you have some uninterrupted time to talk. If one of you has a question about what is said, I request that you hold it until the question period. If you agree to this procedure, I request your permission to hold you to it. Is this acceptable? Do you have other guidelines that might help you discuss more productively?*

Some mediators who wish to establish behavioral guidelines for negotiations list the rules under which they will work and are inflexible on changing them, whereas others ask the disputants to identify and generate their own guidelines to aid them in holding productive discussions. The latter strategy is a first step toward making mutual procedural decisions and developing habits of agreement.

There is clearly no one way to establish behavioral guidelines. In tense situations, disputants may need the mediator to be more directive, whereas in less polarized disputes, the parties themselves may be in total control. Mediators, in establishing guidelines, should be careful not to use authoritarian or command-ridden language. Terms such as *rules* or *terms for negotiation* or even *behavioral ground rules*, which imply regulations that are being forced on the group, should generally be avoided. Noncommanding terms such as *guidelines* or *suggestions for procedure* are often more acceptable to the parties and avoid putting the mediator in an authoritarian position. Once guidelines are established, the mediator should secure an agreement that he or she will be empowered to enforce the agreed terms or procedure.

Answers to Questions

The mediator is now nearing the end of his or her opening statement. At this point, he or she should answer any questions that the parties may have about the procedure to be followed. Questions should be answered to the satisfaction of the disputants before proceeding further. Lack of understanding by a disputant or dissatisfaction with a mediator's answer may lead to a decreased commitment to the process or later resistance.

Commitment to Begin Mediation

Gaining a commitment to begin is the mediator's last move before turning the session over to the parties. The mediator's concluding remarks should outline what has been discussed, set the information-sharing process in motion in a positive way, and motivate the parties to begin discussing their issues. The following is a sample statement concerning commitment and consent:

> *If there are no more questions about the process, I suggest that we are ready to move on to discuss the issues at hand. It is my understanding that you are both (or all) here to work hard and bargain in good faith to achieve a settlement. Are you ready to begin?*

After gaining either verbal or nonverbal assent, the mediator should turn the session over to the disputants.

Opening Statements by Parties

Parties in dispute generally start with opening statements of their own. These statements are usually designed to outline their substantive interests, establish a bargaining procedure, and build rapport with the other side.

Disputants enter negotiations with a variety of levels of information about their own and other parties' issues and preferred solutions. In some disputes, issues and outcome possibilities may be very clear, and negotiators will have to spend little time exploring details of contested issues. In other conflicts, the parties may lack information on a number of dimensions.

Young (1972, p. 57) notes that at the beginning of negotiations, a negotiator may be unclear about

1. "The basic issue(s) at stake"
2. The "range of alternative choices or strategies" available
3. The solutions that will best meet his or her interests or needs
4. The number and identity of people who should be involved in the negotiations (or who will be affected by them)
5. The way that other negotiators will make decisions

The degree of clarity at the start of negotiations varies greatly. At one end of the spectrum are disputant relationships that are very ill-defined. At the other are situations in which strategies, issues, options, and potential outcomes are well known to all negotiators. Parties use opening statements to present and test their views and assumptions at the onset of negotiations.

Mediators should be familiar with the variety of ways in which parties make opening statements so that they are ready to respond. Parties may open negotiations by focusing on substantive issues, negotiation procedures, or moves designed to improve the psychological conditions of disputants.

Openings Focused on Substance

The most common, but not necessarily the most effective, way to open negotiations is to focus immediately on the substantive issues of the dispute. In this approach, the negotiator usually selects several variables—the history of the problem, the reasons for seeking change, the issues, and possibly interests or positions—and orders them in a way that will have the maximum positive effect on the opposing party or parties. Moore (1982b) and Lincoln (1981) list possible combinations:

Focus on history, need, and position. This combination is quite common in many situations and cultures. The negotiator reviews the background of the dispute, outlines how the status quo has caused damage, tells why change is needed, and then proceeds to detail an opening position that he or she feels would solve the problem. This type of opening frequently forces the parties into hard positional bargaining. Singson might use this approach for opening and would detail the history of the Whittamores' coming to the clinic, the legal basis for their contract, and a statement that the contract should be enforced.

Focus on issues. The negotiator may dispense with the history of the problem and proceed directly to a discussion of the issues. The issues may be presented in several ways:

1. They may be left to each side to identify through a verbal presentation of the development of the dispute.
2. They may be outlined by the negotiator in the form of a list that presents the most important issues first, indicating which items deserve the most attention.
3. They may be outlined by the negotiator in an order that places simple and small issues first.
4. They may be presented in random order so that the parties may later jointly organize them.
5. They may be presented in an exhaustive manner that includes the stated or expected issues of the other side—an approach that demonstrates an interest in the opponent's viewpoint.

Whittamore might take the last approach to opening and would list all of the issues that he wants to discuss, as he wants Singson to be aware of all the potential ramifications of the latter's actions.

Focus on merit. In this approach, the negotiator tries to educate the other party about the need for change without disclosing or proposing a position. The major assumption behind this strategy is that if a party can make a convincing case that his or her situation is intolerable and that change is needed, it will be easier to reach an agreement later on a particular solution.

Focus on interests. In this strategy, the negotiator discusses the interests or needs he or she seeks to have satisfied through negotiation. By focusing on interests instead of positions, the groundwork is prepared, but not guaranteed, for possible interest-based negotiations. This approach could be taken by either or both negotiators on their own initiative but might also be initiated by a suggestion from the mediator.

Focus on nonnegotiable position. In cases in which parties are extremely polarized or feel that they have little room for bargaining, the negotiator may dispense with the history of a conflict and the issues involved and present an extreme position instead. This position may or may not be reasonable or negotiable. The tactic will often stalemate negotiations and may force parties to pursue other means of dispute resolution, such as litigation or direct action. If either of the parties in the Whittamore-Singson dispute took this approach, the mediator would probably have to caucus and help him back off of his initial position.

Openings Focused on Procedure

Another way of opening negotiations, which is not as common as substantive openings, is to focus on the negotiation procedure. With this strategy, the time in which the disputants focus on behavioral guidelines is expanded into an extended discussion of procedural steps that the parties will take to resolve their dispute. As discussed in Moore (1982b) and Lincoln (1981), advantages to opening negotiations in this way are that such a focus

- Provides a jointly developed sequence for the negotiation to which all parties are committed
- Allows the parties to practice making decisions as a team
- Provides information about the behavior, attitudes, and trustworthiness of other parties
- Allows parties to practice making agreements on problems that are neither substantively important nor as emotionally charged as the issues in dispute
- Provides an opportunity to build "habits" of agreement
- Demonstrates that agreement is possible and that the situation is not hopeless

Central areas of procedure in which parties may make agreements include the following (Moore, 1982b; Lincoln, 1981):

- How an agenda will be developed
- Negotiation procedures to be followed
- Time frame and schedule for sessions, including beginning and ending times
- How information will be shared among disputants
- Information sharing procedures with constituents or nonparticipating parties
- How legal rights and administrative mandates will be recognized and protected
- Parties' relationships with lawyers
- Parties' relationships with media
- Acceptable and unacceptable behavior (for example, respect for values, personal attacks, attribution of motivation, emotional displays, attitudes toward win-lose solutions)
- How commitment to the procedure and to potential agreements will be maintained
- Determination of participants
- Role of substitutes and observers
- Role of task forces or small work groups
- Size of negotiating teams
- Location of meeting sites
- Maintenance of meeting records
- How procedural and substantive agreements will be enforced

Mediators sometimes encourage negotiators, implicitly or explicitly, to focus on procedural agreements before delving into substance. This is done if the intervenor feels that parties need to build trust or experience in working with one another or would benefit from a more extensive set of procedural guidelines. Parties occasionally begin with this type of opening on their own.

Opening Focused on Psychological Conditions of Disputants

In formal negotiations, the opening that is focused on the psychological conditions of disputants is not as common as substantive or procedural openings. It is more frequently observed in transformative mediation (Bush and Folger, 1994), a form of third-party consultation practiced by organization development specialists (Blake and Mouton, 1984) and by social scientists working in international peacemaking (Rothman, 1992; Kelman, 1991; Burton, 1969; Fisher, 1982; Walton, 1969).

This approach aims to improve the relationship of the disputants before, or as a major element in, discussions of substantive issues or procedure. In its most informal mode, some of the conciliation techniques mentioned in Chapter Seven may be initiated. If the process is conducted more formally, experiences may be planned in which disputants engage in unstructured social activities or take field trips that focus on the topic under discussion, thereby gaining an opportunity to establish and build personal connections. Other means of drawing disputants closer are general personal-sharing groups (Dubois and Mew, 1963), focused-topic discussion groups (Levinson, 1954; Levinson and Sohermerhorn, 1951), intergroup training laboratories (Blake and Mouton, 1984), joint-skill training (Hunter and McKersie, 1992), discussions oriented toward mutual recognition and empowerment (Bush and Folger, 1994), and the performance of common tasks unrelated to the issues in dispute (Fisher, 1978). For example, in a mediation of a public policy dispute, the mediators arranged for all parties to meet the night before the opening session for a casual dinner. The negotiators rode atop a double-decker bus to a Mexican restaurant where they ate, drank, and came to know each other as individuals and not representatives of an interest group. In another dispute involving timber cutting on national forest land, the parties participated in a weekend retreat in which they hiked on land earmarked for a timber harvest. The hike built interpersonal relationships and raised awareness of the land involved in the dispute.

Mediators in marital disputes occasionally spend time before formal divorce negotiations discussing and processing the development and decline of the marriage (Milne, 1981). It is argued that this procedure helps the couple adjust to the fact that they are divorcing.

In their attempts to build more flexible and open attitudes in disputants, mediators often initiate informal moves to promote conciliation. They might encourage active listening, affirmation of some quality of a party that is not related to the issues in conflict, a communication structure that promotes safety, or a deliberate focus on feelings.

Choice of Opening

The choice to focus on substance, process, or the psychological conditions of the disputants depends on

1. The type of dispute
2. The abilities of the disputants to focus on substantive issues
3. The level of emotional intensity of disputants
4. The degree of control the disputants have given to the mediator to design and regulate the process of the meeting
5. The internal and external pressures that are on the negotiators to settle promptly

The mediator should work with the parties to focus on an opening process that will be most successful for them. If the internal or external pressures to reach agreement are high or moderate and emotional tensions are high, the mediator will usually encourage procedural or psychological openings. Parties will often accept this emphasis if they can be convinced that such moves will later enhance the possibility of reaching a substantive settlement.

Transition to Parties' Opening Statements

The mediator shifts from his or her opening statement to a focus on the disputants with a transition statement. A sample transition statement in which the mediator proposes a focus on substance is as follows:

> At this time, I propose that we move into a discussion of the situation that brought you to mediation. (The mediator turns to the party that he or she has previously decided should begin presenting first.) Dr. Whittamore, will you please begin by describing the situation as you see it? Please include some of the historical background of the problem, the issues that you would like to discuss, and the interests or needs you want to have satisfied. At this point, it will be helpful not to identify specific solutions but to merely focus on defining the problem.

The mediator now turns the session over to the first party, who begins his or her opening statement.

Facilitation of Communication and Information Exchange

The most critical task for disputants at this stage of negotiation is to maximize accurate information exchange. They may be hindered in doing so by a number of factors:

Excessive posturing

Extreme demands designed to signal how intensely the parties feel about the issues or how much they want the other party or parties to move

Jumbled or unstructured communication

Inaccurate listening

Intense emotional outbursts

Total dysfunction of one or more parties

The mediator's main task, therefore, is to help the parties communicate about substantive issues in dispute and minimize the psychological damage resulting from emotional exchanges. To facilitate this communication, mediators use a variety of communication techniques, some of which were described in Chapters Five and Seven. Additional communication techniques that may be used include the following:

Restatement. The mediator listens to what has been said and feeds back the content to the party in the party's own words.

Paraphrase. The mediator listens to what has been said and restates the content back to the party using different words that have the same meaning as the original statement. This is often called reframing.

Active Listening. The mediator decodes a spoken message and then feeds back to the speaker the emotions of the message. This is commonly used in conciliation.

Summarization. The mediator condenses the message of a speaker.

Expansion. The mediator receives a message, feeds it back to the listener in an expanded and elaborated form, and then checks to verify accurate perception.

Ordering. The mediator helps a speaker order ideas into some form of sequence (historical, size, importance, amount, and so on).

Grouping. The mediator helps a speaker identify common ideas or issues and combine them into logical units.

Structuring. The mediator assists a speaker in organizing and arranging his or her thoughts and speech into a coherent message.

Separating or fractionating. The mediator divides an idea or an issue into smaller component parts.

Generalization. The mediator identifies general points or principles in a speaker's presentation.

Probing questions. The mediator asks either open-ended or focused questions to encourage a speaker to elaborate on an idea.

Questions of clarification. The mediator asks questions to obtain clarification of particular points.

Mediators use these communication tools to help parties communicate more accurately with each other. Ideally, the parties use them too. Mediators may encourage them to do so by explaining how the tools are used and by commending parties whenever they apply them.

Creation of a Positive Emotional Climate

In addition to facilitating communication, the mediator often must create an emotional climate conducive to clear communication and joint problem solving. Interventions related to promoting a positive emotional climate include

- Preventing interruptions or verbal attacks
- Encouraging parties to focus on the problem and not on each other
- Translating value-laden or judgmental language of disputants into less emotionally charged language
- Affirming clear descriptions or statements, procedural suggestions, or gestures of good faith while not taking sides on substantive issues
- Accepting the expression of feelings and being empathic, though not taking sides
- Reminding parties about behavioral guidelines that they have established

- Defusing specific threats by restating them in terms of general pressure to change
- Intervening to prevent conflict escalation

Cultural Variations

The cultural context—professional, educational, ethnic, gender, and national—may significantly influence the process of beginning the mediation process. It is important for an intermediary to start the discussions in a manner that will be both culturally appropriate and acceptable to the parties. Although it is impossible to describe the wide range of procedures that are used in this stage, there are some approaches that appear quite frequently.

In situations and cultures in which social network mediators play a predominant role, more time may be allocated at the beginning of the mediation session for informal conversation, which is often focused on the connections between the mediator and the parties and between the parties themselves. This time helps to establish or reestablish the relationship between the parties and may also identify mutual bonds or obligations that will encourage settlement. In some cultures, such as many in Latin America and the Middle East, the opening of mediation or negotiations is also accompanied by the consumption of a beverage (and in other cultures, food), which may be provided by the mediator.

In situations where the mediator is in a hierarchical relationship with the parties, or the parties are in a vertical relationship with each other, the opening statement and corresponding process may be more formal and may emphasize the authority of the mediator, the superior-subordinate relationship of the parties to the intermediary, and the differences between the parties themselves. This formality may be seen as a means of leveraging the parties toward an agreement. In some cultures, such an approach may also be necessary to demonstrate respect for the different positions of the parties. Although this may go against norms of more egalitarian societies, it is both acceptable and expected in more hierarchically organized cultures.

The level of detail in which the process and behavioral ground rules are spelled out also varies across cultures. In high-context and fairly homogeneous cultures, where members have many common and unspoken assumptions about how the negotiation process will be conducted, the degree of process explicitness will be less than in low-context cultures composed of members from diverse backgrounds, where parties expect and require detailed descriptions of procedures (Hall, 1989). For example, intermediaries in Japan, a high-context society, may be less procedurally explicit than U.S., Canadian, or Australian mediators, who often work in multicultural settings. In intercultural mediations, the mediator will need to decide how explicit he or she needs to be to adequately inform the parties about how they will proceed.

Patterns of communication may also differ across cultures. Some cultures, such as the majority culture of the United States, are "monochronic," in that events or activities within a human group occur one at time (Hall, 1983). One person talks and the other listens. A number of other cultures, such as many found around the Mediterranean Sea, are "polychronic," in that multiple activities and conversations may occur at once. These communication patterns can significantly affect the type of dialogue that occurs between the mediator and the parties during the opening statement, as well as the discussion or argumentation between the parties. What for one culture appears to be rudeness, interruption, and poor listening will be acceptable overlapping discussion in another. Mediators may need to adjust their communication patterns when working within or between monochronic and polychronic cultures by adopting or adapting to the culture of the parties, by openly discussing and reaching an agreement on communication norms that will be used in the session, or by switching cultures as different parties are related to.

Transition to the Next Stage

If the parties and the mediator have communicated successfully and built some positive feelings between them in this first stage of joint meetings, the groundwork for productive future dialogue has been established. This stage terminates as soon as the parties or the mediator focus on building an agenda or focus on a particular issue or sphere of discussion and move to explore it in depth. Shifts between stages of negotiations are often the most difficult for parties and mediators (Wildau, 1987). As we move to the next chapters, we will explore how mediators can help smooth these transitions and promote productive problem solving.

Chapter Nine

Defining Issues and Setting an Agenda

Negotiation and mediation are problem-solving processes, but they are also, potentially, opportunities for establishing, defining, building, or terminating relationships. Both the problem-solving and the relationship-defining aspects of mediation occur in the context of discussing issues and interests that may be substantive, procedural, or psychological in nature. It is generally helpful to both the parties and the mediator if, early in the negotiations, some if not all of the key issues or topics to be addressed are identified, so that the parties and the intermediary can develop an effective process for discussing them.

If parties are to move toward a settlement of their differences, they must shift procedurally from contentious to cooperative interaction. The three critical tasks negotiators and mediators must accomplish in this stage are (1) identification of broad topic areas of concern to the parties; (2) agreement on the subtopics or issues that will be discussed; and (3) determination of the sequence for discussion of the topics or issues. Coordinated activity by negotiators at this point in the process does not mean that they agree substantively. *Coordination* refers solely to an agreement on the procedure that will be used to handle a topic area or particular issues.

Variables that influence how rapidly and how easily this stage in negotiations can be dealt with include

- The number and complexity of issues involved
- The negotiators' understanding of the conflict's substantive matter
- The clarity of presentation by the parties of each topic or issue

- The capacity of the negotiators to recognize a distinct topic area or issue when it is presented
- The extent of parties' power to persuade other negotiators to accept a topic or issue for inclusion on the agenda
- The degree of psychological or other resistance to collaboration exhibited by one or more parties

Mediators who enter a dispute before topics and issues have been identified and the agenda has been drawn up can help the parties complete these tasks. At this stage, the mediator and the negotiators have similar procedural goals.

Topic Areas and Issues

The content of negotiations varies considerably in terms of the degree of specificity or conceptual definition of topics under discussion. For example, in a community dispute between a group of neighbors and a social service organization that plans to site a health clinic for low-income clients in the group's middle-class neighborhood, the parties may have the following conceptual boundaries for the dispute. The neighbors, who oppose siting the clinic in the neighborhood, might define the boundaries of the discussion as being whether the facility should be sited there at all, what the process for decision making will be, and how their voices can be heard and respected by those in power who will ultimately decide the question. The clinic staff, on the other hand, are probably not concerned with discussing *whether* the facility should be sited in the neighborhood. They want to discuss *how* a building can be leased, how to lower the resistance they are encountering, how to begin to provide services to a clientele in need (and make other community members see this need), and how to establish a positive relationship with the neighbors of the clinic that will enable them to carry out their medical goals. If a representative of each group were asked to identify what the context and range of the negotiations should be, each would answer differently. The neighbors' spokesperson would cite a general topic area: *whether* the clinic should be built. The representative of the clinic staff, however, would focus the discussion on issues related to *how* the clinic could be located in the neighborhood, with community concerns and interests taken into consideration.

The degree of specificity of topic areas or issues that the parties want to discuss varies, of course, from dispute to dispute. Some conflicts begin with a disagreement over a particular point and then move from the specific issue to a more general level of contention, whereas others begin with very general topics of disagreement and gradually become more specific. More will be said about these two dynamics in Chapter Eleven, when we consider what problem-solving technique should be applied to handle a dispute.

Aside from the level of specificity of the dispute, a second kind of distinction can be made: issues can be classified as consensual (interest-based) and dissensual (value-based) (Aubert, 1963).

Consensual or Interest-Based Conflict

Conflicts of interest usually exist in conditions of perceived or actual scarcity in which one or more parties believe that gains for one party may mean a loss for another. Conflicts of interest are often referred to as "competitive cooperation," in that the disputants are collaborating to compete for the same set of goods or benefits.

Because there are numerous types of interests that any given party may have in a dispute, there is often great latitude in trading one set of interests for another so that all parties can be satisfied in a settlement.

Dissensual or Value-Based Conflict

In contrast to conflicts of interest in which a consensus exists between parties about competition for the desired end result or in which enough different interests exist to facilitate a trading process to minimize loss on all sides, dissensual conflicts are based on differences in values. Value disputes focus on such issues as guilt and innocence, what norms should prevail in a social relationship, what facts should be considered valid, what beliefs are correct, who merits what, and what principles should guide decision makers. Disputes over *whether* to build a shelter for the homeless in a middle-class neighborhood, whether to cut down an irreplaceable old growth forest, whether divorcing parents should invite new lovers over when the children live at home, or whether a party should be punished for committing a theft (as opposed to being compelled to make restitution) are generally disputes over values.

Values disputes are extremely difficult to resolve, and intermediaries are usually very careful when working with them to ensure that their actions do not increase the parties' intransigence and adherence to hardline positions. Before examining how mediators help parties identify and frame issues, I would like to take a brief detour and describe several of the most common approaches used by mediators to assist parties in managing values disputes.

First, mediators may try to avoid describing a problem in terms of values. Instead, they encourage the parties to focus on their underlying interests or on what they are trying to achieve, thereby transforming a value dispute into more of an interest-based conflict. For example, in a natural resource conflict over wolf control in Alaska, the mediator helped the parties to reformulate the problem from one of deciding whether wolves should or should not be killed to one of determining how to protect moose and caribou populations from overpredation while protecting the region's wolf population and minimizing the use of lethal control methodologies.

Second, mediators may help parties agree to develop spheres of influence where each has exclusive authority or jurisdiction, and where their respective values will prevail. Such was the approach to conflict management during the Cold War, when the East and the West had physical blocs or territories where their value systems were dominant. On the domestic front, divorcing parents may be encouraged to agree to disagree over values; different norms and rules for their children may apply in the two homes.

Another way of approaching values disputes is for the mediator to determine if there are any superordinate or overriding values held by the parties that can be used to moderate conflicting lower-level values. For example, labor and management may have serious value clashes over what is or is not a management prerogative, but they may also share the superordinate value of keeping the company in business so that everyone can keep his or her job. The identification of a superordinate value may mitigate the intensity of conflict over other less important value disputes.

Before discussing how parties and mediators identify topic areas and issues for negotiation, I reiterate what was stated in relation to conciliation in Chapter Seven: in addition to the two types of issues just described, there are "unnecessary" issues caused by strong emotions, misperception, or poor communication. Such issues are caused by neither conflict of interest nor disagreement over values. I have discussed means to handle these "unnecessary" conflicts in Chapter Thirteen.

Identifying and Framing Issues

In the process of defining the parameters of a dispute, the parties and the mediator engage in a preliminary definition of topic areas and issues that will be the focus of future negotiations. This process has been referred to variously as *framing* or *reframing* (Watzlawick, 1978), *characterizing* (Stulberg, 1981a), *reconceptualizing*, or *redefining* (Boulding, 1962; Sawyer and Guetzkow, 1965) the issues in dispute. Before exploring the moves of framing or reframing a situation, I will briefly explain how parties arrive at their viewpoint of the conflict.

Each disputant comes to the conflict with his or her own individual and subjective picture of what issues are in dispute and what the basis of conflict is (Berger and Luckmann, 1967). Watzlawick (1978, p. 119) describes the individual's condition: "Let us remember: We never deal with reality *per se,* but rather with *images* of reality—that is, with interpretations. Although the number of potentially possible interpretations is very large, our world image usually permits us to see only one—and this *one* therefore appears to be the only possible, reasonable, permitted view. Furthermore, this one interpretation also suggests only one possible, reasonable, and permitted solution."

Framing is summed up in the familiar saying about the difference between an optimist and a pessimist: "The optimist says of a bottle that it is half full; the pessimist sees it as half empty. The same bottle and the same quantity of wine—in other words, the same first-order reality—but two very different world images, creating two very different (second-order) realities" (Watzlawick, 1978, p. 119).

More in line with our focus is the classic dispute in child custody over which parent will receive legal custody of their child. Both parents want to ensure that they will have a high level of involvement in their child's life. They, and in many cases the judicial system, have defined the resolution procedure as a court decision determining who can legally possess the child. There are, however, alternative ways that these parent-parent and parent-child relationships can be framed. If, for example, the struggle over legal custody is defined in terms of maximizing the parent-child relationship, and the concept of legal custody or ownership of the child is reframed in terms of parental rights and responsibilities toward their offspring, the bipolar struggle with only a win-lose outcome is transformed into a more complex issue with multiple variables that may be traded off one against another (Haynes, 1981; Ricci, 1980). By reframing how a dispute is seen and defined by the parties, the parties and the mediator can open the door to more collaborative and mutually satisfactory solutions.

For example, in the Whittamore-Singson case, Singson may frame the problem as "How to enforce the terms of the contract and determine the amount of penalty Whittamore must pay for violating the terms of the agreement." Whittamore might frame the dispute thus: "What is the least amount of compensation I must pay to the clinic that will enable me to practice medicine in the town where my children live?" The mediator, after exploring the issues and interests with the parties, might assist them in reframing the problem in several ways: "How can the clinic and Dr. Whittamore have a mutually beneficial future relationship?" or "If compensation is to be paid so that Whittamore can stay in town, how might fair and objective standards be identified that could guide this calculation?" or "Are there ways that allow Whittamore to achieve the separation and distance he wants from his wife, yet still continue a working relationship with the clinic?"

Variables in Framing and Reframing Issues

When negotiators frame issues in a productive, problem-solving manner, the mediator may be merely an interested observer. However, some disputes become deadlocked because disputants have not discovered a mutually acceptable definition or framing of the issues that will allow them to cooperate. At this point, the mediator's intervention can be invaluable. The mediator may either frame the issues before the parties restrict themselves with a particular definition or may assist the parties in reframing their issues by moving them away from an unproductive definition toward one that will lead to successful problem solving.

When taking the definition of issues put forth by one or more parties and reframing it in terms that are subjectively acceptable to all disputants, the mediator should consider (1) the process for reframing interest-related issues: (2) techniques for reframing value-related issues; (3) the explicitness and timing of reframing; and (4) the appropriate language or syntax used in the redefinition of the situation.

Reframing Interest-Related Issues

The act of reframing itself raises some important questions regarding the mediator's neutrality. The general assumption of mediators when reframing an issue is that they are making such a move "based on some conception (implicit or explicit) of a more constructive or desirable relationship for the original players than the one that they see themselves engaging in at the outset of the interaction. And in this context, the terms 'constructive' and 'desirable' inevitably carry normative content. Be this as it may, mediators constantly redefine the context of disputes in ways that disputants find to be extremely helpful to avoid or overcome impasse" (Young, 1972, p. 59).

In general, reframing interest disputes is easier than reframing value conflicts over such issues as guilt, rights, or facts. In reframing interest disputes, mediators often use a technique that expands issues to provide the parties with more bargaining power. For example, in a labor-management dispute, the union and management are bargaining to a deadlock over a wage increase. The union negotiators must bring to their constituents some tangible benefits from the negotiations. They have selected salary increases as their goal. The mediator can assist the parties in reframing the issue from the problem of a wage increase to the problem of how the union can obtain benefits that its constituents will see are the result of the negotiations. This reframing of the situation allows the negotiator to look for other means of meeting union needs than obtaining an increase in pay.

Reframing interest disputes requires a careful analysis of position statements put forth by the parties and the interests represented by those positions. Shifting from specific interests to more general ones may widen the number of settlement options available.

Occasionally, reframing issues and interests in narrower terms is also effective. For example, consider the case in which several people agreed to purchase a piece of property together that was to be used for cooperative housing. Several months after the purchase, the relationships among the owners deteriorated and one of the partners decided that he wanted his money back. However, this would be possible only by revising the financial contract all the owners had agreed on. The initial issue, stated in the form of a demand, was "I want my money back." The problem as the disputants described it was that one person wanted his money back and was withdrawing from the contract, but the others felt that they could not reimburse him without selling the property. Sale of the property was not acceptable to the other owners. From this either/or situation, the mediator and the parties mutually reframed the issue into smaller, more manageable subissues. How much money? When? In what form? With interest? And so on. The parties were then able to reach agreement on trade-offs for these subissues.

Reframing Value-Related Issues

The difficulty in reframing value conflicts arises from the fact that such issues have a strong tendency to become bipolar, with one side representing right and the other wrong. Disputants place great emphasis on normative judgment, which often makes it difficult to compromise and trade, as can be done with interest-related issues. Even proposing such solutions may provoke escalation. People will claim that their "ideas are not for sale" or that one "can't bargain with the truth" (Aubert, 1963).

Mediators accomplish identification and framing of value-based issues by (1) translating value disputes into interest disputes, (2) identifying superordinate goals, and (3) avoidance. I will discuss each approach in turn.

Pure dissensus in conflicts over values and facts is relatively rare. Usually, value disputes are mixed disputes, in that participants also have some common interests. Mediators who work with value disputes often try to translate values into interests so that the parties have more tangible issues. For example, if a value dispute over authority can be translated into a conflict over the division of power, there are some possibilities for compromise based on a formula for that division. In a hypothetical case, two employees are rivals for promotion in their organization. There is only one position available at the next grade above their current rank. Both employees want the job and claim to be the better candidate. If it is in the company's interest to satisfy both employees, those responsible may explore how the tasks, authority, and status of the job could be divided between the two equally qualified employees. Thus struggle over who is better becomes moot as each employee is rewarded on the basis of interest.

In a real-life dispute, an association of single-family homeowners was confronting a planning department over the construction of multifamily dwellings on the edge of their neighborhood. The single-family homeowners charged that the new construction would change the neighborhood's ambiance and that it would mean an entire shift in lifestyle. On careful examination, lifestyle values were translated into interests—limited noise, no abrupt transitions from single-family to multifamily homes, minimizing the height of new construction to preserve views, and maintaining privacy by avoiding building complexes that overlook the backyards of single-family homes. Given the interests of all parties, a mutually satisfactory development plan was negotiated that met most of the needs described.

A second approach to reframing value disputes is to identify larger superordinate goals with which all parties can identify (Sherif and others, 1961). For example, in a dispute over a dam's location, one party may argue that the proposed construction site damages a pristine wilderness area, whereas the other party argues that it has a mandate to provide water to a nearby city, and that the dam allows the party to fulfill contractual obligations. The mediator looks for a superordinate goal to join the parties in a cooperative effort. A consensus might be obtained on two points: the city needs a certain amount of water, and the wilderness is to be protected. The parties can then participate in a joint search for potential sources of water.

The third strategy for managing value-based issues is to avoid identifying or responding to them directly or to reframe the situation so that parties agree to disagree. Because it is difficult to mediate guilt or innocence, right or wrong, respect or lack of respect, and so on, the mediator may want to avoid these questions entirely and focus only on the dispute's components that can be turned toward interest-based bargaining. If enough issues can be solved with interest-based bargaining, the importance of value differences may fade and will be dropped from a list of demands or topics for discussion.

Explicit-Implicit Reframing and Timing

To resolve disputes over interests or values, parties often must be explicit about the topic areas that divide them. The degree of explicitness, however, may vary over time because of the dynamics of the negotiation process itself or the conscious strategies of the negotiators or the mediator. The mediator should manage the timing of issue identification so that the parties will be most receptive to the way an issue is framed. Parties are often vague at the start of negotiations about the specifics of issues in dispute. Only through a process of discussion and mutual education can the parties jointly define and make explicit the concrete issues that must be resolved.

One party will often precisely name an issue only to have another party repeatedly reject it. After several rounds of proposal rejection and exploration, the parties may finally be able to agree to discuss the issue. The final framing of the issues by the parties, or reframing by the mediator, may be identical to the earlier characterizations. The ultimate acceptance of the framing is a result of timing and the psychological readiness of the parties to accept the definition of the situation. This psychological shift often occurs after dialogue or when the neutral intervenor states the framing. There is research evidence that parties are often willing and able to hear and accept statements worded by the mediator when they are not able to hear or accept the identical statement from another disputant (Rubin and Brown, 1975).

Appropriate Language

One remaining point needs to be covered regarding the framing of issues: the mediator's language. Disputants use language that is judgmental, positional, and biased toward their subjective view. In joint session, mediators usually try to translate the language of the disputants into neutral terms to remove bias, positions, and judgment. Thus, when one party says, "That fat slob hasn't paid his rent money for the past two months," the mediator may translates this as "You are upset that you have not received money that you feel is due to you according to the terms of your rental agreement with Mr. Brown." In this case, the judgmental statement that Brown is a slob is dropped, and the implicit demand on Brown is turned into a statement about the landlord's feelings of deprivation and his need for reimbursement. This, after all, is what concerns the landlord. Reframing the problem in this way also makes Brown feel more comfortable with the issue. The focus is no longer on his character but on the landlord's need to be paid.

In identifying and framing issues, mediators should be careful to state the problem clearly, and in a manner that favors neither side nor makes one party blameworthy. Ideally, the mediator should depersonalize issues and put them outside the relationship between the disputants. The parties can then focus on the topic in a more objective manner (Filley, 1975). Stulberg (1981a) notes that mediators should take great care to avoid "trigger" words or statements that parties may interpret as mediator bias or preconceived judgments as to who is wrong. Many mediators avoid adversarial language, referring to conflicts as *problems,* positions as *viewpoints,* parties as *your group,* and negotiations as *discussions* in order to depolarize and neutralize value-laden and conflict-oriented terminology.

There are times, however, when entirely neutral terminology may not be as effective as more partisan language. If, for example, the parties cannot reach an agreement on issues in joint session, the mediator may call a caucus to discuss the problem of issue identification. The mediator may use language more biased toward the interests or values of the particular party in the caucus to influence that party's decision making. He or she may use the same terminology, syntax, and emotion as the party to promote identification between party and mediator, thereby easing the way to agreement on disputed issues. However, mediators should take care that the way they speak in a caucus is not drastically different from the way they speak in joint session. Otherwise, parties may be confused or feel double-crossed by the shift to more neutral language when they return to joint session.

Determining an Agenda

The agenda the mediator designs before negotiations, as discussed in Chapter Six, is a rough draft to which new information is added from the opening statements of the parties. The negotiating agenda that disputants ultimately follow should be developed and approved by the parties alone, by the parties in conjunction with the mediator, or by the mediator alone (with the consent of the parties). Once issues have been identified, they must be placed in an order for discussion.

There are at least eight different approaches to agenda development in negotiations: (1) ad hoc, (2) simple agenda, (3) alternation of issues, (4) ranking by importance, (5) principled agenda, (6) "easier items first," (7) building-block or contingent agenda, and (8) trade-offs or packaging.

Ad Hoc Development

With ad hoc sequencing, one party proposes that the negotiators discuss an item, the other party or parties concur, and the item is discussed in its entirety until a conclusion has been reached. The parties then mutually agree on another item, and the process is repeated. The parties move through all items in this manner. This model allows for flexibility but also permits and promotes manipulation by parties for placement of agenda items at particularly opportune moments.

Simple Agenda

In the simple agenda method, issues for negotiation are taken, one at a time, in an order prescribed by one or more parties. Generally, the party proposing the agenda has sequenced the items in a manner that will be advantageous to achieving benefits for himself or herself. Typically, each issue is addressed and settled separately.

Gulliver (1979) notes that although this may commonly succeed for decision making in committees and conferences, it can rarely work in negotiations. The chief reason is that it attempts to ignore the essential problems of multiple criteria: that issues are often interconnected in the social life of negotiations and that, in any event, they are necessarily interconnected within the specific context of the negotiations in progress. Parties are aware of this and are unwilling to forfeit advantages that might be gained by getting better terms on one issue through concession (or refusal of it) on another. They wish to explore interconnections without the rigidity of a fixed agenda order.

The simple agenda approach encourages stalling and manipulative tactics in order to gain leverage on items that will come up later on the agenda. Gulliver notes that this procedure tends to subvert the ordering almost immediately.

Alternation of Issues

A third model for agenda construction is the alternating issue approach. In this method, the parties alternate in choosing the topic of discussion. This structural solution allows the parties to proceed and often inhibits the development of deadlocks. Gulliver (1979) says that this process rarely works for long, however, because one or more parties invariably insist on breaking the order.

Ranking by Importance

A fourth model of agenda design is for the parties to pick the one or two items that both consider of greatest importance and place them at the head of the agenda (Gulliver, 1979). The assumption is that if they can agree on these items, the less important items will follow suit. This procedure depends, of course, on the ability of the parties to agree on the most important issues and the order in which they will be addressed. There is evidence that this approach is best utilized when no claims or counterclaims are made or no offense has been alleged, as when parties are attempting to establish a new relationship where only a limited one has existed before.

Principled Agenda

A fifth approach is to define issues in terms of principles or general levels of agreement that will guide the decisions on specific items. The parties jointly establish the principles and then work out in detail how these principles will be applied on specific agenda items (Fisher and Ury, 1981). For example, in negotiations between telephone companies, a public utilities commission, and consumer groups over access charges on interstate phone lines, all parties agreed that the universal telephone service should be maintained. This agreement in principle became the basis for an agenda item in which the negotiators would discuss how universal service could be financed.

The procedure works only under conditions in which the parties are willing and able to negotiate at a high level of generalization or abstraction, and in which they are willing to defer decision making on minor issues until later. This process of approaching a negotiation agenda will be discussed in more detail in Chapter Eleven.

"Easier Items First"

A sixth method of agenda formation is to identify issues on which the parties will most likely reach agreement and that will probably not take long to discuss and settle. These issues are often small, self-contained, less emotion-laden, and not symbolic in comparison with other topics that might be discussed. Some of these simple items may be placed at the beginning of the agenda and others alternated with more difficult items to (1) ensure agreement on some issues early in negotiations; (2) promote a habit of agreement; (3) provide for a backlog of agreements that the parties will be reluctant to lose as the result of an impasse later on; and (4) provide agenda items that can be dropped or traded later, after they have been discussed, as a demonstration of good faith.

Naturally, this strategy is contingent on the ability of the parties to mutually identify simple issues. This is usually accomplished by trial and error, or the mediator may ask parties to identify issues on which they feel ready agreement may be achieved with little effort.

Building Block or Contingent Agenda

A seventh method of agenda construction is the building-block approach. In this process, a party or parties identify which agreements must be made first because the issues involved lay the groundwork or foundation for later decisions. Agenda sequencing depends on which agreements are contingent on previous ones. Contingency may be based on principles, time, payment schedules, and so on. This approach, although fairly complicated and dependent on a high degree of party coordination, does prevent deadlocks due to incorrect sequencing of issues. It will be discussed in more detail in Chapter Eleven.

Trade-offs or Packaging

The final approach to agenda formation is issue trading or packaging. Parties in dispute are sometimes reluctant to settle agenda items one at a time for fear that they will lose leverage on one item if they have settled another one earlier. To avoid this problem, parties link and formulate combinations of issues and offers in return for concessions from the other parties. This means that they negotiate a number of issues simultaneously. Issues may be traded one for another in such a way that equivalence of exchange is attained.

Packaging proposals containing multiple-issue solutions have advantages as an agenda-forming tool: it demonstrates a willingness to trade issues and meet the other party's needs; it may induce an opponent to generate alternative packages; it demonstrates that some concessions are possible if they are linked with specific gains; and it can eliminate some of the difficulty, at least for one party, of producing settlement options. However, packages do have drawbacks. They may be seen as a way of forcing an unfavorable settlement or denying a party the chance to participate in consensus or settlement building. A way to circumvent these drawbacks is to present a series of small packages that are not as comprehensive and are less likely to produce resistance.

Procedural Assistance from the Mediator

The tasks just described can be initiated by either one or more disputing parties or the mediator. Reaching an agreement on an agenda requires coordination between parties that they may not be able to achieve on their own. The mediator may need to suggest a procedure that in his or her judgment will best facilitate the resolution of a critical situation.

If the parties are moving toward a procedure for agenda formation that the mediator feels will be unproductive, he or she should either (1) suggest an alternative method, outlining the basis of its superiority over the one chosen by the parties, or (2) remain quiet, allowing the parties to negotiate and reach an impasse, and then intervene when they are more motivated to use the mediator's services. Selecting the latter strategy must be carefully weighed against the damage inflicted on the relationship of the parties due to failure to bargain.

It is important that the mediator, in making procedural suggestions about the agenda, avoid being maneuvered into the position of forcing a process on the parties (Fisch, Weakland, and Segal, 1982). This situation can only result in loss of credibility, decreased acceptability, more disputant resistance, and less effective later interventions.

Cultural Variations

The prevailing culture may significantly influence the process of defining issues and setting an agenda, and it is important for an intermediary to develop procedures in these two areas that will be both culturally appropriate and acceptable to the parties. I remember one case I mediated where a rapid shift in process was necessary to adapt to the specific professional culture of the parties.

Several years ago, I was asked to intervene in a university graduate department of psychology that was experiencing significant turmoil. The chair of the department had been removed after a conflict between faculty members, and now factions within the department were sabotaging each other and making decision making impossible. Tasks and assignments would be delegated to a faculty member, and when he or she did what was assigned, the results would be rejected, passively resisted, or publicly criticized by other department members.

I was asked by the acting chair and a number of his colleagues to conduct interviews with all key parties, assess their willingness to talk about departmental problems, develop a proposed agenda, and convene a meeting to address identified problems. After holding numerous individual sessions with the parties, I convened a meeting. I began by reporting back on the interviews and proposing an agenda that incorporated the topics that the parties had specifically identified as needing to be discussed. The group immediately balked at the proposal and announced that they were not ready to talk about these issues, even though they had been the ones who had suggested them and individually had approved the agenda. I thought that I recognized a pattern that many people had identified in the interviews, but decided not to argue against their resistance. I decided to "ride the horse in the direction that it was going" and asked them what they wanted to do.

Finally, one person said that she would like to spend the next hour just "talking about their feelings." Although this approach could have represented avoidance of issues, I recognized that many of the department's members were clinical psychologists, and what they wanted was an approach to agenda development that was probably more akin to a group therapy session than a problem-solving mediation—that is, they wanted to be "in their culture" with their dispute, working on feelings first and insights or issues later. I agreed to facilitate the meeting but suggested that they might follow some ground rules, such as talking only about their own feelings and not attributing motives or attacking others. They agreed, and we proceeded. During the hour that they talked, I recorded some of their feelings and related issues and interests on a flip chart, and at the conclusion of this phase of the meeting, they asked me to summarize. I related the history of the conflict as a group story and outlined how it made different people feel, the issues that it raised, and some of the interests that would have to be addressed to resolve past hurts and move ahead to future tasks and better relationships. The group affirmed the summary and agreed to move ahead to problem solving on the issues. By settling into the group's culture and using its familiar norms and procedures, we were able to develop a more acceptable agenda, to define issues out of a discussion of past pain, and to jointly move forward to both problem solving and a clearing of the air for potentially more positive relationships.

There are a number of cultural variations in issue identification and agenda development. Some cultures—such as a number of more traditional Native American, First Nations, New Zealand Maori or other aboriginal tribes or bands—often identify issues through storytelling: a respected party tells the history of the problem and the people involved almost in the manner of relating a legend or odyssey. The issues and interests are encapsulated in the tale being told.

Members of indirect-dealing cultures, or those that try to avoid overt disagreement or conflict, identify issues and set agendas in a variety of ways. Some Asian cultures that are not direct-dealing do not want to identify conflict issues at all but will talk very obliquely and in a circular manner about "difficulties" or "inconveniences." Lederach (1988) also noted this indirectness in Costa Rican disputants; the parties used the words *nails* and *entanglements* to describe issues, problems, or conflicts (the term *conflict* being reserved for violent physical confrontations). Members of other indirect-dealing cultures talk about conflicts in terms of metaphors or attempt to distance themselves from the problem by talking about the people involved in the third person. Yet other indirect-dealing parties, who highly value the preservation of relationships and face, prefer to talk first about a variety of issues that are not conflict-related, especially ones that may affirm the parties' past and future relationships, and only gradually approach areas of disagreement. Easy and less contentious issues are dealt with initially, and only later, after some good feelings have been created and progress made on simpler problems, are harder issues tackled.

Direct-dealing cultures may identify issues and set agendas in a variety of ways, including linear and explicit presentations; brainstorming (identifying and listing issues without immediately discussing or evaluating them); enumerating all topics for discussion on a handout distributed to all parties; listing issues on a wall chart; making specific proposals or advocating specific solutions rather than identifying issues; and proposing principles before identifying specific topics for discussion.

Mediators working within one culture need to develop issue identification and agenda-setting procedures that are culturally acceptable, and when working across cultures, they should help coordinate different and sometimes somewhat incompatible approaches. Ways to accomplish this include

1. Being familiar with the approaches commonly used in the parties' cultures
2. Interpreting and explaining to other parties the rationales for the diverse approaches being used
3. Listening carefully to the parties and articulating issues and concerns in ways that respect sensitivities to overt disagreement and explicitness
4. Drawing out issues from stories and making them more explicit, then suggesting ways to discuss them
5. Facilitating discussions on how issues will be identified and agendas developed.

Chapter Ten

Uncovering Hidden Interests of the Disputing Parties

People negotiate because of interests they want to have satisfied. The negotiation process may be considered to be a game (Cross, 1977) in which one or more parties engage in an educational process, a decoding process, and a bargaining process to present and discover interests and trade promises to meet those interests.

Difficulties in Identifying Issues

Parties in dispute rarely identify their interests in a clear or direct fashion. This lack of clarity occurs because parties

1. Often do not know what their genuine interests are
2. Are pursuing a strategy of hiding their interests on the assumption that they will gain more from a settlement if their genuine goals are obscured from the scrutiny of other parties
3. Have adhered so strongly to a particular position that meets their interests that the interest itself becomes obscured and equated with the position and can no longer be seen as a separate entity, or
4. Are unaware of procedures for exploring interests

I will discuss each of these obstacles to identifying interests.

Lack of Awareness of Interests

Negotiating parties often misperceive what their interests really are. Misperception may result from external factors, such as law, tradition, or advice from friends, that describes how the negotiation game is to be played and completed, or from confusion in the negotiators themselves. In Chapter Nine, I cited a case in which two parents are struggling over the question of who should have legal custody of their child after a divorce. Both parents are excellent child rearers and nurturers, and they are equally qualified to raise the child. They are fighting over a specific solution, sole legal custody, and in the process are damaging their relationship and indirectly harming the child. They each see their interest, and that of the other parent, defined as gaining legal custody of the child. Each parent views settlement outcomes narrowly because of advice from attorneys and relatives and traditional ideas about custody settlement arrangements. In reality, their interests are having time with the child, being involved in decisions about how the child is to be raised, having the chance to go on vacation with the child, and so on. The struggle is over a position—the demand for sole legal custody of the child—not over ways to meet the real substantive, procedural, and psychological interests of each parent. Unless genuine interests are addressed, the parents will remain caught, negotiating over positions that can result only in a win-lose outcome.

In the Whittamore-Singson case, the clinic director may not realize that his interests might be best served by a solution in which the doctor would not leave the clinic until the term of the contract expired, and that such an arrangement could benefit both the clinic and the medical practitioner. Shifting from a focus on compensation for breach of contract and acknowledging the need to satisfy a range of interests—stability at the clinic, cost containment, avoidance of disruptive working relationships, prevention of patient loss, retention of a valued employee, among others—may open new opportunities for problem solving.

Intentional Hiding of Interests

A second reason that interests are difficult to identify is that negotiators often intentionally obscure them. This strategy is often executed by parties with the expectation that it will result in increased gains or better outcomes in negotiations. Parties often see interests, and the degree to which they are met, in terms of positions along a continuum of options. Particular outcomes are more satisfactory or meet more needs than others. Therefore, each party obscures his or her real interests on the continuum of possible settlement options as a means of leveraging the greatest number of concessions from an opponent. Neither party wants to publicly present his or her real interests, or the particular point on the bargaining continuum at which he or she is willing to settle, for fear that they might receive less than they might if their real needs remain unknown.

In the Whittamore-Singson case, Whittamore may be reluctant to disclose how important his interest in staying in town and being near his children really is. He may fear that an untimely revelation of his true interests may reduce his leverage, which is based on Singson's fear that he might leave the area and eliminate the clinic's claim to any compensation. Revealing his interests might give Singson undue power to force a high level of compensation.

Equation of Interests with Positions

A third reason that interests are difficult to identify is that in heated conflict, parties may begin to gradually equate the satisfaction of an interest with a particular position. Separation of the interest from the position becomes difficult. This phenomenon poses a serious challenge to negotiators who are attempting to back off hard-line positions and seek mutually acceptable solutions.

In the Whittamore-Singson case, the clinic director may see financial compensation for violation of the contract as *the* way to meet interests, ignoring the possibility of identifying specific interests and developing a customized solution to satisfy each of them. Unfortunately, the former approach is commonly found in disputes such as divorces, personal injury cases, insurance claims, and so on, where interests (substantive, procedural, or psychological) are often reified into financial solutions. Although financial settlements may satisfy some interests, they rarely address the specific interests—respect, an apology, acknowledgment of harm or inconvenience, and so on—of the parties.

Lack of Awareness of Procedures for Exploring Interests

The final reason that parties often do not directly explore interests is that they are not used to thinking in terms of interests and are not aware of procedures for discovering and discussing them. This often proves to be an insurmountable obstacle in high-tension negotiations.

These four factors—lack of awareness of interests, intentional hiding of interests, equation of interests with positions, and lack of awareness of procedural approaches to interest discovery—are often significant blocks to progress in negotiations and may produce deadlock.

Procedures for Identifying Interests

Negotiators and, if necessary, mediators use two general types of procedures to identify the interests of disputing parties: indirect, low-profile procedures and direct, high-profile procedures.

Indirect procedures are used when parties take a positional bargaining approach to negotiations or try to obscure interests by adhering to rigid positions. Such procedures are also employed when parties seem unsure of their interests, and the trust level is not high enough to merit direct exploration of their needs.

Mediators use *direct procedures* to preempt (Saposnek, 1983) parties from engaging in positional bargaining or to move them toward interest-based bargaining once positional negotiations have begun. Direct procedures are used for the first purpose when parties

1. Are not locked into the process of positional bargaining
2. Are not committed to absolute positions
3. Are aware of the need to separate the identification of interests from adherence to particular positions
4. Are willing to examine their interests explicitly because the trust level is high enough for mutual exploration
5. Have delegated to the mediator the authority to design a structured interest exploration and identification procedure

If parties are already engaged in positional bargaining, direct procedures may be used to identify interests when less direct methods (such as open-ended questioning about interests) have failed; to prevent parties from hardening their adherence to positions; or to manage a large number of parties or issues that are making negotiations cumbersome.

Before exploring direct and indirect moves to identify and explore interests, it is important to note attitudes that lead to a productive exploration of interests.

Positive Attitudes Toward Interest Exploration

Regardless of whether positional or interest-based bargaining is being used, an understanding of interests on the part of negotiators can promote more productive outcomes. Identification of interests is facilitated by open attitudes toward interest exploration. These would include the beliefs that

- All parties have interests and needs that are important and valid to them
- A solution to the problem should meet the maximum number of interests of each party
- Interests can be traded to achieve the most satisfactory combination
- There is probably more than one acceptable solution to a problem
- Any conflict involves compatible interests as well as conflicting ones

Negotiators who hold such attitudes or beliefs about negotiation will be able to make the transition to a focus on interests more easily than disputants who take a narrow view of bargaining.

The critical task facing negotiators at this stage is to gain an understanding of each other's interests. The first step toward doing so is developing an awareness that interests are important. Most negotiators do not distinguish between a solution or position and the specific interest it is designed to satisfy. This linkage prevents creative problem solving.

A mediator may assist parties in overcoming this perceptual block. Before beginning actual interest exploration, mediators can work with parties to change their attitudes and awareness and to encourage acceptance of diverse interests. This can be accomplished through a variety of indirect and direct moves. Indirect moves include modeling behavior that promotes desired attitude change. To increase awareness of the importance of interests, a mediator may state, "All needs and interests of parties are important and valid to them," "We are looking for a solution that allows everyone to have as many needs met as possible," or "There is probably more than one solution that will meet the needs of all parties." Mediators may intervene at even subtler levels by modeling an attitude of expectancy and hope (Freire, 1970). The mediator's expressed attitude often encourages a more conciliatory climate.

Mediators can also confront the need for attitude change more directly. They may explicitly spell out the differences between issues, positions, interests, and settlement options. Or they may state that if a solution cannot be found that meets at least some of the interests of all parties, there will be no settlement. Usually, the more explicit the mediator is about the need for attitudinal change or increase in awareness, the greater the possibility of confrontation between intervenor and disputants. At this point, most mediators prefer low-level, indirect interventions to explicit and direct confrontation over attitudes.

Indirect Procedures for Discovering Interests

I have discussed several indirect and direct moves to induce change in negotiators' attitudes toward interest identification and exploration. I now turn to an examination of procedures for discovering interests.

Mediators may use many of the communication tools outlined in Chapters Seven, Eight, and Nine to identify interests. Particularly helpful tools are active listening, restatement, paraphrase, summarization, generalization, fractionation, and reframing. When used alone or in combination, these tools help disputants and the mediator to decode and uncover interests that are intentionally or unintentionally obscured by negotiators.

One particularly common combination of these tools is the process of *testing* (Moore, 1982b). Testing requires a negotiator or mediator to listen carefully to another negotiator's statements and then to feed back the interest that he or she hears expressed. Through trial and error, the listener can gradually gain an understanding of the other negotiator's needs.

Another method of identifying interests is *hypothetical modeling*

(Pruitt and Lewis, 1977), in which the negotiator or mediator presents a series of hypothetical settlement options or proposals to another negotiator. The questioner does not ask for commitment to, or acceptance of, any of the proposals, but merely an indication of whether the proposal is more or less satisfactory than others under consideration. Repeated proposals that contain a variety of solutions to satisfy another's interests can increase a mediator's or negotiator's understanding of needs to be met without ever having to confront interest identification directly. This approach is often used when a party is hiding interests or when there is not enough trust to explicitly reveal interests.

Direct Procedures for Discovering Interests

Fisher and Ury (1981) advocate direct *questioning* about interests. They suggest that when a disputant presents a position to another party, the recipient or the mediator should directly ask the presenting party why this position is important. Carefully worded questions that demonstrate genuine concern for understanding the other party's perception of the situation can be used to encourage revelation of important interests.

Because the intervenor has credibility as an impartial party, disputants may be more open to directly identifying and discussing their interests with him or her than with another party. The mediator plays a valuable role in this situation because he or she can help the parties explore the substance and salience of each other's interests while minimizing the risks of full disclosure to an adversary. These conversations are often held during a caucus.

Another common procedure is the *interest-oriented discussion*. The mediator in this process requests that disputants refrain from discussing issues or positions and focus instead on the general interests or elements that would make a settlement satisfactory. Through careful questioning, the mediator moves the parties from a discussion of general interests to more concrete and explicit interests.

Brainstorming is a process in which items are rapidly generated by a group. Brainstorming separates generation from evaluation, giving the group multiple options to consider. (See Chapter Eleven for instructions on how to conduct a brainstorming session.) Brainstorming can be conducted by negotiators in joint session or in caucus. The procedure is one of the most common direct moves to identify interests.

Brainstorming was used to identify the interests of parties in a complicated dispute over water supply to an urban area. The mediators carefully divided the thirty-two negotiators into groups of eight. Each group had members who represented diverse views on the questions of water supply, containing at least one water supplier, one consumer, one environmentalist, and one person from the agricultural or rural community. The groups were instructed to list without evaluation the various interests that would have to be met if an agreement were to be reached. A mediator and a recorder worked with each small group to record the interests on a wall chart that everyone could see. These lists were then presented to the entire group to educate all negotiators about the general interests that would have to be addressed.

Positions, Interests, and Bluffs

A mediator's involvement does not mean that parties will be candid about their interests. Parties may engage in bluffing activity. "A party to negotiation is engaged in bluff when he asserts or implies that he will do what he does not intend to do at the time the assertion is made" (Stevens, 1963). Bluffs may also involve a party's misrepresentation of interests to convince another disputant that only a settlement with certain criteria will meet the party's needs. In ideal negotiation situations, bluffing is not possible because all disputants have accurate knowledge of the interests, settlement options, power, and preferences for behavior of the other parties. In reality, however, these variables are not known (or not completely known), and bluffing is common. This seems to be the case especially when there is no external deadline or factors that force the parties to be candid and to come to terms with their differences.

To work, bluffs must be credible. One party must be perceived by another to have the authority, capacity, and will to carry out a threatened action in order to satisfy a particular interest. Mediators should probe and question parties in joint session, but more often in a caucus, to determine if a threat or a position is a genuine stance that represents the party's true intentions or is a bluff to mislead an opponent. If the latter is true, the mediator should assess with the bluffing party (1) the long-term effect a bluff will have on the relationship of the parties and (2) the potential cost to the negotiators of letting the bluff go unchallenged by the mediator. This last outcome can have drastic effects on negotiations if the parties reach an impasse based on a false claim.

If in the process of position and interest exploration a mediator discovers that a party has been bluffing and sending inaccurate messages about his or her interests, and this appears to be having detrimental effects on the negotiation process, the mediator may decide to help the bluffing party shift from the artificial posture toward a more accurate presentation of his or her interests. Procedures used by mediators for this purpose are persuasion and rationalization (Stevens, 1963). Persuasion and rationalization refer to activities designed to influence or control the course of actions or operations of another negotiator, alter a party's preferences, or change how a party perceives the negotiation environment. A rationalization is a logical and plausible argument for a shift in position or approach. A rationalization for a change of position may be presented to a negotiator engaged in bluffing, to other concerned parties, to observers, or to a negotiator's constituency as a means of explaining a shift in position or to stress the importance of heretofore undisclosed interests. The rationalization may be presented by the negotiator or by the mediator. Ideally, the negotiator makes the presentation, because it will increase his or her commitment to the move. However, in some disputes, the negotiator may need to save face (Brown, 1977). In such a situation, the mediator may want to present the newly identified position, interest, or move to help explain or share the responsibility for the shift.

Regulatory negotiations between certain industry groups, a public utility commission, and consumer advocates provide an example of how mediators use persuasion and rationalization to help bargainers identify genuine interests and avoid impasse. One issue facing the negotiators was how they were to pay for mediation. Industry representatives believed that participants in the negotiations should "pay to play." They took the hard-line position that if public interest groups did not contribute toward the costs of mediation, then they should not be represented. The public consumer advocates indicated that they could not afford to contribute and intimated that if they were required to pay, they would boycott the negotiations and attack the proposed settlement later when it was presented to the public utility commission for consideration.

The mediators saw that each interest group was escalating its threats (and bluffs) to push the other party to accept its position. The mediators, in reflecting on the industry group's interests, asked its representatives whether they saw payment as a party's indication of commitment to the process and assurance that the party would not sabotage or delay settlement. The industry representatives replied that they did. The mediator asked the consumers why they believed they need not pay. The consumer advocates replied that because theirs was a nonprofit group, it did not have assets to fund the process, and that in principle, advocacy groups should not have to fund alternative regulatory negotiations when they would normally have free access to the regulatory hearing process.

The mediators asked the industry group if it was reasonable or fair to insist that groups lacking funds pay to participate. They also asked the consumer groups if they could find a means other than a financial contribution to indicate that they were committed to the process and were bargaining in good faith. The consumer group representative made a public statement that she was committed to the process and asked if, in return, the industry groups would allow a nonprofit group to have a place at the table. The rationalization that made it possible to disconnect financial contributions from good-faith bargaining enabled the parties to reach agreement.

Interest Identification, Acceptance, and Agreement

Once the mediator and the negotiators have identified the interests of the parties, they will confront one or more of the following situations. Interests may be (1) *mutually exclusive* in that satisfaction of one party's needs precludes the satisfaction of another's interests; (2) *mixed* in that the parties have some compatible and some competing needs; or (3) *compatible* in that they have similar and nonexclusive needs. A particular case illustrates how the division of interests applies.

An author was working on the staff of a research organization, preparing a book that would describe state-of-the-art practice in a human relations field. He had worked for many months on the project and was pleased with the product. As the book neared completion, the organization's director issued a memorandum informing the staff that in the future, no individual authors' names would appear on publications produced by the agency. The author responded with a countermemorandum that argued in favor of having the author's name on the book, citing the precedent of other agency publications.

In this dispute, it appeared that the positions of the parties were mutually exclusive. A careful examination of the interests, however, indicated room for cooperation. Both parties had *compatible interests* in that they wanted to see the book published and distributed. Publication would financially and professionally benefit both. The parties also had *mixed interests*. The research organization was opposed to the author taking all the credit for the work. The director sought to build his agency's credibility and wanted the book to be seen as an agency product. He was not willing to give away all the credit but was willing to share it. He also wanted the staff to enjoy working for the agency. The author, meanwhile, wanted to take credit but was not willing to push the issue so far that he risked losing his job.

There was clearly a mixed set of interests that allowed for competition and cooperation, but both parties believed that incompatible or exclusive interests predominated in the dispute. The director wanted the agency's name on the cover and sought to have the work identified as a team project. The author wanted only his name on the cover. It seemed like a win-lose dispute.

The parties agreed to negotiate on the issue of identification of authorship. They acknowledged that they had a common interest in publishing and distributing the book as soon as possible. The author accepted that the agency should get credit for sponsoring the research as long as he was given credit for producing it. The director conceded that the author was the primary researcher for the book, but he wanted the team that had performed some of the preliminary work to be given credit also. The author agreed that this was fair and suggested that he include this point in an acknowledgments section at the beginning of the book. His proposal was accepted.

The process of deciding what was to go on the cover was more difficult. Both parties acknowledged that they wanted a particular name on the cover. A variety of options were explored. The final decision was that both the agency and the author would be credited on the cover. The agency's name was to be in larger type, and the author was to be identified by his agency title. The two parties agreed that their interests were satisfied by this solution.

This case study illustrates several approaches that mediators can use to work with the interests of disputing parties. First, the mediator should work with the parties to jointly identify interests. A party's willingness to identify and explore his or her interests and those of others does not necessarily mean that he or she agrees with the needs of other disputants. Creighton (1972, p. II–8) makes explicit the difference between acceptance of information (emotions, in this case) and agreement. "You express acceptance when you say: 'I understand that you feel such-and-such a way about this topic.' You express agreement when you say: 'You couldn't be more right, I feel that way too.' In the first you accept that the other person feels the way he does, but in agreement you *ally* yourself with the other person."

At this stage, the mediator should be more concerned with negotiators accepting information about interests than with obtaining agreement. Although agreement with the interests of other parties greatly facilitates a party's progress through later negotiation stages, agreement at this point is not mandatory. Parties can accept that others have interests that are different from theirs and still search for mutually acceptable solutions.

Next, the mediator should identify and make explicit compatible or complementary interests. This enables the parties to change their assumptions about the conflict's purity, builds a habit of agreement, and promotes cooperation. Finally, the mediator should focus on mixed and mutually exclusive interests. I will discuss measures to handle such interests in later chapters. Using a process of interest-based bargaining, trade-offs, and compromise, the mediator can help parties to progress and agree on even the most difficult of incompatible interests.

Framing Joint Problem Statements in Terms of Interests

During the process of discussion of parties' issues, an individual party's interest will often be revealed, identified, or defined. Mediators generally restate for each party the interests that they have heard and then proceed to the next task of problem solving: framing joint problem statements. This is another way of defining an issue, but in a manner that incorporates the individual and joint interests that the parties want addressed.

Joint problem statements include the interests of both or all parties in one comprehensive statement. For example, the mediator in the Whittamore-Singson case, after having both parties articulate their interests and restating them back, might encourage the parties to reframe those interests as a new issue in the following manner: "How could we state this problem in a way that identified both of the sets of interests that you want to satisfy?" After further discussion, the doctors might arrive at the following framing: "How can Dr. Whittamore remain in town, maintain his relationship with his children, and continue to practice medicine, while at the same time the clinic minimizes staff disruptions due to strained relations between the spouses, continues to have Whittamore provide medical services to its patients, and preserves the terms of the contract that were designed to protect the clinic from patient loss, unexpected staff recruitment costs, unpredictable employment conditions, and competition from doctors that it had helped to establish in the community?"

As can be seen from the above, joint framing includes all parties' interests and often enables negotiators to commit to work on a common problem because they believe that their needs will be respected, if not met by, the solutions that will be developed. Once agreement is reached on the joint problem statement, the parties can proceed to explore the issue and interests in more detail; look for objective standards, criteria, or principles that could provide a framework for a solution; generate specific settlement options; or construct a package agreement. More will be said about these activities in subsequent chapters.

Chapter Eleven

Generating Options for Settlement

So far, the parties have defined the parameters of their dispute, clarified issues, developed an agenda, and through joint education and questioning, identified common and conflicting interests. Now, the central task of negotiators and mediators is to develop mutually acceptable settlement solutions.

Mediators and parties are required to generate settlement options either because the positions put forth in opening statements are unacceptable to one or more parties or because the parties have focused only on identifying issues and interests and have not yet explored any concrete settlement possibilities.

To develop options, the parties must be aware of the need for a range of alternatives from which to choose, they must be flexible enough in their stated positions to be able to disengage themselves from unacceptable proposals if necessary, and they must be aware of option generation procedures. In this chapter, I will discuss

1. The development of an awareness of the need for options
2. Detachment of parties from unacceptable positions
3. Strategies of option generation
4. Procedures for developing options
5. Types of settlement options

Development of an Awareness of the Need for Options

Awareness of the need for multiple settlement options is not an inherent characteristic of negotiators engaged in intense disputes.

Disputants often enter negotiations with a preconceived belief that they have already discovered the best solution for all concerned, and all that remains is to persuade—or if necessary, coerce—the other party into agreement or submission. For another negotiator or the mediator even to suggest that alternative solutions are available or desirable may be abhorrent to a negotiator committed to a particular solution. Only after persuasion and pressure fail to convince other parties of the merits of the position being advocated will an entrenched negotiator consider other options.

Negotiators and mediators begin their search for settlement options with the development of an awareness that multiple choices are needed from which to select the ultimate solution. The mediator may elicit this awareness, or it may develop through the process of the negotiators' interactions. In the latter case, awareness of the need for alternatives may result from a strong negative response to an opening statement or position.

Opening statements are often an expression of a party's maximal position and frequently do not take others' needs and interests into consideration. They are designed to educate parties about how strongly the disputant feels about an issue or to express how far the party wants an opponent to yield. For these reasons, opening statements and the positions expressed therein are rarely accepted by other disputants as final representations of ways to satisfy genuine interests. It is generally both understood and expected that parties will adhere to the practice of making a large initial demand (or conversely, a low initial offer). Once a proposal is rejected, one or more parties usually propose another solution or state a counterposition.

Occasionally, however, the party who put forward a proposal or position does not recognize its categorical rejection and doggedly adheres to it. The party ignores the need for alternative proposals, assuming that if the right persuasive technique is used or the proper influence exerted, the other party will concede. Such a posture often results in a deadlock.

At this point, other negotiators or the mediator must convince the intransigent negotiator that his or her belief that the other parties will eventually accept the current position is inaccurate, and that there is a need for alternatives.

Detachment of Parties from Unacceptable Positions

Parties commit themselves to a position for a variety of reasons:

- It meets intangible psychological needs.
- They feel it is the best solution.
- They believe other parties do not know what is best for them.
- They believe they can weaken resistance if they continue to argue their position.
- They believe they have the power or influence to force their solution on the other parties.

Negotiators and mediators faced with an intransigent party need to assess why that party adheres so strongly to his or her position. They must then determine how they might encourage the party to explore other options. Negotiators and mediators use a variety of strategies to persuade a party to reverse commitment to a stated position.

Psychological Means of Reducing Commitment

Most psychological approaches to reducing *positional* commitment begin with identification of the psychological needs of a recalcitrant party through active listening, restatement, and summarization. Either a disputant or the mediator can verbally identify the psychological needs of the party.

The second step is to gain a commitment from all parties to explore settlement options that will meet those needs. This does not imply agreement that the need will be satisfied in the way demanded; the parties are simply expressing a willingness to examine other solutions that will meet the need. If a disputant can be convinced that his or her need has been heard and will at least be considered in alternative solutions, he or she will often agree to suspend for the moment advocacy of an intransigent position.

It is often the mediator's task to persuade other parties to consider the needs of a recalcitrant negotiator. Parties may be very reluctant to respect and consider a psychological need that they believe to be irrationally founded. Mediators may have to assist parties in assessing the cost of failure to consider another's need, in determining if the parties actually have a choice, and in deciding what the risks of impasse will be.

Procedural Means of Reducing Commitment

Procedural methods for reducing commitment are steps that increase the likelihood of finding a solution that meets needs and satisfies interests. Parties often adhere to positions because they see no other ways to develop new ones. Introducing a logical or acceptable problem-solving process may allow a disputant to abandon a position. The party may do so because he or she likes the proposed process and considers it fair. I will examine procedural means of reducing commitment later in this chapter.

Leverage to Reduce Commitment

Parties do not always respond to psychological moves or procedural proposals to satisfy needs. Negotiators may have to resort to leverage or means of influence to shift an intransigent party from a hard-line position. There are four ways to reduce commitment to an unacceptable position:

1. One negotiator can convince another that the latter has overestimated the cost to the first party of maintaining a position. For example, an employee might say to a former employer: "I know that you think the cost of going to court will deter me from filing this wrongful termination suit. Well, it won't. In fact, I've asked my brother who is a lawyer to represent me and he said he would do it for free. It won't cost me anything but time to fight this, and I've got a lot of that these days!"

2. One negotiator can convince another that the latter has underestimated the costs involved in maintaining a position. Thus, the representative of a public interest group might say to a developer: "Look, if you won't put up a larger performance bond that will assure us that the mined land will be reclaimed as you promised, we will oppose your permit. We are prepared to go to court if necessary, and will even use direct action. Are you prepared for a delay of several years while we fight this out in the legal system? If time is money to you, it will cost you a lot more if you don't settle soon."

3. One negotiator can convince another that the former's position or interests are more important than the latter had initially realized. For example, the seller of a home might say to a prospective buyer: "I realize that when you look at this home, what you see is a nice Victorian house. To me, it's much more than that. It's my

family legacy. It was built by my grandfather and willed to me. That is why I'm unwilling to change the terms of the sale."

4.   One negotiator can convince another that the latter's interest or position is not as important as he or she originally believed, and that his or her needs can be met satisfactorily in another way. For example, a wife might say to her husband in child custody negotiations: "You say you want legal custody of Jamie so that you can be involved in decisions about his religious upbringing. What happens if I agree that the religious arena of his life is for you to decide? Isn't the religious training issue more important to you than legal custody?"

The mediator can aid parties in exerting any of these means of leverage. In addition, he or she may use other motivational tactics that will be discussed in detail in Chapter Fifteen.

Strategies for Option Generation

Once parties are aware of the need for a range of settlement options from which to choose, they must select a specific issue to discuss and a strategy for the generation of possible solutions.

The focus of the option generation procedure depends on the way the issue is defined, the type of solution desired, and the way option generation fits into the overall strategy of reaching an agreement. Settlement options can be generated with respect to a specific issue that is merely a component of a larger issue, or in relation to a general principle. These two basic strategies are similar to the building-block approach and the agreement in principle or formula approach to agenda formation discussed in Chapter Nine (Fisher and Ury, 1981; Zartman and Berman, 1982). The approaches can be used in combination within any given negotiation session or on a particular issue. I will discuss these two overall strategies and then proceed to explore specific activities mediators and negotiators use to develop settlement options.

Building-Block Approach to Settlement

The *building-block approach* requires disputants to divide an issue into subissues or component parts. Fisher (1964) refers to this procedure as *fractionation*. Usually, these smaller components are more manageable tasks for problem solving. Each of the subissues is resolved in turn and its solution combined with those of previous issues. This approach allows the parties to build an elaborate and complete settlement. They may accept as final their agreement on each subissue or may delay final settlement until a comprehensive agreement can be reached on all the issues in dispute.

Issues are divided into smaller components because (1) disputants may see and understand smaller issues more easily than those that are complex and many-faceted; (2) dividing issues into components prevents moves to join or link unrelated subjects, which may block agreement; and (3) dividing issues into components may depoliticize or isolate issues that prevent settlement.

There are two ways to divide issues into smaller components. The first is for the mediator to suggest that the definition of what is being discussed be narrowed. The second is for the mediator or a negotiator to ask parties to look at an issue and split it into component subissues. Obtaining the involvement of the parties in subissue definition can create greater commitment to the process.

Fractionation and the building-block approach are illustrated in a negotiation over how privacy could be maintained for single-family homeowners if condominiums were built close to their residences. The mediators and the parties divided the problem of privacy into several subissues: visual privacy, auditory privacy, and congestion. To achieve visual privacy, the parties generated solutions that (1) reduced building height so that second-floor dwellers in the condominiums could not see into the backyards or windows of the single-family homes; (2) provided for berms and fences to shield single-family homes from the sight of the condominiums; (3) graduated building heights so that condominiums closest to single-family homes were one story in height and those further away were two and three stories high; and (4) shielded lights in the condominium parking lot to prevent them from shining into the windows of the single-family homes. Similar solutions were generated to handle auditory and congestion problems. By dividing the issue into smaller pieces and solving the component parts, the parties were ultimately able to forge a comprehensive settlement.

Agreement in Principle Approach to Settlement

The second major strategy for defining options and progressing toward a settlement is the *agreement in principle* or *formula* approach. This procedure requires negotiators to create or identify a bargaining formula or set of general principles that will guide the shape of the final settlement. This approach is the polar opposite of the building-block approach in that it requires negotiators to reach a general level of agreement and then initiate steps to define the specifics. The approach is often appropriate when underlying values of the disputants are similar or when superordinate goals can be identified.

The agreement in principle or formula approach to settlement is often not as familiar to disputants as the building-block approach. The mediator may have to be more directive in educating the parties about the procedure. He or she may directly reframe the central issue in broader terms and then encourage the parties to generate general principles of agreement or may explain the philosophy behind the strategic approach and turn the implementation over to the negotiators.

An example of the agreement in principle approach is provided by the Metropolitan Water Roundtable negotiations in Denver, Colorado, between water suppliers, environmentalists, ranchers, and recreation interests. The parties were initially stalled over whether additional water was needed in the Denver area and over a proposal to construct a dam at a particular site.

After an intensive educational process, all the parties agreed that the water was needed, that some of it could be obtained through conservation, and that a dam was probably required somewhere on the eastern side of the Rocky Mountains. After agreeing on these three principles, the parties began to investigate how the water needs could be met through a variety of sources (conservation, groundwater, transbasin exchanges), where a dam might be sited, and how large it should be. By reaching a series of agreements in principle on several different levels, the parties were able to progress toward agreement.

General Procedures for Generating Options

Once parties have decided on the level of settlement option—general or specific—that is desired, mediators or negotiators need to devise a procedure to generate the options. There are two general approaches: (1) bargaining based on positions and counterpositions and (2) a collaborative search for options, that is, interest-based bargaining.

Positional Bargaining

In positional bargaining, the parties assume that the way to present settlement options is to exchange proposals and counterproposals. If there are two parties to the dispute, the normal dynamic is for them to alternately offer proposals and counterproposals so that no more than two proposals to resolve a given issue are considered at any given time. Ideally, each proposal brings the parties closer to a settlement or settlement range because of increased satisfaction of interests for both sides (Stevens, 1963). The settlement range refers to a number of possible solutions, any one of which is regarded by both parties as preferable to a stalemate.

There are several limiting characteristics to positional bargaining. First, only two proposals or positions are generally examined at one time. This two-sided view tends to limit the number of options explored by the parties and inhibits the development of solutions to meet specific needs.

Second, the two-sided view discourages the integration of ideas and encourages negotiators to view proposals as total packages requiring yes or no responses. Parties fail to realize that proposals can be combined or recombined to create new options.

Third, two-sided negotiations, with only two possible proposals, tend to produce win-lose or "right" and "wrong" attitudes toward concessions or counterproposals; a win for one party is viewed as a loss by the other. Parties conducting positional bargaining often commit themselves psychologically to their proposal and view acceptance of another's position as an abandonment of principles.

Fourth, positional bargaining encourages evaluation of the proposals at the same time that the options are generated. Simultaneous generation and evaluation of only two options tend to lock the parties into mutually exclusive positions and militate against the thoughtful consideration of new ideas.

Because the proposal-counterproposal procedure places limits on the negotiating process, negotiators may wish to shift to an interest-based bargaining strategy. Such a shift, though more difficult to accomplish in negotiations in which parties have already used positional bargaining, is nevertheless not impossible. The transition from positional bargaining to interest-based bargaining can be greatly facilitated by the presence and intervention of a mediator.

Interest-Based Bargaining

Interest-based negotiation, a procedure that promotes integrative bargaining in which the interests of all parties are combined and addressed in jointly developed solutions, is often superior to positional bargaining in generating settlement options. Interest-based bargaining works most effectively under certain specific conditions: (1) the resource or interests over which the parties are negotiating must be divisible or negotiable in such a way that a gain for one party does not necessarily mean a loss for another; (2) there must be enough trust and spirit of cooperation to enable the parties to develop a joint solution; (3) one party must not have, exhibit, or be willing to exercise overwhelming power or influence to force a decision in his or her favor; and (4) the parties must be aware of a procedure to develop options that all perceive as equitable and fair. I will examine each of these points in turn.

Many negotiators, when entering a dispute, assume that the parties have entirely conflicting interests and that the outcome will yield more benefits to one party than to another. They are prepared to play a win-lose game.

Most conflicts, however, are not pure; the relationship of the parties is not purely conflictual, and all interests are not mutually exclusive. This mixed characteristic applies even to such apparently finite commodities as money. Some negotiators assume that money is finite and that an increase for one side inevitably means a loss for another. The assumption means that a compromise in which each party receives some but not all of what he or she desires is the only possible option. This type of dispute is often referred to as a *half-a-loaf dispute* (Warren, 1978). However, people may have multiple interests in financial disputes besides a particular sum of money. Monetary disputes can be subdivided into issues of the timing, rate, and form of payment so that a win-win outcome that satisfies many interests is possible.

Seemingly pure conflicts can in many cases be transformed into disputes in which all parties can win more than if they had merely divided available resources in some sort of compromise. Negotiators can accomplish this shift themselves, but often they are locked into the perception of a pure conflict. At this point, the mediator can intervene and reframe the issue so that the parties see it in a new way.

Mediators use several techniques to produce win-win options. One important technique is *expansion of the resource* (Pruitt and Lewis, 1977). Union-management negotiations, for example, have a history of deadlock when the parties negotiate solely on the wage increase issue. However, by adding issues such as cost-of-living benefits, insurance options, goodwill, working conditions, or increased productivity, the mediator may change a win-lose negotiation into a situation in which a mutually satisfactory outcome is a possibility.

Mediators also assist parties in *logrolling* (Pruitt and Lewis, 1977)—trading items that are valued differently by the parties. Logrolling allows each party to offer components that are valued less than those offered by the other party. The difference in items to be exchanged and their desirability to the recipients makes agreement possible. Logrolling was utilized in a case in which an employer hired a consultant and had not been explicit about the terms for contract termination. The consultant, who was working in good faith, put in more time than the employer wished to pay for. The consultant felt that the employer owed additional pay, but the employer refused because she was not satisfied with the work. The consultant then hired a collection agency, which contacted the employer and demanded payment.

By this time, the parties had developed an extremely antagonistic relationship and could not talk to one another. Not wanting to deal with the collection agency, the employer contacted a mediator. The employer realized that she would probably have to pay something to settle the dispute, but she did not want to pay the consultant for unsatisfactory work. The mediator discovered that the consultant was more concerned with the principle that the employer should pay her debts than with receiving the small sum due to him.

The mediator, operating on the principle that honoring the debt was the important issue, asked the consultant whether having the employer pay the disputed amount to another party, such as a charity, might meet his needs. The consultant agreed. The mediator then discussed this solution with the employer, who was willing to pay as long as she could choose the charity. The parties ultimately agreed on this solution. By logrolling, trading components of differing importance to the negotiators, the mediator was able to assist the parties in meeting each other's strongest interest without compromising on principles.

A further technique is *alternation*. When there is no way to expand resources, the parties may alternate between the options each of them favors. In an alternating scheme, neither side forsakes his or her *preferred option*, but each is allowed to enjoy it at a different time. For example, to settle a domestic conflict over where to vacation, a couple might go to the mountains this year and to the seashore next year, thus meeting the husband's interest in mountain climbing and the wife's interest in beachcombing. Alternating schemes will be more integrative than simple compromise when the resource that is sought cannot be divided into parts without excessive loss of value to the negotiators.

The final procedure for interest-based bargaining is *designing new and specifically integrative interest-based solutions*. Such solutions meet the needs of each party, but not at the expense of another's needs. The classic illustration of this type of solution, related by many mediators, is the conflict between two children who are fighting over the last orange left in the fruit bowl. Each child adamantly demands that he or she get the orange. The wise mother intervenes and offers to help the children decide who should get it. At first examination, it appears that each child has equal claim to the orange. What should the mother do? She could halve the orange and give each child a piece. She could even alternate who slices and who chooses which piece goes to whom to increase the children's perception of procedural fairness. However, the mother is dissatisfied with these solutions and pursues the exploration of each child's interests in more depth. After several minutes of discussion, she discovers that one child wants to eat the fruit and the other wants the rind to prepare a cake icing. She helps the children agree to split the orange and satisfy all of their needs.

Mediation, through careful data collection and option generation, can often help parties build solutions of this type. It challenges disputants to overcome apparent barriers to settlement that would require them to settle for less than they could attain if they produced a truly integrative solution.

Trust has already been discussed in great detail in Chapter Seven. Interest-based bargaining requires the development of at least a minimal level of trust. To accomplish this end, mediators should utilize techniques described in the earlier chapter.

Parties must have some means of influencing each other if they are even to begin formal negotiations. The threat or exercise of power may, however, inhibit interest-based bargaining.

The mediator can reduce or prevent the effects of threats or exercises of power by (1) ignoring them and persuading the other parties to do the same; (2) minimizing them by translating the threat into nondetrimental terms; (3) educating the parties about the cost of making perceived or actual threats; or (4) in extreme cases, helping another party to realize and exercise its power to counter the threat or display. This last strategy tends to maintain polarization and competition rather than promote cooperation. I will discuss contingent moves mediators can initiate to respond to power problems in Chapter Fifteen.

Parties often remain locked in positional bargaining merely because they are not aware of alternative means of negotiating. Mediators can assist people in shifting from positional to interest-based bargaining by suggesting means to accomplish cooperative option generation.

A mediator's procedural suggestions for achieving this transition may have several advantages over moves initiated by the disputants themselves. First, research shows that suggestions by an impartial third party may be more readily trusted and accepted by disputants than those suggested by a party with substantive concerns in the conflict's outcome (Rubin and Brown, 1975).

Second, the mediator's suggestions may, because of his or her professional stature and experience, be accorded more credibility. The parties may be more willing to try a procedure because they believe the mediator would not make a poor suggestion (Rubin and Brown, 1975; Brookmire and Sistrunk, 1980).

Third, the mediator can take some responsibility for the success or failure of a negotiation procedure (Stevens, 1963). Parties are often reluctant to initiate new methods because they might have to bear the ill will of other parties or their constituents if the procedure does not work. The mediator, by sharing the responsibility, takes the burden on himself or herself and removes the party from the risk of blame.

Finally, a mediator may be of assistance because he or she expends the time and energy to identify the appropriate procedure. Often, parties could develop a process that would suit their needs if given the necessary time and resources, but these are not always available. Mediators can accelerate the transition and avoid the accumulation of additional negative experiences that may result from a struggle over procedure by providing a viable process for option generation.

Specific Option Generation Procedures

Parties in mediation using an interest-based approach to bargaining have used numerous processes to generate settlement options. These procedures have several characteristics in common. First, they attempt to generate several options so that the parties can move from a bipolar view of solutions to a multipolar view (Maier and Hoffman, 1960). Second, they attempt to separate the stage of generating options from the later evaluation or assessment stage. This separation ensures that the search process will be more comprehensive and complete and not inhibited by premature judgments. Third, they focus the effort of the negotiators on the issue or problem and not on the other party. The dispute is depersonalized so that the parties aim their attacks not at the people in the negotiations but at the issues that divide them (Chandler, 1945; Fisher and Ury, 1981; Walton and McKersie, 1965; Filley, 1975). I will now discuss twelve common procedures mediators or negotiators can use to generate settlement options.

Ratification of the Status Quo

This procedure is one of the simplest and easiest ways to begin to develop options and reach an early agreement on selected issues. It is commonly used by parties who have a past or current relationship in which they have established patterns of interaction or developed solutions to problems that they would like to formalize and keep in a future relationship. To initiate this option, the mediator asks the parties to identify what agreements they have reached previously or what is working in the relationship that they want to continue and include in their final agreement. Often the parties will name a number of things, and the mediator will then work with them to develop acceptable wording that can be incorporated into a new settlement agreement.

Development of Objective Standards for an Acceptable Agreement

Though it does not result in a specific option or options, the development of standards for an agreement establishes the parameters for later option generation. To initiate this process, the parties or mediator propose to identify criteria or objective standards that could be used to shape a final agreement. These criteria should be ones that would be widely seen to be fair, that are based on historical precedent or tradition, or that are commonly used to establish value. Once a list is generated and discussed, the mediator helps the parties to reach a consensus on the criteria to be adopted. This procedure was used to help resolve a dispute over thermal impacts on fish of solar-heated water released from a hydropower dam. The parties, state and federal agencies and the private power producer, identified a number of criteria that they would use to shape the final agreement. The criteria included absence of significant impact on other agreements reached regarding the operation of the dam, maximization of the number of recreational fishing days downstream, calculation of the impact on fish in specific sections of the stream, and compensation of the state for fish lost because of temperature increases specifically attributable to the dam.

Open Discussion

Open discussion is still one of the best means of developing options. However, for free and creative discussions to occur, parties need to feel that they can share ideas without prematurely committing themselves to them. Mediators can assist in this regard by setting ground rules that allow parties to propose and explore ideas without any expectation of commitment. The mediator may also facilitate discussions to keep the parties on track, focus them on specific topics, summarize the conversation, and test for and identify areas of consensus.

Brainstorming

Brainstorming is a procedure in which a group of people generate a variety of ideas or options for consideration. The mediator or a negotiator begins the process by framing an issue as a "problem." A problem is often stated as a *how* question. How can enough resources be found to send a wife to school so that she can be self-supporting? How can an outstanding bill be paid by a company with limited assets? How can a popular recreation area be maintained while still allowing companies to explore for minerals?

The parties are then instructed to speak one at a time and suggest as rapidly as possible a number of solutions that might meet the needs of the parties. The mediator should instruct them to avoid stating purely self-serving options and should caution them against making verbal or nonverbal judgments of practicality or acceptability during the session. He or she should inform them that assessment and evaluation of the options will be initiated after they have generated a substantial number of solutions and should encourage them to build and modify each other's ideas as long as the results move them toward an option that might meet more of their interests. The mediator should record suggestions on a pad or wall chart, taking care to record accurately and keep the session going. When the parties have generated a satisfactory number of options or have exhausted their ideas, they may shift to an assessment procedure.

Brainstorming can be done (1) by all disputants together, (2) by individuals or teams from a particular party, (3) by subgroups within a team, or (4) by subgroups composed of delegates or representatives of each of the parties. Brainstorming as individuals, teams, or team subgroups may be used when disputants do not trust other parties and are uncomfortable disclosing options publicly but want to expand their range of settlement possibilities. The mediator may randomly assign members of opposing parties to subgroups when he or she or a negotiator wants to maximize participation and increase personal contact between disputants by using small groups. Brainstorming in a subgroup with specifically assigned membership may be used to group or more evenly distribute moderates from opposing negotiating teams. Moderate team members are more likely than hard-line negotiators to come up with integrative solutions that will meet the needs of all parties.

Nominal Group Process

Building on the basic concept of small-group process that individuals invent and groups evaluate, the nominal group process seeks to maximize individual creativity to help a group solve a problem (Delbecq, Vandeven, and Gustafson, 1975). In this process, the issue is stated as a "how" problem, and individuals make their own lists, within a specific time limit, of all the possible solutions they can imagine. They then form small subgroups of about five members each, where ideas are shared one at a time and recorded. These ideas are then elaborated on, discussed, and assessed for merit in the small groups. Potential mutually acceptable options are then brought to the larger group for discussion and consideration.

Plausible Hypothetical Scenarios

Parties may occasionally be encouraged to generate settlement options by engaging in hypothetical scenario development. The mediator states the issue as a "how" problem and then charges individuals or small groups to develop hypothetical scenarios, in narrative form, in which the problem is overcome. Scenarios should describe how procedural, substantive, and psychological interests would be met. This approach, when used in small groups composed of disputants from all parties, often produces greater commitment to cooperative solutions. Once the scenarios are developed, the groups may present each one until the negotiators have heard all the possibilities. The parties then assess whole scenarios and individual components for their relevance as solutions to the dispute.

Model Agreements

This procedure seeks out agreements made in other disputes, where the parties were in a similar predicament to that faced by the current disputants. Those agreements are then explored and modified to meet the needs of the present situation. The procedure is often employed in business disputes in which past contract language can be used as a basis for the development of a customized agreement in the new, different situation.

Linked Trades

The linked trades procedure involves the identification of potential linkages of issues and the trading of specific items that each party values differently. The mediator asks the parties to identify interests that they would trade for specific desired benefits. By generating such possible trades, the mediator and the parties may be able to develop potential deals that can then be modified to better meet each party's interests.

Single Text Negotiating Document

Plausible hypothetical scenarios can often be developed into a single text negotiating document (Fisher and Ury, 1981). Either a party or the mediator may initiate this procedure. The first step is to identify the interests of all parties. The initiator then develops a text or proposal that might satisfy the majority of the interests and resolve the dispute. This document becomes a draft settlement text that is circulated among the parties for comments and revision. Each party should have an opportunity to modify the text to better meet his or her needs. Gradual revision often results in a single text that is acceptable to all disputants.

President Carter used this procedure in 1978 to negotiate the Camp David accords between Israel and Egypt. A similar procedure was used in the Law of the Seas negotiations. The single-text approach is helpful for two-party disputes and almost a necessity for a multiparty dispute.

Procedural Solutions to Reach Substantive Agreements

Options may be generated through procedural solutions when parties perceive different probabilities or risks attached to the outcome of a dispute and/or when the future is unknowable. The parties work to develop a fair procedure that can be used either at the present time or in the future to arrive at a substantive answer. For example, neighbors who oppose the opening of a mine because they fear it will lower their property values or adversely affect the environment may be able to support the development if the mine operator puts up a large enough performance bond to compensate them for any potential losses. Naturally, this process would have to specify the time when the evaluation would be made, how the baseline data for property values would be established, how differences in projected and actual values would be determined, and how funds would be allocated.

Package Agreements

The solution of a dispute sometimes lies in the construction of a total comprehensive agreement that addresses all parties' key issues and interests. This procedure is generally used only when parties have exchanged enough information to develop mutually acceptable packages. Packages generally strive to balance gains and losses for all parties so that the settlement in its totality is jointly accept-able. Packages can be constructed in joint session, in caucuses, or in smaller, mixed-interest groups. The procedure was applied in 1993–94, in U.S. Environmental Protection Agency regulatory negotiations on the control of emissions from the manufacturing of wood furniture. The parties first compiled a list of all their inter-ests. They then developed a matrix showing how well various options met those interests. Finally, the parties negotiated a per-mutation of these options that was acceptable to all.

Use of Outside Experts or Resources

Parties are often frustrated by a myopic view of the conflict when attempting to generate viable options. This condition may result from their proximity to, or lack of objectivity toward, issues in dis-pute. Disputants may also be limited by their own experiences or may possess inadequate data. The use of outside resources, initiated by either the parties or the mediator, may be of great assistance to the negotiations. Often the mediator, because of his or her per-ceived neutrality, can increase the acceptability of such a move.

Outside resources may take the form of written material or experts in the topic under discussion. For example, in child cus-tody disputes, mediators may want the couple to read *Mom's House, Dad's House* (Ricci, 1980) or *Joint Custody and Co-Parenting* (Galper, 1980) so that they may obtain ideas outside of mediation on how to establish a new parenting relationship. For companies trying to negotiate the structure of a new employee-management grievance procedure, representatives may want to consult books on organi-zational dispute resolution (Bazerman and Lewicki, 1983; Blake and Mouton, 1984).

Outside resource persons may be substantive or procedural experts on the issue. Among those who may have data to con-tribute are lawyers, assessors, or accountants; parties who have had similar conflicts and have resolved them, such as government offi-cials, managers, or parents; and individuals from other disciplines or backgrounds.

Forums for Option Generation

Options are generally developed in joint session, in caucuses, or in subgroups composed of representatives of the major parties.

Joint sessions are generally used when the whole group is some-what comfortable working together, when the knowledge or exper-tise of many people is needed to develop multiple options, or when the parties are uncomfortable delegating option generation to a smaller or mixed-interest group.

Caucuses are used when parties are not comfortable exploring options in front of each other; when suggesting options with a con-tending party present may be perceived as risking a premature commitment; when a party needs privacy to figure out what options he or she wants to explore in joint session; or when mutual option generation may reveal information that a party wants to remain confidential.

People in conflict are often hindered from generating op-tions because groups are too large to be conducive to problem solving, high-level interaction, or candor. This may be especially true for multiparty public disputes. Small, informal discussion groups are often helpful for option generation. In disputes with multiple parties, the entire group may delegate subissues or prob-lems to small working groups or committees, charging them to propose an integrative solution that can be referred back to the main group for final decision. Generally, these subgroups are composed of representatives of the major interest groups. This approach was used by provincial labor negotiators in Saskatch-ewan, Canada, as a means of developing options in collective bar-gaining negotiations. Subgroups composed of key negotiators from each side and some of each party's constituents developed some very creative options that were later accepted by both labor and management.

Types of Settlement Options

Settlement options must satisfy the substantive, procedural, and psychological interests of the parties if they are to be considered as acceptable solutions to the conflict. The degree to which inter-ests are met determines how strong the agreement will be. Nego-tiators and mediators formulate settlement options by varying a number of factors. The goal is to create a package that meets the needs of all parties at an acceptable level.

Fisher (1978) identified some of the variables that determine how strong an agreement will be:

Stronger Agreements Are:	*Weaker Agreements Are:*
Substantive. They define specific tangible exchanges (money, services, labor, and so on) that will result from negotiations.	*Procedural.* They define the way or process by which a decision is to be made.
Comprehensive. They include a resolution of all issues in dispute.	*Partial.* They do not include a resolution of all issues in dispute.
Permanent. They resolve for all time the issues in dispute.	*Provisional.* They may be temporary or trial decisions that may be subject to change in the future.
Final. They include all the details in their final form.	*In-principle.* They include general agreements, but the details remain to be worked out.
Nonconditional. They provide for the termination of the dispute without the requirement of future conditional performance.	*Contingent.* They state that the conclusion of the dispute is contingent on additional information or future performance by one or more parties.
Binding. They are formal contracts that bind the parties to certain actions. (Often, people agree to be bound and to adhere to the terms of a settlement if they can identify consequences of nonperformance.)	*Nonbinding.* They make recommendations or requests only; the parties are not legally obliged to comply.

Mediators generally want to help the parties to reach the strongest agreement possible, but it may not always be feasible to develop a settlement with all the characteristics listed in the left-hand column. For example, a mediator may not be able to obtain a substantive agreement on the value of a piece of property but may be able to establish a procedure for assessing the land's value that all parties will accept. The mediator in another case may not be able to obtain a permanent decision about where a child will live after his parents divorce, but may be able to reach settlement on a trial solution that will be periodically evaluated and changed if necessary.

A procedural solution that partially settles issues, that is provisional, that is contingent on future performance, that elaborates general principles, and that is nonbinding may be the strongest agreement possible and is preferable to no solution at all. The mediator, by experimenting with the form of settlement options, can assist the parties in negotiating the strongest agreement possible, while tailoring it to their specific needs and interests.

Option Generation in the Whittamore-Singson Case

In the Whittamore-Singson mediation that we have been following in previous chapters, the disputing doctors worked in earlier stages of the process to gain a common understanding of the issues, explore their interests, and agree on a joint problem statement. But after further discussion, the mediator discovered that Singson was not totally confident that a solution could be found in which Whittamore stayed in town and continued to practice medicine and the clinic's interests would be satisfied. The mediator acknowledged this concern and suggested that they explore the development of three possible settlement frameworks: (1) Whittamore stays in town, practicing medicine and maintaining a connection with the clinic that would not violate the terms of the contract; (2) Whittamore stays in town, opening his own practice and compensating the clinic for ending his employment prior to the contracted date; and (3) Whittamore moves out of town (beyond the minimum distance specified in the contract), practicing medicine and maintaining contact with his children. All parties agreed to this approach.

In addressing the first framework, the mediator asked the parties to generate some options that would address the issue of limiting the Whittamores' contact with each other and yet allowing Andrew to continue to practice with clinic staff. The processes that they used to develop options included brainstorming and, later, discussion to refine the possible solutions that had been proposed.

To address the second framework, the mediator asked the parties to identify some of the elements that would need to be taken into consideration when calculating the amount of compensation to be paid to the clinic. Through listing, discussion, and the use of the building-block approach, the following factors were identified:

Potential patient loss

Costs of recruiting a new doctor

Coverage of medical services between the time that Whittamore left the clinic and the time that a new doctor's services could be procured

Adverse precedent costs to the clinic if other doctors would follow Whittamore's example and leave the clinic before their contract was fulfilled

Costs of setting up a new practice

Timing of compensation payments

Both doctors agreed that these components needed to be discussed further and proceeded to talk about each one in detail. On the issue of recruitment, they agreed that advertising costs, several recruitment trips (air fare and per diem payments), and site visits by at least two prospective candidates would have to be paid for. The doctors reached a deadlock on the amount of advertising costs to be included in the financial settlement and agreed to have a mutually respected staff member at the clinic compile some realistic figures. They also disagreed over how many site visits would be necessary. After caucuses with the mediator, they finally agreed that there could be up to three, but if there were fewer, that the costs would be prorated. They then developed some numbers to cover each of these costs.

Regarding the costs of potential patient loss, the disputants agreed to explore two potential procedural solutions. The first would have Whittamore continue to serve the clinic's patients in his new practice but pay the clinic a percentage of fees collected from those clinic patients until the end of the contract period. This would compensate the group practice for patient recruitment costs and for helping to establish the doctor's new practice. The second option was a flat fee based on data and a formula from other medical clinics that had lost patients to doctors who left the group practice.

After addressing each of the issues listed earlier and developing cost figures, Singson and Whittamore put together a total financial package that they continued to discuss and fine-tune.

With the first two frameworks discussed, there was little interest in pursuing the third—Whittamore leaving the area altogether. The doctors agreed to take a break in negotiations so that they could consider and evaluate the options and to meet again the following week, when they would try to reach a conclusion.

Cultural Variations in Option Generation

Option generation is one of the stages of the mediation process that is most strongly influenced by culture. Professional culture (legal, business, education), organizational culture (corporate, governmental agency, nongovernmental organization), or ethnic, regional, national, or class culture often influences parties' preferences and comfort in using different methods, as well as their skills in doing so.

In the past, American legal culture has been strongly oriented toward positional bargaining as a procedure for developing options. International studies have identified national preferences for particular approaches in specific settings. Negotiators from the People's Republic of China, for example, often seem to prefer positional bargaining for the resolution of both political and economic disputes (Pye, 1982; Seligman, 1989). The Japanese in commercial situations frequently prefer informal discussions away from joint session as means of developing settlement options, with formal meetings being used to ratify agreements reached in earlier dialogues (Graham and Sano, 1984). And North American businesspeople often like brainstorming or highly linear and systematic approaches.

Mediators working across cultures should take time to explore with the parties their familiarity with and preferences for various option generation procedures and then develop approaches that will be culturally acceptable. In some cases, a different approach will have to be used with each party in caucus to accommodate cultural diversity.

Reaching a Settlement

Part Four

Reaching a Settlement

Chapter Twelve

Assessing Options for Settlement

The stage of assessing options is procedurally similar to the pre-negotiation stage of searching for a dispute resolution approach and arena, which was discussed in Chapter Four.

Parties are engaged in

1. Reviewing their interests
2. Assessing how these interests can be met by solutions developed through positional or interest-based generation procedures
3. Determining the costs and benefits of selecting or not selecting one of the solutions
4. Determining the best alternative to a negotiated settlement
5. Beginning the process of modifying, integrating, combining, dropping, and trading options to reach a final settlement

The major differences between the assessment process and the earlier stage are that (1) the amount of time that has already been invested in negotiation often encourages parties to reach a negotiated settlement; (2) the parties may jointly assess options rather than conduct their evaluation in isolation from each other; and (3) the focus of the parties is primarily on the content of the negotiations rather than the procedure.

The central task of the parties at this stage is to assess how well their interests will be satisfied by any one solution or any combination of the solutions that have been generated collaboratively or offered by one party. The mediator's task is to help the parties evaluate the options and to assist them in determining the costs and benefits of acceptance or rejection.

Because assessment procedures have already been discussed in detail in Chapter Four, they will not be reexamined here. However, two concepts and related series of activities need to be explored further: the establishment of a settlement or bargaining range and the consideration of the best alternative to a negotiated agreement (Fisher and Ury, 1981).

The Settlement Range

The *settlement range* is a range of options, any one of which the disputants would prefer to embrace rather than accept the consequences of a breakdown of negotiations. The settlement range is often referred to as the *bargaining range* when applied to options generated by positional bargaining. I will now examine how parties recognize when they have produced, by means of positional bargaining or cooperative problem solving, options that fall within the settlement range.

Creation and Identification of a Bargaining Range

Positional bargainers generally assume that they are negotiating about a finite or fixed-sum resource: money, time, or tangible objects. Thus, the total value available to all parties cannot be increased. This assumption is not always valid, but I will consider it here as a hypothetical given. If parties are negotiating for fixed shares of a finite resource, a gain for one party must mean a loss for another. If parties are to reach an agreement on the division of the resource, they must reach a compromise position.

Possible outcomes in fixed-sum negotiations are plotted in Figure 12.1. In this figure, the vertical axis represents gains for Party A and the horizontal axis represents equivalent gains for Party B. If the parties are to divide a fixed-sum resource, the division will have to occur at some point along the diagonal line *xy*. Some of the settlement options are identified at points along the line, with point 5, 5 considered an equal distribution of the resource. On this continuum of distribution, parties usually identify a point that is a preferred solution or target. That point becomes their goal in subsequent negotiations.

Figure 12.1. Possible Outcomes in Fixed-Sum Negotiations.

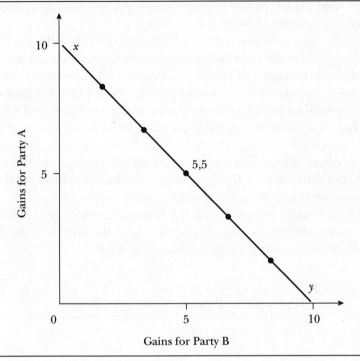

The *target point* is *the* preferred distribution of resources, in which the party's compensation is considered to be the best that could be obtained under the circumstances. It is also a point of aspiration. Targets may be developed on the basis of the gut-level feelings or high aspirations of a party, or they may be the result of highly sophisticated calculations and analysis.

In addition to target points, negotiators may have upper or lower limits that are often called *resistance points.* The upper limit indicates the maximum that a party will pay or give in settlement. The lower limit is the minimum that a party will accept.

Between the target point and the resistance point is the settlement or bargaining range—a field of options that, although satisfactory, provide different degrees of benefits for each negotiator. Because each party has a range of preferred options, the goal of each disputant is to (1) discover the other party's settlement range,

(2) determine if there is an overlap with his or her own settlement range, and (3) maximize his or her own gains within the range of possible outcomes if there is an overlap.

In the best possible case, the disputing parties will have overlapping settlement ranges so that there are mutually satisfactory solutions or divisions of resources. Figure 12.2 illustrates how the options of two parties may be compatible. Parties in positional bargaining, with or without the assistance of the mediator, will ideally be able to identify a mutually acceptable settlement range and make proposals between the boundaries established by their resistance points. When settlement ranges overlap, parties must decide how they will make a final decision on the distribution of the resource within their general area of agreement.

Occasionally, parties reach the assessment stage and discover that their settlement ranges do not overlap (see Figure 12.3). This condition is known as a *negative settlement range*.

Figure 12.2. Positive Settlement Range.

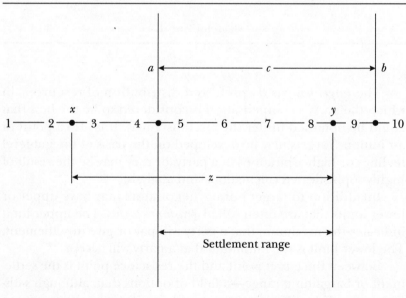

a = Party A's resistance point x = Party B's target
b = Party A's target y = Party B's resistance point
c = Acceptable options for Party A z = Acceptable options for Party B

When a party discovers that a negative settlement range exists, he or she has several procedural options:

1. Continue to negotiate and make subsequent proposals in the hope that the other parties will shift their target and resistance points so that a positive settlement range is created
2. Change his or her own target point and resistance point and continue to offer new proposals that demand fewer concessions from other negotiators
3. Expand the number of issues to allow for trade-offs on other interests that will compensate for losses on the fixed-sum variable
4. Cease negotiations

The mediator can assist the party in assessing the feasibility and desirability of pursuing any or all of these four options.

Figure 12.3. Negative Settlement Range.

a = Party A's resistance point
b = Party A's target
c = Acceptable options for Party A

x = Party B's target
y = Party B's resistance point
z = Acceptable options for Party B

Settlement Range and Cooperative Problem Solving

Reaching a settlement range when parties are engaged in interest-based bargaining involves a somewhat different procedure from the one used in positional bargaining. Although the concept of the settlement range remains valid, options that the parties consider do not necessarily fall along a continuum in which one party gains value at the expense of another. The outcome in interest-based bargaining represents a compromise only in a worst-case scenario. The norm appears to be solutions that, in the long run, are more satisfactory than the status quo for all parties concerned. Figure 12.4 identifies the field in which this type of outcome can be found.

In Figure 12.4, the diagonal line *xy* represents a division of values in which parties reach some compromise in an apparently fixed-sum negotiation. The point 5, 5 represents an equal division

Figure 12.4. Cooperative Problem-Solving Settlement Range.

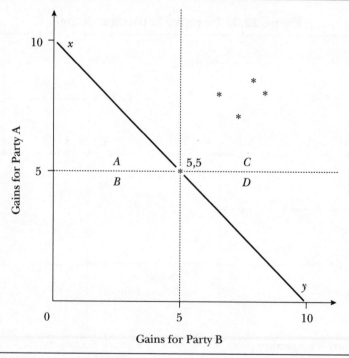

Note: Asterisks indicate cooperative problem-solving settlement options.

of the contested resources. The solutions sought by interest-based bargaining are those found in quadrant C, which represent greater joint satisfaction of interests by settlement than any distribution of benefits along the xy range.

Recognition of the Settlement Range

In some negotiations, parties have little difficulty recognizing their arrival at a settlement range. Either through prenegotiation planning in which a range was established or in the process of interaction, all parties may recognize that they have reached a field in which any settlement is preferable to no agreement.

Occasionally, however, parties have perceptual difficulties in recognizing a settlement range. This condition may be due to misperception of what is an acceptable field of settlement or to the existence of a negative settlement range. The mediator's intervention to prevent an impasse at this stage of negotiations may be crucial. I will discuss here how mediators respond to the first problem.

Identification of the Acceptable Field of Settlement

The problem of identification here is similar to perceptual or attitudinal problems identified earlier in negotiations. For example, it is necessary to be aware of the importance of interests and to recognize when a party should shift from an initial position to a new one. The mediator, through public and private discussions with the disputing parties, often has the most accurate perception of what the settlement range will be for all the negotiators. The problem for the intervenor is to communicate to disputants that a bargaining range has been reached without disclosing or determining the precise outcome of the dispute.

Mediators should attempt to make the parties aware that they have reached a settlement range by indirectly questioning them about how well their interests or needs can be met by the available solutions. Mediators can also ask in caucus whether a party is willing to lose one of the available options as the result of an impasse. If the party responds that he or she is not willing to risk the impasse, the mediator knows that the party has reached a point equal to or better than his or her resistance point. The party has moved into an acceptable range of options. The same procedure is then repeated with the other parties, generally in caucuses.

Once the mediator identifies that an acceptable settlement range has been reached, he or she may privately—or on occasion, publicly—announce to the parties that the conditions for settlement do exist. Perhaps more commonly, the mediator may quietly lead the parties into the settlement procedures that will be described in Chapter Thirteen.

Moderation of Inflated Expectations

Most of the discussion so far has concerned disputes in which the parties have been willing to acknowledge that they have moved into a settlement range. In some disputes, however, parties have inflated expectations, have their hopes raised, and subsequently make unreasonable demands. Such behavior may prevent disputants from progressing into an acceptable settlement range. In order to avoid this, mediators should try to persuade the party with inflated expectations either that his or her demand is out of line with what is attainable in reality or that the other party has reached his or her bottom line and cannot offer any more. Both strategies are designed to raise the specter of impasse—a specter that will dissipate only if the unrealistic party modifies his or her position.

The mediator often accomplishes the first strategy—convincing a party that his or her demands are unrealistic—by asking one or more of the following questions:

- If you were in the other party's situation, would you accept the proposals that you are making now, or would you expect that more should be offered in exchange for an agreement?
- Is the offer fair? Will those whom you respect, the community or the public, perceive it as such?
- Is the offer in line with community, legal, or other norms?
- Is the demand that you are making in line with other negotiated settlements or court decisions on similar issues or under similar conditions?
- Do you have the power to force the issue?
- What are the benefits to you of pursuing your present course? Are there any risks?

If the mediator cannot, by careful questioning, induce the party to decide to moderate inflated hopes or positions, he or she may have to use information about the other side as a lever of influence. Transmitting specific information about one party's position or means of influence is always problematic for mediators. The mediator may not have an accurate assessment of a party's position or influence or may be the victim of a party's bluffing tactics. Before telling a party that another party has reached his or her bottom line and cannot offer any more, the mediator should be certain that there are no additional offers to be made. The party to whom the request is being directed should generally be given an opportunity to make additional offers before the mediator transmits the message of total commitment to the other party. Generally, most of this activity occurs within a caucus. Once a mediator has gained permission to transmit a final offer, he or she may convey it to the party who has inflated expectations. The form in which a final offer is transmitted may vary according to specificity, timing (when it must be accepted), and implications for rejection (Fisher, 1978; Walton and McKersie, 1965).

Mediators should be cautious and use this tactic only as a last resort. If the party with inflated expectations does not shift position, an impasse occurs. Mediators should usually try to keep parties uncommitted to particular solutions for as long as possible so that the parties do not become entrenched in an untenable position. However, if disclosure of a party's bottom line is successful, the intransigent party may revise his or her demands and progress into a mutually acceptable settlement range.

Negative Settlement Range

Unfortunately, negotiations do not always result in a positive settlement range. I have discussed the interventions that a mediator makes when there is a perceptual problem in recognizing an existent settlement range. I now turn to strategies when the problem is not perceptual—when the differences are real and there are no mutually acceptable solutions.

The major strategic intervention mediators make when a negative settlement range is present is to assist the parties in determining their "best alternative to a negotiated agreement" (BATNA)

(Fisher and Ury, 1981). In defining the BATNA, the mediator returns to the process of selecting an approach and arena of conflict as outlined in Chapter Four. Separately or jointly, the mediator and the parties should discuss procedural options available to them should negotiations fail, and potential substantive and psychological outcomes that might result from these different approaches. Parties may at this time decide either to terminate negotiations and move to other resolution approaches or to reassess their positions and proposals and move toward an acceptable settlement. Often, a careful and realistic assessment of each party's best alternative to a negotiated agreement brings all the disputants back to negotiation with a renewed commitment to reaching a mutually acceptable agreement (Lax and Sebenius, 1985).

Option Evaluation in the Whittamore-Singson Case

In the Whittamore-Singson dispute, the parties developed a range of settlement options, including one with and one without compensation. As both of these options were generated primarily in joint session, the parties also began the evaluation process together. They discussed which option would best preserve their relationships with each other and with the clinic and staff, which would be most cost-effective for each of the parties, which would address concerns about precedent, and so on. In the end, they tentatively agreed on the option of Whittamore continuing to practice with the clinic, but at a satellite office, until the contract expired. But they both needed to explore this solution with other concerned parties before a final agreement could be reached. Singson wanted to confer with his board, legal counsel, and other physicians; and Whittamore with the mediator, his lawyer, and his soon-to-be ex-wife. Whittamore's meeting with the mediator was brief and focused primarily on how Whittamore might approach his estranged wife to discuss the potential settlement option.

Culture and the Assessment of Settlement Options

Culture is often a critical factor in how parties assess settlement options, for culture usually shapes the standards and criteria that parties use to define fairness, justice, efficiency, or implementability. Some cultures that are dominated by the rule of law, such as mainstream North American culture, often use legal standards—that is, calculations of what one might gain in court—to determine the acceptability or fairness of an outcome. In such contexts, parties are bargaining in the shadow of the law.

Other cultures might use traditional law or customary practices to evaluate outcomes. For example, the parties may want to determine how close the agreement comes to the way the problem was handled in the past or the way similar disputes have been handled. In traditional or indigenous societies, age-old standards are invoked when decisions are made.

Some cultures use a person's rank or status to determine what would be a fair distribution of resources or benefits, with higher rank carrying a greater entitlement. This was the case in a number of Tswana disputes in Southern Africa (Comaroff and Roberts, 1981).

Finally, parties may use standards and criteria that are particular to their ethnic group or religion. A few years ago, while working in Sri Lanka, I observed a mediation in which the parties settled after the mediator explored with one of them the merit that he would accrue if he reached a negotiated settlement. The mediator later explained to me that among Sri Lankan Buddhists, storing up merit by doing good deeds was seen as desirable because it enabled one to avoid reincarnation, get off the wheel of life, and reach nirvana more rapidly.

These examples illustrate how important it is for mediators to explore with parties the specific standards and criteria they are using when determining the acceptability of an agreement. Understanding their conceptual framework may help the intervenor to work successfully within their world view, to interpret one party's logic and rationale to others, and ultimately to facilitate agreement.

Chapter Thirteen

Conducting Final Bargaining

Final bargaining involves activities initiated late in negotiations to reduce the scope and number of differences between negotiators and to progress toward agreement and termination of the conflict. Gulliver (1979, pp. 161–162) identifies four situations in which negotiators find themselves in the final bargaining stage:

1. The bargaining range may have been so narrow that the advantages to be gained from bargaining have become small, even trifling, given the agreement already achieved. . . . What remains to be done is a clearing up of minor details and a joint commitment to the culminating outcome.
2. The bargaining range may have been narrowed, or the bargaining formula may have already established much agreement in principle and orientation, but the details of terms need to be worked out.
3. In a third bargaining situation, although something like a viable bargaining range has been discovered, albeit roughly and with unclear limits, considerable differences may remain between the parties. In principle, any point within the range is mutually preferable to no agreement, yet considerable gain or loss of advantage can still result from final agreement on a particular point.
4. No viable range has been discovered and it may well not exist. Here although the parties are deliberately working toward agreement and are making "real" proposals for an outcome, their preference sets and expectations are still not altogether clear.

Parties who find themselves in the first situation usually reach agreement easily. Their relationship is cordial, the acceptable options are clear, and the procedural route to completion of the negotiations is uncomplicated and direct. The remaining situations, however, are more problematic for negotiations, and a mediator's intervention may be needed to prevent deadlock. I will focus the following discussion on procedures negotiators and mediators can use to accomplish final bargaining in the last three situations.

There appear to be four major patterns of moves negotiators use during the final stage of bargaining: (1) incremental convergence (Gulliver, 1979; Walton and McKersie, 1965); (2) a delay of agreement and then a final leap to a package settlement (Zartman and Berman, 1982); (3) development of a consensual formula; and (4) procedural means to reach agreements (Fisher, 1978; Zartman and Berman, 1982). In this chapter, I will first explore these approaches to final settlement and then examine the crucial factor of timing to see how the mediator uses deadlines to bring negotiations to a conclusion.

Incremental Convergence

In incremental convergence, the parties make gradual concessions within the bargaining range until they reach a mutually satisfactory compromise position. Parties may isolate concessions to a single issue or link issues to balance losses and benefits.

If the disputants have adhered to positional bargaining, the mediator's main task is to assist them in making offers that will be acceptable to the other party and to prevent them from prematurely committing to a position that will be difficult to back away from later in negotiations.

Offers are the specific terms of a position that a party presents as a possible solution to an issue. Especially in positional bargaining, an offer frequently implies some form of concession or trade a party is willing to make in exchange for an acceptable reciprocal offer or agreement. Parties engaged in positional bargaining face several problems that may inhibit them from making offers:

Reluctance to Overconcede or Reveal Bargaining Positions

At this point in negotiations, parties may be reluctant to make offers that go beyond their opening positions, even if they have discovered an opponent's settlement range. They do not want to concede more than necessary, nor do they want to indicate the bargaining positions within their own settlement range. This situation can result in endless avoidance behavior and a lack of commitment to a specific proposal.

In this situation, mediators should assist parties in developing tentative or hypothetical offers that can be used to test for potential agreement while not formally committing a party to a specific solution. Tentative or probing offers can be designed by a negotiator, the mediator, or both. Such offers can vary in degree of specificity, resources exchanged, time of performance, and implications if the offer is accepted in a timely manner. This allows a party more flexibility in exploring the settlement range without prematurely committing to a position. The mediator might say, "I'd like to try out a possible settlement option. If you find it to be reasonable, I will explore its acceptability with the other party." Tentative offers can often be explored with the other party by having the mediator shuttle between the parties, testing areas of agreement without formally committing a party to a specific solution.

Fear of Being Perceived as Weak

A second factor that inhibits parties in initiating offers is the fear of being perceived as weak (Rubin and Brown, 1975). People in conflict often do not want others to see them being "forced" to make a concession. They fear that concession making will become—or will be perceived to be—a pattern, and that the opponent will hold out on later issues expecting similar compliant behavior. There is evidence in pure game theory that concession making may be perceived as a sign of weakness (Deutsch, 1974); however, in actual negotiations in which there is personal interaction, making the first offer or concession can be turned into an asset rather than a liability. The classic case is Anwar Sadat's initiative in proposing to Menachem Begin that they begin discussions on a Middle East peace plan. Sadat's proposal to travel to Israel to talk was a potent first offer, and a definite sign of strength.

Mediators can aid a party in making a first offer by helping to frame the offer in such a way that the concession becomes an initiative of strength, not weakness. Through framing, the party can make explicit the fact that he or she is making an offer or concession to demonstrate good faith, to show a willingness to take the other's needs into consideration, to encourage the other party or parties to make similar moves, or to establish a trading arrangement in which a concession is made on one issue in exchange for a concession on another. The mediator may coach and assist the party in framing the offer so that the other party will perceive it favorably. The mediator may also prime the recipient so that the offer will be accepted or reciprocated.

Negative Transference
Parties often reject an offer not because of its substantive content but because of their attitude toward its initiator. The mediator can help negotiators avoid this pitfall by proposing one party's ideas to the other as if they were his or her own. This eliminates the possibility that the other party will perceive offers as "partial, biased, or tainted more because of their source than because of their substantive content" (Young, 1972).

Fear of Rejection and Impasse
Parties are often discouraged from making offers because they fear rejection and stalemate. They may prefer to continue discussions rather than reach impasse. Mediators can assist parties in overcoming this obstacle by testing the ideas of the parties in private and bringing to the joint session only those points on which the parties can agree. The mediator can encourage the parties to make the offers or may make the offers for them. It is generally preferable for the parties to make the offers as this increases their commitment to proposals and maintains the mediator's impartiality toward the substance of the negotiations.

Public Pressure on Negotiators
In cases in which negotiators represent a constituency, the parties may be constrained from making public offers because of possible personal repercussions from unpopular concessions. This is often the case in labor-management negotiations when a union team feels constrained by the union membership from making an offer that the team feels is reasonable and acceptable. Here, the mediator can make a proposal and become a negotiator's scapegoat. Negotiators can agree to the concession and later claim that they

agreed because the mediator requested concurrence, not because they initiated it or the other party forced them to agree.

The Mediator as Coalition Former. Closely related to the scapegoat function of the mediator is the role of coalition former. The mediator's presence and his or her suggestions of offers can cause the disputants to reevaluate their relationship to each other and the issues that divide them. "One possibility is, of course, that the two original contestants both become antagonistic towards the third person and decide to agree so as not to let the newcomer influence the settlement" (Aubert, 1963, p. 35). The mediator can induce this situation by proposing one or more solutions that are more extreme than either party is willing to accept. In this situation, they may be forced into a coalition to moderate the mediator's exaggerated position.

Loss of Face

Another block to parties initiating offers is the issue of "saving face" (Brown, 1977). Mediators can assist parties in making new offers by providing them with rationalizations for shifts in positions and by reframing the situation so that an offer does not result in a loss of dignity. This strategy also aids parties in abandoning untenable postures.

The six blocks described here can all be impediments to the initiation of offers that lead to incremental convergence of positions. Appropriate mediator intervention, however, can minimize the negative effects and ease the decision-making process of positional bargaining.

Leap to Agreement

The leap-to-agreement approach to final bargaining is characterized by a strategy of opening with a high demand, offering few concessions, and then making a final leap toward a package that meets the negotiators' demands (Zartman and Berman, 1982). Leaps to agreement usually occur when (1) negotiators consciously pursue a hard-line strategy to educate an opponent about a principle; (2) negotiators want to use deadline pressure to force an agreement; or (3) all options are equally acceptable (or unacceptable) and no one proposal has superior merit.

The leap model of negotiation is often characterized by "package deals" or "yesable proposals" that attempt to incorporate the needs of all parties into one acceptable linked package (Fisher, 1969). Advantages to this approach are that

1. It prevents incremental concession making that may result in expectations of more concessions.
2. It allows a party to make a point about the strength of his or her commitment to an issue or principle.
3. By turning the task of developing a comprehensive solution over to one party, it attempts to eliminate part of the difficult task of jointly drafting an agreement.
4. It demonstrates that acceptable trade-offs are possible.
5. It may incline a party toward agreement when a deadline is close and there is no time to develop a counterproposal.

This approach does, however, have some drawbacks. Intransigence on a position and lack of progress early in a negotiation may cause the other party to adhere to its position and may also foster increasing hostility over the procedure used to resolve the dispute rather than over the issues themselves. Presenting a package late in negotiations may also cause problems because the opposing party may believe that he or she has not had an opportunity to participate in formulating the plan for the settlement. Rejection thus may be based on procedural participatory factors rather than the proposal's substantive content.

The Mediator and Leaps to Agreement

The leap to agreement approach may have both positive and negative impacts for negotiators, as described previously. Mediators can either promote or inhibit the use of this procedure, depending on the dynamics of the negotiation session. If the procedure is being used by a party in final bargaining and is causing damage to negotiations, the mediator can notify the party in caucus of the detrimental effect on the other party. If, on the other hand, the hard-line procedure of delaying commitment is educating the other party on a particular principle or point, and if the mediator has learned that the other party is progressing toward agreement, the process can be encouraged.

The mediator can also use the leap to agreement tactic by delaying a party's presentation of a solution until the mediator is certain that the other party will agree to a particular proposal. At that time, the mediator can ask one of the parties to make the proposal, or he or she may make it. With agreement ensured, the parties can leap to a one-step settlement.

Formulas and Agreements in Principle

I have already discussed at some length the procedures used to reach a bargaining formula or an agreement in principle. This strategy is one of progressing from the most general level of agreement to more specific details of a settlement. The mediator may initiate this approach early in negotiations, even as early as the stage of defining dispute parameters, or it may appear as late as final bargaining, after more specific options have been generated and assessed.

The procedures for reaching a formula settlement are somewhat like those used in constructing a puzzle. First, the outside boundary—the general agreement—is constructed. The outside pieces determine the overall boundaries of the settlement. The negotiators then construct various packages that will fit into this framework. The formula development process is conducted by consensus and usually entails modification, refinement, and synthesis of proposals or, occasionally, the exchange of small incremental pieces. The process often involves the creation of multiple levels of agreements with increasing specificity.

The Mediator and Formula Construction

Parties often begin building a formula or attempt to develop agreements in principle early in negotiations. This process usually starts during the stage of defining dispute parameters, when the parties attempt to outline the boundaries, both conceptual and substantive, within which they will negotiate. The development of a formula or agreement in principle may later become much more explicit during the process of defining issues and interests.

In final bargaining, formula development or agreements in principle are primarily useful in preventing deadlocks. Formulas may be designed to define principles by which a limited resource within a bargaining range can be divided or to set forth procedures for combining solutions that meet the needs of all parties. Mutual decision about a formula or agreement in principle "is desirable . . . because a formula or framework of principles helps give structure and coherence to an agreement on details, helps facilitate the search for solutions on component items, and helps create a positive, creative image of negotiation rather than an image of concession and compromise" (Zartman and Berman, 1982, p. 93).

Parties with extensive experience with or bias toward positional bargaining are often not aware of the merits of establishing a bargaining formula or agreements in principle to reach final settlement. Mediators can often assist parties by educating them about the approach and by identifying such a formula in much the same manner as an intervenor is able to help identify interests.

Zartman and Berman (1982) maintain that the recognition of a common formula depends on three elements: (1) a shared perception or definition of the conflict; (2) an understanding of the primary and underlying values or interests that give meaning to the issues under discussion; and (3) an applicable criterion of justice. By the final bargaining stage, it would be hoped that the parties had developed a shared perception or definition of the conflict. If they have not, the mediator should refer them back to the previous stages of issue and interest identification. Interests and underlying values must be satisfied or be met by a settlement. The formula must contain provisions for responding to the primary and secondary interests of the disputants or it will be unacceptable.

The third component of a formula is a mutually accepted standard of justice. Zartman and Berman (1982) identify five types of justice: substantive, procedural, equitable, compensatory, and subtractive. *Substantive justice* refers to a concrete objective outcome that the parties believe is fair. *Procedural justice* refers to the process by which a solution is reached and the settlement is carried out. Most disputants expect the same procedure to be in effect for both parties, or if the procedure is to be different, the reasons for the difference should be mutually acceptable. *Equitable justice* refers to the "apportionment of shares on the basis of each party's particular characteristics" (Zartman and Berman, 1982, p. 104). The basis of equity will vary from dispute to dispute; it may be need, power, historic precedent, size, or amount of resources available to divide.

Compensatory justice refers to payments that remedy an unequal distribution of resources. Compensatory justice is usually an issue when one party has been deprived as a result of a previous relationship with the other. For example, a husband may agree to pay spousal support and fund his ex-wife's school expenses so that she can earn an income and attain a standard of living equal to what she was accustomed to in the marriage. A developer may monetarily compensate the immediate neighbors of an unpopular new facility needed by the community, for potential damages to their lifestyle (O'Hare, Bacow, and Sanderson, 1983). *Subtractive justice* refers to equal denial to all parties of a resource, so that no one wins. This component of a formula is used when parties attach a higher priority to denying the other parties access to a resource than to possessing it themselves. For example, if in a divorce property settlement the couple cannot decide which of them should take their antique brass bed, both may agree to sell it and deny possession to each other rather than agree that one of them should have it.

Procedural Means of Reaching Substantive Decisions

Occasionally, negotiators are unable to make a decision on a particular substantive issue, and the impasse delays the settlement of the entire conflict. Inability to agree may be based on psychological unwillingness to settle a dispute, reluctance to agree to a point for fear of constituency disapproval, multiple solutions that are equally acceptable (or undesirable), and so on. Regardless of the reason that agreement cannot be reached, the parties may still be under pressure to find some solution to their impasse. To break the deadlock, they may turn to a procedural solution to the substantive problem. This process was discussed briefly in Chapter Eleven, on option generation, but it should now be explored in more detail.

Procedural solutions are process decisions that parties make to resolve disputes without directly deciding the issue. Generally, the process determines a substantive answer. There are four common types of procedural approaches to resolving substantive impasse: the procedural time line approach, third-party decision makers, arbitrary decision-making procedures, and postponement or avoidance.

Procedural Time Line Approach

The procedural time line approach requires negotiators to develop a process and time line for particular substantive agreements and to define specific advantages, consequences, or penalties for parties meeting or failing to meet the agreed deadlines. Time determines the substantive outcome. For example, if parties are negotiating payment, they may agree that if payment is received before a specific date, it will be of a certain amount. If payment is received after that date, a penalty charge will be imposed. A party then has a choice about when to pay. The procedural time line approach allows the parties to avoid reaching a specific substantive decision on issues and creates instead a procedural formula governing how the decision will be made.

Third-Party Decision Makers

Parties who reach an impasse on a substantive question can turn the problem over to a third party other than the mediator. The most common form of third-party decision making is performed by a judge or jury. Disputants are legally bound by the decision of the impartial third party. Another third-party structure is arbitration, which was defined in Chapter One. Mediators often suggest referral to an arbiter or judge of issues over which parties are deadlocked.

Other third-party decision makers who can assist parties in breaking deadlocks include property appraisers, custody evaluators, and other technical experts. Parties can agree to engage the assistance of third parties and to abide by their recommendations. In a business dispute over the division of common property, the parties disagreed about what the property was worth. They decided to submit the problem to two appraisers who were mutually acceptable and to average the answers received. Thus a mutually acceptable and fair process provided a substantive answer that both parties could accept.

Mechanical Decision-Making Procedures

Parties often wish to make a decision on issues in which there is an equal chance of winning or losing or in which the outcome is of little consequence to the disputants. Negotiators or mediators frequently resort to procedural mechanisms that automatically result in a decision.

Mechanical decision making is appropriate when the difference between the parties is not large, and therefore the loss for either would not be great, or when the probability of reaching a decision by another means has an equal chance of loss or gain for one of the parties. Parties split the *difference* in order to maximize their rewards and minimize their losses.

Negotiators may also choose to take turns in satisfying their interests—for example, by alternating the selection of items to be inherited from an estate—or to use games of chance such as flipping coins or drawing lots or straws. These procedures provide each disputant with an equal chance to win rewards. The process, not the disputants, decides the outcome. The mediator may impartially supervise the process to ensure fairness.

Postponement, Avoidance, and Issue Abandonment

Parties may also break a deadlock by postponing or avoiding a decision or by abandoning an issue. Postponement may mean delaying a decision until the other party is more psychologically disposed toward an issue or is represented by a different person. Postponement may also be used to allow time for the development of new proposals or arguments, the mobilization of power or resources, or the reconfiguration of external structural variables or influences on the conflict. In one public policy dispute, the parties decided to hold off on making an agreement until an election had occurred and the disposition of the newly elected officials could be determined.

Postponement may be used in conjunction with third-party decision making. In cases in which parties cannot reach agreement on a particular issue and in which failure to agree on that issue may result in total impasse, negotiators may decide to forge a general agreement and defer decision making on the particular point until the specific conflict arises at a later date. They may designate one component of a dispute for referral to an arbiter or judge for final resolution. This approach avoids total deadlock and allows agreement to be reached in the absence of a full consensus on all issues.

At the start of negotiations, parties raise a number of issues or demands that they want addressed. Each issue can be ranked according to its importance in terms of the overall settlement. It is not unusual for negotiators to include one or more bogus or throwaway issues that are made to appear important so that they can be used for educational or trading purposes. A party uses throwaway issues as part of an initial large demand to educate his or her opponents about how many concessions will have to be made for a settlement to be reached. Throwaway issues are used in final bargaining as chips that are traded for desirable concessions. They are useful only if the other party believes that they are genuine and valuable. If this illusion can be maintained throughout negotiations, a bargainer may truly have a tradable commodity.

The manner in which throwaway issues are used varies. They may be used as an early concession to demonstrate goodwill; they may be offered later in exchange for the withdrawal of another negotiator's demand; or they may be deployed as positive tradable items. Negotiators will often mutually agree to abandon issues in an "I'll get rid of mine if you'll get rid of yours" manner.

On occasion, the mediator is in the best position to manage the dropping of issues. He or she should determine with the parties in caucus whether they require acknowledgment in joint session that they have abandoned the demands or issues or whether they prefer merely not to mention them. If they prefer acknowledgment, the mediator can help establish the conditions for the abandonment of issues or demands.

Deadlines

Timing is a critical component in final bargaining and settlement. Cross (1969, p. 13) notes, "If it did not matter *when* the parties agreed, it would not matter whether they agreed at all." Time is both an important motivational factor for negotiators and a variable that helps determine how well their interests will be met. In final bargaining, time may be managed for the purpose of inducing a settlement. The most common form of time management at this stage is the deadline.

Deadlines are limits that delineate the period of time in which an agreement must be reached. Deadlines perform an important function in the settlement of a variety of issues. "Of the 85,420 federal civil cases that were filed in the United States in 1975, only

9 percent were disposed of by trial" (Shallert, 1982, p. 255). Lawyers often settle legal cases in the days or hours before the court date. Much of the impetus for out-of-court settlement comes from the unpredictable outcome of court proceedings and the potential for negative consequences if the parties engage in direct litigation. The deadline of a court date motivates parties to settle.

Deadlines play an equally important function in prompting the settlement of labor-management disputes. The eleventh-hour settlement before a strike deadline is well known. The same dynamics are common in nearly all other types of negotiations. Stevens (1963, p. 200) argues: "An approaching deadline puts pressure on the parties to state their true positions and thus does much to squeeze elements of bluff out of the later steps of negotiation. However, an approaching deadline does much more. . . . It brings pressures to bear which actually change the least favorable terms upon which each party is willing to settle; thus, it operates as a force tending to bring about conditions necessary for agreement."

An understanding of deadlines and how they can be used is an invaluable tool for negotiators and mediators. It is beneficial to discuss several characteristics and variables of deadlines that affect their utility in negotiations.

Internally and Externally Established Deadlines

A party can establish his or her own deadline, or outside forces may determine when negotiation ceases. A contract deadline, an ultimatum imposed by an outside agency, and an impending court date are examples of externally imposed constraints.

External deadlines are often important to negotiation strategies. Shapiro (1970, p. 44), in referring to negotiations in which one party represents a constituent group, observes that "any settlement made without the pressure of a last minute crisis leaves the negotiators open to attack by the people they represent, who may feel that they could have gotten a more favorable contract if only their negotiators had bluffed the other side right down to the final moment."

Coordinated and Uncoordinated Deadlines

Deadlines can be symmetrical or asymmetrical in that the parties may have either the same time limits or different ones. For some

parties, a delay in decision making may result in increased benefits, whereas for others a rapid decision may be essential (Lake,
1980).

Actual and Artificial Deadlines

Parties may be constrained by deadlines that correspond to particular events beyond which they have little control, or they may
be influenced by artificial time constraints that are almost arbitrarily established by one or more parties.

An artificial deadline was created during negotiations between
environmentalists, industry representatives, and two U.S. governmental agencies over restrictions on oil and gas development on
federal lands. The environmentalists stated that if they did not note
progress in the talks within six weeks, they would cease negotiating. They arbitrarily set a deadline in order to encourage industry
and government representatives to reach an agreement.

Rigid and Flexible Deadlines

The rigidity/flexibility variable is closely related to the distinction
between actual and artificial deadlines. Although rigid deadlines
are usually viewed as the stronger impetus for settlement because
they provide fixed time boundaries that the parties dare not over-
step, more flexible deadlines, at least at the eleventh hour, may
allow the parties necessary latitude to effect a decision. Parties
often need additional time to reconsider a last-minute proposal or
to gain constituent or bureaucratic approval to reach a final settlement. Mutually determined extensions of deadlines may be a
prerequisite for a settlement.

Deadlines With and Without Consequences

Deadlines promote settlements primarily because they usually imply
negative consequences if the time limit is transgressed. Possible consequences include the termination of negotiations, a stalemate, a
loss of gains already achieved, a withdrawal of an offer, acceptance
of another party's offer, a court suit, a strike, and other undesirable
outcomes. Although a deadline does not have to imply dire consequences such as threat or actual imposition of negative sanctions,
it must present the possibility of a worse option than if settlement
were reached. Negotiators and mediators often manipulate the

explicit or implicit consequences of not settling before a deadline because known or unknown consequences may incline another party toward agreement.

Explicit or Vague Deadlines

Deadlines may be explicitly defined or may remain vague. The appropriate strategy depends on the particular negotiation. Explicit deadlines create a definite point at which settlement must be reached. Though providing a positive benefit in creating motivation for settlement, explicit deadlines may also create resistance because of a perceived threat of negative consequences; they may promote unwise decisions because there is not enough time to consider all options; and they may encourage an excessive willingness to settle at the sacrifice of principle. Negotiators usually argue for explicit deadlines only when all parties will bear the negative consequences of a failure to reach agreement within the prescribed time. An example of this situation is a strike in which both labor and management stand to lose if a new contract is not negotiated.

Nonexplicit deadlines, on the other hand, may be used to imply that the negotiator is willing to talk as long as necessary to reach an acceptable settlement. Such deadlines can be used to the advantage of negotiators who know that an opponent is under pressure to settle by a certain time. The appearance of unlimited time for discussion may motivate an opponent to settle early in order to curtail rising costs that result from delay. However, even if time is an important factor for negotiators, a party may gain more in the end by concealing his or her deadline. Cohen (1980), a business negotiator, describes a case in which he lost thousands of dollars because he discussed his time constraints too openly and his opponent discovered his settlement deadline. His opponent was willing to talk for a longer period of time than was available to Cohen, and thus forced him to make concessions to reach an agreement before his deadline—the departure of his plane.

Mediators and Deadline Management

Mediators can significantly assist negotiators in managing deadlines by making them aware of internal or external deadlines or assisting them in setting artificial deadlines when none exist. When appropriate, mediators may also make rigid deadlines more flexible, assist the parties in avoiding negative moves related to time, and enhance the usefulness of deadlines.

Making Parties Aware of Deadlines

Parties are often not aware of the existence or consequences of deadlines. This is especially the case when the deadlines are externally imposed or implicitly assumed. In final bargaining, mediators often remind negotiators that a deadline is approaching and that positive benefits may be lost or negative consequences incurred from a failure to settle. This function should not be construed to mean that the mediator should reveal a hidden deadline that is crucial for another party to meet his or her interests. Mediators should take great care not to reveal confidential information about a party's time constraints lest they unduly influence the settlement and create a mediator-induced imbalance in the power relationship between the parties. The mediator should, however, bring to the consciousness of the negotiators the explicit time parameters that affect final bargaining.

Assisting Parties in Establishing a Deadline

The presence of a deadline often enhances a negotiation's outcome. Deadlines can be created by parties who have the capacity to reward or punish other disputants for their performance with respect to time parameters. They can also be established by external constituencies—bureaucratic authorities or collectives of interested parties—or by external events. Finally, the mediator's moves can create deadlines. I will examine each of these means of defining time boundaries for negotiation and the mediator's role in influencing them.

The mediator, if he or she deems it advisable or necessary, may encourage one or more parties in a dispute to establish a deadline. This move may be made in caucus or in joint session and may be developed unilaterally or multilaterally. There are some situations in which it is appropriate for the mediator to suggest that only one party set a deadline, whereas in others, a cooperatively established time limit may be necessary to motivate all disputants to reach agreement. However, a mediator's suggestion in a caucus that only one party set a deadline may be seen as undue manipulation of the negotiation process and may represent a loss of neutrality; it may also carry the risk of exposure in joint session. This step is taken only with great care.

If a jointly established deadline is desirable, the mediator can assist the parties in deciding the criteria to be used in determining the deadline. Relevant factors may include time needed to learn about or study the issue; time for ratification of an agreement by a constituency; availability of necessary data; and structural constraints such as court dates, business schedules, and even changes of season.

Persons or events external to negotiations may also establish deadlines. Mediators often help parties negotiate with superiors or constituencies not directly involved in the mediation regarding the establishment of time parameters. Such externally imposed boundaries are often beyond direct control of negotiators but may be needed to motivate other parties to settle.

Although mediators rarely control external events that impose deadlines on negotiations, they can translate the consequences of these events to the parties to encourage them to settle within an agreed period of time. For example, if economic forces allow an offer to be made for only a limited period, the mediator may inform the parties of this fact. Raising awareness about an imminent court date that cannot be changed is another means of deadline leverage.

The mediator can also create his or her own deadline if such a move appears to be the only means of settlement. This can be done in several ways. First, the mediator can make all parties aware that a settlement is possible and that he or she thinks it can be accomplished within a specific period of time. The mediator can request that parties reach agreement within these time parameters. Deadlines imposed by the mediator may encourage the parties to negotiate more expeditiously. For example, some commercial mediators structure a limited number of sessions within which the parties must agree or cease mediation.

Second, the mediator can announce that he or she will make a public statement after a certain date that the parties are not negotiating in a timely and serious manner. Third, a mediator may threaten to leave the negotiations at a certain time unless the parties agree to honor a deadline (Kolb, 1983). This threat creates a functional deadline to which the parties must respond if they want to retain the mediator's services.

Mediators can impose deadlines on parties only if (1) the mediator's threat is credible; (2) the parties are willing to agree to the mediator's request or demand; and (3) the services of the mediator are genuinely needed or desired. The mediator's expendability or his or her failure to carry out a threat may lead to either a loss of credibility or the mediator's exit.

Lack of a deadline may not be the problem in a dispute. Parties may believe they face a rigid deadline, and the time parameter itself raises the specter of deadlock. The mediator's task in this situation is to create a more flexible time frame, which can be accomplished by several different methods.

First, the mediator may find ways to actually extend the time available for negotiation. Specific procedural agreements may be proposed to postpone the deadline so that parties have more time to make a decision. A suggestion to this effect by the mediator rather than by one of the parties often makes the proposal more palatable to the disputants and also avoids the appearance that if the deadline is extended, one party will make a concession. Another mediator tactic, which is often used in labor negotiations, is to "stop the clock." In this maneuver, the mediator obtains agreement to continue negotiations and to temporarily ignore the passage of time and the consequences of exceeding the deadline. Negotiation is extended without publicly disavowing that a deadline exists. This approach works as long as progress toward agreement is being made. If not, a party may unilaterally terminate negotiations after the deadline has been passed and thus incur the consequences of deadlocked negotiations. A third move mediators can use to create more flexibility in deadlines is to delay the time or date by which a specific component of a decision is to be made or is to go into effect. This allows the parties more time to work out controversial details of a particular problem and still reach general agreement.

Avoiding Deadline Dangers

There are several dangerous but common moves that negotiators may make in conjunction with deadlines. Among these are exposure of another party's deadline, games of "chicken," threats of dire consequences if agreement is not reached before the deadline, unrealistically quick agreements because of a false momentum toward the deadline, and manipulation of embarrassment to force an agreement. Mediators can help parties avoid pitfalls in each of these situations.

"Chicken" is a strategy in which each party delays making concessions until the deadline is imminent. The tension of intransigence will supposedly force another negotiator's will to fail so that he or she will make concessions rather than risk deadlock or negative costs if the deadline passes. Unfortunately, no party may be willing to break the cycle of resistance, and then all parties are forced to carry out threats and endure consequences that no one wanted. Mediators may help parties avoid playing "chicken" with deadlines by (1) publicly labeling the strategy; (2) privately working with each party to assess the costs of pursuing such a tactic; and (3) figuring out ways that parties can abandon extreme positions and make offers that will allow them to maintain their dignity.

Threats made close to deadlines seem to be especially common when parties experience intransigence from other negotiators and impasse is looming. Generally, mediators discourage parties from making threats and encourage them to make positive offers to induce agreement. This is both a more constructive and a less risky tactic.

A deadline's presence occasionally forces parties to reach unrealistic and unimplementable agreements. Parties begin a process of agreeing and become so involved in the excitement and dynamics of settlement that they formulate impracticable agreements. When a mediator recognizes this pattern, he or she should temper the enthusiasm of the disputants by utilizing reality testing, by asking questions that raise doubts, by encouraging the parties to seek more information, or by physically separating parties into caucuses so that they can more realistically assess the settlement without the stress of the presence of other negotiators.

Kheel, a labor mediator, has used this delaying tactic both to avoid untenable agreements and to psychologically encourage settlement (Shapiro, 1970). Kheel separates parties, assuring them that they are "not ready to settle," until they virtually demand to return to joint session to make an agreement. After the delay, in which the real merits of the settlement are analyzed, the parties are ready to make a solid and realistic agreement.

Parties are often embarrassed if they ask to delay settlement until they can be more certain of a proposal's merits. Other negotiators can manipulate such embarrassment to force an untimely agreement. Mediators can legitimize delay and prevent the manipulation of embarrassment by publicly calling for more time to reasonably consider a proposal. As an impartial intervenor, the mediator may even claim a personal lack of understanding of the settlement in order to delay a decision and provide the parties with more time for deliberation.

Enhancing the Usefulness of Deadlines

Mediators can assist parties in enhancing the positive use of deadlines in several ways. First, they can help parties to design offers that contain fading opportunities. They can also create artificial mileposts by which to measure progress before the ultimate deadline is reached. Each milepost marks a certain number of benefits that an opponent will receive if he or she settles at that time. The longer the settlement is delayed, the fewer benefits are offered.

An example of the first strategy occurred at a dinner party I attended one winter. Parents of several children attending the function told them that they had had enough hors d'oeuvres for the evening, but the children wanted more. At a certain point, more firewood was needed to heat the room. The children were offered the option of having more hors d'oeuvres if they would each bring in one log. They protested, started delaying tactics, and said they really didn't want to go out into the cold and get the wood. One of the guests changed the terms of the bargaining by saying that if the children did not bring in the wood in five minutes, he would do so; thus the offer of more food would no longer be available. The children decided that the proposed exchange was worthwhile and carried in the wood before the adult could do so.

Culture, Time, and Deadlines

Culture often significantly influences how parties view time, and consequently deadlines. Generally, people from cultures that see time as a limited commodity and an item to be saved or spent sparingly value efficiency, rapid agreement, and timeliness. Such cultures frequently expect and allocate shorter periods of time for negotiations and often set hard and fast deadlines.

Many other cultures see time as an unlimited resource; they believe that problem solving should not be rushed and will all occur in good time. It is not that these cultures do not have deadlines, but that their deadlines are more distant than is common in more speedy cultures.

When disputants are out of sync in their sense of time and timeliness, additional conflicts may result. For example, North Americans often complain of the time it takes to reach an agreement in many Latin American and Asian countries and grouse that if deadlines are set, they are ignored. This cultural problem is generally due to different expectations regarding the meaning, value, and use of time.

When working in intercultural disputes, mediators need to become aware of the different expectations that parties may have for the use of time and deadlines (to say nothing of clashes with mediators' own expectations in this regard). Mediators may need to act as cultural interpreters and time negotiators in order to coordinate the parties' activities in the context of time.

| Chapter Fourteen |

Achieving Formal Agreement or Settlement

The final stage of mediation requires disputants to formalize the agreement and design an implementation and monitoring procedure. Success in this final stage ensures both an immediate settlement and an agreement that will hold over time.

Depending on the situation and the culture, the formalization of the agreement may occur either before or after the development of the implementation and monitoring plan.

Implementing the Agreement

Implementation refers to procedural steps that disputants or mediators take to operationalize an agreement and to terminate a dispute (Coser, 1967). Implementation is discussed here as a specific phase of negotiation and a separate set of mediator interventions because it poses critical problems that must be overcome if the agreement is to endure.

The success of a substantive agreement frequently depends on the strength of the implementation plan. Parties may fail to reach substantive agreement because they cannot conceive how it could be implemented. Later, parties may fail to adhere to a poorly conceived plan. Insufficient consideration of implementation may result in settlements that create devastating precedents, and these may engender reluctance to negotiate in the future. Other possible results are damaged interpersonal relationships and losses in money, time, or resources. For these reasons, mediators may need to carefully assist parties in devising reasonable, efficient, and effective implementation procedures.

There are two types of procedures for executing agreements: "A self-executing agreement is one which is either: (1) carried out in its entirety at the time it is accepted, or (2) formulated in such a way that the extent to which the players adhere to its terms will be self-evident. A nonself-executing agreement, on the other hand, is one which requires continuing performance which may be difficult to measure in the absence of special monitoring arrangements" (Young, 1972, p. 58).

An example of a self-executing agreement is the mediated settlement of a dispute over the amount of legal fees a client was to pay a lawyer. Once the parties agreed on the amount, the client wrote the lawyer a check for the amount owed. The payment immediately terminated the dispute.

The negotiated settlement of visitation terms for the child of a divorcing couple illustrates a non-self-executing agreement. Because visitation will occur over many years, the agreement will not be carried out in its entirety when the negotiation terminates. The parents will need to cooperate over time to ensure that both the spirit and the specific terms of the agreement are fulfilled. Frequent conflicts over visitation rights illustrate the difficulties of interpreting and complying with non-self-executing agreements.

A self-executing agreement is clearly a stronger and more effective means of ensuring that a settlement will be managed according to the negotiated terms. Compliance is tangible and immediate, and chances of violation are minimized. Mediators can often significantly assist parties in designing self-executing implementation plans so that the conflict can be terminated rapidly and there is no need for the settlement to be extended over time.

However, not all conflicts can be terminated or settlements completed in a self-executing and immediate manner. Certain agreements—regarding child or spousal support payments, house or car payments, monitoring of environmental mitigation measures, and ongoing work relationships—may inherently or structurally require performance over a long period of time.

Compliance is difficult to measure in non-self-executing agreements, and this type of agreement often results in later discord due to differing interpretations. In disputes in which a self-enforcing agreement cannot be reached, the parties often prefer not to settle at all or to use other settlement procedures rather than negotiate an agreement that may not be implemented or in which compliance is difficult to determine. In such cases, disputants may fail to agree not because they are unable to reach a substantive settlement on issues in dispute, but because they do not trust each other to perform according to the plan over time (Schelling, 1956).

Mediators and negotiators should consider eight factors that are important for the successful implementation of a settlement:

1. A consensual agreement about the criteria used to measure successful compliance
2. The general and specific steps required to implement the decision
3. Identification of the people who have the power to influence the necessary changes
4. An organizational structure (if applicable) to implement the agreement
5. Provisions that will accommodate both future changes in the terms of the agreement and changes in disputing parties themselves
6. Procedures to manage unintended or unexpected problems, or violations of the settlement, that may arise during implementation
7. Methods to monitor compliance, as well as the identity of the monitor(s)
8. Determination of the monitor's role (for example, whistleblower or enforcer)

Criteria for Compliance and Implementation Steps

The probability of noncompliance by one or more parties may increase in rough proportion to (1) the number and complexity of issues in dispute; (2) the number of parties involved; (3) the degree of psychological tension and distrust; and (4) the length of time during which the obligations of the agreement must be performed. This does not mean that the parties will intentionally violate the agreement, but that structural variables can make violation more likely. Negotiated or mediated agreements are not inherently more prone to noncompliance than other forms of dispute resolution processes. In fact, research indicates that mediated agreements have a high compliance rate (Cook, Rochl, and Shepard, 1980; Pearson, 1984; Bingham, 1984). However, because negotiated settlements are often conducted on an ad hoc basis, they are more susceptible to violation than conflict resolution approaches with strictly defined implementation procedures, such as judicial or legislative decision.

To mitigate this inherent weakness, mediators generally encourage disputants to strictly define both the criteria and the steps to be used in implementing their decisions. Mediators usually assume that the degree to which compliance criteria and steps are defined determines how well substantive or procedural disputes due to misinterpretation of agreements can be avoided. Of course, implementation steps can be so strictly defined that they hinder more than help, and parties can use highly defined agreements to create problems for each other. Minor infractions can escalate into another full-scale conflict or to claims of compliance in bad faith. However, this does not appear to be the norm.

Criteria for evaluating implementation steps are similar to those used to evaluate the effectiveness of a substantive settlement. Implementation steps should be (1) cost-efficient; (2) simple enough to be easily understood, yet detailed enough to prevent loopholes that cause later procedural disputes; (3) realistic in their demands on or expectations of parties; and (4) if necessary, able to withstand public scrutiny of standards of fairness.

Monitoring the Performance of Agreements

Agreements that must be performed over time frequently have self-contained evaluation procedures and structures. Parties often strictly define standards and schedules of performance, and periodic meetings are held to review compliance. The performance agreement may be monitored by the parties themselves, by a joint committee composed of party representatives (in complex multiparty disputes), or by a third party who is usually not the mediator—for example, a governmental agency, a respected third party, a court, or an independent monitoring committee (Straus, Clark, and Suskind, n.d.).

In one complex dispute involving seventy city government employees, the parties established an ongoing monitoring committee to ensure that all participants complied with tasks, responsibilities, and a work schedule that had been established. An annual meeting was set up, in which all the parties were to report on their progress and reach additional decisions as new issues developed.

If an independent third party is to effectively conduct monitoring, the monitoring body must be an individual or group that the disputants respect and trust. Its membership may vary according to the type of dispute. Community disputes may call for a large committee. Straus, Clark, and Suskind (n.d.) urge that "a committee of this type should include prominent community leaders, agency representatives, and technical advisors committed to the consensus that has been reached and to implementing the terms of the bargain. The membership of such a committee should be approved by all parties to the negotiation (and might include some of them)" (p. V–55).

In small interpersonal disputes or in intraorganizational conflicts, the monitor may be one or two individuals who are trusted by the disputing parties. For example, a divorcing couple may designate mutually respected relatives to monitor compliance with visitation terms.

If monitoring is to be effective, parties must clearly define the performance standards by which compliance is measured, the role of the monitors, and the limits of the third party's authority. Careful definition of these variables minimizes problems with the monitoring committee's or individual's functioning at a later time.

The degree of responsibility given to monitoring committees or individuals assigned to oversee implementation varies from one case to another. Monitors may merely review progress and confirm or deny that compliance has occurred, or they may actually oversee implementation of the agreement.

Another role for monitors is to activate or participate in a grievance procedure conducted by the parties themselves or by a third party. A grievance procedure is a process disputants resort to when disagreements arise during or as a result of settlement implementation. The establishment of a grievance procedure is often a functional prerequisite for initial settlement. Parties often believe that a grievance procedure gives them a way to redress new problems, to modify an agreement if necessary, or to avoid abandoning the entire settlement because of difficulty implementing a small component of the accord.

Grievance procedures vary in form and process. The procedure may be no more than a general agreement to reopen negotiations or return to mediation before pursuing other options such as litigation, or it may specifically define the method of settling a new conflict. Many labor-management, commercial, and interpersonal contracts provide for either renegotiation, mediation, or binding arbitration to resolve a dispute. Courts are including or requiring similar procedures in some mediated settlements of family disputes.

In cases such as the Whittamore-Singson dispute, the parties work to negotiate a detailed agreement with a time line for implementation. They also include a grievance mechanism that provides an option to return to mediation if the settlement is found to be unsatisfactory or needs modifications to achieve implementation.

Culture and Implementation

In many North American mediations between members of dominant ethnic groups, the implementation and monitoring procedures are considered to be part of the immediate negotiations, and agreements reached about these issues are incorporated into the final settlement agreement. In other cultures, implementation and monitoring may be seen as yet another negotiation or as an ongoing process of bargaining that follows the formalization of an initial substantive, procedural, or psychological agreement. For example, in many Asian countries, or in negotiations involving Asian nationals (Japanese or Chinese in particular), the negotiation of specific types of agreements may occur in phases. A first phase may conclude with an affirmation by all parties that a positive relationship exists and with an agreement that the parties will pursue further discussions. This phase and all subsequent phases are often marked by a ritual ceremonial meeting or meal. A second phase of negotiations may conclude with a set of agreements in principle that will guide the parties' future relationship. The third phase may result in significant substantive agreements, but with few details about how they will be implemented. This phase is generally celebrated with an "official" social occasion and meal that involves the key spokespersons or dignitaries from the various sides. The final phase is often a series of ongoing negotiations to work out the details and modify the existing agreement to meet unforeseen changing circumstances. This phase of negotiations may not have a formal ending, as the working out of the relationship between the parties is considered to be part of day-to-day activities.

As these descriptions indicate, cultural expectations are crucial elements in implementation. For example, if Western and Asian negotiators are not familiar with each other's expectations for the content and phasing of implementation activities, extreme frustration or additional conflict may arise. The Westerner will be striving for a highly defined agreement that includes a detailed implementation plan. After the agreement is formally recognized, negotiations are considered to be over. The Asian party may be expecting a series of negotiations, with each phase recognized by a ritual meeting; the final agreement will be only generally defined because the details will be worked out during the life of the agreement. Such differences in expectations have resulted in serious tensions between parties in a number of international joint ventures in the automobile industry. Mazda and the United Automobile Workers (UAW) encountered problems in implementing new labor-management relations because of different expectations about the schedule for working out details of the labor contract and because of the Japanese tendency to informally modify agreements to meet changing circumstances (Fucini and Fucini, 1990). Chrysler also had difficulties in China with the phasing and timing of negotiations, and lacked understanding of the role of ritual occasions that recognize the establishment of a relationship, the affirmation of general principles, the substantive agreement, and ongoing mini-negotiations to address day-to-day problems (Mann, 1989).

Needless to say, a mediator working in intercultural negotiations needs to understand parties' expectations and procedures for the work of implementation. In many cases, the mediator may have to act as a cultural interpreter between the parties, explain their different assumptions and approaches, and assist them in working together to implement the agreement.

Formalizing Settlement

The final steps of negotiating or mediating a dispute focus on formalizing the settlement. This phase depends on (1) the implementation of commitment-inducing procedures that will enhance the probability of adherence and (2) some form of symbolic con-flict termination activity.

Commitment-Inducing Procedures

Negotiated settlements endure not only because their implemen-tation plans are effectively structured and meet the interests of the parties but because parties are psychologically and structurally committed to the agreement. Negotiators and mediators should be particularly concerned in this last phase of negotiations with building in psychological and structural factors that will bind the parties to the negotiated settlement. Commitment-inducing pro-cedures can be voluntary and implemented unilaterally by the par-ties or can be involuntary measures executed by an external party.

Voluntary Commitment Procedures

Voluntary commitment procedures are activities initiated by the mediator or the negotiators that enhance the probability that the disputants will voluntarily comply with the settlement. Specific mea-sures include

- Private oral exchange of promises between disputants in the mediator's presence
- Private oral exchange of promises between disputants in the presence of authority figures or parties whose disapproval the disputants would fear should they violate the agreement (relatives, workplace superiors, mentors, religious leaders, and so on)
- Public oral exchange of promises (press release or press conference)
- Symbolic exchange of gifts, tokens of affection, first pay-ments, early payment (Fisher, 1969), and so on, as an indi-cation of bargaining in good faith and willingness to fulfill commitments
- Symbolic gestures of friendship that demonstrate a willingness to take personal risk in order to implement the negotiated settlement
- Informal written agreements (memorandums of understanding)
- Formal written agreement (contract, covenant, and so on)

Voluntary agreements and commitment-inducing activities should not be underestimated as means of ensuring compliance. In a 1980 study measuring agreement compliance in mediated cases at neighborhood justice centers with informal or unenforced commitment procedures, between 81 and 95 percent of respondents stated that they had honored all the terms of their agreement. (A total of 315 respondents from the various centers answered this question.) In response to another question answered by a total of 286 people, between 52.4 and 74.1 percent of respondents agreed that the other party or parties had honored all the terms of their agreement (Cook, Rochl, and Shepard, 1980, p. 56). Labor-management settlements have much higher rates of compliance. These data indicate that there is significant voluntary adherence to the terms of negotiated settlements.

A review of fifty-one studies of the process and outcome of family mediation found that the parties reached complete agreement in between 40 percent and 60 percent of the cases and partial agreement in 10 to 20 percent of the conflicts. "These overall agreement rates varied between 50 percent and 80 percent, with most studies closer to the higher than the lower figure" (Benjamin and Irving, 1995, p. 57). These rates tended to be consistent regardless of whether the services were provided by a court-based or private program, whether participation was mandatory or voluntary, or whether little or intense family conflict was involved. A handful of the studies looked at satisfaction compliance and post-mediation reescalation of family disputes from four months to two years after the last session was held. Forty to sixty percent of the parties remained satisfied with both the process and the outcome of mediation, and all of the studies found higher rates of satisfaction than in control groups that had used litigation as a means of settling their differences.

Satisfaction can generally be correlated with compliance. "In addition several studies noted that a substantial portion of clients, in the 40 percent–65 percent range, had made changes to the terms of their agreement by mutual consent" (Benjamin and Irving, 1995, p. 63). The authors of the report also found that relitigation rates among couples that had participated in mediation were extremely low, and much lower than among families that had used litigation to resolve their initial conflicts. Benjamin and Irving (1995, p. 64) conclude that "mediated agreements tend to endure and their terms and conditions are typically complied with."

Externally Executed Commitment Procedures

On occasion there are problems with voluntary compliance. Negotiators and mediators often attempt to overcome these weaknesses with structural and external enforcement provisions that enhance the probability of compliance.

Parties may initiate mutually binding commitment procedures that, once established, are structural assurances that the settlement will be maintained. These structural assurances determine that performance of settlements will be enforced, and that the parties will not have to rely exclusively on promises of good faith or the unpredictable pressures of public opinion. There are a variety of structural means of inducing commitment.

Legal contracts are the most common way of ensuring commitment to an agreement in many situations and cultures. A legal contract is an agreement between two or more parties that is judicially enforceable. Contracts are characterized by an exchange of consideration, a promise, or an act that one party agrees to perform in return for promises or acts from another. For example, several professionals wanted to establish a private group practice. One of their prospective partners was better known and earned a larger income. They wanted to resolve how they were to invest capital in the practice and the terms for payment of each partner. They hired a mediator to help resolve their differences over financial arrangements and to draft a memorandum of understanding that they would later ask a lawyer to formalize as a contract. All parties wanted to have their financial rights protected by a formal and legal agreement.

Legal contracts generally provide parties with a judicial recourse should one or more parties fail to honor promises. Parties who have suffered what they consider a breach of contract can sue another party for redress of grievances. If the suit is successful, the plaintiff or party initiating the suit can receive one of three possible types of remedies (Straus, Clark, and Suskind, n.d., pp. V–58–59):

- Damages—financial compensation for the consequences of the defendant's breach

- Recision of the contract—the court voids the contract and releases the plaintiff from his or her contractual obligations
- Specific performance—the court orders the defendant to comply with the terms of the contract

Negotiated agreements do not automatically become contracts enforceable under law. The enforceability of contracts depends both on the laws and rules of the legal jurisdiction in which they are promulgated and the forms that the contracts take.

Although a verbal agreement may be considered a legal contract, especially if made in the presence of witnesses, a written document is safer. Written documents that are to become contracts must contain at minimum (1) the *name* (or kind of contract); (2) the *parties*, including date and place of agreement; (3) *recitals* that detail the relationship of the parties and describe the contract's function; (4) the *promise clause*, which describes the exchanges the parties are to make; and (5) *closing* and *signatures* (Brown, 1955).

In addition to the contents of the agreement, the way the settlement is written can make a difference in its acceptability and later compliance. Saposnek (1983, p. 102) identifies four additional factors to consider in drafting agreements: (1) the clarity of the clauses; (2) the degree of detail in the clauses; (3) the balance of concessions; and (4) "the attitude and perspective connoted."

Clarity of clauses refers to writing that precludes the possibility of diverse interpretations or misinterpretations. Mediators should work with the parties to clarify their intentions and then—either alone or in collaboration with the parties—draft the memorandum of understanding, which will later become a contract, so that loopholes are eliminated. The mediator should ask himself or herself and the parties where later interpretation problems might exist and try to eliminate them in the initial draft (Salacuse, 1989).

- *Degree of detail in the clauses* refers to the specificity of the agreement. Usually, the more precise the terms of settlement, the less likely that interpretation conflicts will arise. In disputes in which the parties are highly emotional and in which there is little trust, strictly worded agreements that specify all details may be crucial in terminating the dispute.

In disputes in which the parties have a positive relationship, however, detail can sometimes be viewed as a disadvantage. A detailed agreement may suggest lack of trust or inability to solve new problems that may arise in the future. One party may also use the detailed agreement to harass the other so that the terms are honored to an excessive degree. Fanatical adherence to an agreement's details can cause another party to resist compliance and thus promote additional discord. The mediator, in drafting an agreement, must clearly consider the abilities of the parties to negotiate later details if they are needed, the degree of trust of the parties, and the tendency of the parties to use an agreement as a weapon against their opponents. Specificity may either encourage or discourage future conflict.

• *Balance of concessions* refers to the equity of the exchanges made by the parties. The written agreement should clearly identify what is to be exchanged, and it should be written so that the settlement does not appear one-sided. The document may alternate parties from one exchange clause to the next to maintain the perception of balance. The exchanges need not be equal in number, but the importance of the interests satisfied must be equivalent if renewed conflict is to be avoided. The mediator will often have to search for the terms that will facilitate exchange.

On occasion, a psychological concession such as "John acknowledges that Philip was proceeding in good faith" can be traded for a specific substantive exchange. Equality of exchange can also be maintained by mentioning both parties in the clause— for example, "Neither Paul nor Mary will make disparaging remarks about the other parent in the presence of the children." With equal treatment for the two parties, an acceptable exchange may be made.

• A *positive attitude and perspective* are the final consideration in drafting an agreement. A settlement document is an affirmation of the willingness and ability of the parties to cooperate. The document should note and encourage cooperative attitudes and behaviors. In the recitals—the preamble to the section that details precise exchanges—the mediator may include a statement about the willingness of the parties to end the dispute, their commitment to bargaining in good faith, their dedication to complying with the agreement, and their commitment to cooperative problem solving.

In a business relationship, the statement may read, "After a period of bargaining in good faith, labor and management have agreed to the following terms that both expect to result in mutual benefit." In a custody case, the parents may affirm, "Both of us love our children very much and want to arrange for a living situation that will provide them with stability and continuity with both parents, their extended families, their neighborhood, and friends. We make the following agreements because we believe that they are the best possible arrangements for the children and for each of us."

It should be noted that specific kinds of disputes and particular cultures may merit different kinds of written documents. In some cases, informal minutes or a memorandum of understanding may be all that is expected or needed by the parties. In other situations, a more formal document may be needed, both to detail the terms of the settlement and for ritual purposes. Elaborate settlement documents, on high-quality paper with the parties' signatures or seals, may serve to induce commitment. Settlement agreements in some of the phases described under "Culture and Implementation" may also be expected.

It has already been noted that cultures may differ in their expectations concerning the levels of detail and closure on issues described in a written settlement document. The mediator may have to work with the parties to coordinate their expectations and to develop a document that is mutually acceptable in these respects. The mediator may also have to work with translators to ensure that different versions of the document, if written in more than one language, are congruent and have the same meanings to all parties.

Judicial supervision is a second structural means to bind parties to agreements. If disputing parties reach a negotiated settlement while awaiting a court hearing, they may stipulate to the court the terms of their agreement, and the court will then include these terms in the final decree. This is common practice in many countries—for example, in mediated business disputes or divorce settlements. Generally, the parties take their agreement to their respective lawyers, who may change the wording to comply with legal standards and practice and then submit the document to the court as a stipulated settlement.

A second example of judicial supervision of negotiated settlements is the process used in the selection of representatives to negotiations that will affect classes of people in complex disputes.

Straus, Clark, and Suskind (n.d., pp. V–61–62) suggest that legislation could be passed that would establish "a process whereby a court supervises the selection of representatives to act as agents of recognized diffuse interests. This is precisely the procedure currently employed to appoint representatives in class action suits." A similar procedure has been used to appoint the guardian *ad litem* to represent a child's interests in mediated disputes involving termination of parental rights (Mayer, 1985).

Administrative or legislative action sometimes follows from negotiated settlements and serves to enforce compliance. (Many administrative and legislative bodies commonly use negotiation procedures in their daily operations, but here I refer to extra-parliamentary negotiations.) Negotiated settlements that involve regulatory or policy content have routinely been recommended for inclusion in new agency policies or regulations or in legislative bills. A negotiated settlement that is drafted into a bill or regulation and becomes law can be enforced by appointed officials.

Executive action is also used in some instances to formalize negotiated settlements and bind the parties to adhere to them. This is especially the case when negotiations are sponsored by an elected or appointed executive. The settlement of conditions for the issuance of general dredge and fill permits on Sanibel Island in Florida was negotiated under the supervision of the U.S. Army Corps of Engineers—and was subsequently approved and implemented by them.

Economic incentives or constraints are another structural device that encourages adherence to the terms of a settlement. Two economic approaches are common: agreement on indemnification and performance bonds (Straus, Clark, and Suskind, n.d.).

- *Agreement on indemnification* refers to a commitment by the parties to the amount and form of compensation if one or more parties fail to comply with the terms of the agreement. Agreement on indemnification pressures the parties to adhere to the agreement because the costs of not doing so are specified before the breach of contract occurs. However, this succeeds only when conditions of violation are easily identified or measured. An example of agreement on indemnification can be found in the terms of settlement between the developer of a shopping center and residents of the surrounding neighborhood, who argued that they would be adversely affected by the mall's presence. The developer agreed to protect land values of residential property owners by guaranteeing a sale of the property at a fair market price to be determined by an appraisal before the mall's construction. The developer agreed to buy the properties or pay the difference between the actual selling price and the appraised value if the former price was lower. This offer was to be in effect for five years after the mall's construction (Baldwin, 1978).

• Performance bonds are one step beyond agreements on indemnification in that they require a party to post a bond or reserve a specific sum of money to ensure that assets are available to pay for noncompliance. The use of performance bonds is an ancient method of ensuring adherence to agreements. Fifteenth- and sixteenth-century Japanese warlords required performance bonds in the form of relatives of their subordinates. The warlords would hold these relatives captive in their capital cities; if a functionary did not perform his contractual duties, his relatives would be put to death.

Performance bonds today are usually funds held in escrow by a financial institution. The release of the bond is effected by an appointed neutral party who establishes that the terms of the settlement have been violated. This third party may be a monitoring committee established by the parties themselves or an independent, publicly recognized authority.

In the case of the shopping center described above, the developer agreed to construct a fourteen-foot-high landscaped berm as a boundary between the development and the residential neighborhood. A $100,000 letter of credit was deposited at a local bank to guarantee construction funds.

Symbolic Conflict Termination Activities

Whereas some social processes have definite beginnings and endings, others have no precise points at which they may be said to have started or terminated. Coser (1967, p. 47) observes that social conflicts "follow a law of social inertia insofar as they continue to operate if no explicit provision for stopping their course is made by the participants. Whereas in a game, for example, the rules for the process include rules for its ending, in social conflict explicit provisions for its termination must be made by the contenders."

Unlike lower animals, human beings have not devised regularized communication patterns to symbolize when a conflict should or has in fact ceased. Failure to define when a dispute has ended or when a negotiated settlement has been reached can result in unnecessary extended conflict. The forms that symbolic conflict termination activities take clearly depend on the context in which the dispute occurs and the degree of common acceptance of the symbols.

Negotiators and mediators often try to create activities that symbolically indicate termination of a conflict. Handshaking, formal signing procedures, toasts, and celebratory meals are common ways of jointly affirming the termination of a dispute. One mediator provided a divorcing couple with a bottle of champagne to acknowledge the end of a successful child custody negotiation. In a large community dispute over county land use, the participants celebrated successful completion of negotiations with a banquet that all parties attended.

In the Whittamore-Singson dispute, the parties would normally opt for either the development of a new written contract, or a modification of the old one, that details the terms of the agreement and the steps of implementation. This document would probably be drafted by the attorneys of one or both parties and couched in legal language based on the memorandum of understanding reached by the parties in mediation and drawn up by the mediator. There is commonly a joint signing ceremony in which the agreement would be sealed by a handshake between the parties. There might also be some witnesses present, to confirm that a settlement has been reached.

Although negotiators themselves may identify and initiate some ritual act or behavior that they believe will terminate a conflict or negotiation, lack of common perceptions as to the meaning of the act, persisting antagonism, or lack of innovative skills on the part of the other side may inhibit its acceptance. Mediators can often help the parties to plan or structure termination signals, rituals, or ceremonies that will be mutually acceptable and meaningful. Naturally, the type of initiative that a mediator takes will depend on the situation, the relationship of the parties, and the authority the parties have vested in him or her to design such activities.

Culture and Achieving Agreement

Culture may be a factor in considering the design of symbolic dispute termination activities. Ritual meals, with special menus, symbolic speeches, blessings by priests, prayers, or other symbolic acts may be appropriate if participating parties attach importance to them. An interesting ritual closure occurred in a recent case in Thailand, in which two families had fought a long and lethal feud over land rights and timber sales. After concluding substantive negotiations, the mediator, a Buddhist priest, invited the parties to attend a ritual ceremony to end the conflict. He asked them to bring a weapon that they would surrender at the ceremony to symbolize the giving up of violent means of resolving differences. At the gathering, the weapons were placed in a box, and sacred water was poured on them. All parties were asked to drink from the box to symbolize the end of the dispute and their mutual bond. The priest knew that this ritual—which had been performed in times past by a Thai king—would have meaning to the parties and would act on them as a strong inducement to keep their commitments.

Chapter Fifteen

Strategies for Dealing with Special Situations

The previous chapters have focused for the most part on noncontingent mediator strategies. These interactions between the mediator and a single party or between the mediator and multiple disputants are performed regardless of the type of dispute, the number or variety of issues, or the number of parties.

I now turn to contingent strategies and activities—interventions a mediator makes to respond to specific or unusual problems posed by disputants or to conditions that are not present in every negotiation (Smart, 1987). In examining contingent activities, I will discuss interventions that are applicable to two-party conflicts and to disputes involving negotiation teams and their constituents.

It is impossible to identify and describe all of the contingent strategies and activities mediators initiate to respond to specific situations. The most comprehensive listings to date of contingent strategies are those developed by Fisher (1978), Maggiolo (1972), and Wall (1981). There are, however, five categories of contingent strategies and activities that are particularly common:

1. The caucus technique
2. Techniques using mediator power and influence
3. Techniques for managing the power relations between parties
4. Techniques used with multiperson negotiation teams
5. Techniques used with teams when wider constituencies are involved

Caucuses

In a caucus, the disputants are physically separated from each other and direct communication between parties is intentionally restricted (Moore, 1987; Bethel, 1986). Caucuses are initiated in response either to external forces that affect the negotiators and the general conflict situation or to problems arising from issues, events, or dynamics in the joint session.

Factors That May Necessitate a Caucus

External forces—political, economic, and social and cultural pressures—can all create changes during negotiations. More easily catalogued are the internal dynamics between negotiators that may require a caucus. There are three general categories of internal dynamics: (1) problems with the *relationships* between the parties or within a team; (2) problems with the *negotiation process;* and (3) problems with *substantive issues* under discussion.

Numerous problems in the relationships between team members or opponents may lead to the holding of a caucus. The parties or the mediator may initiate a caucus for any of the following reasons: to allow intense emotions to be vented without escalating differences between the parties; to clarify perceptions or misperceptions; to change unproductive or repetitive negative behavior; or to diminish and limit unhelpful communications.

Procedural problems may also call for a caucus. The parties or the mediator may hold a private meeting to clarify or assess the negotiation procedure used by one or all parties; to design new procedures, either for negotiations within a group or for joint negotiations; or to break the flow of negative procedures. Caucuses can also be called by parties or the mediator to explore substantive issues such as definition of interests, clarification of positions, identification of new offers, or weighing of another party's proposals.

In addition, mediators can use a caucus to

- Provide the parties (or the mediator) with a pause if the pressure to progress in joint session is too intense and is not promoting productive exchange
- Refocus the motivation of the parties on why a settlement is important and what alternatives to negotiated settlement exist

- Conduct reality testing of a party's proposals
- Encourage a party who is in doubt about whether his or her interests can be satisfied by pursuing present unsatisfactory tactics to persevere or try a new negotiation approach.
- Act as a sounding board for a party
- Uncover confidential information that may not be revealed in joint session
- Control communication between parties so that they focus exclusively on substance and eliminate all emotional communication as conveyed by speech or nonverbal signals
- Educate an inexperienced disputant about negotiation procedures or dynamics
- Prevent a party from making premature concessions or a premature commitment in joint session, or from adhering to an untenable or hard-line position
- Develop a single-text negotiating document when parties are too numerous, issues too complex, or emotions too heated for face-to-face encounters
- Develop settlement alternatives in an environment that separates the process of option generation from that of evaluation
- Determine if an acceptable bargaining range has been established (or create one)
- Design proposals or offers that will later be brought to joint session
- Test the acceptability of one party's proposal by presenting the offer to another party as an option the mediator himself or herself has generated
- Make appeals to common principles or superordinate goals
- Express their own perceptions of the situation and possibly make suggestions for settlement options

Timing

Caucuses can be held at almost any time in negotiations. If they are initiated early, it is usually for the purpose of venting emotions, designing negotiating procedures, or identifying issues. Caucuses held in the middle of negotiations typically focus on preventing premature commitment to a position, identifying interests, generating alternatives, and testing bargaining ranges. Those held at the end of negotiations usually are designed to break deadlocks, develop or assess proposals, develop a settlement formula, or achieve a psychological settlement. Clearly, there is no correct time to call a caucus because its necessity is highly dependent on the needs and skills of the individual negotiators and mediator. In some disputes, there may be numerous caucuses, whereas in others, caucuses may not be used at all.

Mediators should take care not to schedule caucuses prematurely, when parties are still capable of working productively in joint session, nor too late, after unproductive hostile exchanges or actions have hardened positions.

Location

For caucuses to be most effective, they need to provide a genuine separation of the parties. This usually means separate rooms where parties neither see nor hear each other, and where they feel safe to discuss issues or problems candidly. Mediators responsible for selecting the negotiation site should provide facilities that have spaces for caucuses. Inadequate sites may necessitate returning to a party's headquarters or to neutral ground where confidentiality can be ensured.

Protocol

Although the caucus is a technique commonly used to facilitate productive negotiations, there are few standards for implementation that apply to all situations. Tasks that must be undertaken by mediators who initiate a caucus include

- Educating the parties about the technique
- Overcoming resistance of the parties to separate meetings
- Making the transition to the caucus
- Deciding which party to caucus with first
- Determining the duration of the caucus
- Determining what is said in the caucus
- Facilitating the return to joint session

Although the caucus is familiar to the experienced negotiator, novices may not be aware of its usefulness. Mediators should explain at the start of negotiation and in their opening statements that caucuses may be held at some time during mediation, and that either the parties or the mediator may initiate them.

Parties occasionally resist caucusing with a mediator. This resistance may be associated with concerns about confidentiality, fear of coalition formation between the mediator and the other party (Simmel, 1955), or political problems with constituencies that can result from private meetings (Maggiolo, 1972). The mediator does not want to create unnecessary barriers between himself or herself and one or more parties by pushing disputants to use an unacceptable technique. Mediators should explain the general reasons for the caucus before using the technique and should allow disputants to make an independent decision about whether to meet in private at the specific time that a caucus might be needed. If the parties do not consider a caucus necessary, the mediator should accede to their choice. However, if the mediator believes that failure to caucus will eventually lead to a breakdown in negotiations, he or she may refuse to mediate unless the parties meet separately.

Progress from joint session to caucus must be conducted smoothly so that the flow of negotiations is not interrupted. Parties may initiate caucuses by formally calling for a time to meet privately or by asking for informal breaks. Mediators use the same procedures. When caucuses are formally called, a specific duration for the separate meetings is often jointly established. To make this transition, the mediator can say, "You have been discussing this issue together for quite a while. I believe that it might be helpful to take a break so that you can reflect on the available options in private. During this time, I would like to speak to each of you privately and explore whether there is any additional room for movement. I estimate that I will talk to each of you for about ten minutes."

Mediators can use several informal guidelines to determine which party to meet first. In early caucuses, the mediator usually meets first with either the initiator of the dispute or the party that called for the caucus. Caucuses held later in negotiations follow a different rule. "If neither side has indicated any flexibility in their bargaining position, the first caucus should be held with the party appearing most inflexible. In such situations, some movement is necessary if negotiations are to proceed along fruitful lines" (Maggiolo, 1972, p. 53). If, however, the mediator perceives that one of the parties is extremely upset or is exhibiting emotional distance from or hostility toward the mediator, the intervenor may choose to caucus with that party first.

There is no general rule for duration of a caucus. Some mediators argue that private meetings should be held for as long as necessary to accomplish a desired purpose (Maggiolo, 1972), whereas others argue for brief, time-specific meetings. Common practice and courtesy dictate that if a caucus is to take more than an hour, a formal break should be called in negotiations so that the party with whom the caucus is not being held is not kept waiting.

Regardless of how long a caucus with one party lasts, the mediator should confer with the other party before reconvening joint sessions. Meeting with the other party demonstrates equitable and impartial behavior and may also be an occasion to test options that have developed in the first caucus. Meeting with the other party can alleviate curiosity about what has occurred in the first caucus, maintain the trust relationship between the intervenor and the parties, and help educate disputants about what will transpire when they return to joint session.

Unless specified otherwise, conversations held between the mediator and disputants in caucus are considered confidential. Confidentiality generally encourages parties to be more candid in conversations with the mediator and enables them to explore options that entail more risk.

In caucus, mediators can play stronger roles as allies to parties and can be more supportive than is acceptable in joint session. This often enables parties to progress and to find acceptable options that they resisted in joint session. Care must be taken, however, not to form so close a relationship with the party that neutrality is lost. Similarly, the mediator must not lose the capacity to separate from the party and assume responsibility for the following joint session.

Mediators can also be more firm with a party in caucus than they can in joint session. They can undertake reality testing, propose hypothetical options, and question a party's judgment in caucus, which they cannot do in joint session. They can protect the negotiator's integrity while asking firm questions and creating doubt about the viability of adhering to hard-line positions.

Information shared with mediators in caucus is often crucial to reaching agreements. However, the confidentiality barrier may inhibit such information from being used to its best effect. The mediator can pursue several strategies to overcome this barrier.

First, he or she may directly obtain the party's permission to disclose the information to the other side by explaining how it will be used and what benefits could result.

Second, the mediator may explain that he or she would like to talk with the other party about information discussed in the caucus and ask, "Is there anything that we have talked about that you would not like me to disclose?" This process allows the party to specifically identify what he or she wishes to remain confidential and gives the mediator the authority to disclose other information as he or she sees fit.

Third, the mediator may take an idea generated with one disputant and claim it as his or her own when talking with another disputant. This conceals the proposal's connection with the originating party—making it perhaps more acceptable—and enables the mediator to test a possible settlement without committing any of the parties to it. If both parties agree to a solution but do not realize that the other is in agreement, the mediator must then decide who is to propose the solution, and how it is to be framed.

It is crucial that the party who proposes a solution developed in caucus assume ownership of it and not present it simply in order to please the mediator. Furthermore, the party must be able to defend the offer in joint session. This is true whether or not the mediator knows that the proposal is acceptable to the other side. The mediator may otherwise be accused of forcing his or her own preferences on the disputants.

During caucuses with the parties, the mediator should determine how the parties will be brought together again in joint session. Factors to consider include how to (1) explain the purpose and results of the caucus; (2) determine which party speaks first after the caucus; and (3) decide how offers will be made after the caucus. Many of these strategic questions must be answered while the caucuses are in session so that the mediator can prepare the parties for their next moves.

Although there are no firm rules for mediator and negotiator activities that result from a caucus, there are some general guidelines. Parties with greater power are often able to make the first move or offer after a caucus without losing integrity or advantage. They may have greater resources and therefore may be able to be magnanimous, or they may have sufficient self-confidence or sufficient respect from other parties that they will not lose face or status by making the first move. Parties with offers contingent on another party's offer should speak only after the opponent's offer has been made. Simultaneous offers (with both parties putting written offers on the table at the same time) or incremental alternating offers (in which the parties alternate providing benefits to each other) may also be used. Mediators should take care to sequence speakers to ensure that the order of presentation does not prejudice a party's interests, and that a party does not inadvertently offer premature concessions.

Caucuses and Manipulation

Although the caucus is one of the most common and effective contingent strategies, it is not without problems. Caucuses provide mediators with the greatest opportunity to manipulate parties into an agreement because disputants do not have the advantage of face-to-face communication to test the accuracy of information exchanged.

Keltner (1965, pp. 74–75) notes that

> in separating the parties during negotiations the mediator establishes himself as the main channel of communication between the parties. For example, in a separate session with the company the mediator expresses doubts that the offer that he is asked to carry to the union will be accepted, thereby *minimizing* the possibility of acceptance. Shortly thereafter he will meet the union and will *maximize* the desirability of acceptance of the proposal. This control and manipulation of the channel of communication and the introduction into it, thereby, of evaluative material provides him with some strength in bringing the parties closer together toward an area of agreement.

The ability to control, manipulate, suppress, or enhance data, or to introduce entirely new information, gives the mediator an inordinate amount of influence over the parties. The ethics of such control and the proper role of the intermediary are hotly debated topics among mediators (Stevens, 1963). Young (1972, p. 57) observes that "it is difficult for an intermediary to engage in such manipulative activities without exhibiting some degree of partiality among the original players, either explicitly or implicitly. This raises a variety of problems concerning the acceptability of partial behavior on the part of intermediaries. And it may generate additional tactical rigidities in the interactions among the original players if they become concerned with actual or perceived partiality on the part of an intermediary."

An additional problem in caucuses arises with tensions between pushing for disclosure and encouraging retention of information. The majority of mediators treat communications in the caucus as confidential. Parties occasionally reveal information to the mediator that may place him or her in a potentially compromising position. For example, a husband may tell a mediator that he has a hidden bank account that his wife does not know about and that he does not want to include in the financial settlement. Or a party may acknowledge to a mediator that he or she has lied or made a false claim in the joint session that will adversely affect the outcome for the other party. These examples illustrate how the mediator, by using a caucus and assuring confidentiality, may place himself or herself in an ethical bind. Should confidentiality be the mediator's highest value, or should full disclosure of information relative to a fair settlement of the dispute have primacy? There is probably no single right answer to this question, but because of problems created by the commitment to confidentiality, many mediators take great care when using the caucus. Some mediators tell the parties what they are willing or not willing to hear, and where the limits of confidentiality end. Several ethical codes or model standards require that the mediator disclose the limits of confidentiality at the beginning of the mediation session and carefully describe when confidentiality will be broken. Lack of full financial disclosure, child abuse, or imminent physical danger, for example, are legitimate grounds for breaking confidentiality, according to the *Model Standards of the Association of Family and Conciliation Courts* (1984).

Other mediators refuse to assure confidentiality in caucuses and use them merely to discuss issues without the tension induced by the physical presence of the other party. Although this procedure is an exception, not the rule, it does protect the mediator from being placed in the bind just described.

Regardless of its susceptibility to confidentiality problems and manipulation, the caucus remains one of the major contingent mediator strategies. In many disputes, settlement would be impossible if separate meetings were not conducted.

Mediator Power and Influence

Ideally, all disputes should be resolved by rational dialogue and goodwill. However, mistrust and power imbalances prevent this in a significant number of conflicts. Parties often resort to the exercise of power to determine the outcome of negotiations. Mediators, too, use various means of influence to change the dynamics of bargaining (Mayer, 1987). For mediators to be effective, they must know how to manage the means of influence and power the parties exercise and how to exert pressure themselves.

Power or *influence* is the capability of a person or group to modify the outcome of a situation—that is, the benefits received by another and the costs inflicted, in the context of a relationship (Thibaut and Kelly, 1959). The capacity to influence the outcome for another party depends on the exercise of various means of pressure or persuasion that either discourage or encourage the possibility of various options. Mediators, although neutral in relationship to the parties and generally impartial toward the substantive outcome, are directly involved in influencing disputants toward settlement. In this section, I will examine two topics related to the mediator's exercise of power or influence. First, I will identify the forms that mediator influence takes, and second, I will explore how this influence may be exercised when parties have equal and unequal power.

Influence is usually designed to change the viewpoint or condition of another. Means of influence can be placed on a continuum that indicates the amount of leverage or pressure that is being applied to encourage change and the degree of directiveness of the initiator. Usually, directiveness and pressure are directly correlated. Thus, at one end of the continuum, the means of influence exert low pressure toward change, and the person using the leverage is not very directive. At the other end, the pressure is intense, and the initiator is extremely directive.

Mediators generally use twelve forms of influence to incline parties toward agreement. I will examine each of these means and indicate where they lie on this continuum.

Management of the Negotiation Process

In every dispute, the mediator exerts a specific degree of control over the sequence of negotiation and problem-solving steps and the management of individual agenda items. He or she must choose—on the basis of the situation, the parties, and the issues in dispute—whether to have limited influence and make few procedural suggestions (either general or specific); to be moderately influential and provide some structure; or to be highly influential, with much directiveness and a highly detailed procedure over which parties have a low degree of control. Kolb (1983) notes this continuum in her description of labor-management mediators. She found some to be "orchestrators," who made less directive procedural interventions, and others to be "deal-makers," who were highly directive and controlled both the process and substance under discussion. A similar continuum is common in family disputes. Coogler (1978) illustrates the more directive end of the continuum, and Stulberg (1981a) is probably at the other end.

Communication Between and Within Parties

The mediator can manage both communication behavior and structure in negotiations. Communication behavior can be managed by using techniques of active listening and reframing for the purpose of clarification and problem definition. The structure of communication may be modified by asking the parties to meet together, to talk directly to each other, to talk only to the mediator in each other's presence, or to caucus and communicate only through the intervenor. In caucus, the mediator has extensive control over what will or will not be communicated and can frame information exchange so that it is more likely to be accepted. The mediator can exert great influence by being very directive about communicative behavior or structure, or may play a much less directive role and still be effective.

Physical Setting and Negotiations

Mediators may modify the physical setting to encourage parties to settle. Seating arrangements, table shape, room size, availability of caucusing space, and removal of the negotiations from the scene of conflict can all affect outcome. Highly directive intervenors may use one or many of the above activities to influence settlement.

Timing in Negotiations

Decisions on timing govern the start of negotiations and their duration, the imposition or removal of deadlines for settlement, and the issuing of specific communications and offers. Mediators can be directive or nondirective in their control of timing, depending on their assessment of the parties and the situation.

Information Exchanged Between Parties

Negotiation involves a constant flow of information among the parties and the mediator. However, the content and form of that information vary, depending on the situation. Fisher (1978, pp. 141–142) developed an "asking ladder" that depicts the ways in which information is given or received in terms of the initiator's degree of directiveness. The ladder ranges from requests for information to general suggestions, specific suggestions, concrete proposals, and demands. Mediators usually make less directive moves with respect to information; they usually ask questions and make suggestions rather than issue demands or force parties toward specific substantive conclusions. They may, however, play more directive roles in helping parties to identify what information needs to be exchanged, what form it should take, and how it will best be heard or received by other parties. Mediators may also occasionally refer parties to sources of needed information.

Associates of the Parties

Certain people wield *associational influence* on disputants to the extent that their opinions or actions affect the parties' attitudes or behavior. Associates include friends, colleagues, family members, other members of a disputing group, and constituents. Mediators should assess when these associates should be included or excluded from the negotiations in order to induce settlement. The trusted words of a professional colleague or the involvement of a stepparent or grandparent in family negotiations may be all that is needed to change the dynamics of the dispute and incline the parties toward settlement. The mediator can often engineer the form and effect of associational influence.

Experts

Mediators can often influence the parties to settle by involving in negotiations people with particular expertise or areas of knowledge. The mediator can play either more directive or less directive roles in identifying the need for substantive, procedural, or psychological experts; in encouraging their use; and in proposing procedures for selecting them.

Authority

Authority refers to a widely recognized right or legitimate power to exercise influence or make a decision. Authority can be vested either in an institution or in a person's formal role. Mediators may exercise authority as a result of their affiliation with a mediation agency or, occasionally, a governmental body. Because of the prestige of their institutional connections, mediators who work for the Federal Mediation and Conciliation Service or those who are connected with a court or district attorney's office may be able to exercise more influence than the independent mediator without such affiliation. Parties may defer to the mediator on procedural and sometimes substantive issues because they acknowledge his or her skill, knowledge, and legitimate authority to be involved in a dispute.

Mediators may also call on other authorities to influence negotiators. They may appeal to a party's constituencies, superiors, judges, creditors, custody evaluators, or others to exert pressure on parties to settle. When a mediator obtains outside authorities, he or she is being highly directive. Although the mediator's goal may be gentle persuasion of a difficult party, an external authority's pressure is almost tantamount to coercion. Mediators should take extreme care when involving authority figures directly in negotiations.

Habits of Disputants

Many people in conflict have long-standing relationships in which routine patterns of behavior have been established. Business colleagues, lawyers, teachers, students, and spouses all develop relational routines that, for better or worse, are accepted as normal.

Mediators can often appeal to personal habits to reach settlement. For example, business disputants may be open to continuing their established accounting practices; divorcing spouses may readily agree that both should continue to make proportional financial contributions toward child support. Agreement to ratify some element of the status quo is often the first decision that parties may reach.

Parties' Doubts

Probably no negotiated agreement is ever reached without some doubt on the part of the parties that a better settlement might have been obtained if they had been firmer, had bargained longer, or had pursued another means of dispute resolution. Doubt, however, was their rationale for pursuing a negotiated settlement. If they had been certain that they could have reached a more satisfactory agreement by negotiating in a different way or pursuing another approach to dispute resolution, they probably would have done so.

Mediators often use doubt to influence parties toward settlement. Doubt about the viability of a position or settlement option can be raised or explored in joint session—where both parties must bear the potential negative consequences—but more often, the mediator instills doubt in one or more parties in a caucus. By raising questions about potential outcomes that the party may not like, the mediator can often moderate a party's position and incline him or her toward mutually acceptable settlement possibilities. For example, a mediator might ask

- Do you think you can win in court (or other public setting, such as before a commission or in the legislature)?
- How certain are you? Ninety percent? Seventy-five percent? Fifty percent?
- What risk are you willing to take?
- What if you lose?
- What will your life be like then?
- What impact do you think your victory in court (or other arena) will have on your ongoing relationship with the other party?
- Will you ever be able to work together again?
- Who else might be affected?
- What would they think of your position?
- Would you be proud to publicly announce this stance?
- Would others whom you respect feel it is reasonable?
- If you were in the other party's place and this proposal were made to you, would you accept it?
- Could you accept it over the long run?

Through careful questioning that may vary in degree of directiveness, the mediator may begin to create doubt in a party's mind about the feasibility of his or her adherence to an option. If misused, this technique obviously approaches manipulation and raises questions about the ethics of mediator influence.

Rewards or Benefits

Generally, mediators only indirectly influence the rewards that a party receives as a result of negotiation. The other party or parties to the dispute are usually the grantor of those benefits. The major exception to this rule is in international disputes in which the mediator is a representative of a powerful interest or nation and has resources at his or her command to bestow benefits such as foreign aid, military assistance, or recognition if the parties settle.

Mediators do, however, have some indirect rewards to offer as inducements to settlement. The mediator's friendship, respect for a person or point of view, interest in a party's personal well-being, or affirmation of how a point was settled can all induce a disputant to agree. The mediator's relationship with the parties is often the only positive reward that he or she can offer in negotiations. If the disputants value this, they may behave in ways that will encourage the mediator to continue his or her positive response.

Another indirect means of rewarding a party is to identify the benefits that the disputant could receive as a result of a settlement and to help him or her visualize what it would be like to have that settlement. Mediators can verbally project the beneficial outcome. If the disputants perceive the mediator's vision as adequate reward for settlement, they may move forward to agreement.

Coercive Influence

Coercive influence refers to the use of force to change another's opinion or behavior against his or her will. Coercive influence depends on decreasing a party's choices for settlement and then increasing the damage that the party will incur if he or she does not accept the designated outcome. Because mediation is voluntary and the mediator serves the parties, he or she usually has few direct coercive techniques available to influence disputants. Exceptions include some court-related mediators who are on occasion empowered by statute to make recommendations to the judge if the parties cannot settle; international mediators with powerful superiors who can damage recalcitrant parties; and intervenors practicing "med-arb," a mediation-arbitration hybrid in which the parties agree to allow the intervenor to mediate until an impasse occurs, at which time the mediator becomes an arbiter and decides the conflict's outcome.

There are, however, several indirect coercive techniques that may incline the parties toward settlement. A mediator's display of impatience or displeasure, as indicated by nonverbal communication or verbal statements, may "coerce" a party to move toward agreement. This may be especially true when a party wants the intervenor's respect or wants to maintain the respect of his or her group, and when this respect may be eroded by continuing an unpopular course of action. Mediator or peer approval—or its withdrawal—can be very important in moderating hard-line positions.

The mediator's most direct and coercive means of influencing parties is to threaten to withdraw from negotiations, or to actually do so. This is the ultimate act of disapproval and denial of service to the parties. In one case, a mediator believed that the parties were not negotiating in good faith and were delaying settlement. He announced that he wanted to terminate his participation because the parties did not seem to be making progress. He offered the parties his business card, told them to call him when they were ready to talk, and walked toward the door. He never reached it. The parties called him back and settled immediately.

Withdrawal or the threat of withdrawal is risky for the mediator and the parties because it may precipitate a breakdown in negotiations. Threats to withdraw succeed only if the parties consider the mediator unexpendable, and if they believe the threat. If these conditions are not met, the parties may even welcome the mediator's departure. Mediators should exercise care in using this technique because it can backfire and leave them out of the negotiations. Even if it works, the tactic may create resentment or later resistance from the parties.

Power Balance Between Parties

Parties exercise the same twelve forms of influence or power, but they are usually much more overt, directive, and coercive than the intervenor in their means of influencing each other, and they have specific substantive gains that they wish to achieve. Exercising power, however, may or may not achieve these desired results.

Power is not a characteristic of an organization or person but is an attribute of a relationship. A party's power is directly related to the power of an opponent. Power relations generally occur in two forms: *symmetrical,* or equal, and *asymmetrical,* or unequal, levels of influence (Bagozzi and Dholakia, 1977).

Symmetrical Power Relations

Practical experience and social psychological experimentation indicate that when negotiators have an equal or symmetrical power relationship, they behave more cooperatively, function more effectively, and behave in a less exploitive or manipulative manner than when there is an asymmetrical power relationship (Rubin and Brown, 1975). Disputes in which parties have roughly equal power tend to be most amenable to mediation.

Mediators working with parties of equal power usually attempt to improve the cooperative behavior of the parties, enhance the perception of equal power in the relationship, and limit the expression of coercive power in negotiations. The most common influence problems that disputants with equal power encounter are perceptual difficulties between the parties with respect to symmetry and the negative residue of emotions resulting from past exercise of coercive power within the relationship.

Perception of power symmetry is usually dependent on the ability to measure or project the potential outcome of a dispute if one or more parties decide to exercise their power. For example, if two people contest a piece of property, and both know that the other has unlimited funds, equally qualified lawyers, and case law to back up their arguments, the perception of each other's power may be relatively easy to determine. This is true because the variables by which power is measured—capital, personnel, and case law—are the same for each party and are known.

However, what if the sources of power are different so that the types of power and even the standards of measurement are not the same and are not known by each party? For example, in some labor-management negotiations, labor must assess management's ability to carry on production in the event of a strike, management's staffing capabilities, product stockpiles, and public demand for the product. The employer must assess the number of employees who are willing to strike, the assets available to the union and its allies to sustain a strike, the climate of public opinion regarding the merits of the dispute, and so on. In this instance, the basis of power is different for the two parties, as are the variables used to measure that power.

When parties have different bases of influence, a power assessment problem often develops. This often results in a breakdown in negotiations. Parties return to negotiations only after they have exercised and tested their power and have developed a more accurate assessment of the power of the other parties. For example, many divorcing spouses attempt to negotiate issues, fail, and hire lawyers. A large proportion of these cases settle before the case actually opens. The act of testing the strength and will of an opponent to go to court may be an important step in developing an accurate perception of another disputant's power.

Unfortunately, testing power often involves the exercise of coercive power and tends to produce negative effects on the ability of the parties to negotiate. Even in symmetrical relations, exercise of power—especially coercive power—may lead to increased resistance to settle or an irreversible breakdown of negotiations.

Mediators in disputes in which symmetry is hard to determine because of different power bases or measures should attempt to help the parties to assess each other's power without encouraging the parties to resort to coercion.

Changing a perception about power, especially when the parties have symmetrical relationships, is usually accomplished by developing an accurate power assessment mechanism or by changing conditions so that power is irrelevant. In the first method, mediators can privately encourage a party to list his or her own sources or bases of power and then identify the costs and benefits of exercising it (Fisher, 1969; Bellows and Moulton, 1981). The party then uses the same procedure for assessing the opponent's power. The process may be repeated, if necessary, with the other side. A cross-reference of costs and potential outcomes will usually incline parties toward a mutual recognition of symmetrical power relations.

The second technique requires parties to shift their focus from power relationships to interests. By calling attention to the process of how needs can be satisfied, the mediator often can persuade the parties to avoid emphasis on how they can force the opposing party into submission.

Asymmetrical Power Relations

Although symmetrical power relations seem to be the optimal relationship for effective bargaining, this type of relationship is not the norm. Parties differ in the form or amount of power or influence they possess in relation to one another.

Mediators in disputes in which parties have asymmetrical or unequal power relationships face two kinds of problems: (1) perceptual problems—situations in which the stronger party believes that the weaker party has equal power, or situations in which the weaker party has an inflated view of his or her strength; and (2) extremely asymmetrical relationships—situations in which a party is in a much weaker position, and both parties know it.

Mediators work with both weaker and stronger parties to minimize the negative effects of unequal power. In a situation in which the balance of power is unequal, the weaker party bluffs about his or her power, and the stronger party accepts the bluff, the mediator should usually meet with the bluffing party to educate him or her about the potential costs of being found out or called on to carry out the bluff. The other party's discovery of the deception can lead to a deterioration in relationships and may lead to retaliation if the victim of the bluff is the stronger party.

If the party can be convinced that the costs of bluffing are too high, the mediator and the party should jointly search for a way to retreat from the bluff or minimize the importance of power dynamics in the context of the negotiations. Retreating from a bluff or minimizing the effects of bluff can often be achieved by ceasing to make threatening statements or false promises and by providing a plausible rationalization for the change in stance or position.

In power situations in which parties appear to have an asymmetrical relationship and the bases of power are different, the mediator may attempt to obscure the strength or influence of both parties. He or she can pursue this strategy to create doubt about the actual power of the parties by questioning the accuracy of data, the credibility of experts, the capability of mobilizing coercive power, or the degree of support from authority figures. These techniques will prevent the parties from ascertaining the balance of power. If a party cannot determine absolutely that he or she has more power than another, he or she usually does not feel free to manipulate or exploit an opponent without restraint.

By far the most difficult problem mediators face regarding power relationships is a huge discrepancy in strength of the parties' means of influence. The independent mediator, because of his or her commitment to neutrality and impartiality, is ethically barred from direct advocacy for the weaker party, yet is also ethically obligated to assist the parties in reaching an acceptable agreement.

Wall (1981) argues that the mediator's primary task is to manage the power relationship of the disputants. In unequal power relationships, the mediator may attempt to balance power. "To strike the balance, the mediator provides the necessary power underpinnings to the weaker negotiator—information, advice, friendship—or reduces those of the stronger" (p. 164).

If this strategy is adopted, the mediator should undertake moves to assist the weaker party in mobilizing the power he or she possesses. The mediator should not, however, directly act as an organizer to mobilize or develop new power for the weaker disputant unless the mediator has gained the stronger party's approval. To act as a secret advocate puts the mediator's impartiality and effectiveness as a process intervenor at risk.

Empowering moves may include

- Assisting the weaker party in obtaining, organizing, and analyzing data and identifying and mobilizing his or her means of influence
- Assisting and educating the party in planning an effective negotiation strategy
- Aiding the party in developing financial resources so that he or she can continue to participate in negotiations
- Referring the party to a lawyer or other resource person
- Encouraging the party to make realistic concessions

Wall (1981) notes that stronger parties often welcome a mediator's involvement in power balancing. The mediator can assist a weaker party who is unorganized and unable to negotiate in preparing for a productive exchange that will benefit both parties. This role of the mediator as organizer has been practiced in husband-wife disputes (Haynes, 1981), labor-management conflicts (Perez, 1959), community disputes (Lincoln, 1976), large-scale environmental contests (Dembart and Kwartler, 1980), and interracial disputes (Kwartler, 1980).

Multiperson Negotiation Teams

When negotiations are between more than two disputants, interpersonal dynamics become exponentially more complex. This section will detail one format for additional negotiators: the formation of a team. The next section of the chapter will deal with an extension or expansion of the team and will describe mediator moves designed to assist negotiators in multiparty disputes.

Basis for Team Formation and Mediator Moves

A negotiation team is a group composed of two or more people who share similar experiences, interests, likes, dislikes, or sentiments. People form teams to negotiate issues of concern for a variety of reasons. A team may be a coalition of weaker parties who are trying to increase their influence. Alternatively, a team may be a group of people who want to verbally represent a broader viewpoint or include more diversity of opinion or expertise than a sole negotiator. Teams may also be selected for negotiation because the team members do not trust one person to negotiate for their interests. And finally, teams may be formed to provide a more efficient representative body for wider constituencies such as community groups or labor unions.

By the time a mediator is asked to assist in a dispute, the parties have usually already formed teams. The mediator must then work with the people whom the parties have selected. Occasionally, however, a mediator may enter a dispute before team formation has occurred. In that case, he or she may significantly assist disputants in forming negotiation teams.

Although the mediator cannot and should not select the negotiating team's members, he or she may suggest criteria for selection. A team member should understand the various issues in the dispute, be able to identify and articulate his or her own interests and those of other team members, and represent the concerns of a broader constituency, if one exists. Other team members and the wider constituency should have confidence in each team member so that agreements reached at the negotiating table will be credible and acceptable to those represented by the team (McSurely, 1967). Rapport, credibility, and the capacity to deal with people who are on an opposing team are also possible criteria. A team composed of people who cannot negotiate or who will be unacceptable to the other side is useless. It makes no sense for negotiations to break down over a question of personnel if competing interests are the principal issues that divide the parties.

In addition to suggesting general criteria for the selection of team members, the mediator may also help directly with team formation. In initiating negotiations between black and white student groups in a highly polarized and volatile school desegregation dispute, Lincoln (1976) urged each group to select a team of respected representatives who would be able to advocate for their interests. Fear that the representatives would not be good enough negotiators and would embarrass the group spurred the youths to select the most qualified people to be on the teams.

Although most mediators do not play this extreme catalytic role, they can make significant procedural suggestions. Mediators can often suggest the number of representatives appropriate to the dispute, the type of expertise that would be beneficial, and a decision-making process for selecting team members. One mediator was called into a complex housing dispute by a large group of disgruntled renters as they were about to meet with their landlord. She decided that this undifferentiated group would not be able to bargain effectively with the landlord and also saw that the tenants' disorganized state and raucous manner might even provoke more resistance from their opponent. She refused to mediate the case until the tenants had organized themselves and selected a bargaining team. After indicating possible criteria for team membership, including some of those listed earlier, she suggested a specific number of representatives and a manner of deciding whom to appoint.

Team Dynamics and Mediation Strategies

Once the disputants have selected a team, the mediator should carefully analyze and assess the group's crucial dynamics, individual and group interests, the personal behavior patterns of individual members (including the way they interact with people on their own and the opposing team), and the team decision-making structure (Anacona, Friedman, and Kolb, 1991).

A negotiating team, when viewed by an opponent, may appear monolithic, unified, and unshakable in its commitment to a stated position or option. Usually, however, this is not the case. Negotiation teams are composed of individuals with varying interests. The members may vary in their strength of commitment to their own needs, to those of other team members, or to group interests as a whole. Mediators should carefully assess the spectrum of interests within a team to determine the potential for noncompetitive interests, both within each team and between the teams.

Negotiation styles of team members are often closely related to how they believe their interests can best be achieved (Frost and Wilmot, 1978; Rubin and Brown, 1975). Mediators should assess the relative degrees of collaborative and competitive behavior within the team. Colosi and Berkeley (1980) identify three types of team members: stabilizers, nonstabilizers, and quasi-mediators. Stabilizers are those committed to negotiations and a settlement, often at any cost. Nonstabilizers may not be committed to negotiations, may be disruptive, and may be unwilling to settle, regardless of the offer. The quasi-mediator wants to build a realistic and workable settlement that meets as many needs as possible for all the parties. The quasi-mediator is the mediator's ally and will work to forge an agreement. They may alternately support each other to bolster their respective proposals or activities.

Mediators should look for quasi-mediators with moderate interests and collaborative styles within a team because he or she will need their assistance in moving the team toward agreement.

Negotiating team members also have diverse means of influence or power that they bring to the negotiation table. Mediators should assess the influence relationships that exist between team members in an effort to understand internal team dynamics.

A group's decision-making methods are often closely related to its power relationships (Brett, 1991). In general, negotiation teams tend to make decisions either by *fiat, hierarchical decision making,* or *consensus.*

Hierarchical decision making occurs when one or more team members make a decision that is accepted or deferred to by others on the basis of the decision maker's legitimate authority or ability to coerce or grant benefits to other members. This decision-making model is characteristic of bureaucratically organized institutions such as government agencies, businesses, or churches. The process works well only when adherence of team members to the decision maker's choices can be ensured by the means of influence just described. If allegiances cannot be ensured, the team's cohesion will suffer greatly under the stress of joint sessions.

The second method of decision making within a team is consensus. Consensus involves a synthesis of the ideas and interests of all team members, leading to a broad, general agreement on issues. Consensus may be used because team members hold a philosophical commitment to the process, or it may be the only functional way that the group can reach agreement. In negotiations in which team members are representatives of independent groups, or in which no one group is either dominant in terms of power or recognized as the central decision maker, consensus may be the only way a group can develop a coalition with a common purpose.

The third process, voting, is generally not an effective procedure for decision making within teams. A vote taken within a team may cause irreparable divisions that may result in decreased team cooperation in joint sessions, direct collaboration with an opponent, or rejection of the negotiation process itself. Divisions caused by voting and majority rule can be avoided only if the team makes decisions by consensus or if one party has either legitimate authority or coercive power to make binding decisions for the team.

Negotiators are often unfamiliar with appropriate internal decision-making procedures. Mediators may be called on as process advisers to in-team negotiations and may even mediate disputes within a team. The inability of a negotiation team to manage internal conflict and make group decisions can be as detrimental to successful negotiations as an impasse in joint session.

The mediator's role in helping negotiation teams to make decisions can vary significantly—from that of an educator who informs the parties about appropriate decision-making procedures, to a process observer who makes an occasional procedural suggestion to assist parties in bargaining more effectively, to an actual facilitator of team meetings (Kolb, 1983). The role of the mediator in in-team meetings often depends on the team's knowledge of, and sophistication in, internal negotiation processes, the amount of commonality of interest between team members, and the facilitative skills of the team members. In community disputes in which negotiators are appointed informally, have little experience in working together, and have little or no experience in either in-team or joint-session negotiations, the mediator may play a significant role in internal team bargaining. He or she may both educate the team members about how to negotiate and how to facilitate meetings (Doyle and Straus, 1976; Coover, Deacon, Esser, and Moore, 1977).

Types of Team Negotiations

The addition of multiple negotiators to a dispute not only increases the complexity of in-team negotiation but also widens the range of possible interactions between people on two or more opposing teams. In two-person negotiations, the two central actors are the primary channels through which communications flow. Additional participants both increase the amount and complexity of the communications and raise the problem of coordinating communication. Lincoln identifies three types of negotiation that occur at meetings of disputants in which each party has multiple representatives (Lincoln, n.d.).

Bilateral bargaining takes place when there are two sides, and communication occurs primarily between the spokespersons of the two groups. Bilateral bargaining is often considered "official" communication between the teams, as it is most likely to express either the consensus of the teams or the team position as expressed by the hierarchical decision maker.

Alongside the official communications that pass between the teams may be two types of unilateral bargaining. *Unilateral conciliatory bargaining* is commonly initiated by a quasi-mediator or by a member of a team who has some common interest or bond with a member of another. Conciliatory bargaining is usually conducted, either publicly or privately, with the negotiating team's explicit or implicit consent. The goal of conciliatory bargaining is to find a formula or option that will satisfy both parties. The conciliatory bargainer is not primarily motivated by personal gain.

In contrast to conciliatory bargaining, *unilateral vested-interest bargaining,* or under-the-table bargaining, is almost invariably motivated by a particular negotiator's drive for personal gain. This objective may even be sought at the expense of the interests of fellow team members. Vested-interest bargaining is nearly always conducted covertly, although occasionally there may be a public sellout by one member of a team.

Mediators can play an important role in facilitating bilateral bargaining and conciliatory bargaining, as well as in inhibiting unilateral vested-interest bargaining. They can influence effective bilateral negotiations by assisting and supporting the major spokespersons for each side. Kolb (1983) notes that in disputes in which the spokespersons are skilled in negotiation, the mediator need only affirm and support them in the activities they are pursuing. In doing so, the mediator conveys to the team that their leader is on the right track. In cases in which the spokespersons are not expert negotiators, the mediator may have to coach them on how to carry out their roles. Such coaching may include process suggestions, education about specific tactics, and questions to help clarify interests and goals.

Mediators also help team members communicate to the other team more clearly. By using some of the communication skills mentioned in earlier chapters, mediators can also assist teams conducting conciliatory bargaining. They can also aid quasi-mediators to develop internal team agreement. Quasi-mediators may be encouraged to communicate to the other team messages that promote positive relationships, as well as moderate proposals that meet the interests of all parties.

Teams with Constituents

Members of negotiating teams often do not make the final decision in a dispute. Teams are frequently responsible to other parties who have not been present at negotiations. Typically, the individuals or groups that have final authority to ratify a decision reached through negotiations form either a "bureaucratic constituency" or a "horizontal constituency."

A *bureaucratic constituency* consists of a hierarchy of decision makers who may or may not be present at negotiations and who must sign an agreement or signify final approval before it is considered valid. Bureaucratic constituencies are most common when one party is a governmental agency, a hierarchically organized company or industry, or a bureaucratically organized institution such as a hospital or social service agency.

Final approval of a settlement by persons not present may be a formal or legal requirement or a negotiating tactic a team employs to weaken an opponent's direct influence (Cohen, 1980; Stevens, 1963). A negotiator's argument that he or she is not empowered to make the final decision may provide that team with additional leverage. For example, a team may be able to claim that a higher authority does not approve of a proposed settlement and thus eke additional concessions from the other side. A further advantage may be gained from the additional time that is required for bureaucratic review or approval; this time may be used to bolster a negotiating position. Not having an authoritative decision maker at the table may also alleviate pressure on a negotiator to produce a final decision, and additionally may hinder the development of trust between teams.

A *horizontal constituency* is one that is not organized in a bureaucratic manner. Relatives, coworkers, public interest groups, tenants' unions, prisoners, and even industry associations may be organized in this manner. Negotiating teams that are responsible to horizontal constituencies usually must gain approval of a negotiated settlement through some form of ratification process. Voting is probably the most common procedure used, although consensus may also be employed. For voting or consensus to work, however, the members of the constituency must all accept it as the process for settlement approval. The absence of an acceptable ratification and commitment-ensuring procedure is one of the principal causes of breakdown in negotiations in which one of the teams is both horizontally organized and responsible to a horizontal constituency.

The lack of procedure for constituent approval can end in disaster. One of the many reasons why negotiations between inmates and correctional authorities at Attica Prison and New York State failed in the late 1960s was the absence of a procedure by which inmates could ratify any agreements that were reached (New York State Special Commission on Attica, 1972; Wicker, 1975). This problem is often common among public interest groups, either when they do not have institutional means for ratifying negotiated settlements or when ratification does not bind and commit all members to adhere to an agreement. Constituency ratification problems, however, are not confined to public interest groups. In mediated negotiations over information exchange and stipulations pertaining to oil and gas drilling in federal Wilderness Study Areas, environmentalists challenged Independent Petroleum Association of the Mountain States and Rocky Mountain Oil and Gas Association, the two industry associations involved, to explain how they would gain individual company ratification and commitment to any agreement. Both organizations, although maintaining a hierarchically organized staff, had horizontally organized constituent companies. Neither organization had a formal method for obtaining constituency approval of, or commitment to, negotiated settlements. Ironically, the environmental groups had decision-making structures that were similar to those of the industry organizations and encountered the same problems.

The mediator's primary role is not to work with the constituents of a negotiator or negotiating team. However, some efforts in this area may be necessary to attain a settlement's approval.

First, mediators may assist negotiating teams in identifying and organizing their constituents. They may aid teams in defining to whom they are responsible and who should ultimately be involved in final ratification and decision making (Straus, Clark, and Suskind, n.d.). This task may be relatively easy when teams are hierarchically organized or responsible to a bureaucratic constituency, and extremely difficult when the team and constituency are horizontally organized. The task may be especially complex when a negotiating organization has elements of both models. In some unions, for example, agreements reached in negotiation must be approved by the executive committee, the union president, and the union members at large.

Second, mediators may assist negotiators in explicating to each other the constraints imposed by their various bureaucratic or horizontal constituencies and the ratification procedures that will be used at the time of settlement. Early notification of both the procedure to be used for approval of a settlement and the time necessary to achieve ratification can reduce unnecessary conflicts that may arise from false procedural expectations.

Third, mediators may work with negotiators or negotiating teams to develop specific procedures for notifying constituent groups about developments in negotiations. Constituent groups often expect their representatives or negotiation teams to bring back for their approval a settlement that resembles the team's opening position. This is usually an unrealistic expectation.

Constituencies, like negotiators, must be educated about the composition of a realistic and probable settlement. Constituent education must occur throughout the negotiation process so that the final proposed settlement that reaches the constituency is not a surprise, and so that the constituency has an opportunity to contribute ideas and comments during bargaining. For the constituency to reach substantive, procedural, and psychological closure on any given issue or package of issues, it must believe that the substantive deal is the best that could have been negotiated given the options available, the power constellations of the parties, and external social forces. The constituency must also feel that its negotiators used the best process at their disposal and that constituents had adequate opportunity to contribute to the negotiations. It must also trust its representatives and believe that they have bargained in good faith to obtain the best solution possible.

In some disputes, the negotiators take full and adequate responsibility for educating and obtaining input from their constituency. In other conflicts, lack of negotiating experience, failure to understand the importance of the educational process, poor procedures, or constraints on negotiation privacy result in distance between negotiators and constituents. This distance may have serious effects on the ratification of an agreement.

To avoid settlement rejection, mediators can occasionally intervene between negotiators and their constituencies either before and after the announcement of the terms of settlement. They may also attempt to convince negotiators that a potential option for settlement is acceptable to their constituency (Stevens, 1963), and they may assist in developing procedures to promote constituent input to the negotiation team.

Fourth, the mediator may assist the negotiator or negotiating team in convincing a recalcitrant constituency that the negotiator or team has done as much as possible to promote the interests of constituents (Kerr, 1954). This may entail discussing the merits of the substantive proposals and contrasting them with what the opponent originally offered, discussing the effectiveness of negotiation strategies, and verifying the integrity and commitment of the negotiators.

So far, this section has focused on what a mediator does to assist a negotiator in working with his or her constituency. The mediator may also work with a constituency to modify the behavior of a negotiator or negotiating team. A mediator, through either public or private statements, may indicate to a constituency that a negotiator is being too firm and may suggest that the constituents encourage the negotiator to abandon a hard-line position (Shapiro, 1970). The mediator may also appeal directly to the constituents for concessions that will advance negotiations (Douglas, 1962).

Chapter Sixteen

Toward an Excellent Practice of Mediation

As the field of mediation has developed, procedures have become more formalized and in some places roles professionalized, and practitioners have taken a number of initiatives to promote excellent practice. These have included the development of

1. Conflict management and mediation associations and organizations, which promote networking and information exchange
2. Codes of ethics and model standards of practice, which define ethical behavior and clarify good performance
3. Training seminars and educational programs, which prepare intermediaries in relevant approaches and skills
4. Qualifications and standards for practice in specific arenas

This chapter details some of these activities as they have occurred in North America, as well as in other countries around the world.

Associations and Conferences

The development of associations in the field of voluntary dispute resolution first occurred in North America, in the area of arbitration. In 1947, a group of professional arbiters formed the National Academy of Arbitrators, but this organization failed to meet the needs of a growing number of mediators and other intermediaries who wanted an association that would provide an opportunity for their professional development. In 1972, the Society of Professionals in Dispute Resolution (SPIDR) was created to "promote the peaceful resolution of disputes." This membership association, which was originally composed of mediators, arbiters, ombudspersons, and others who were working in the field as paid professionals, now has a much broader membership. As of 1995, SPIDR had over 3,300 members from the United States, Canada, and a host of other nations. SPIDR holds annual international and regional meetings and has spearheaded the development of codes of ethics, practice guidelines, qualifications, and competencies, both in the field in general and in several practice areas. The organization has also established informal mentoring programs at conferences and an ethics committee to address members' ethical concerns.

In 1980, a second dispute resolution association, the National Conference on Peacemaking and Conflict Resolution (NCPCR) was founded, primarily to provide a forum where public and community sector mediators could share ideas, experiences, and skills. Since its founding, membership has expanded to include mediators from all sectors of the field. Participants at its conferences, which are held approximately every eighteen months, closely mirror the membership of SPIDR, with the exception that there are fewer attendees from the labor and commercial sectors. NCPCR's major function is to provide ongoing education and skills training through speakers, panel discussions, and brief workshops.

In the early 1980s, two organizations for family mediators emerged, primarily oriented around two early practitioners in the field. Ultimately, these two organizations merged to form the Academy of Family Mediators (AFM). Initially, membership in this organization was limited to those who had had academic training in the legal, therapeutic, and social work fields; experience or training in mediation was not emphasized. The criteria for membership have since been considerably broadened, and AFM members now include intermediaries from a wide range of backgrounds who handle many types of interpersonal disputes. AFM has become a leader in developing criteria for membership in a professional mediation organization that are based on direct experience in the field. It has also set minimal standards for instructors and content in family mediation training programs. The organization has an annual conference.

In the area of court-based family mediation programs, the Association of Family and Conciliation Courts (AFCC) has provided a significant degree of leadership. AFCC produces a number of publications and holds an annual conference.

Since the founding of these professional associations, a number of specialized organizations has been formed to address particular areas of practice or practitioners with specific foci. In the area of education, the National Association of Mediation in Education (NAME) was formed to meet the need of dispute resolution practitioners in primary, secondary, and university settings. The Section on Alternative Dispute Resolution of the Association of American Law Schools was established to promote the sharing of information among law professors teaching courses on conflict management and mediation.

Lawyers have been very active in the field of dispute resolution, and along with active involvement in many of the organizations already mentioned, have formed a number of organizations to meet their specific professional needs. The Section of Dispute Resolution of the American Bar Association (ABA) publishes a newsletter and other literature and has sponsored conferences on targeted topics in the field. The Family Law Section of the ABA serves to link lawyer-mediators who practice in the family arena.

In the early 1980s, public policy and environmental mediators started a very loose association that sponsored invitational conferences, but by the 1990s, the group had become a special sector within SPIDR. This sector has primarily focused on defining the field of environmental and public dispute resolution, sharing strategies and skills, and developing a compendium of competencies and skills that constitute best practice (Society of Professionals in Dispute Resolution, 1995).

In recent years, an informal association of state-based mediation programs, primarily working in the arenas of public disputes and dispute systems design, has been convened by the National Institute of Dispute Resolution. This association was the initial catalyst for the development of a number of state-related dispute resolution programs.

In addition to associations of mediation practitioners, an informal network has emerged of universities that have mediation and theory-building programs financially supported by the William and

Flora Hewlett Foundation. The Harvard Program on Negotiation and George Mason University have also convened gatherings of university faculty who either coordinate programs or conduct courses in U.S. or international universities. In Canada, the University of Victoria's Institute for Dispute Resolution, as well as Conrad Grebel College and Queens University, have developed courses and other professional programs in the area of dispute resolution and mediation.

Other associations that emerged in the late 1980s include specialized associations for community mediators, victim-offender mediators, and commercial mediators. Also, a large number of state-level mediation associations have formed across the United States.

Canada has several mediation organizations—including The Network: Interaction for Conflict Resolution and Family Mediation Canada—as well as a network of mediators who have handled farmer-lender disputes. A number of mediation associations have also been set up in several Canadian provinces. These associations, which meet the specific needs of Canadian mediators, have provided a valuable network for the sharing of information and the provision of services across the nation.

The emergence of this array of mediation organizations in North America has spurred the founding of a number of international conference-based organizations worldwide. The Asia-Pacific Organization for Mediators (APOM) held its first conference in Manila in 1985. Attended by private mediators, program-based mediators, and program organizers from several Pacific nations, the conference provided a forum for the exchange of experiences and set the stage for the development of new mediation programs in the region. The tradition of this organization/conference was continued by a 1994 conference, "Conflict Resolution in the Asia-Pacific Region: Culture, Problem Solving and Peacemaking," held in Penang, Malaysia. The gathering, which was sponsored by the Asia Foundation, Univeristi Sains Malaysia, and the Asia Pacific Peace Research Association, was attended by close to one hundred practitioners from most Asian and Asia Pacific nations.

The first European Conference on Peacemaking and Conflict Resolution was held in Antalya, Turkey, in 1992, and a subsequent conference was held in San Sebastian, Spain, in 1994. The 1996 European conference will be held in Varna, Bulgaria. This

conference-based organization has linked Western European conflict management specialists and mediation practitioners and has
recently reached out to bring in a number of Eastern European
practitioners.

The first Latin American Conference on Peacemaking and
Conflict Resolution is scheduled for 1996. This gathering will bring
together a wide variety of community and government-related
mediators to discuss the broadening of applications in these southern countries.

In addition to the international and regional associations just
described, a number of national associations have been developed
in the Asia Pacific region and Western Europe. These organizations may focus on general practice or on specialized fields of
mediation and dispute resolution. In Australia, the Australian Dispute Resolution Association (ADRA) and the Conflict Resolution
Network, and in New Zealand, the Arbitrators' Institute of New
Zealand have conducted conferences and established networks
and are working on the development of ethical standards and
high-quality performance in the delivery of services. In Europe,
there are a number of mediation associations and organizations,
including Mediation UK in Great Britain, Centro Italiano Per la
Promozione della Mediazione in Italy, the Bundesverband für
Familienmediation in Germany, the Mediation Network for Northern Ireland, Gernika-Gogoratuz in Spain, and the Umut Foundation in Turkey.

South Africa, too, has developed a national association of conflict managers and mediators: the South African Association for
Conflict Intervention. Established in 1989 by intermediaries
opposed to the apartheid system, this organization provided a
forum for the exchange of ideas on successful conflict handling,
mediation strategy development, and dispute systems design. Many
members of this organization were active in helping parties to institute and operate local and regional peace committees that were
part of the National Peace Accord between the major conflicting
parties in the country.

Codes of Ethics and Standards of Practice

As the dispute resolution field has developed, practitioners, members of the public, other concerned professionals, and government

agencies in North America have become interested in formulating clear ethical standards for practice. The motivation for this initiative has been a desire to educate the public and mediation practitioners about ethical practice, to ensure that work with clients is conducted according to the highest ethical standards, and to protect the reputation of the profession from being sullied by less than responsible practitioners.

The ethical standards that have been developed in North America and most other societies have been designed to address the roles and responsibilities of independent or professional mediators in relation to their clients and the broader society (Grebe, 1989). It should be noted that ethical standards developed for independent mediators are not always applicable to—and often do not fit—the roles and activities of many social network or authoritative mediators. To date, there are no formal codes of conduct for these latter types of intermediaries.

The first codes of ethical standards for intermediaries were developed in the United States and Canada, but a number of other countries and regions have since used the drafting of codes as a way of establishing the profession and defining good practice. This activity has been most common in areas where the independent mediator is the typical practitioner.

The first code of ethics was developed by the Federal Mediation and Conciliation Service of the U.S. government. Among other things, this code covered the responsibilities of the mediator to the disputing parties, to the negotiation process, to other mediators, to his or her agency, to the profession, and to unrepresented third parties.

The first code for general mediation practice at the state level was developed in the state of Colorado (Moore, 1982a). It was rapidly followed by model standards of practice or ethical standards formulated by the American Arbitration Association, the Association of Family and Conciliation Courts, the Academy of Family Mediators, the American Bar Association Family Section, the Society of Professionals in Dispute Resolution, as well as by a number of state codes.

The Ethical Standards of Professional Responsibility of SPIDR, which were approved in 1986, cover the largest number of mediation practitioners in the field and address standards for intermediaries serving in a variety of capacities. The standards state that neutrals have ethical obligations "to the parties, to the profession and to themselves. They should be honest and unbiased, act in good faith, be diligent, and not seek to advance their own interests at the expense of their parties.'" Further, "neutrals must act fairly in dealing with the parties, have no personal interest in the terms of the settlement, show no bias toward individuals and institutions involved in the dispute, be reasonably available as requested by the parties, and be certain that the parties are informed of the process in which they are involved." (The full text of the standards appears in Resource A.)

Among the responsibilities that the intermediary has to the parties are

1. An obligation to remain impartial and maintain "freedom from favoritism or bias either by word or by action, and a commitment to serve all parties as opposed to a single party"
2. Assurance of informed consent to guarantee that participants understand the "nature of the process, the procedures, the particular role of the neutral, and the parties' relationship to the neutral"
3. Disclosure of the limits, if any, of confidentiality, and a commitment to hold confidences once given
4. Avoidance of conflict of interest or its appearance
5. Implementation of the process in a timely manner
6. Assistance in conducting a process and a settlement that they will hold as their own, and in which the neutral "has no vested interest"

In addition to these responsibilities to the parties, neutrals are advised to consider—and where appropriate, raise with the principal parties—the interests of unrepresented parties and to educate the principals about the use and impact of multiple dispute resolution procedures. Intermediaries are advised to accept only those cases where they have sufficient knowledge and expertise in terms of process and substance, to engage in an ongoing process of professional development, and to assist in the development of new practitioners in the field.

Intermediaries are expected to disclose to the parties at the beginning of any intervention the "bases of compensation, fees, and charges." Where appropriate, they should provide *pro bono* services. No commissions are to be paid or received by an intermediary for the referral of clients.

Where more than one intermediary is working on a case, all have an ethical obligation to inform each other of their involvement and to maintain a cordial and professional relationship.

Finally, advertising is to be accurate with respect to services offered and should not promise a favorable outcome to a particular side.

No code of ethical standards can cover all circumstances, nor will the rules be totally clear when applied to real-life disputes. This is especially the case when there are tensions between different ethical precepts. A commitment to confidentiality may conflict with the risk of adverse impacts on unrepresented third parties. The mediator's capacity to remain neutral may be undermined by past, present, or potential future relations with one or more of the parties. At times, an intervenor may wonder whether his or her assistance, motivated by the desire to see a settlement, is shading into unacceptable coercive influence. A mediator who has industriously and in good faith acquired expertise in a new area of practice may wrestle with the question of whether he or she has enough knowledge to begin to offer services in that area. And then there are the cases in which the mediator's commitment to impartiality is tested by an agreement that he or she feels is grossly unfair, unconscionable, or lacking in durability.

To assist practitioners who have encountered ethical dilemmas, SPIDR has established an ethics committee to which questions can be referred for an advisory opinion. Currently, there are no means of securing a binding judgment from the committee that enforces an opinion or imposes sanctions on an errant practitioner. Although it is possible to go to court to seek a judicial decision regarding possible malpractice, there have been very few suits over violations of ethical standards in mediation, and in the few cases that have gone to trial, most have either been dismissed or decided in favor of the intermediary.

Training, Education, and Professional Development

A significant component in the establishment of both ethical and excellent practice is the development of high-quality training and professional development programs. Seminars and courses on mediation have been routinely conducted in the United States since the early 1970s. This practice has now expanded to the point that training programs are readily available on a wide range of topics and practice areas across North America, and increasingly worldwide. As well as general mediation seminars, there are specialized programs on the mediation of interpersonal, family, divorce, parent-child, victim-offender, student-student, neighborhood, consumer, commercial, employment, grievance, discrimination, collective bargaining, environmental, and public policy disputes.

As formal educational programs on mediation have developed, a number of key issues in training have emerged. These include

1. Criteria for trainee selection
2. Forums and formats for training
3. Content, methodology, and duration of programs
4. Qualifications of trainers and instructors
5. Consumer criteria in program selection

Criteria for Trainee Selection

Obviously, anyone should be able to obtain training and education as a mediator. The world needs proficient and effective intermediaries in any number of arenas to help resolve a wide range of disputes. But the question is often raised, Who will make a good mediator? Simkin (1971) listed eighteen qualities sought in a mediator, including

The patience of Job

The physical endurance of a marathon runner

The guile of Machiavelli

The personality-probing skills of a good psychiatrist

The hide of a rhinoceros

Demonstrated integrity and impartiality

Fundamental belief in human values and potentials tempered by ability to assess personal weaknesses as well as strengths

Hard-nosed ability to analyze what is available in contrast to what
  might be desirable

Sufficient personal drive and ego, qualified by a willingness to be
  self-effacing

   Some mediation organizations, in seeking either potential
trainees or staff, try to screen applicants for these and other qualities using interviews, life experiences, questionnaires, requests for
case examples where the applicant has helped people in disputes,
quick-decision problem-solving exercises, and role-playing. Although these methods may begin the screening process, the best
measure is probably performance in simulations during a mediation training seminar or demonstrated proficiency in actual cases
after training or apprenticeship. Many organizations train a pool
of mediators and make selections for volunteers and staff on the
basis of performance in the seminar.
   Since the mid-1980s, there has been an ongoing controversy
regarding who should receive training and be able to practice as a
mediator in professional settings. The crux of this issue is whether
previous education and professional training should be used as
adequate or relevant criteria for entry into practice as a mediator.
The issue has become especially important as other professions
and professionals who also see themselves as conflict resolvers have
sought to stem the loss of their clients to mediation practitioners,
limit entry into the mediation field, or capture the mediation profession as their own. Unfortunately, some states have begun to
restrict the practice of mediation to those with professional qualifications that have little relationship to knowledge or proficiency
in the practice of mediation.
   The SPIDR Commission on Qualifications, after careful deliberation on this matter, "found no evidence that formal academic
degrees, which obviously limit entry into the dispute resolution
field, are necessary to competent performance as a neutral. There
is impressive evidence that individuals lacking such credentials
make excellent dispute resolvers and that well designed training
programs, which stress the specific skills and techniques of mediation and arbitration, are of critical importance in attaining competence. As a consequence, SPIDR recommends: Qualifications

based on performance" (Society for Professionals in Dispute Resolution, 1989). The commission also emphasized training by qualified and competent trainers, performance-based testing, and continuing mediation education as means of promoting mediators' competence.

Forums and Formats for Training

Currently, there are six paths that an individual may take to obtain knowledge and skills in mediation theory and practice:

1. Short courses on mediation and other dispute resolution procedures offered by associations and conferences, some in the dispute resolution field and some not
2. Longer training programs (several days to one or more weeks) on general mediation process or on particular topics, offered by experienced public or private mediation practitioners, organizations, and firms
3. Conflict management certification programs composed of multiple courses, offered by a number of junior and four-year colleges and universities
4. Courses in professional schools
5. University degree programs in conflict theory, analysis, and practice
6. Mentoring programs in which prospective practitioners learn mediation skills and practice as apprentices to experienced mediators

In general, short courses are appropriate for presenting overviews of the conflict management field and mediation practice, introductions to new areas of practice, and in-depth treatment of advanced topics. They are generally not adequate, in and of themselves, to train participants to be mediators.

Longer programs, lasting approximately forty hours, in mediation process and individual dispute resolution topics are currently the most common vehicle for formal training. Since the mid-1980s, a wide range of courses has been developed and offered on a regular basis by a number of reputable nonprofit and for-profit organizations. Some of these courses are presented by staff of community mediation programs; others are conducted by professional conflict management and mediation firms. Often, the programs are combined with internships or volunteer mediation opportunities so that trainees can more easily make the transition into practice. These programs vary significantly in quality and depth and in the experience of trainers. Prospective consumers of such programs should ask, Are the trainers practicing mediators? In general, the higher-quality seminars are taught by individuals who are experienced mediators as well as good educators.

In the late 1980s, several colleges and universities began to offer certificate programs in conflict management and mediation. In this context, *certification* means satisfactory completion of a prescribed number of hours of course work and does not necessarily imply a specific level of competence as a mediator. The faculty in these programs may be practicing mediators from the local community who teach on a part-time basis, but as in a number of university-based and professional-school courses described below, instructors may be academics with little experience of actual mediation practice.

Professional schools of law, business, social work, and urban planning have also begun to offer courses on mediation and other types of dispute resolution (Savage, 1989). Some of these are overview seminars that educate students about a range of conflict management procedures, whereas others focus specifically on mediation. These academic programs provide an in-depth study of the mediation process. Some schools have instituted mediation clinics or teamed up with local community mediation centers as a way of integrating theory with practice.

A significant number of colleges and universities have begun to offer courses on dispute resolution and mediation, and a small number have specialized degree programs in conflict analysis or conflict management. A study undertaken by George Mason University identified hundreds of institutions of higher learning that offered courses in conflict management, peace studies, and mediation. Most of these courses provide good theoretical information. Generally, more training and practice beyond these seminars is necessary before participants are ready to serve in a professional capacity.

Degree programs, both undergraduate and graduate, that combine theory and practice are still few in number. Most programs teach a variety of dispute resolution procedures, of which mediation is one. The programs that appear to best prepare participants for work in the field are those that have an active clinical practice component. Of note in this area is George Mason University's Institute for Conflict Analysis and Resolution, which offers comprehensive master's and Ph.D. programs, and a consortium of universities in the Boston area, loosely associated with Harvard's Program on Negotiation, that offers a number of cross-registered courses and degree programs in traditional subjects with an emphasis on dispute resolution.

Content, Methodology, and Duration of Programs

Content of training programs and courses is related to the competencies that individuals will need to perform well as intermediaries, to the specific types of disputes or issues they will handle, and to the setting in which they plan to work. Training programs developed in the 1970s tended to focus on general concepts and skills, but more recent educational programs have included both general and issue- or context-specific skills and content.

In 1989, the SPIDR Commission on Qualifications prepared a report that identified a number of competencies for intermediaries in general, and mediators in particular:

a. Skills necessary for competent performance as a neutral include:
 (1) General
  (a) ability to listen actively;
  (b) ability to analyze problems, identify and separate the issues involved, and frame these issues for resolution or decision making;
  (c) ability to use clear, neutral language in speaking and (if written opinions are required) in writing;
  (d) sensitivity to strongly felt values of the disputants, including gender, ethnic, and cultural differences;
  (e) ability to deal with complex factual materials;
  (f) presence and persistence, i.e., an overt commitment to honesty, dignified behavior, respect for the parties, and an ability to create and maintain control of a diverse group of disputants;
  (g) ability to identify and to separate the neutral's personal values from issues under consideration; and
  (h) ability to understand power imbalances.

(2) For mediation
   (a) ability to understand the negotiating process and the role of advocacy;
   (b) ability to earn trust and maintain acceptability;
   (c) ability to convert parties' positions into needs and interests
   (d) ability to screen out non-mediable issues;
   (e) ability to help parties to invent creative options;
   (f) ability to help the parties identify principles and criteria that will guide their decision making;
   (g) ability to help parties assess their non-settlement alternatives;
   (h) ability to help the parties make their own informed choices; and
   (i) ability to help parties assess whether their agreement can be implemented.

b. Knowledge of the particular dispute resolution process being used includes
   (1) familiarity with existing standards of practice covering the dispute resolution process; and
   (2) familiarity with commonly encountered ethical dilemmas.

c. Knowledge of the range of available dispute resolution processes, so that, where appropriate, cases can be referred to a more suitable process;

d. Knowledge of the institutional context in which the dispute arose and will be settled;

e. In mediation, knowledge of the process that will be used to resolve the dispute if no agreement is reached, such as judicial or administrative adjudication or arbitration;

f. Where parties' legal rights and remedies are involved, awareness of the legal standards that would be applicable if the case were taken to a court or other legal forum; and

g. Adherence to ethical standards [Society of Professionals in Dispute Resolution, 1989].

Most reputable mediation training programs present content that develops the general competencies—concepts, approaches, procedures, and skills—just described and then supplement this with material on specific issues and contexts.

As the field has grown, there has been an increase in the number of specialized mediation training programs that prepare trainees to handle disputes in specific arenas. Of note are child custody and divorce, family, parent-child, neighborhood, victim-offender, consumer, school-based, organizational, personnel griev-ance, discrimination, labor-management (collective bargaining), commercial, public policy, and environmental mediation semi-nars. Some of these programs may be taken as free-standing edu-cational programs, whereas others, such as those dealing with environmental and public policy mediation, are advanced pro-grams and should ideally be taken after completion of a basic medi-ation process seminar.

Procedures used to teach the competencies identified by the SPIDR are fairly diverse, but some general conclusions can be drawn about the educational goals embraced by most mediator trainers and mediation training programs. First, prospective medi-ators need to learn a concrete process that can be used by both the intermediary and conflicted parties for approaching and resolving disputes. Second, contingent approaches and skills for handling special problems need to be acquired. Third, the process needs to be presented in or embedded in a specific context, and related substantive information also needs to be learned. Finally, ethical dilemmas related to the specific area of practice need to be raised and explored so that new practitioners will be prepared for certain problems that may arise. Most mediator trainers believe that learn-ing all these things can best be accomplished by combining didac-tic presentations and practice sessions so that trainees have an opportunity to try out and integrate materials presented in the training.

Among the teaching methodologies commonly used in medi-ation training are

Lectures on a variety of topics

Conflict analysis exercises to develop the ability to understand the causes and dynamics of disputes

Negotiation simulations to teach the dynamics and procedures of advocacy

Mediation demonstrations by trainers to model approaches and skills

Strategy design sessions to show how interventions are planned and implemented

Demonstrations and practice sessions on the caucus process

Case study presentations by trainers and trainees to explore the dynamics of conflict escalation and resolution

Presentations and practice sessions on co-mediation exercises

Discussions to explore the forms and exercise of parties' and mediators' influence and power

Quick-decision problems or role-plays to help trainees learn to think on their feet and respond to unanticipated problems

A number of two-party and (where appropriate) multiparty simulations

Discussions and presentation of ethical problems in the prospective field of practice

A little more probably needs to be said about role-plays and simulations. Most mediation trainers generally believe that practicing mediation procedures and skills through simulations is one of the best ways to learn intervention techniques and strategies. Simulations provide an opportunity for experimentation, practice, and creativity in a safe forum, where there is no risk of harm to real parties. Simulations are best conducted when observed and debriefed by an experienced mediator-coach.

Since the early 1980s, there has been extensive discussion among practitioners in the field about how long an individual should undergo training before he or she is ready to work professionally. To date, there is no consensus on this question, but experience and practice are beginning to provide some answers. Most independent and government-affiliated community mediation programs have training seminars that last thirty-two to forty hours or more. Many of the programs also provide and require additional training in the family or civil areas and continuing mediation education programs throughout the year.

Family mediation is generally seen as a specialized and technical area of practice that requires more training, and a number of states and associations have begun to set some standards for both the duration and the content of such training. The Academy of Family Mediators has advocated a minimum of forty hours of training for those wishing to practice in family or divorce mediation.

Court-based mediation training programs, like the community

and family sectors, have also been active in establishing minimal training standards. This trend has probably been influenced by the fact that clients participating in such programs often have less say over who their mediator is, and governmental agencies feel compelled to develop minimal service and quality standards.

To date, there are no commonly recognized standards for the duration of commercial, employment, Equal Economic Opportunity (discrimination), public policy, or environmental training programs. Some programs, especially in the area of commercial and employment mediation, are often only a day or two in length, and it is questionable whether they adequately prepare a practitioner to work effectively with clients. Most practitioners in these arenas believe that longer programs are preferable.

In addition to formal training programs conducted in a classroom setting, a number of individuals and organizations provide and rely on mentoring or co-mediation opportunities to develop new mediators' strategies and skills. The U.S. Federal Mediation and Conciliation Service has relied almost exclusively on mentoring programs to train new mediators. In this training model, a novice is apprenticed to an experienced intermediary and works side-by-side with him or her for a year or more, or until such time that the senior practitioner believes the apprentice is ready to practice independently. The mentoring or apprenticeship program gradually moves the novice from observer to recorder to back-up mediator to co-mediator, and finally to lead mediator under the supervision of the senior practitioner.

A number of programs and projects also use co-mediation as a means of on-the-job training. A novice may be paired with a senior mediator, or two novices may work under the supervision of a senior practitioner. These models provide new mediators with opportunities to work with disputants. They also ensure that clients receive high-quality services.

Qualifications of Trainers and Instructors
As more mediators have been trained, and more training programs have sprung up, a concern has developed—both among consumers and trainers—as to the qualifications, expertise, and experience of individuals offering such programs. Professional associations such as SPIDR have advocated that instructors should have practical

experience in the area that they are teaching, and associations such as the Academy of Family Mediators have begun to certify training programs on the basis of both content and the experience of instructors.

Consumer Criteria in Program Selection

Potential consumers of mediation training programs are often confused by the number and variety of training options available to them. The following questions are presented as a guide for individuals or organizations seeking to evaluate the quality of the various seminars being offered. Although no individual program will possess all of the qualities outlined here, an acceptable program should meet a significant number of these criteria.

Instructors

1. Are the trainers practicing mediators?
2. How many years have they been in practice?
3. Do the trainers meet the standards established for membership in SPIDR, the international professional association for conflict managers? These standards are as follows:

> A member must establish qualifications as a neutral or impartial person with a minimum of three years substantial experience:
>
>   a) As an official or professional employee or ombudsperson of a local, state, provincial or federal governmental or private agency or corporation with the primary purpose of resolving disputes. The conflicts may be in such areas as labor relations, the environment, prisons or mental health facilities. The work of the applicant may also involve resolution of community, family/interpersonal, homeowners' warranty/other consumer, intergovernmental, regulatory, educational/student, and intracorporate disputes.
>
>   b) As a neutral practitioner engaged primarily in the resolution of disputes.
>
>   c) As a teacher of a curriculum directly related to the negotiation, arbitration, mediation or conciliation processes.

4. Have the trainers handled cases in the arena (labor, family, environmental, personnel, insurance claims, farmer-lender, com-

munity, and so on) in which they are conducting training or in another arena that is similar in substance or complexity?

5. Do the trainers have substantive knowledge of the arena in which they are training?

6. If the trainers are working in a substantive field that is new to them, do they have adequate access to substantive resource people who can educate them about the new arena for which they are training conflict managers?

7. Have the trainers conducted other dispute resolution training programs in the arena covered by the present course? Where mediation or facilitation is being applied to a new arena, such prior experience may not be possible. In this case, past programs in similar areas are good indicators of trainer performance and seminar quality.

8. Do the trainers have any formal academic training in conflict management procedures? Academic training can indicate a stronger understanding of conflict and conflict management theory.

9. Are the trainers experienced at working as a team so that the program's content has continuity and there is coordinated interaction between the trainers?

Program

1. Does the program present to the participants an overall framework for analyzing the diverse causes of conflict? Conflict is usually caused by multiple factors, and these need to be understood by the prospective mediator.

2. Does the program enable the participants to understand what they bring—past experience, skills, values, and biases—to the conflict situation and the role of the mediator? People are motivated to be mediators or conflict managers by a variety of factors—some good, others not so good. A training program should provide a forum for exploring trainees' backgrounds, motivations, strengths, and weaknesses as conflict managers.

3. Does the program educate the trainees about theories, dynamics, strategies, and tactics of *negotiation?* Because mediation and facilitation are extensions of the negotiation process, mediators and facilitators need to understand the dynamics of negotiation.

In particular, they should understand positional and interest-based bargaining assumptions and procedures.

4. Does the program provide demonstrations, either live or on videotape, of conflict management procedures as used by experienced practitioners? Trainees often learn conflict management skills by watching experienced negotiators, mediators, or facilitators resolve a dispute. Demonstrations by trainers are generally a component of high-quality programs.

5. Does the training program present an understandable and practical step-by-step model of dispute resolution? Trainees initially need a simple procedural framework to guide their conflict management efforts.

6. Do trainees have an opportunity to practice individual tasks or stages of the conflict management process? Skills are best learned by isolating specific manageable "pieces" or behaviors and practicing them until proficiency is attained.

7. Do the trainees have an opportunity to engage in role-plays or the simulated resolution of disputes? Do they have an opportunity to play the role of negotiator (disputant), mediator, or facilitator for an adequate period of time and become proficient in the requisite skills? One study of mediators found that their success rate drastically increased after they had handled five cases. Most conflict management skills are best learned by "hands on" practice. How many simulated cases does each trainee get to participate in, and how much time does he or she spend in the role of the conflict manager? Most high-quality forty-hour programs have five to ten hours of simulations.

8. Do trainees receive one-on-one feedback about their performance from their trainers or coaches? Conflict management procedures and skills are best learned through practice and feedback on performance. The quality of the seminar is greatly enhanced if trainees receive individualized coaching rather than being trained exclusively in a large group.

9. Are trainees taught to use specific conflict management procedures such as active listening, reframing, giving clear and direct messages, procedures for moving disputants from positional to interest-based bargaining, and the caucus technique? Are trainees taught how to overcome substantive, procedural, and psychological barriers to settlement and how to manage negotiator, mediator,

or facilitator power? Knowledge and skill in using the above behaviors and procedures makes for more sophisticated and effective conflict managers.

10. Does the training seminar contain substantive presentations relevant to the field for which the trainee is being prepared? In order to help parties resolve their conflicts, mediators and facilitators need some substantive knowledge about the issues in a dispute and possible resolutions. Procedural knowledge alone may not be enough to move the parties toward settlement.

11. Does the training program provide a procedure for moving from training to practice? Seminars should teach trainees how to set up a practice, integrate their new skills on the job, or define the way they will work in an established program.

12. Does the training program educate the trainees about the need for ongoing conflict management education and provide for some means of supervision or quality control, such as co-mediation, supervision by an experienced practitioner, or group supervision? New mediators and facilitators generally need assistance to effectively practice their newly learned skills. Means to obtain supervision and assistance in intervention strategy design should be addressed in the training program.

13. Does the training program address some of the critical ethical problems, questions, and dilemmas involved in the practice of conflict management? Does the seminar familiarize the participants with relevant standards of practice and codes of ethics? The Standards of Practice of the Society of Professionals in Dispute Resolution, the Code of Ethics for Labor Mediators, the Model Standards of Practice for Family and Divorce Mediation and the Model Standards of Practice for Child Custody Evaluation of the Association of Family and Conciliation Courts, the Standards of Practice of the Academy of Family Mediators, and the American Bar Association's Standards for Divorce Mediators are guidelines for ethical practice.

14. How long is the training seminar? Basic mediation training programs should be thirty-two to forty hours. This standard has been adopted by numerous practitioners, one of the major professional associations, and a large number of state and private mediation programs.

15. What kinds of written materials are provided to trainees? Seminar workbooks and handouts should be useful as training aids

and be comprehensive enough to serve as "refreshers" after the seminar is finished. Trainees should also be provided with an up-to-date bibliography that can aid them in conducting further studies of the dispute resolution process.

Promoting the Field and Ensuring Competence and Quality

As the field of mediation has matured, there has been increasing interest, both within the profession and among governmental agencies, in promoting the use of alternative dispute resolution, ensuring that practitioners are competent, and guaranteeing the provision of quality services to the public (Gentry, 1994). This concern has led to a significant increase in legislation to promote and regulate the field. "As of 1988, roughly 35 states and the District of Columbia had adopted some type of statutory authority for mediation. At least nine states had adopted comprehensive statutes to define and encourage the development of 'alternative' dispute resolution methods" (*Dispute Resolution Forum*, 1989, p. 5).

In 1990, the U.S. Congress passed the Administrative Dispute Resolution Act, which encouraged the use of alternative dispute resolution and mandated each federal agency to "adopt a policy that addresses the use of alternative means of dispute resolution (ADR) and case management" (Administrative Dispute Resolution Act, 1990). Executive orders encouraging the use of ADR were issued during the Bush administration, and in 1993, President Clinton issued an executive memorandum directing "each agency to explore and, where appropriate, use consensual mechanisms for developing regulations, including negotiated rulemaking" (President, 1993).

As of the late 1980s, "at least 21 states provide for mediation of labor disputes, usually by state boards of mediation. At least ten states have statutes specifically addressing mediation of family disputes, including issues of divorce, separation, child custody, and visitation rights. Individual states authorize or require the use of mediation in other specific types of dispute—for example, foreclosures by lenders against farm property and the siting of hazardous waste facilities" (*Dispute Resolution Forum*, 1989, p. 5).

Because of the push to use alternative dispute resolution procedures, and especially mediation, there has been a strong need to develop qualifications for mediators. In 1992, SPIDR appointed a new Committee on Qualifications and authorized its members to reexamine emerging qualifications issues. After two-and-a-half years of deliberations, the committee, composed of U.S. and Canadian practitioners and mediation program administrators, issued a report, *Ensuring Competence and Quality in Dispute Resolution Practice*, which was a response to the need of policy makers, governmental agencies, and others to identify qualifications that would "ensure skillful, honorable and effective dispute resolution" (Society of Professionals in Dispute Resolution, 1995). The report recommends a set of guidelines to help organize the discussion of the ingredients of practitioner competence. Among these guidelines are the following:

1. The formation of standards of competence and qualifications should be undertaken through a process of consultation with all stakeholders and should provide for ongoing review and revision.

2. Programs should clearly state their qualifications and ethical standards, and their goals and values in a manner that can be understood by practitioners, parties and the public.

3. In a pluralistic society, the development of qualifications standards must reflect an understanding of the context, the diversity of stakeholders, and respect for the variety of values and goals of all parties.

4. The context of the dispute resolution service must be examined and understood because it determines what should be considered competent practice in that context.

5. The multiple paths to becoming a competent practitioner ought to be recognized, maintained and expanded. Some combination of natural aptitude, skills, knowledge, and attributes acquired through an appropriate combination of dispute resolution training, education and experience is the best route to ensuring practitioner competence.

6. No one method of assessment should be relied on because it may lead to emphasis of one measure of competence at the expense of other valuable measures. Use of a combination of measures of competence also will reduce the likelihood of inadvertent discrimination.

7. Assessing competence is key to enduring quality service delivery and is a shared responsibility of practitioners, programs, dispute resolution associations and parties [Society of Professionals in Dispute Resolution, 1995, p. 2].

In addition to these recommendations, the committee developed a seven-step framework of questions to assist the concerned parties that were listed earlier in analyzing, within specific contexts, how high quality and competence can be achieved. Each step requires an answer to a central question and a number of subquestions. These include (Society of Professionals in Dispute Resolution, 1995, pp. 2–4)

1. "What Is the Context?" (the social and cultural setting, the parties' relationships to each other, the disputants' values, the nature of the dispute, the types of procedures available, and the program context)
2. "Who Is Responsible for Ensuring Competence?" (practitioners, consumers, program administrators, associations)
3. "What Do Practitioners and Programs Do?" (practitioner tasks to provide procedural, substantive, and relationship-building assistance, and program tasks to provide services, such as case assessment and assignment, training, and monitoring and evaluating practitioners)
4. "What Does it Mean to Be Competent?" (knowledge of and ability to effectively apply mediation concepts and skills to assist in the prevention and management of disputes)
5. "How Do Practitioners and Programs Become Competent?" (identification of a variety of paths including life skills, past experience, formalized training, apprenticeships, group supervision, peer review, and degree programs)
6. "How Is Competence Assessed? (assessment of practitioners and programs by a variety of concerned parties—practitioners, programs, organizations, and mediation participants—at various times in a practitioner's career or in the life of an organization)
7. "How Should Assessment Tools Be Used to Assure Quality?" (use of tools to support program goals, to determine admittance to organizations, to make referrals, to develop rosters, to obtain funding, or to improve practice)

In general, the committee found that certification, which recognizes that a practitioner "has achieved a level of competence and met certain standards of education, training and experience," can help ensure that qualified individuals are providing services to the public and can enhance the stature of the profession (Society of Professionals in Dispute Resolution, 1995). However, the committee was opposed to licensure—"governmental permission to practice based on a prescribed level of education, experience and training"—because of the risk of creating arbitrary standards, the possibility that the field might be dominated by one group or profession, and the danger that standards might inappropriately "freeze" both who is allowed to act as a mediator and how the profession is practiced.

Challenges for the Growth and Development of Mediation

Conflict is an omnipresent phenomenon in human interaction. Conflicts can lead to productive and positive changes or growth or to the destruction and degradation of relationships. A significant variable in the outcome of a dispute is the means that the participants use to resolve their differences. Now, more than ever before, there is a need for dispute resolution procedures that assist parties in meeting their needs, satisfying their interests, and reaching voluntary agreements that minimize physical and psychological harm. Mediation is one process that can make an important contribution to peaceful dispute resolution.

The use of mediation has grown tremendously during the ten years since this book was first published. Its practice has expanded not only in North America, where the procedure has been highly articulated and applied to diverse problems, but also in Africa, the Asia Pacific region, Latin America, the Middle East, and Western and Eastern Europe. Arenas of practice have grown to encompass all areas of life—interpersonal, familial, communal, educational, occupational, medical, commercial, local, urban, regional, national, ethnic, international, and environmental.

For mediation to achieve even broader utilization as a means of voluntary dispute resolution, several developments will need to occur. First, the public needs more education about the availability of mediation and its ability to address problems of frequent concern. Mediation is currently underutilized not because of its lack of applicability but because those involved in disputes are not aware of mediation's benefits. Public education about the process should become a priority among mediators and others interested in peaceful dispute resolution.

Second, more research needs to be conducted on mediation formats, procedures, strategies, and tactics, and the findings disseminated. More information is needed about how mediators enable parties to manage intense emotional multiparty conflicts, imbalances of power, and communication problems. Great progress has been made in this area over the last ten years, through both practitioner and academic publications, and this work needs to continue.

Third, mediation must become more highly institutionalized. It must be incorporated as a significant component of organizational dispute resolution systems at all levels of society. Mediation has for too long been conducted on an ad hoc basis. Fortunately, in the last decade, formalized training has given mediation much wider acceptability, and the increase in the number of organizations that now incorporate services on a routine basis is an indication of this trend.

Fourth, funding must be developed that will promote the growth of mediation organizations and agencies in the private and public sectors. Funding must come from governmental agencies, the business sector, foundations, and individuals who will utilize mediation on a fee-for-service basis. Only through funded institutionalization will mediation become readily accessible to a broader public.

Finally, participants in conflicts, mediators, and other professionals need to search for new arenas in which mediation can be applied. Following the Gandhian example, we need to conduct "experiments in truth" to discover appropriate new applications for mediation. Although mediation is not a panacea and does not guarantee perfect settlements in all conflicts, it is a tool that has wider application than is currently recognized.

In conclusion, I will identify seven major areas where advancement is needed and where I believe growth will occur in the field of mediation during the next decade:

1. *Ethnic disputes.* The late 1980s and early 1990s have produced some of the most brutal incidents of violence between

ethnic groups that have been seen since the Second World War (Brown, 1993, Horowitz, 1985). Ethnic cleansing in new states carved from the former Yugoslavia, genocidal killings in Rwanda, decades-long guerrilla war between the government and Indians in Guatemala, disputes in India between the government and separatist groups in Kashmir and the Punjab, civil war in Liberia and Somalia, ethnic conflicts in Afghanistan, Tajikistan, and Turkey, and civil war between Sinhalese and Tamils in Sri Lanka are large-scale examples on the international front.

But conflicts with strong ethnic components are not found just in war-torn countries. Ethnic disputes occur on a smaller scale in most multicultural countries: attacks on Turks and foreigners in Germany and France; disputes between members of different tribal or ethnic groups in South Africa; violations of the land or water rights of Native American, First Nations, and other aboriginal peoples in a number of countries; beatings of African Americans by members of other races and police in the United States; conflicts between Korean store-owners and African-American youth in New York or Los Angeles; racial discrimination in the workplace.

Certain conflicts with ethnic components have been handled and resolved creatively. The relatively peaceful transition to democracy in South Africa, breakthroughs in the Middle East conflict, and innovative mediation work in cases of alleged discrimination in a number of countries all exemplify this. However, the field is still in its infancy and desperately needs more research, experimental applications, and aggressive initiatives. Effective use of mediation, especially when combined with procedures to establish and build relationships and to foster interest-based bargaining, offers the promise of helping entrenched parties to deal with and manage disputes that include ethnic differences.

2. *Psychological and relationship barriers to agreement making.* Closely related to some of the ethnic disputes just described is the resolution of what have come to be called intractable disputes (Kriesberg, Northrup, and Thorson, 1989). These are conflicts where trust, respect, and cognitive empathy or understanding between parties are so lacking that disputants are unable to move toward discussion of, or agreement on, any substantive issues that divide them. They are locked into a cycle of negative intimacy that, without assistance, they appear to be unable to break out of. This

dynamic commonly occurs in the context of diplomatic relations, ethnic group interactions, labor-management bargaining, superior-subordinate relationships, community disputes, divorce, and a range of other group and interpersonal confrontations. Until new procedures are developed to break this type and cycle of negative conflict, many disputes will remain both unmanageable and unresolvable. This topic will be a critical research focus and area of experimentation in the future. It is probable that mediation, with a greater emphasis on the establishment and building of relationships and the development of cognitive empathy, will be able to make a greater contribution to unlocking these intractable disputes.

3. *Violent conflict.* Again related to the preceding points is the need to find alternative means of regulating and resolving violent disputes. These would include creative approaches to deescalating potential violence, shifting to nonviolent means once violence has actually occurred, and addressing postviolence trauma and relationships. In the international arena, research and interventions in preventive diplomacy (Evans, 1993) and the development of peace accord systems that utilize mediation on the ground (Moore, 1993) are significant new steps toward control of violent conflict. On the domestic front, they are matched by initiatives to prevent gang violence, stem spousal and child abuse, and promote reconciliation between victims and offenders. More work needs to be done to explore the roles of third parties and mediation in such contexts.

4. *Education for creative conflict management.* The development of more nonviolent cultures will require structured educational initiatives to teach people how to work through their conflicts more effectively, more productively, and with less harm to each other. This effort should start with the youngest of children, but should also be presented in all phases of education and life. Students need to be introduced to mediation principles and procedures early in their education so that they can apply them throughout their lives. Additional formal courses of instruction need to be developed for secondary, undergraduate, graduate, and professional schools, and public seminars need to be provided for those not in schools.

Teaching people from various cultures how to handle conflict more effectively and nonviolently will also mean further research into how different cultures successfully manage disputes. Sometimes, procedures may be borrowed by one culture from another, but often, prescriptive solutions from one society cannot be transferred or imposed in their totality. More elicitive approaches to research and conflict analysis will have to be used, in which people from diverse cultures are asked to decode their own patterns of dispute escalation and deescalation and their successful management and resolution methods. This will ensure that appropriate, effective, and culturally acceptable procedures are being developed and taught (Lederach, 1995).

5. *Dispute systems design.* The trend of designing dispute resolution systems that incorporate mediation as one of the central procedures is already significantly under way for a variety of types of disputes and in a number of public and private organizations. Systems that utilize mediation have been developed to handle large numbers of employment disputes, charges of discrimination, consumer complaints, and environmental controversies. Organizational leaders, personnel, and mediators will increasingly appreciate the multiplier effect of systems that channel disputes to appropriate procedures and intermediaries and facilitate the resolution of multiple conflicts as opposed to the mediation of single disputes on an ad hoc basis. In the future, many mediators will be called on to design and implement dispute management and resolution systems as well as being requested to mediate individual cases. The creation of such systems can exponentially increase the number of conflicts that are addressed and resolved and can substantially broaden public exposure to, and awareness of, cooperative means of managing differences.

6. *Conflict management and public governance.* Although there appears to be a worldwide trend toward more democratic decision making within organizations and governments (Huntingdon, 1991), there also seems to be a growing level of dissatisfaction both with the forms of participation that are prescribed or allowed and with the adversarial and often ineffective nature of decision-making processes. Citizens, government officials, coworkers, and managers are increasingly seeking means to build consensus agreements that a broad spectrum of people can support and to move beyond adversary democracy (Mansbridge, 1983). This is an arena where mediation has a lot to offer.

Mediation has been used effectively to build consensual decisions on a wide range of public policy, regulatory, site-specific, and organizational issues. There is every reason to believe that this trend will continue into the next century, and that the range of applications will become even more diverse. Mediation has the potential to provide an alternative to divisive politics in a number of arenas and to help build social consensus on critical issues of concern.

7. *Conflict management and the global environment.* Social conflicts are often played out in the context of a natural environment that sets significant parameters for what is and is not possible. As worldwide awareness of the interlocking relationship between our social and natural worlds increases, there will be a greater impetus to explore how more sustainable societies can be developed, both at local and global levels. Mediation has been an effective procedure for addressing certain critical environmental issues and will increasingly be used to handle major problems such as transboundary air pollution, global warming, and limited water resources. Large environmental issues, more and more of which are of a transboundary nature, will be highly appropriate for mediation because no one international actor has either the authority or the power to impose a unilateral decision.

Today, people around the world are in need of effective means to help manage and resolve conflicts in all aspects of their lives. Mediation has proven itself in the past to be a helpful tool in accomplishing this goal in a variety of situations and cultures. It is my hope that the detailed elaboration of the mediation process found in this book will help both disputants and intermediaries to develop better, more creative, and more acceptable solutions to joint problems, and more positive working relationships between and among the people of the world.

Professional Practice Guidelines

The Society of Professionals in Dispute Resolution (SPIDR) Ethical Standards of Professional Responsibility

The Society of Professionals in Dispute Resolution (SPIDR) was established in 1973 to promote the peaceful resolution of disputes. Members of the Society believe that resolving disputes through negotiation, mediation, arbitration, and other neutral interventions can be of great benefit to disputing parties and to society. In 1983, the SPIDR Board of Directors charged the SPIDR Ethics Committee with the task of developing ethical standards of professional responsibility. The Committee membership represented all the various sectors and disciplines within SPIDR. This document, adopted by the Board on June 2, 1986, is the result of that charge.

The purpose of this document is to promote among SPIDR Members and Associates ethical conduct and a high level of competency among SPIDR Members, including honesty, integrity, impartiality and the exercise of good judgment in their dispute resolution efforts. It is hoped that this document also will help to 1) define the profession of dispute resolution, 2) educate the public, and 3) inform users of dispute resolution services.

Application of Standards

Adherence to these ethical standards by SPIDR Members and Associates is basic to professional responsibility. SPIDR Members and

Associates commit themselves to be guided in their professional conduct by these standards. The SPIDR Board of Directors or its designee is available to advise Members and Associates about the interpretation of these standards. Other neutral practitioners and organizations are welcome to follow these standards.

Scope

It is recognized that SPIDR Members and Associates resolve disputes in various sectors within the disciplines of dispute resolution and have their own codes of professional conduct. These standards have been developed as general guidelines of practice for neutral disciplines represented in the SPIDR membership. Ethical considerations relevant to some, but not to all, of these disciplines are not covered by these standards.

General Responsibilities

Neutrals have a duty to the parties, to the profession, and to themselves. They should be honest and unbiased, act in good faith, be diligent, and not seek to advance their own interests at the expense of their parties'.

Neutrals must act fairly in dealing with the parties, have no personal interest in the terms of the settlement, show no bias toward individuals and institutions involved in the dispute, be reasonably available as requested by the parties, and be certain that the parties are informed of the process in which they are involved.

Responsibilities to the Parties

1. *Impartiality.* The neutral must maintain impartiality toward all parties. Impartiality means freedom from favoritism or bias either by word or by action, and a commitment to serve all parties as opposed to a single party.

2. *Informed Consent.* The neutral has an obligation to ensure that all parties understand the nature of the process, the procedures, the particular role of the neutral, and the parties' relationship to the neutral.

3. *Confidentiality*. Maintaining confidentiality is critical to the dispute resolution process. Confidentiality encourages candor, a full exploration of the issues, and a neutral's acceptability. There may be some types of cases, however, in which confidentiality is not protected. In such cases, the neutral must advise the parties, when appropriate in the dispute resolution process, that the confidentiality of the proceedings cannot necessarily be maintained. Except in such instances, the neutral must resist all attempts to cause him or her to reveal any information outside the process. A commitment by the neutral to hold information in confidence with the process also must be honored.

4. *Conflict of Interest*. The neutral must refrain from entering or continuing in any dispute if he or she believes or perceives that participation as a neutral would be a clear conflict of interest and any circumstances that may reasonably raise a question as to the neutral's impartiality.

The duty to disclose is a continuing obligation throughout the process.

5. *Promptness*. The neutral shall exert every reasonable effort to expedite the process.

6. *The Settlement and Its Consequences*. The dispute resolution process belongs to the parties. The neutral has no vested interest in the terms of a settlement, but must be satisfied that agreements in which he or she has participated will not impugn the integrity of the process. The neutral has a responsibility to see that the parties consider the terms of a settlement. If the neutral is concerned about the possible consequences of a proposed agreement, and the needs of the parties dictate, the neutral must inform the parties of that concern. In adhering to this standard, the neutral may find it advisable to educate the parties, to refer one or more parties for specialized advice, or to withdraw from the case. In no case, however, shall the neutral violate Section 3, Confidentiality, of these standards.

Unrepresented Interests

The neutral must consider circumstances where interests are not represented in the process. The neutral has an obligation, where in his or her judgment the needs of parties dictate, to ensure that such interests have been considered by the principal parties.

Use of Multiple Procedures

The use of more than one dispute resolution procedure by the same neutral involves additional responsibilities. Where the use of more than one procedure is initially contemplated, the neutral must take care at the outset to advise the parties of the nature of the procedures and the consequences of revealing information during any one procedure which the neutral may later use for decision making or may share with another decision maker. Where the use of more than one procedure is contemplated after the initiation of the dispute resolution process, the neutral must explain the consequences and afford the parties an opportunity to select another neutral for the subsequent procedures. It is also incumbent upon the neutral to advise the parties of the transition from one dispute resolution process to another.

Background and Qualifications

A neutral should accept responsibility only in cases where the neutral has sufficient knowledge regarding the appropriate process and subject matter to be effective. A neutral has a responsibility to maintain and improve his or her professional skills.

Disclosure of Fees

It is the duty of the neutral to explain to the parties at the outset of the process the bases of compensation, fees, and charges, if any.

Support of the Profession

The experienced neutral should participate in the development of new practitioners in the field and engage in efforts to educate the public about the value and use of neutral dispute resolution procedures. The neutral should provide *pro bono* services, where appropriate.

Responsibilities of Neutrals Working on the Same Case

In the event that more than one neutral is involved in the resolution of a dispute, each has an obligation to inform the others regarding his or her entry in the case. Neutrals working with the same parties should maintain an open and professional relationship with each other.

Advertising and Solicitation

A neutral must be aware that some forms of advertising and solicitation are inappropriate and in some conflict resolution disciplines, such as labor arbitration, are impermissible. All advertising must honestly represent the services to be rendered. No claims of specific results or promises which imply favor on one side over another for the purpose of obtaining business should be made. No commissions, rebates, or other similar forms of remuneration should be given or received by a neutral for the referral of clients.

Mediation Services Agreement
Sample Waiver and Consent Form

The purpose of this waiver and consent form is to ensure that you, our client, understand the nature of our service and the responsibilities you have to maintain the confidentiality of the mediation process.

Your Initials

_____ I understand that CDR Associates offers neither legal advice nor legal counsel.

_____ I agree that I will not, at any time (before, during, or after mediation of this dispute), call the mediator as an adversarial witness in any legal or administrative proceeding concerning this dispute.

_____ I agree that I will not subpoena or call for the production of any records, notes, or work product of the mediator in any legal or administrative proceeding that arises before, during, or after the mediation of this dispute. However, any agreement resulting from mediation that is intended by the parties to have legal effect and to be legally enforceable may be subpoenaed, called for, or produced in any proceedings to which it is relevant, unless the agreement specifically provides otherwise.

I have read the above and have no further questions regarding the confidentiality of this process.

_____

Signature

_____

Date

Settlement Documentation Form

Sample Memorandum of Understanding

This is a memorandum of understanding regarding the revision of the contract of employment between Dr. Richard Singson, director of and representative for the Fairview Medical Clinic, 3504 Arizona Avenue, Smithville, Colorado, and Dr. Andrew Whittamore, a physician working at the same clinic.

Because of personal difficulties between Dr. Andrew Whittamore and his wife, Dr. Janelle Whittamore, who also works at Fairview Medical Clinic, it is agreed by Dr. Singson and Dr. Andrew Whittamore that the latter should continue to practice medicine for the Fairview Medical Clinic, but that his principal office should not be at the clinic's address listed above. This arrangement will allow the Whittamores the physical separation that they both desire.

The following points detail the agreements reached by Dr. Andrew Whittamore and the clinic regarding establishment of a separate office.

1. Dr. Andrew Whittamore will remain an employee of the Fairview Medical Clinic for the next two-and-a-half years, although his practice will not be at the clinic's address listed above.

2. Dr. Andrew Whittamore will find new office space on his own time. The time frame for the search is left up to Dr. Whittamore.

3. Dr. Andrew Whittamore's current desk and office furniture will be moved from the clinic to his new office.

4. Dr. Andrew Whittamore will pay one-half of the cost for all new equipment purchased for his new office. The cost of the

equipment will be prorated and deducted from his salary on a monthly basis over the next two-and-a-half years. The furniture will remain the property of the clinic.

5. Moving expenses will be equally borne by the clinic and Dr. Andrew Whittamore.

6. The clinic will continue to provide Dr. Whittamore with a full-time nurse-receptionist.

7. Dr. Whittamore will continue to have full access to the laboratory, staff, and facilities of the clinic.

8. All billing from Dr. Whittamore's practice will be managed by the bookkeeper for the clinic.

9. Dr. Whittamore will duplicate at his own expense all new patient records developed through his separate practice and file records in the central file of the clinic. Duplicate reports on patient care should be submitted to the clinic by the end of each month.

Both doctors agree to comply fully with this agreement and expect that the arrangement will be mutually beneficial. Should problems arise in the implementation of the agreement, both doctors agree to return to mediation before pursuing another course of dispute resolution.

It is the understanding of Drs. Whittamore and Singson that this agreement will be reviewed by their respective lawyers before it becomes effective.

In the event any future dispute arises in regard to the provisions of this agreement or otherwise related to our revision of the employee contract which we cannot settle ourselves, we agree to enter into mediation before seeking a solution in court.

Each of us has considered the implications of this agreement, has discussed it with our own legal counsel, and considers it to be a fair and equitable arrangement. We intend for this agreement to be a final settlement of all issues pertaining to the employee contract.

Richard Singson, M.D.	Andrew Whittamore, M.D.
(for Fairview Medical Clinic)	
Date	Date
Attorney/Witness	Attorney/Witness
Date	Date

List of Professional Associations

Associations/Organizations

Academy of Family Mediators
4 Militia Drive
Lexington, MA 02173
(617) 674–2663
(617) 674–2690

American Arbitration Association, National Office
1150 Connecticut Avenue, Sixth Floor
Washington, DC 20036
(202) 296–8510

American Bar Association
Section of Dispute Resolution
1800 M Street, N.W.
Washington, DC 20036
(202) 662–1680

Arbitrators' Institute of New Zealand
16 Palmer Street
PO Box 1477
Wellington
NEW ZEALAND
64 4 385 4178
64 4 385 7224

Association of Family and Conciliation Courts
329 W. Wilson Street
Madison, WI 53703
(608) 251–4001

Australian Dispute Resolution Association
17 Randle Street
Surry Hills, NSW 2010
AUSTRALIA

Bundesverband für Familienmediation
c/o Dr. Hans Georg Maehler
Suedliche Auffahrtsallee 57
D-80639 München
GERMANY

Bureau of National Affairs, Inc. (BNA PLUS)
1231 25th Street, N.W.
Washington, DC 20037
(800) 452–7773
(202) 452–4323

Centro Italiano Per la Promozione della Mediazione
via Giolitti, 21
Torino 10123
ITALY
39 11 814 2726
39 11 839 5577

Conflict Resolution Network
P.O. Box 1016
Chatswood NSW 2057
AUSTRALIA
61 2 412 2584
61 2 413 1148

Family Mediation Canada
123 Woolwich Street, Second Floor
Guelph, ON N1H 3V1
CANADA
(519) 836–7750
(519) 836–7204

Gernika-Gogoratuz
Foru Plaza z/g
Gernika-Lumo Bizkaia 48300
SPAIN
34 4 625 3558
34 4 625 6765

Mediation Network for Northern Ireland
74 Dublin Road
Belfast BT2 7HP
NORTHERN IRELAND
44 232 438 614
44 232 314 430

Mediation UK
82A Gloucester Road
Bishopston
Bristol BS7 8BN
ENGLAND
44 117 924 1234
44 117 944 1387

Nairobi Peace Initiative
P.O. Box 14894
Nairobi
KENYA
254 2 482 08

National Association of Mediation in Education (NAME)
425 Amity Street
Amherst, MA 01002
(413) 545-2462

National Conference on Peacemaking and Conflict Resolution
(NCPCR)
4400 University Drive
Fairfax, VA 22030-4444
(703) 934-5140

National Institute of Dispute Resolution (NIDR)
1901 L Street, N.W., Suite 600
Washington, DC 20036
(202) 466-4764

The Network:. . .for Conflict Resolution
Conrad Grebel College
Waterloo, ON N2L 366
CANADA
(519) 885 0800
(519) 885 0806

Society of Professionals in Dispute Resolution (SPIDR)
815 15th Street, N.W., Suite 530
Washington, DC 20005
(202) 783–7277

South African Association for Conflict Intervention (SAACI)
c/o Welma de Beer
41 Rhyn ave
Bayswater 9301
SOUTH AFRICA
27 51 311 423
27 51 313 696

Umut Foundation
Resit Galip Caddesi, Hereke Sokak No. 10
G.O.P. Ankara
TURKEY
2321000/2002
011 90 312 447 10 36

Professional Journals

Canadian Arbitration Journal
Arbitration and Mediation Institute of Canada Inc.
P.O. Box 462, Station U
Toronto, ON M8Z 5Y8
CANADA
(416) 849–8993

Mediation Quarterly
Jossey-Bass Inc., Publishers
350 Sansome Street
San Francisco, CA 94104
(415) 433–1767

Missouri Journal of Dispute Resolution
Center for the Study of Dispute Resolution
University of Missouri, Columbia
School of Law and Missouri Law Review
104 Hulston Hall
Columbia, MO 65211
(314) 882–6487

Negotiation Journal: On the Process of Dispute Settlement
Plenum Publishing Corporation
233 Spring Street
New York, NY 10013
(212) 620–8000

Ohio Journal
The Ohio State University School of Law
1659 N. High Street
Columbus, OH 43210
(614) 292–2631

Newsletters

American Bar Association
Section of Dispute Resolution
1800 M Street, N.W.
Washington, DC 20036
Dispute Resolution (newsletter)
(202) 662–1680

Bureau of National Affairs, Inc. (BNA PLUS)
1231 25th Street, N.W.
Washington, DC 20037
(800) 452–7773
(202) 452–4323

Conflict Resolution Consortium
The Florida State University
500 Miccosukee Road, Suite A
Tallahassee, FL 32308
Florida Growth Management (newsletter)
(904) 644–2560

Conrad Grebel College
Waterloo, ON N2L-3G6
CANADA
Interaction for Conflict Resolution (newsletter)
(519) 885–0880

Council of Better Business Bureaus, Inc.
Alternative Dispute Resolution Division
4200 Wilson Boulevard, Suite 800
Arlington, VA 22203
BBB Solutions (newsletter)
(800) 537–4600

Mediation Development Association of British Columbia
P.O. Box 2309
Vancouver, BC V6B-3Y4
CANADA
The Mediator (newsletter)
(604) 241–1460

Mennonite Central Committee
21 S. 12th Street,
P.O. Box 500
Akron, PA 17501–0500
Conciliation Quarterly Newsletter (newsletter)
(717) 859–3889

National Association of Mediation in Education (NAME)
425 Amity Street
Amherst, MA 01002
The Fourth "R" (newsletter)
(413) 545–2462

National Institute of Dispute Resolution (NIDR)
1901 L Street, N.W., Suite 600
Washington, DC 20036
Dispute Resolution Forum (newsletter)
(202) 466–4764

Program on Negotiation at Harvard Law School
513 Pound Hall
Harvard University
Cambridge, MA 02138
Consensus (newsletter)
(617) 495–1684

RESOLVE
Center for Environmental Dispute Resolution
2828 Pennsylvania Ave., N.W., Suite 402
Washington, DC 20007
Resolve (newsletter)
(202) 944–2300

Training Resources

CDR Associates
100 Arapahoe Avenue, Suite 12
Boulder, CO 80302
(303) 442–7367
(303) 442–7442
(800) MEDIATE

References

"AAA Designs ADR Insurance Procedures." *Dispute Resolution*, 1984, *13*, 12.

Acland, A. *A Sudden Outbreak of Common Sense: Managing Conflict Through Mediation*. London: Hutchinson, 1990.

Administrative Dispute Resolution Act, Federal Register, 23 Jan., 1990.

Afzal, M. "Community-Based Conflict Resolution (Pakistan Experience)." In C. Pe, G. Sosmeña, and A. Tadiar (eds.), *Transcultural Mediation in the Asia-Pacific*. Manila, Philippines: Asia-Pacific Organization for Mediators, 1988.

Aiken, M., and Mott, P. "Locating Centers of Power." In M. Aiken and P. Mott (eds.), *The Structure of Community Power*. New York: Random House, 1970.

American Arbitration Association. *An Overview of Mediation*. New York: American Arbitration Association, n.d.

Aminuddin, M. *Malaysian Industrial Relations*. New York: McGraw-Hill, 1990.

Anacona, D., Friedman, R., and Kolb, D. "The Group and What Happens on the Way to 'Yes.'" *Negotiation Journal*, 1991, *7*(2), 155–173.

Antoun, R. *Arab Village*. Bloomington: Indiana University Press, 1972.

Araki, C. "Dispute Management in the Schools." *Mediation Quarterly*, 1990, *8*(1), 51–62.

Argyris, C. *Intervention Theory and Method: A Behavioral Science View*. Reading, Mass.: Addison-Wesley, 1970.

Aryal, L. "Mediation in Nepal." In C. Pe, G. Sosmeña, and A. Tadiar (eds.), *Transcultural Mediation in the Asia-Pacific*. Manila, Philippines: Asia-Pacific Organization for Mediators, 1988.

Assefa, H. "The Politics of Reconciliation." *Track Two*, 1994, *3*(4), 1–7.

Association of Family and Conciliation Courts. *Model Standards of the Association of Family and Conciliation Courts*. Portland, Oreg.: Association of Family and Conciliation Courts, 1984.

Aubert, V. "Competition and Dissensus: Two Types of Conflict and Conflict Resolution." *Journal of Conflict Resolution*, 1963, *7*(1), 26–42.

Auerbach, J. *Justice Without Law: Resolving Disputes Without Lawyers*. New York: Oxford University Press, 1983.

Augsburger, D. *Conflict Mediation Across Cultures.* Louisville, Ky.: Westminster/ John Knox Press, 1992.

Awad, M. Conversation with the author regarding Palestinian dispute resolution processes, Cyprus, summer 1994.

Bach, G., and Goldberg, H. *Creative Aggression: The Art of Assertive Living.* New York: Doubleday, 1974.

Bacow, L., and Wheeler, M. *Environmental Dispute Resolution.* New York: Plenum, 1984.

Bagozzi, R., and Dholakia, R. "Mediational Mechanisms in Interorganizational Conflict." In D. Druckman (ed.), *Negotiations: Social Psychological Perspectives.* Newbury Park, Calif.: Sage, 1977.

Baldwin, P. (ed.). *Environmental Mediation: An Effective Alternative?* Palo Alto, Calif.: RESOLVE, Center for Environmental Conflict Resolution, 1978.

Barnes, B. E. "Conflict Resolution Across Cultures: A Hawaii Perspective and a Pacific Mediation Model." *Mediation Quarterly,* 1994, *12*(2), 117–133.

Barsky, A. "Issues in the Termination of Mediation Due to Abuse." *Mediation Quarterly,* 1995, *13*(1), 19–35.

Bazerman, M., and Lewicki, R. (eds.). *Negotiating in Organizations.* Newbury Park, Calif.: Sage, 1983.

Behn, R., and Vaupel, J. *Quick Analysis for Busy Decision Makers.* New York: Basic Books, 1982.

Bellman, H. "Mediation as an Approach to Resolving Environmental Disputes." In *Proceedings of the Environmental Conflict Management Practitioners Workshop.* Florissant, Col., Oct. 1982.

Bellows, G., and Moulton, B. "Assessment: Framing the Choices." In G. Bellows and B. Moulton (eds.), *The Lawyering Process.* Mineola, N.Y.: Foundation Press, 1981.

Benjamin, M., and Irving, H. "Research in Family Mediation: Review and Implications." *Mediation Quarterly,* 1995, *13*(1), 53–82.

Berger, P., and Luckmann, T. *The Social Construction of Reality: A Treatise on the Sociology of Knowledge.* New York: Doubleday, 1967.

Berkowitz, L. "Stimulus/Response: The Case for Bottling Up Rage." *Psychology Today,* 1973, *7*(2), 24–31.

Bernard, S., Folger, J., Weingarten, H., and Zumeta, Z. "The Neutral Mediator: Value Dilemmas in Divorce Mediation." *Mediation Quarterly,* 1984, no. 4, 61–74.

Bethel, C. "The Use of Separate Sessions in Family Mediation." *Negotiation Journal,* 1986, *2*(3), 257–271.

Bianchi, H. "Returning Conflict to the Community: The Alternative of Privatization." Unpublished manuscript, Amsterdam, Netherlands, 1978.

Biddle, A., and others. *Corporate Dispute Management 1982*. New York: Bender, 1982.

Bingham, G. "Does Negotiation Hold a Promise for Regulatory Reform?" *Resolve*, 1981, *10*, 1–8.

Bingham, G. *Resolving Environmental Disputes: A Decade of Experience*. Washington, D.C.: Conservation Foundation, 1984.

Blake, R., and Mouton, J. S. "Union Management Relations: From Conflict to Collaboration." *Personnel*, 1961, *38*, 38–51.

Blake, R., and Mouton, J. S. *Solving Costly Organizational Conflicts: Achieving Intergroup Trust, Cooperation, and Teamwork*. San Francisco: Jossey-Bass, 1984.

Blake, R., Mouton, J., and Sloma, R. "The Union-Management Intergroup Laboratory: Strategy for Resolving Intergroup Conflict." In W. Bennis and others (eds.), *The Planning of Change*. Troy, Mo.: Holt, Rinehart & Winston, 1961.

Blake, R., Shepard, H., and Mouton, J. *Managing Intergroup Conflict in Industry*. Houston: Gulf, 1964.

Bluehouse, P., and Zion, J. "Hozhooji Naat'aanii: The Navajo Justice and Harmony Ceremony." *Mediation Quarterly*, 1993, *10*(4), 321–325.

Bonner, M. *Group Dynamics*. New York: Ronald Press, 1959.

Boulding, K. *Conflict and Defense*. New York: HarperCollins, 1962.

Brett, J., "Negotiating Group Decisions," *Negotiation Journal*, 1991, *7*(3), 291–310.

Brett, J., and Goldberg, S. "Mediator Advisors: A New Third Party Role." In M. Bazerman and R. Lewicki (eds.), *Negotiating in Organizations*. Newbury Park, Calif.: Sage, 1983.

Bronstein, R. "Mediation and the Colorado Lawyer." *Colorado Lawyer*, 1982, *11*(9), 2315–23.

Brookmire, D., and Sistrunk, F. "The Effects of Perceived Ability and Impartiality of Mediators and Time Pressure on Negotiation." *Journal of Conflict Resolution*, 1980, *24*(2), 311–327.

Brown, B. "Face Saving and Face Restoration in Negotiation." In D. Druckman (ed.), *Negotiations: Social Psychological Perspectives*. Newbury Park, Calif.: Sage, 1977.

Brown, D. "Divorce and Family Mediation: History, Review, Future Directions." *Conciliation Courts Review*, 1982, *20*(2), 1–37.

Brown, L. D. *Managing Conflict of Organizational Interfaces*. Reading, Mass.: Addison-Wesley, 1983.

Brown, L. M. *How to Negotiate a Successful Contract*. Englewood Cliffs, N.J.: Prentice-Hall, 1955.

Brown, M. (ed.). *Ethnic Conflict and International Security*. Princeton: Princeton University Press, 1993.

Burgess, H. *The Foothills Water Treatment Project: A Case Study in Environmental Mediation.* Cambridge: Environmental Negotiation Project, Laboratory of Architecture and Planning, Massachusetts Institute of Technology, 1980.

Burrell, N. A., and Vogl, S. M. "Turf-Side Conflict Mediation for Students." *Mediation Quarterly,* 1990, 7(3), 237–250.

Burton, J. *Conflict and Communication: The Use of Controlled Communication in International Relations.* London: Macmillan, 1969.

Bush, R., and Folger, J. *The Promise of Mediation: Responding to Conflict Through Empowerment and Recognition.* San Francisco: Jossey-Bass, 1994.

Carpenter, S., and Kennedy, J. "Information Sharing and Conciliation: Tools for Environmental Conflict Management." *Environmental Comment,* 1977, 22–23.

Carpenter, S., and Kennedy, J. "Conflict Anticipation: A Site Specific Approach for Managing Environmental Conflict." Paper presented at fall meeting of the Society for Mining Engineers of AIME, Tucson, Ariz., Oct. 1979.

Carter, J. *Keeping the Faith: Memoirs of a President.* New York: Bantam Books, 1982.

CDR Associates. *Designing Dispute Resolution Systems.* Boulder, Colo.: CDR Associates, 1992.

CDR Associates. "Dispute Resolution and School Restructuring Project." Report to the National Institute for Dispute Resolution, Jan. 27, 1993.

CDR Associates. Wolf summit materials. Boulder, Colo.: CDR Associates, 1993.

CDR Associates. Furbearer dialogue materials. Boulder, Colo.: CDR Associates, 1995.

Chandler, J. P. (ed.). *Teachings of Mahatma Gandhi.* Lahore, India: Indian Printing Works, 1945.

Civil Rights Act, Title X. *U.S. Code,* vol. 42, sec. 2000 (1964).

Clark, P., and Cummings, F. "Selecting an Environmental Conflict Management Strategy." In P. Marcus and W. Emrich (eds.), *Working Papers in Conflict Management.* New York: American Arbitration Association, 1981.

Clark-McGlennon Associates. *Patuxent-River Cleanup Agreement.* Boston: Clark-McGlennon Associates, 1982.

Coates, R., and Gehm, J. "Victim Meets Offender: An Evaluation of Victim-Offender Reconciliation Programs." In M. Wright and B. Galaway (eds.), *Mediation and Criminal Justice.* London: Sage, 1989.

Cohen, A., and Smith, R. "The Critical-Incident Approach to Leadership

Intervention in Training Groups." In W. Dyer (ed.), *Modern Theory and Method in Group Training.* New York: Van Nostrand Reinhold, 1972.

Cohen, H. *You Can Negotiate Anything.* Secaucus, N.J.: Lyle Stuart, 1980.

Colosi, T., and Berkeley, A. "The Negotiating Table: Bridging Troubled Waters." Unpublished manuscript, American Arbitration Association, Washington, D.C., 1980.

Comaroff, J., and Roberts, S. *Rules and Processes: The Cultural Logic of Dispute in an African Context.* Chicago: University of Chicago Press, 1981.

Comeau, E. "Procedural Controls in Public Sector Domestic Relations Mediation." In H. Davidson and others (eds.), *Alternative Means of Family Dispute Resolution.* Washington, D.C.: American Bar Association, 1982.

Connors, J. "Resolving Disputes Locally in Rural Alaska." *Mediation Quarterly,* 1993, *10*(4), 367–385.

Constantino, C., and Merchant, C. S. *Designing Conflict Management Systems: A Guide to Creating Productive and Healthy Organizations.* San Francisco: Jossey-Bass, 1995.

Coogler, O. J. *Structured Mediation in Divorce Settlement.* Lexington, Mass.: Lexington Books, 1978.

Cook, J., Rochl, J., and Shepard, D. *Executive Summary Final Report.* Washington, D.C.: Neighborhood Justice Field Institute, U.S. Department of Justice, 1980.

Coover, V., Deacon, E., Esser, C., and Moore, C. W. *Resource Manual for a Living Revolution.* Philadelphia: New Society, 1977.

Corcoran, K., and Melamed, J. "From Coercion to Empowerment: Spousal Abuse and Mediation." *Mediation Quarterly,* 1990, *7*(4), 303–316.

Cormick, G. "Mediating Environmental Controversies: Perspectives and First Experience." *Earth Law Journal,* 1976, *2,*

Cormick, G. "Intervention and Self-Determination in Environmental Disputes: A Mediator's Perspective." *Resolve,* 1982, *11,* 1–7.

Cormick, G., "Strategic Issues in Structuring Multi-Party Public Policy Negotiations." *Negotiation Journal,* 1989, *5*(2), 125–132.

"Corps of Engineers Early Resolution Program." Circular 690–1–690. Washington, D.C.: Corps of Engineers, 1993.

Coser, L. *The Functions of Social Conflict.* New York: Free Press, 1956.

Coser, L. *Continuities in the Study of Social Conflict.* New York: Free Press, 1967.

Creighton, J. *Communications.* Tulsa, Okla.: Synergy, 1972.

Crohn, M. "Dispute Resolution in Higher Education," *Negotiation Journal,* 1985, *1*(4), 301–305.

Cross, J. *The Economics of Bargaining.* New York: Basic Books, 1969.

Cross, J. "Negotiation as a Learning Process." *Journal of Conflict Resolution,* 1977, *21*(4), 581–606.

Crowfoot, J. "Negotiations: An Effective Tool for Citizen Organizations?" *The NRAG Papers,* 1980, *3*(4).

Curle, A. *Making Peace.* London: Tavistock, 1971.

Dahl, R. *Who Governs? Democracy and Power in an American City.* New Haven, Conn.: Yale University Press, 1961.

D'Antonio, W., Loomis, C., Form, W., and Erickson, E. "Institutional and Occupational Representations in Eleven Community Influence Systems." *American Sociological Review,* 1961, *26*(3), 440–446.

Daily, J., "The Effects of Anger on Negotiations over Mergers and Acquisitions." *Negotiation Journal,* 1991, *7*(1), 31–39.

Dauer, E. "National Practitioner Data Bank: Implications for Reaching Settlement in Medical Malpractice Cases." In *Proceedings, 22nd Annual SPIDR Conference, Dallas, Texas, 1994,* as cited in D. Joseph, "Health Care Conflict Management Education," unpublished, 1994.

Davis, A., and Gadlin, H. "Mediators Gain Trust the Old-Fashioned Way—We Earn It!" *Negotiation Journal,* 1988, *4*(1), 55–62.

Davis, R., Tichane, M., and Grayson, D. "The Effects of Alternative Forms of Dispute Resolution on Recidivism in Felony Offenses Between Acquaintances." Unpublished manuscript, Brooklyn Dispute Resolution Center, 1980.

deLeon, Linda, "Using Mediation to Resolve Personnel Disputes in a State Bureaucracy." *Negotiation Journal,* 1994, *10*(1), 64–86.

Delbecq, A., Vandeven, A., and Gustafson, D. *Group Techniques for Program Planning.* Glenview, Ill.: Scott, Foresman, 1975.

Dembart, L., and Kwartler, R. "The Snoqualmie River Conflict: Bringing Mediation into Environmental Disputes." In R. Goldmann (ed.), *Roundtable Justice: Case Studies in Conflict Resolution.* Boulder, Colo.: Westview Press, 1980.

Deutsch, M. "Trust and Suspicion." *Journal of Conflict Resolution,* 1958, *2*(4), 265–279.

Deutsch, M. "The Effect of Motivational Correlation upon Trust and Suspicion." *Human Relations,* 1960, *13*(2), 125–139.

Deutsch, M. "Conflicts: Productive and Destructive." *Journal of Social Issues,* 1969, *25*(1), 7–41.

Deutsch, M. *Resolution of Conflict.* New Haven, Conn.: Yale University Press, 1974.

Dewdney, M., Sordo, B., and Chinkin, C. "Contemporary Developments in Mediation Within the Legal System and Evaluation of the 1992–93 Settlement Week Program." Sydney, Australia: Law Society of New South Wales, 1994.

Dhammapada Commentary, as cited in J. McConnell, *Mindful Mediation: A Handbook for Buddhist Peacemakers.* Bangkok, Thailand: Buddhist Research Institute, 1995.

Dispute Resolution Forum. Washington, D.C.: National Institute for Dispute Resolution, 1989.

Doelker, R. E., Jr. "Mediation in Academia: Practicing What We Preach." *Mediation Quarterly,* 1989, 7(2), 157–161.

Douglas, A. *Industrial Peacemaking.* New York: Columbia University Press, 1962.

Downing, T. "Strategy and Tactics at the Bargaining Table." *Personnel,* 1960, 37(1), 58–63.

Doyle, M., and Straus, D. *How to Make Meetings Work.* Chicago: Playboy Press, 1976.

Drake, W. "Statewide Offices of Mediation." *Negotiation Journal,* 1989, 5(4), 359–364.

Dubois, R., and Mew, S. L. *The Art of Group Conversation.* New York: Association Press, 1963.

Eckhoff, T. "The Mediator, the Judge, and the Administrator in Conflict Resolution." *Acta Sociologica: Scandinavian Review of Sociology,* 1966–67, *10,* 148–172.

Ehrman, J., and Lesnick, M. "The Policy Dialogue: Applying Mediation to the Policy Making Process." *Mediation Quarterly,* 1988, no. 20, 93–99.

Ellis, D., and Stuckless, N. "Pre-Separation Abuse, Marital Conflict Mediation and Post-Separation Abuse." *Mediation Quarterly,* 1992, *4*(17).

Epstein, A. "Dispute Settlement Among the Tolai." *Oceana,* 1971, *41*(4), 157–170.

Erickson, S., and McKnight, M. "Mediating Spousal Abuse Divorces." *Mediation Quarterly,* 1990, 7(4), 377–388.

Evans, G. *Cooperating for Peace.* St. Leonards, Australia: Allen & Unwin, 1993.

Fagan, and Gehm, J. *Victim-Offender Reconciliation and Mediation Program Directory.* Valparaiso, Ind.: PACT Institute of Justice, 1993.

Faulkes, W. "Mediation in Australia: State of the Art 1987." In C. Pe, G. Sosmeña, and A. Tadiar (eds.), *Transcultural Mediation in the Asia-Pacific.* Manila, Philippines: Asia-Pacific Organization for Mediators, 1988.

Faulkes, W. "The Modern Development of Alternative Dispute Resolution in Australia." *Australian Dispute Resolution Journal,* 1990, *1*(2), 61–68.

Felsteiner, W., and Williams, L. "Mediation as an Alternative to Criminal Prosecution." *Law and Human Behavior,* 1978, *2*(3), 223–244.

Feuille, P. "Why Does Grievance Mediation Resolve Grievances?" *Negotiation Journal,* 1992, 8(2), 131–145.

Feuille, P., and Kolb, D. "Waiting in the Wings: Mediation's Role in Grievance Mediation." *Negotiation Journal,* 1994, *10*(3), 249–261.

Filley, A. *Interpersonal Conflict Resolution*. Glenview, Ill.: Scott, Foresman, 1975.

Fisch, R., Weakland, J., and Segal, L. *The Tactics of Change: Doing Therapy Briefly*. San Francisco: Jossey-Bass, 1982.

Fisher, L. "Family (Divorce) Mediation in the United States of America." *Australian Journal of Dispute Resolution*, 1991, *2*(3), 186–197.

Fisher, R. "Fractionating Conflict." In R. Fisher (ed.), *International Conflict and Behavioral Sciences: The Craigville Papers*. New York: Basic Books, 1964.

Fisher, R. *International Conflict for Beginners*. New York: HarperCollins, 1969.

Fisher, R. *International Mediation: A Working Guide*. New York: International Peace Academy, 1978.

Fisher, R., and Brown, S. "How Can We Accept Those Whose Conduct is Unacceptable?" *Negotiation Journal*, 1988, *4*(2), 125–136.

Fisher, R., and Ury, W. *Getting to Yes: Negotiating Agreement Without Giving In*. Boston: Houghton Mifflin, 1981.

Fisher, R. J. "Third Party Consultation: A Method for the Study and Resolution of Conflict." *Journal of Conflict Resolution*, 1982, *16*(1), 67–94.

Folberg, J., and Milne, A. *Divorce Mediation: Theory and Practice*. New York: Guilford Press, 1988.

Folberg, J., and Taylor, A. *Mediation: A Comprehensive Guide to Resolving Conflicts Without Litigation*. San Francisco: Jossey-Bass, 1984.

Freedman, L., Haile, C., and Bookstaff, H. *Confidentiality in Mediation: A Practitioner's Guide*. Washington, D.C.: American Bar Association, 1985.

Freire, P. *Pedagogy of the Oppressed*. New York: Herder and Herder, 1970.

Freud, S. *A General Introduction to Psycho-Analysis*. Garden City, N.Y.: Garden City Publishing, 1943. (Originally published 1920.)

Frost, J., and Wilmot, W. *Interpersonal Conflict*. Dubuque, Iowa: Brown, 1978.

Fucini, J., and Fucini, S. *Working for the Japanese*. New York: Free Press, 1990.

Galper, M. *Joint Custody and Co-Parenting: Sharing Your Child Equally. A Source Book for the Separated or Divorced Family*. Philadelphia: Running Press, 1980.

Galtung, J. "On the Meaning of Nonviolence." In J. Galtung (ed.), *Peace: Research-Education-Action*. Copenhagen, Denmark: Ejlers, 1975.

Gardner, L. "Mediation Triage: Screening for Spouse Abuse in Divorce Mediation." *Mediation Quarterly*, 1990, *7*(4), 365–376.

Gentry, D. B. "The Certification Movement: Past, Present, and Future." *Mediation Quarterly*, 1994, *11*(3), 285–291.

Ginsberg, R. B. "American Bar Association Delegation Visits the People's Republic of China." *American Bar Association Journal,* 1978, *64,* 1516–25.

Girdner, L. "Mediation Triage: Screening for Spouse Abuse in Divorce Mediation." *Mediation Quarterly,* 1990, *4*(17).

Goffman, E. *The Presentation of Self in Everyday Life.* New York: Doubleday, 1959.

Goffman, E. *Strategic Interaction.* Philadelphia: University of Pennsylvania Press, 1969.

Goldberg, S. "Grievance Mediation: A Successful Alternative to Labor Arbitration." *Negotiation Journal,* 1989, *5*(5), 9–15.

Golten, M. M., and Mayer, B. S. *Child Protection Mediation Project Manual.* Boulder, Col.: CDR Associates, 1987.

Gordon, T. *Leadership Effectiveness Training.* New York: Wyden, 1978.

Graham, J., and Sano, Y. *Smart Bargaining: Doing Business with the Japanese.* New York: Ballinger, 1984.

Grebe, S. C., "Ethical Issues in Conflict Resolution: Divorce Mediation." *Negotiation Journal,* 1989, *5*(2), 179–190.

Gulliver, P. H. *Neighbors and Networks.* Berkeley: University of California Press, 1971.

Gulliver, P. H. *Disputes and Negotiations.* San Diego, Calif.: Academic Press, 1979.

Gunning, I. "Mediation as an Alternative to Court for Lesbian and Gay Families: Some Thoughts on Douglas McIntyre's Article." *Mediation Quarterly,* 1995, *13*(1), 47–52.

Hall, E. T. *The Hidden Dimension.* New York: Doubleday, 1966.

Hall, E. *The Dance of Life.* New York: Anchor Press/Doubleday, 1983.

Hall, E., and Hall, M. *Hidden Differences: Doing Business with the Japanese.* New York: Doubleday, 1987.

Hamilton, P. "Counseling and the Legal Profession." *American Bar Association Journal,* 1972, *58,* 39–42.

Hamzeh, A. "The Role of Hizbullah in Conflict Management Within Lebanon's Shi'a Community." Unpublished manuscript, American University of Beirut, 1994.

Harter, P. "Regulatory Negotiation: The Experience So Far." *Resolve,* 1984, *16,* 1–10.

Haygood, L. "Negotiated Rule Making: Challenges for Mediators and Participants." *Mediation Quarterly,* 1988, *20,* 77–91.

Haynes, J. *Divorce Mediation: A Practical Guide for Therapists and Counselors.* New York: Springer, 1981.

Haynes, J. *Fundamentals of Family Mediation.* Albany: State University of New York Press, 1994.

Henley, N. *Body Politics—Power, Sex, and Nonverbal Communication.* Englewood Cliffs, N.J.: Prentice-Hall, 1977.

Henry, J., and Lieberman, J. *The Manager's Guide to Resolving Legal Disputes.* New York: HarperCollins, 1985.

Herat, P. B. "Community-Based Dispute Resolution in Sri Lanka." *Forum* (National Institute of Dispute Resolution), winter 1993.

Hinde, R. (ed.). *Nonverbal Communication.* Cambridge, England: Cambridge University Press, 1972.

Hokanson, J. "Psychophysiological Evaluations of the Catharsis Hypothesis." In J. Hokanson and E. Megargee (eds.), *The Dynamics of Aggression.* New York: HarperCollins, 1970.

Horowitz, D. *Ethnic Groups in Conflict.* Berkeley: University of California Press, 1985.

Hourani, A. *A History of the Arab Peoples.* New York: Warner Books, 1991.

Hughes, M. "Beating Diversity Adversity in the Battle Against AIDS," *Consensus,* 1995, no. 28, 5–8.

Hunter, F. *Community Power Structure: A Study of Decision Makers.* Chapel Hill: University of North Carolina Press, 1953.

Hunter, L., and McKersie, R. "Can 'Mutual Gains' Training Change Labor-Management Relationships?" *Negotiation Journal,* 1992, *8*(4), 319–330.

Huntington, S. *The Third Wave: Democratization in the Late Twentieth Century.* Norman: University of Oklahoma Press, 1991.

Ihromi, T. "Informal Methods of Dispute Settlement in Indonesia." In C. Pe, G. Sosmeña, and A. Tadiar (eds.), *Transcultural Mediation in the Asia-Pacific.* Manila, Philippines: Asia-Pacific Organization for Mediators, 1988.

Interim Rules 1992. Part 21 of the Industrial Court (Interim) Rules, Appendix A to the Industrial Court Rules (Transitional) (Australia) Regulation 1992.

International City Managers' Association. *Municipal Human Relations Commissions: Organizations and Programs.* Report no. 270. Chicago: International City Managers' Association, 1966.

Irving, H. *Divorce Mediation: A Rational Alternative to the Adversary System.* New York: Universe Books, 1980.

Islam, A. "Status of Mediation in Bangladesh in the Sub-Continental Settings." In C. Pe, G. Sosmeña, and A. Tadiar (eds.), *Transcultural Mediation in the Asia-Pacific.* Manila, Philippines: Asia-Pacific Organization for Mediators, 1988.

Jackins, H. *The Human Side of Human Beings.* Seattle: Rational Island Press, 1978.

Jennings, M. K. *Community Influentials: The Elites of Atlanta.* New York: Free Press, 1964.

Joseph, D. "Health Care Conflict Management Education." Unpublished, 1994.

Kelly, H. "A Classroom Study of the Dilemmas in Interpersonal Negotiations." In K. Archibald (ed.), *Strategic Interaction and Conflict: Original Papers and Discussion*. Berkeley, Calif.: Institute of International Studies, 1966.

Kelman, H. "Interactive Problem solving: The Uses and Limits of a Therapeutic Model for the Resolution of International Conflicts." In V. Volkan, J. Montville, and D. Julius (eds.), *The Psychodynamics of International Relationships*. Vol. 2. Lexington, Mass.: Lexington, 1991.

Keltner, J. "Communications and the Labor-Management Mediation Process: Some Aspects and Hypotheses." *Journal of Communication*, 1965, *15*(2), 64–80.

Kerr, C. "Industrial Conflict and Its Mediation." *American Journal of Sociology*, 1954, *60*, 230–245.

Kessler, S. *Creative Conflict Resolution: Mediation*. Unpublished workbook. 1978.

Klugman, J. "Negotiating Agreements and Resolving Disputes Across Cultures." *Mediation Quarterly*, 1992, *9*(4), 387–390.

Khor, K. "Cost Savings Propel Proliferation of States' Conflict Resolution Programs," *Consensus*, 1995, no. 27, 1–12.

Kochan, T., and Jick, T. "The Public Sector Mediation Process: A Theory and Empirical Examination." *Journal of Conflict Resolution*, 1978, *22*(2), 209–237.

Kochman, T. *Black and White Styles in Conflict*. Chicago: University of Chicago Press, 1981.

Kolb, D. *The Mediators*. Cambridge, Mass.: MIT Press, 1983.

Kolb, D., and Sheppard, B. "Do Managers Mediate, or Even Arbitrate?" *Negotiation Journal*, 1985, *1*(4), 379–388.

Kosambi Jataka, no. 428, Bk. IX, 486–90, n.d.

Krapp, T. Presentation at the First European Conference on Peacemaking and Conflict Resolution, Antalya, Turkey, May 1992.

Kraybill, R. "Institutionalizing Mediation as an Alternative Dispute Settlement Mechanism: An Ethical Critique." In R. Kraybill and L. Buzzard (eds.), *Christian Conciliation Sourcebook*. Oak Park, Ill.: Christian Legal Society, 1979.

Kriesberg, L. *The Sociology of Social Conflicts*. Englewood Cliffs, N.J.: Prentice-Hall, 1973.

Kriesberg, L., Northrup, T., and Thorson, S. (eds.). *Intractable Conflicts and Their Transformation*. Syracuse, N.Y.: Syracuse University Press, 1989.

Kwartler, R. "This Land Is Our Land: The Mohawk Indians v. the State of New York." In R. Goldmann (ed.), *Roundtable Justice: Case Studies in Conflict Resolution*. Boulder, Colo.: Westview Press, 1980.

Labor-Management Relations Act (Taft-Hartley Act). *U.S. Code*, sec. 203(b) (1947).

Lake, L. *Environmental Mediation: The Search for Consensus.* Boulder, Colo.: Westview Press, 1980.

Lake, R. *Resolving Locational Conflict.* New Brunswick, N.J.: Center for Urban Policy Research, 1987.

Landsberger, H. "Final Report on a Research Project in Mediation." *Labor Law Journal,* 1956, 7(8).

Lansford, H. "The Metropolitan Water Roundtable: A Case Study in Environmental Conflict Management." Boulder, Colo.: ACCORD Associates, 1983.

Laue, J. "Using Mediation to Shape Public Policy." *Mediation Quarterly,* 1988, no. 20.

Laue, J., and Cormick, G. "The Ethics of Intervention in Community Disputes." In G. Bermont and others (eds.), *The Ethics of Social Intervention.* New York: Wiley, 1978.

Lax, D., and Sebenius, J., "The Power of Alternatives or the Limits to Negotiation." *Negotiation Journal,* 1985, 1(2), 163–179.

Lederach, J. P. *"La regulacion del conflito: interpersonal y de grupos redudidos"* ["The Regulation of Conflict: Interpersonal and Small Groups"]. Unpublished manuscript, University of Colorado, 1984.

Lederach, J. P. "Mediation in North America: An Examination of the Profession's Cultural Assumptions." Paper presented at the National Conference on Peacemaking and Conflict Resolution, Denver, Colo., 1985.

Lederach, J. P. "Of Nails, Nets, and Problemas." Ph.D. dissertation, University of Colorado, 1988.

Lederach, J. P. "Comprehensive Approach in Somalia." Presentation at the North American Conference on Peacemaking and Conflict Resolution, May 1993.

Lederach, J. P. *Preparing for Peace: Conflict Transformation Across Cultures.* Syracuse, N.Y.: Syracuse University Press, 1995.

Lemmon, J. (ed.). "Community Mediation," special issue of *Mediation Quarterly,* 1984, no. 5.

Lemmon, J. *Family Mediation Practice.* New York: Macmillan, 1985.

Leone, A. "Is ADR the Rx for Malpractice?" *Dispute Resolution Journal,* 1994, 4(3), 7–13.

LeResche, D. Editor's Notes. *Mediation Quarterly,* 1993, 10(14), 327–337.

Levinson, D. "The Intergroup Relations Workshop: Its Psychological Aims and Effects." *Journal of Psychology,* 1954, 38, 103–126.

Levinson, D., and Sohermerhorn, R. "Emotional Attitudinal Effects of an Intergroup Relations Workshop on Its Members." *Journal of Psychology,* 1951, 31, 243–256.

Levy, J. "Conflict Resolution in Elementary and Secondary Education." *Mediation Quarterly,* 1989, 7(1), 73–87.

Li, M. Q. "Mediation in China." In C. Pe, G. Sosmeña, and A. Tadiar (eds.), *Transcultural Mediation in the Asia-Pacific*. Manila, Philippines: Asia-Pacific Organization for Mediators, 1988.

Li, V. *Law Without Lawyers: A Comparative View of Law in China and the United States*. Boulder, Colo.: Westview Press, 1978.

Lincoln, W. F. *Mediation: A Transferable Process for the Prevention and Resolution of Racial Conflict in Public Secondary Schools*. New York: American Arbitration Association, 1976.

Lincoln, W. F. "Presenting Initial Positions." Unpublished manuscript, National Center for Collaborative Planning and Community Services, Watertown, Mass., 1981.

Lincoln, W. F. "Types of Negotiations." Unpublished manuscript, National Center for Collaborative Planning and Community Services, Watertown, Mass., n.d.

Lovell, H. "The Pressure Lever in Mediation." *Industrial and Labor Relations Review*, 1952, *6*(1), 20–29.

McCarthy, J. (ed.). *Resolving Conflict in Higher Education*. New Directions for Higher Education, no. 32. San Francisco: Jossey-Bass, 1980.

McCarthy, J., and others. *Managing Faculty Disputes: A Guide to Issues, Procedures, and Practices*. San Francisco: Jossey-Bass, 1984.

McConnell, J. *Mindful Mediation: A Handbook for Buddhist Peacemakers*. Bangkok, Thailand: Buddhist Research Institute and Manachula Buddhist University, 1995.

McCreary, S. "Independent Fact Finding as a Catalyst for Cross-Cultural Dialogue." *Cultural Survival*, 1995, *19*(3), 30–32.

Macduff, I. "Mediation in New Zealand: Legislating for Community?" In C. Pe, G. Sosmeña, and A. Tadiar (eds.), *Transcultural Mediation in the Asia-Pacific*. Manila, Philippines: Asia-Pacific Organization for Mediators, 1988.

Macduff, I. "Resources, Rights and Recognition." *Cultural Survival*, 1995, *19*(3), 30–32.

McIntyre, D. "Gay Parents and Child Custody: A Struggle Under the Legal System." *Mediation Quarterly*, 1994, *12*(2), 135–149.

McIsaac, H. "Mandatory Conciliation Custody/Visitation Matters: California's Bold Stroke." *Conciliation Courts Review*, 1983, *19*(2), 51–73.

McSurely, A. *How to Negotiate*. Louisville, Ky.: Southern Conference Educational Fund, 1967.

McWhinney, R., and Metcalf, K. Conversations with the author at the annual meeting of the Association of Family and Conciliation Courts, Denver, Colo., May 1984.

Maggiolo, W. *Techniques of Mediation in Labor Disputes*. Dobbs Ferry, N.Y.: Oceana, 1972.

Maier, N., and Hoffman, L. "Quality of First and Second Solutions in

Group Problem Solving." *Journal of Applied Psychology*, 1960, *44*, 278–283.

Mann, J. Beijing Jeep. New York: Simon & Schuster, 1989.

Mansbridge, J. *Beyond Adversary Democracy*. Chicago: University of Chicago Press, 1983.

Mansfield, E. "Balance and Harmony: Peacemaking in Coast Salish Tribes of the Pacific Northwest." *Mediation Quarterly*, 1993, *10*(4), 339–353.

Marcus, L., and others. *Renegotiating Health Care: Resolving Conflict to Build Collaboration*. San Francisco: Jossey-Bass, 1995.

Maslow, A. *Toward a Psychology of Being*. New York: Van Nostrand Reinhold, 1968.

Matz, D. "ADR and Life in Israel." *Negotiation Journal*, 1991, *7*(1), 11–16.

Mayer, B. S. "Conflict Resolution in Child Protection and Adoption." *Mediation Quarterly*, 1985, no. 7, 69–81.

Mayer, B. S. "The Dynamics of Power in Mediation." *Mediation Quarterly*, 1987, no. 16, 75–85.

Mayer, B., Wildau, S., and Valchev, R. "Promoting Multi-Cultural Consensus Building in Bulgaria." *Cultural Survival*, 1995, *19*(3), 64–68.

Mayor's Office, City of Portland, Oregon. *Police-Citizen Mediation Program*. Portland, Oreg.: Mayor's Office, 1994.

Meeks, G. "Negotiating a State Environmental Quality Act: The Arizona Groundwater Case." *Mediation Quarterly*, 1988, no. 20, 57–73.

Mernitz, S. *Mediation of Environmental Disputes: A Sourcebook*. New York: Praeger, 1980.

Milne, A. "Family Self-Determination: An Alternative to the Adversarial System in Custody Disputes." Paper presented at the winter meeting of the Association of Family and Conciliation Courts, Fort Lauderdale, Fla., Dec. 1981.

Model Standards of the Association of Family and Conciliation Courts. Association of Family and Conciliation Courts. Portland, Ore.: 1994.

Moore, C. W. *Mediator Checklist*. Denver, Colo.: Center for Dispute Resolution, 1981.

Moore, C. W. *Code of Professional Conduct*. Denver, Colo.: Colorado Council of Mediation Organizations and the Center for Dispute Resolution, 1982a.

Moore, C. W. *Natural Resources Conflict Management*. Boulder, Colo.: ACCORD Associates, 1982b.

Moore, C. W. "The Caucus: Private meetings That Promote Settlement." *Mediation Quarterly*, 1987, no. 16, 87–101.

Moore, C. W. "Obstacles to Effective Divorce Mediation." In J. Folberg and A. Milne (eds.), *Divorce Mediation*. New York: Guilford Press, 1988.

Moore, C. W. "Utilizing Negotiations to Resolve Complex Environmental Disputes." In W. Viessman and E. Smerdon, *Managing Water-*

Related Conflicts, New York: American Society of Civil Engineers, 1989.

Moore, C. W. *Corps of Engineers Uses Mediation to Settle Hydropower Dispute.* Ft. Belvoir, Va.: Institute for Water Resources, Case Study 91-ADR-CS6, 1991.

Moore, C. W. "Implementing Peace Accords on the Ground." *Track Two,* 1993, *2*(2), 10–13.

Moore, C. W., and Santosa, A. "Developing Appropriate Environmental Conflict Management Procedures in Indonesia." *Cultural Survival,* 1995, *19*(3), 23–29.

Morrow, D., and Wilson, D. "Three Into Two Won't Go? From Mediation to New Relationships in Northern Ireland." *Forum* (National Institute of Dispute Resolution), 1993.

Mulcahy, N. "Conciliation and Race Complaints." *Australian Dispute Resolution Journal,* 1992, *3*(1), 21–30.

Muntarbhorn, V. "Prospects and Trends of Mediation as an Alternative to Dispute Resolution in Thailand." In C. Pe, G. Sosmeña, and A. Tadiar (eds.), *Transcultural Mediation in the Asia-Pacific.* Manila, Philippines: Asia-Pacific Organization for Mediators, 1988.

Nader, L. "Styles of Court Procedure: To Make the Balance." In L. Nader (ed.), *Law in Culture and Society.* Chicago: Aldine, 1969.

Nathan, L. "An Imperfect Bridge: Crossing to Democracy on the Peace Accord." *Track Two,* 1993, *2*(2), 1–5.

Nelson, M., and Sharp, W. R. "Mediating Conflicts of Persons at Risk of Homelessness: The Helping Hand Project." *Mediation Quarterly,* 1995, *12*(4), 317–325.

New York State Special Commission on Attica. *Attica: The Official Report of the New York State Special Commission on Attica.* New York: Praeger, 1972.

O'Hare, M., Bacow, L., and Sanderson, D. *Facility Siting and Public Opposition.* New York: Van Nostrand Reinhold, 1983.

Orenstein, S. G. "The Role of Mediation in Domestic Violence Cases." In H. Davidson and others (eds.), *Alternative Means of Family Dispute Resolution.* Washington, D.C.: American Bar Association, 1982.

Owen, D. *Balkan Odyssey.* New York: Harcourt Brace & Company, 1995.

Patai, R. *The Arab Mind.* New York: Charles Scribner's Sons, 1983.

Pe, C., and Tadiar, A. *Katarungang Pambarangay: Dynamics of Compulsory Conciliation.* Quezon City, Philippines: Publishers' Printing Press, 1988.

Pearson, J. "Divorce Mediation: Strengths and Weaknesses Over Time." In H. Davidson and others (eds.), *Alternative Means of Family Dispute Resolution.* Washington, D.C.: American Bar Association, 1982.

Pearson, J. "Denver Child Custody Project: Final Report to the Piton Foundation and Colorado Bar Association." Denver, Colo.: Center for Policy Research, 1984.

Perez, F. A. "Evaluation of Mediation Techniques." *Labor Law Journal,* 1959, *10*(10), 716–720.

Phear, W. P. Conversation with the author at a meeting of the Association of Family and Conciliation Courts, Ethics Working Group, Keystone, Colo., Mar. 1984.

Polsby, N. "How to Study Community Power." *Journal of Politics,* 1960, *22,* 474–484.

President. Memorandum on Use of Alternative Dispute Resolution. *Federal Register,* September 30, 1993.

Princen, T. *Intermediaries in International Conflict.* Princeton, N.J.: Princeton University Press, 1992.

Pruitt, D. *Negotiation Behavior.* San Diego, Calif.: Academic Press, 1981.

Pruitt, D., and Lewis, S. "The Psychology of Integrative Bargaining." In D. Druckman (ed.), *Negotiations: A Social Psychological Perspective.* Newbury Park, Calif.: Sage, 1977.

Pye, L. *Chinese Commercial Negotiating Style.* Cambridge, Mass.: Oelgeschlager, Gunn & Hain, 1982.

Quayle, D. "Less Litigation, More Justice." *The Wall Street Journal,* Aug. 14, 1991, p. A8.

Rapoport, A., and Chammah, A. M. "Sex Differences in Factors Contributing to the Level of Cooperation in the Prisoner's Dilemma Game." *Journal of Personality and Social Psychology,* 1965, *2,* 831–838.

Ray, L., and Smolover, D. *Consumer Dispute Resolution: Exploring the Alternatives.* Washington, D.C.: American Bar Association and U.S. Department of Consumer Affairs, 1983.

Reeves, J. "ADR Relieves Pain of Health Care Disputes." *Dispute Resolution Journal,* 1994, *49*(3), 14–20.

Renouf, E. "Family Conciliation/Mediation in Australia: Which Way Forward?" *Australian Dispute Resolution Journal,* 1991, *2*(2), 108–116.

Reynolds, W., and Tonry, M. "Professional Mediation Services for Prisoners' Complaints." *American Bar Association Journal,* 1981, *67,* 294–297.

Ricci, I. *Mom's House, Dad's House.* New York: Collier Books, 1980.

Richardson, J., and Margulis, J. *The Magic of Rapport: The Business of Negotiation.* New York: Avon Books, 1984.

Richardson, S., Dohrenwend, B. S., and Klein, D. *Interviewing: Its Forms and Functions.* New York: Basic Books, 1965.

Riley, H., and Sebenius, J. "Stakeholder Negotiations over Third World Natural Resource Projects." *Cultural Survival,* 1995, *19*(3), 39–43.

Riskin, L. "Mediation and Lawyers." *Ohio State Law Journal,* 1982, *43,* 29–60.

Roberts, K., and Lundy, C. "The ADA and NLRA: Resolving Accommodation Disputes in Unionized Workplaces." *Negotiation Journal,* 1995, *11*(1), 29–41.

Rogers, C. "The Non-Directive Method as a Technique of Social Research." *American Journal of Sociology,* 1945, *50*(4), 279–283.

Ross, H. "Aboriginal Australian's Cultural Norms for Negotiating Natural Resources." *Cultural Survival,* 1995, *19*(3), 33–38.

Rothman, J. *From Confrontation to Cooperation: Resolving Ethnic and Regional Conflict.* Newbury Park, Calif: Sage, 1992.

Rowe, M. "Harassment: A Systems Approach." Unpublished manuscript, Massachusetts Institute of Technology, 1994.

Rowe, M. "Dispute Resolution in the Non-Union Environment." Unpublished manuscript, Massachusetts Institute of Technology, 1995.

Rubin, J. (ed.). *Dynamics of Third Party Intervention: Kissinger in the Middle East.* New York: Praeger, 1981.

Rubin, J., and Brown, B. *The Social Psychology of Bargaining and Negotiation.* San Diego, Calif.: Academic Press, 1975.

Salacuse, J. "Your Draft or Mine?" *Negotiation Journal,* 1989, *5*(4), 337–341.

Saposnek, D. T. *Mediating Child Custody Disputes: A Systematic Guide for Family Therapists, Court Counselors, Attorneys, and Judges.* San Francisco: Jossey-Bass, 1983.

Savage, C. A. "Future Lawyers: Adversaries or Problem Solvers? Two Law School Programs in Alternative Dispute Resolution." *Mediation Quarterly,* 1989, *7*(1), 89–101.

Sawyer, J., and Guetzkow, H. "Bargaining and Negotiating in International Relations." In H. Kelman (ed.), *International Behavior: A Social Psychological Analysis.* Troy, Mo.: Holt, Rinehart & Winston, 1965.

Schein, E. *Process Consultation: Its Role in Organization Development.* Reading, Mass.: Addison-Wesley, 1969.

Schelling, T. "An Essay on Bargaining." *American Economic Review,* 1956, *46*(3), 281–306.

Schelling, T. *The Strategy of Conflict.* Cambridge, Mass.: Harvard University Press, 1960.

Schön, D. *The Reflective Practitioner: How Professionals Think in Action.* New York: Basic Books, 1983.

Schreiber, F. B. *Domestic Disturbances: Officer Safety and Calming Techniques.* St. Cloud, Minn.: Center for Studies in Criminal Justice, St. Cloud University, 1971.

Schwarz, A. *Nation in Waiting: Indonesia in the 1990's.* St. Leonards, Australia: Allen & Unwin, 1994.

Seligman, S. *Dealing with the Chinese: A Practical Guide to Business Etiquette in the People's Republic Today.* New York: Warner Books, 1989.

Shallert, E. "Settlement of Civil Litigation in Federal Courts: The Judge's Role." Unpublished paper, Cambridge, Mass., 1982.

Shanahan, J., and others. *Negotiated Investment Strategy.* Dayton, Ohio: Kettering Foundation, 1982.

Shapiro, D., Sheppard, B., and Cheraskin, L., "Business on a Handshake." *Negotiation Journal,* 1992, *8*(4), 365–377.

Shapiro, F. "Profiles: Mediator." *New Yorker,* Aug. 1, 1970, pp. 36–58.

Sharp, G. *The Politics of Nonviolent Action.* Boston: Porter Sargent, 1973.

Shaughnessy, E. *Conflict Management in Norway: Practical Dispute Resolution.* Lanham, Md.: University Press of America, 1992.

Shaw, M. "Mediating Between Parents and Children." In H. Davidson and others (eds.), *Alternative Means of Family Dispute Resolution.* Washington, D.C.: American Bar Association, 1982.

Sherif, M., and others. *Intergroup Conflict and Cooperation: The Robbers Cave Experiment.* Norman: University of Oklahoma Book Exchange, 1961.

Shonholtz, R. "Neighborhood Justice Systems: Work, Structure, and Guiding Principles." *Mediation Quarterly,* 1984, no. 5, 3–30.

Shonholtz, R. (ed.). "Developing Mediating Processes in the New Democracies." Special issue of *Mediation Quarterly,* 1993, *10*(3).

Shook, V., and Kwan K. "Straightening Relationships and Resolving Disputes in Hhawai'i: Ho'Oponopono and Mediation." In C. Pe, G. Sosmeña, and A. Tadiar (eds.), *Transcultural Mediation in the Asia-Pacific.* Manila, Philippines: Asia-Pacific Organization for Mediators, 1988.

Shourie, H. "Mediation Sans Legislation: An Experiment in India." In C. Pe, G. Sosmeña, and A. Tadiar (eds.), *Transcultural Mediation in the Asia-Pacific.* Manila, Philippines: Asia-Pacific Organization for Mediators, 1988.

Shrestha, K. "Community Forestry in Nepal: An Overview of Conflicts." Unpublished paper presented at a conference on community forestry in Kathmandu, Nepal, January 1995.

Simkin, W. *Mediation and the Dynamics of Collective Bargaining.* Washington, D.C.: Bureau of National Affairs, 1971.

Simmel, G. *Conflict and the Web of Intergroup Affiliations.* New York: Free Press, 1955.

Simokaitis, M. *Preparing for Negotiations.* St. Louis, Mo.: Washington University Community Crisis Intervention Project, n.d.

Skratek, S. "Grievance Mediation: Does it Really Work?" *Negotiation Journal,* 1990, *6*(3), 269–280.

Slaiku, K. "Designing Dispute Resolution Systems in the Health Care Industry." *Negotiation Journal,* 1989, *5*(4), 395–400.

Slatts, H., and Porter, K. *Traditional Decision Making and Law.* Yogyakarta, Indonesia: Gadja Mada University Press, 1992.

Smart, L. "Mediator Strategies for Dealing with Dirty Tricks." *Mediation Quarterly,* 1987, no. 16, 53–63.

Smith, M., and Sidwell, J. *Training and Implementation Guide for Student Mediation in Secondary Schools.* Albuquerque, N.M.: New Mexico Center for Dispute Resolution, 1990.

Smith, W. "Effectiveness of the Biased Mediator." *Negotiation Journal,* 1985, *1*(4), 363–372.

Society of Professionals in Dispute Resolution. *Qualifying Neutrals: The Basic Principles.* Report of the SPIDR Commission on Qualification. Washington, D.C.: Society of Professionals in Dispute Resolution, 1989.

Society of Professionals in Dispute Resolution. *Ensuring Competence and Quality in Dispute Resolution Practice.* Washington, D.C.: Society of Professionals in Dispute Resolution, 1995.

Sommer, R. "Further Studies of Small Group Ecology." *Sociometry,* 1965, *28,* 337–348.

Sommer, R. *Personal Space: The Behavioral Basis of Design.* Englewood Cliffs, N.J.: Prentice-Hall, 1969.

Stamato, L., and Jaffe, S. "Mediation and Public Policy: Variations on a Consensus Theme," *Mediation Quarterly,* 1991, *9*(2), 165–178.

Steinmetz, S., and Straus, M. *Violence in the Family.* New York: Harper-Collins, 1974.

Stevens, C. *Strategy in Collective Bargaining Negotiations.* New York: McGraw-Hill, 1963.

Stevenson, E. "The Use of Community Mediation in the Family Mediation Centre (NSW)." *Australian Dispute Resolution Journal,* 1990, *1*(1), 24–30.

Stewart, C., and Cash, W. *Interviewing: Principles and Practices.* Dubuque, Iowa: Brown, 1974.

Straus, D. "Managing Environmental Complexity: A New Look at Environmental Mediation." *Environment Science and Technology,* 1979, *13*(6), 661–665.

Straus, D., Clark, P., and Suskind, L. *Guidelines to Identify, Manage and Resolve Environmental Disputes.* New York: Research Institute, American Arbitration Association, n.d.

Straus, M. "A Sociological Perspective on the Prevention and Treatment of Wifebeatings." In M. Roy (ed.), *Battered Women.* New York: Van Nostrand Reinhold, 1977.

Stulberg, J. *Citizen Dispute Settlement: A Mediator's Manual.* Tallahassee, Fla.: Supreme Court of Florida, 1981a.

Stulberg, J. "The Theory and Practice of Mediation: A Reply to Professor Suskind." *Vermont Law Review,* 1981b, *6*(1), 85–117.

Sullivan, T. *Resolving Development Disputes Through Negotiations.* New York: Plenum, 1984.

Survey Research Center. *Interviewer's Manual.* Ann Arbor: Survey Research Center, Institute for Social Research, University of Michigan, 1969.

Suskind, L. "Environmental Mediation and the Accountability Problem." *Vermont Law Review,* 1981, *6*(1), 1–47.

Suskind, L. "NIDR's State Office of Mediation Experiment." *Negotiation Journal,* 1986, *2*(4), 323–327.

Suskind, L., Babbit, E., and Segal, P. "When ADR Becomes the Law: A Review of Federal Practice." *Negotiation Journal,* 1993, *9*(1), 59–75.

Suskind, L., and Cruikshank, J. *Breaking the Impasse: Consensual Approaches to Resolving Public Disputes.* New York: Basic Books, 1987.

Talbot, A. *Settling Things: Six Case Studies in Environmental Mediation.* Washington, D.C.: Conservation Foundation, 1983.

Thibaut, J., and Kelly, H. *The Social Psychology of Groups.* New York: Wiley, 1959.

Thomas, K. "Conflict and Conflict Management." In M. Dunnette (ed.), *Handbook of Industrial and Organizational Psychology.* Skokie, Ill.: Rand McNally, 1976.

Tomain, J. "Land Use Mediation for Planners." *Mediation Quarterly,* 1989, *7*(2), 163–173.

Umbreit, M. *Victim Offender Mediation: Conflict Resolution and Restitution.* Washington, D.C.: National Institute of Corrections, U.S. Department of Justice, 1985.

Umbreit, M. *Victim Meets Offender: The Impact of Restorative Justice and Mediation.* Monsey, N.Y.: Criminal Justice Press, 1994.

Ury, W., Brett, J., and Goldberg, S. *Getting Disputes Resolved: Designing Systems to Cut the Costs of Conflict.* San Francisco: Jossey-Bass, 1988.

Valtin, R. "The 'Real and Substantial' Benefits of Grievance Mediation." *Negotiation Journal,* 1993, *9*(2), 179–184.

Van Hook, M. P., "Resolving Conflict Between Farmers and Creditors: An Analysis of the Farmer-Creditor Mediation Process." *Mediation Quarterly,* 1990, *8*(1), 63–72.

Van Zandt, H. "How to Negotiate in Japan." *Harvard Business Review,* Nov.–Dec. 1970, 45–56.

Viessman, W., and Smerdon, E. *Managing Water-Related Conflicts.* New York: American Society of Civil Engineers, 1989.

Volpe, M. R., and Witherspoon, R. "Mediation and Cultural Diversity on College Campuses." *Mediation Quarterly,* 1992, *9*(4), 341–351.

Von Benda-Beckmann, K. *The Broken Stairways to Consensus: Village Justice and State Courts in Mjnangkabau.* Cinnaminson, N.J.: Foris Publications, 1984.

Vorenberg, E. W. *State of the Art Survey of Dispute Resolution Programs Involving Juveniles.* Dispute Resolution Papers, Section 1. American Bar Association, Special Committee on Alternative Means of Dispute Resolution (Division of Public Service Activities), 1982.

Votchal, V. "The Movement Toward Conflict Resolution in the Former Soviet Union." *Forum* (National Institute for Dispute Resolution), winter 1993.

Wall, J. "Mediation: An Analysis Review and Proposed Research." *Journal of Conflict Resolution*, 1981, *25*(1), 157–180.

Walton, J. "Substance and Artifact: The Current Research on Community Power Structure." *American Journal of Sociology*, 1966, *71*(4), 430–438.

Walton, R. *Interpersonal Peacemaking: Confrontations and Third Party Consultation.* Reading, Mass.: Addison-Wesley, 1969.

Walton, R., and McKersie, R. *A Behavioral Theory of Labor Negotiations.* New York: McGraw-Hill, 1965.

Warhaftig, P. "Gang-Related Conflict Resolving Process." *Conflict Resolution Notes*, 1995, *13*(1), 4–5.

Warren, C. "The Hopeful Future of Mediation: Resolving Environmental Disputes Outside the Courts." In P. Baldwin (ed.), *Environmental Mediation: An Effective Alternative?* Palo Alto, Calif.: RESOLVE, Center for Environmental Conflict Resolution, 1978.

Watzlawick, P. *The Language of Change.* New York: Basic Books, 1978.

Wehr, P. *Conflict Regulation.* Boulder, Colo.: Westview Press, 1979.

Weidner, H., and Fietkau, H. J. "Environmental Mediation: The Mediation Procedure on the Waste Management Plan in the District of Neuss, North Rhine-Westphalia." Berlin, Germany: Social Science Research Centre, Berlin, 1995.

Werner, L. *International Politics: Foundations of the System.* Minneapolis: University of Minnesota Press, 1974.

Westin, A., and Feliu, A. *Resolving Employment Disputes Without Litigation.* Washington, D.C.: Bureau of National Affairs, 1988.

Wheeler, M. Lecture in divorce mediation seminar. Boulder, Colo.: 1982.

Wicker, T. *A Time to Die.* New York: Quadrangle/New York Times, 1975.

Wildau, S. T. *Guidelines for Mediating Domestic Violence Cases.* Denver, Colo.: Center for Dispute Resolution, 1984.

Wildau, S. "Transitions: Moving Parties Between Stages." *Mediation Quarterly*, 1987, no. 16, 3–13.

Wildau, S., and Mayer, B. "Introduction to Dispute Systems Design." In CDR Associates, *Designing Dispute Resolution Systems.* Boulder, Colo.: CDR Associates, 1992.

Wildau, S., Moore, C., and Mayer, B. "Developing Democratic Decision-Making and Dispute Resolution Procedures Abroad." *Mediation Quarterly*, 1993, *10*(3), 303–320.

Williams, G. *Legal Negotiations and Settlement.* St. Paul, Minn.: West, 1983.

Wilson, I. "The Waitangi Tribunal." *Australian Dispute Resolution Journal*, 1992, *3*(4), 240–254.

Wixted, S. "The Children's Hearings Project: A Mediation Program for Children and Families." In H. Davidson and others (eds.), *Alternative*

Means of Family Dispute Resolution. Washington, D.C.: American Bar Association, 1982.

Yang, J. "Role of the Korea Legal Aid Center in Promoting Mediation as an Alternative to the Court." In C. Pe, G. Sosmeña, and A. Tadiar (eds.), *Transcultural Mediation in the Asia-Pacific.* Manila, Philippines: Asia-Pacific Organization for Mediators, 1988.

Young, O. "Intermediaries: Additional Thoughts on Third Parties." *Journal of Conflict Resolution,* 1972, *16*(1), 51–65.

Zartman, I. W., and Berman, M. *The Practical Negotiator.* New Haven, Conn.: Yale University Press, 1982.

Ziegenfuss, J. *Organizational Troubleshooters: Resolving Problems with Customers and Employees.* San Francisco: Jossey-Bass, 1988.

Name Index

Subject Index